THE INTERNATIONAL GUIDE TO
MANAGEMENT CONSULTANCY

The Evolution, Practice and Structure of Management Consultancy Worldwide

Consultant Editors
Barry Curnow & **Jonathan Reuvid**

Endorsed by
The International Council of Management Consulting Institutes (ICMCI)

European Federation of Management Consulting Associations (FEACO)

All-Japan Federation of Management Organizations (Zen-Noh-Ren)

THE INTERNATIONAL GUIDE TO
MANAGEMENT CONSULTANCY

Every possible effort has been made to ensure that the information contained in this book is accurate at the time of going to press, and the publishers cannot accept responsibility for any errors or omissions, however caused. No responsibility for loss or damage occasioned to any person acting or refraining from action as a result of the material in this publication, can be accepted by the editors or publisher.

First published in 2001

Apart from any fair dealing for the purposes of research or private study, or criticism or review, as permitted under the Copyright, Designs and Patents Act, 1988, this publication may only be reproduced, stored or transmitted, in any form or by any means, with the prior permission in writing of the publishers, or in the case of reprographic reproduction in accordance with the terms of licences issued by the Copyright Licensing Agency. Enquiries concerning reproduction outside those terms should be sent to the publishers at the undermentioned address:

Kogan Page Limited
120 Pentonville Road
London N1 9JN

© Kogan Page and contributors, 2001

British Library Cataloguing in Publication Data

ISBN 0 7494 3561 5

Typeset by Saxon Graphics Ltd, Derby
Printed and bound in Great Britain by Clays Ltd, St Ives plc

Contents

Dedication		ix
About the Editors		xi
Contributors' Notes		xii
Forewords:	President, ICMCI	xix
	Chairman, Zen-Noh-Ren	xxi
	Chairman, FEACO	xxiii
Introduction: The Editors		1

Part one	***The evolution and practice of management consultancy globally***	5
1.1	The international consulting industry today *Barry Curnow and Jonathan Reuvid*	7
1.2	The evolution of management consultancy: its origins and global development *Matthias Kipping*	20
1.3	Multinational management consultancies: world market leaders *Mick James*	33
1.4	The impact of the IT revolution and e-business on management consultancy *Fiona Czerniawska*	42
15.	Sustainability and management consultancy *Adrian Henriques*	48
1.6	The Delphi Study and beyond: scenarios for the consulting market in 2010 *Mike Jeans*	56

Part two	**Ethics and Best Practice**	63
2.1	Competition and objectivity: management consultancy, auditing and outsourcing *Bruce Petter*	65
2.2	Professionalism in best practice: consultancy and competence in the new e-economy *Barry Curnow*	70
2.3	Ethical norms and guidelines *C. Paul Lynch*	82
2.4	Higher education opportunities in management consulting *Sally Woodward and Alan Williams*	99
2.5	What is the case for regulating management consultants? *Ian Barratt*	114

2.6	Developments in management consultancy – from stagnation to evaporation or condensation? *Hans de Sonnaville*	122
2.7	Corporate governance – structures, processes and functions *Daniel Summerfield*	138

Part three *A client's guide to management consultancy* 149

3.1	The client-consultant relationship: setting the guidelines *Barry Curnow*	151
3.2	Selecting and appointing a management consultant *Barry Curnow*	156
3.3	How to get value from a management consultant *E. Michael Shays*	170
3.4	Managing the consultancy assignment in progress *Barry Curnow*	175
3.5	Phases of the client-consultant relationship *Barry Curnow*	186
3.6	Evaluating advice and recommendations *Jonathan Reuvid and John Mills*	195
3.7	Appreciative Inquiry: building on strengths in your organisation *Anne Radford*	202
3.8	The consultant's role in managing change *E. Michael Shays*	214
3.9	Closing off the consultancy assignment *Barry Curnow*	227

Part four *Key consultancy activities* 235

4.1	Strategy *Martin Whitehill*	237
4.2	Marketing *David Hussey*	246
4.3	Organisational change *Colin Coulson-Thomas*	255
4.4	Organisation and culture change in post-merger integration *Geoffrey Kitt*	263
4.5	Leadership in corporate transformations *Philip Channer and Jonathan Reuvid*	274
4.6	Coaching in management development *Myles Downey*	285

4.7	Supporting employees around the world *Michael Reddy*	295
4.8	Communication consultancy *Colette Dorward*	303
4.9	Customer relations *Clive Bonny*	312
4.10	Information and knowledge management *Colin Coulson-Thomas*	323
4.11	m-commerce: the next wave of management consulting *Thomas Korseman & Daniel Shepherd*	334
4.12	ERP to e-business – the opportunities *Sarah Taylor and Barry Curnow*	344

Part five	***Consulting internationally***	355
5.1	Consulting in developing economies and third world countries *Colin Adams*	357
5.2	Selected International management consultancy market profiles	367

The EU

Austria *Herbert Bachmaier*	367
Germany *Klaus Reiners*	370
Greece *Yiangos Charalambous*	375
Ireland *Peter Nolan*	379
Netherlands *Robert Florijn*	383
United Kingdom *Ian Barratt*	383

Scandinavia

Denmark	390
Norway	393
Sweden	396
Flemming Poulfelt	

Other Western Europe

Switzerland *André Wohlgemuth*	402

Central & Eastern Europe

Bulgaria	408
Hungary	409
Poland	411
Romania	412
Russia	413
Slovenia	413

József Poór

The Middle East

Jordan	417

Hatem Abdel Ghani

Africa

Nigeria	420

David Iornem

South Africa	426

Angelo Kehayas

The Americas

Brazil	428

Eduardo de Macedo Rocha

Canada	431

Heather Osler

USA	445

Asia & Australasia

Regional overview	446

Walter E. Vieira

Australia and New Zealand	451

Richard Elliott

China PRC	457

Li Yong

Hong Kong & Pearl River Delta	462

Gregg Li

Japan	473

Matsui Shigeki

Appendices

I	ICMCI Membership	497
II	FEACO Membership	503
III	Zen-Noh-Ren Membership	507

Dedication

In memory of Paul Noboru Yamada (1948–2000) friend and supporter of ICMCI, who brought Zen-Noh-Ren and the Japanese Management Consulting community to membership in ICMCI in 1999. Paul will be remembered fondly by consultants all over the globe for his professionalism, his humour and his friendship.

Paul was honoured in Japan by over 1000 people who attended his memorial service, and in the United States where a portion of his ashes together with an ICMCI seal and CMC pin were placed in a crypt in San Francisco, California.

About the editors

Barry Curnow is a *consultants' consultant* based in London and specialises in strategic advisory work for professional service firms. He is First Vice Chairman of the International Council of Management Consulting Institutes (2001–3), Principal of the Maresfield Curnow School of Management Consulting, a past president of both the IMC and the Chartered Institute of Personnel and Development in the UK and a former chairman of Hay-MSL. He was previously a worldwide partner and main board director of the Hay Group in Washington DC, Chairman of Hay Pacific in Hong Kong and managing director of Hay UK. A graduate of the Universities of Exeter and London, he is the joint author of three books and numerous articles and teaches consulting at City University Business School. barry-curnow@compuserve.com

Jonathan Reuvid graduated in economics from Oxford and was employed as an economist by the French national oil company, Total, at the time of its UK market entry. From there, he moved into investment banking, financial consultancy and marketing strategy. After seven years working for the engineering division of the US multinational Barnes Group with European general management responsibility, he engaged in the development of joint ventures and technology transfers in northern China, where he remains involved. In 1989, Jonathan embarked on a new career in business publishing, editing and writing a series of international business books with Kogan Page. He has a developing interest in the delivery of business briefings and adult learning on the Internet.

Contributors' notes

Hatem Abdel Ghani is executive director of the Institute of Management Consultants of Jordan.

Colin Adams has been the chief executive of BCB for over six years and has introduced major changes to the association. He was also instrumental in a substantive change in the management structure including the introduction of an Advisory Council and member-elected Board. In the last two years BCB was the major player in the formation of the Kosovo Government/Private Sector Task Force and subsequently the equivalent for the Former Republic of Yugoslavia, a group that has been instrumental in many British companies winning work. Since his appointment, he has visited some forty countries.

Herbert Bachmaier is a graduate of Vienna University and is active in professional methods of education. In 1982 he entered the Austrian Economic Chamber and from 1982–1986 was Speaker in the 'Innungsgruppe VIII' of the Trade, Crafts and Service Industry (Metal Groups) ministries. Since 1986 he has been the manager of the Skilled Workers Association, handling entrepreneurial advice and IT as well as advertising and market communication.

Ian Barratt is a graduate of Oxford University and a Fellow of the Royal Society of Arts. Originally a career civil servant, he was deputy general secretary of the Association of Chief Police Officers from 1994 until he joined the UK Institute of Management Consultancy as chief executive in January 2000.

Clive Bonny is owner-manager of SMP, a strategic enterprise which coaches individuals & advises organisations how to develop themselves. Initial consultations are available at no charge at www.consult-smp.com, email clivebonny@aol.com.

Philip Channer spent 10 years in consumer goods sales and marketing and then 20 years as a management consultant, working with top teams to implement sustainable personal and organisational change. He now works as a coach and mentor as director of executive development with Coutts PDC, and as a psychotherapist.

Yiangos Charalambous, FCCA, is vice president of the newly elected board of directors of SESMA.

Dr Colin Coulson-Thomas is chairman of ASK Europe plc, Adaptation Ltd, CotocoLtd, Creative Database Projects Ltd, and other companies and chairman of the judges for the eBusiness Innovations Awards. He is professor of competitiveness at the UK's National Centre for Competitiveness, leads the 'winning business' research programme and is author of *Individuals and Enterprise* (Blackhall Publishing, 1999), *The Information Entrepreneur* (3Com Active Business Unit, 2000), and *Shaping Things to Come* (Blackhall Publishing, 2001). He can be contacted on + 441 733 361 149 or adaptationltd@cs.com

Dr Fiona Czerniawska is director of the Management Consultancies' Association think tank. She is also the founder and managing director of Arkimeda and lectures regularly at various business schools. Her publications include *Business in a Virtual World: Exploiting the Competitive Advantage of Information* (with Gavin Potter) and *Management Consultancy in the 21st Century*. Her next book, *Management Consultancy: What Next?* will be published in November 2001.

Colette Dorward was a founder and, latterly, chief executive, London, of Smythe Dorward Lambert, the UK's leading internal communication management consultancy. She works across a variety of sectors, advising on employee communications and cultural change. She is co-author of *Corporate Reputation – the new strategic asset* (Hutchinson/Random Century).

Myles Downey is a coach, consultant, speaker and writer. He works internationally with a small number of clients with the aim of re-creating work so that it is productive, fulfilling and a joy. He is director of studies at The School of Coaching, which he established with The Industrial Society, author of *Effective Coaching* (published by Orion) and an exponent of The Inner Game.

Richard Elliott has over 20 years of consulting experience and leads project teams of up to 25 specialists focusing on growth and development in Australasia. He is the chief executive of Pacific Southwest Strategy Group. He is currently chairman of ICMCI, convenor of the 2001 Sydney Congress and chairman of the Resources Committee and the Communications Committee.

Robert Florijn is chairman of the Dutch National Institute of Management Consultants.

Adrian Henriques is an independent consultant on corporate responsibility, social accountability and sustainability with a business and NGO background. He is a council member of the Institute of Social and Ethical Accountability, an associate fellow of Warwick Business School's Corporate Citizenship Unit, and a member of the Global Reporting Initiative Steering Committee and the Association of Chartered Certified Accountants Social and Environmental Committee. He is the author of the forthcoming book *Sustainability: A Management Guide*. Website: www.henriques.co.uk

David Hussey is a well known international authority on strategic management, with experience as both a practitioner and a consultant to major companies in many industries. He is author or editor of around 30 books on strategy or related subjects. One of the founders of the Strategic Planning Society, and a director of the Japan Strategic Management Society, he is currently visiting professor in strategic management at Nottingham Business School.

David Iornem is the director general of the Institute of Management Consultants in Nigeria.

Mick James is a freelance business writer and editor. He is the author of management reports such as *Management Consultancy 2010* (Lafferty) and the *Winning New Business in Professional Services* titles for Policy Publications, covering PR, marketing, advertising, management consultancy and accountancy. His work appears in a wide range of business and professional titles: he currently writes regularly *for Sunday Business*, *Professional Recruiter* and *Knowledge Management*, as well as producing case studies, reports and newsletters for private clients. He began his journalistic career in IT titles, then edited *Management Consultancy* magazine for 6 years before going freelance.

Mike Jeans KPMG, is Master of the City of London Company of Management Consultants and a past president of both IMC, UK and CIMA.

Angelo Kehayas is the chairman of Cinergi Holdings. He has 24 years' experience in the information, financial and manufacturing industries. He has founded and led consulting business units in IBM and Unisys and has consulted for Deloitte and Touche. He has established numerous entrepreneurial businesses of which Cinergi is the most recent. Angelo has been involved in the commercialisation of certain state corporations, where re-engineering played a major role. He has been a registrar, vice president, national president and executive director of the Institute of Management Consultants, South Africa. He is the only individual to receive the honorary award for outstanding achievement and service to the consulting profession.

Geoffrey Kitt leads the organisation change competence for IBM Global Services Mergers and Acquisitions practice covering Europe, the Middle East and Africa. His consulting experience spans a range of disciplines including strategy, information systems, business process re-engineering, organisational change and development and culture change. He has for some time been interested in the role of organisation culture in securing competitive advantage and he is also a proponent of lean, agile organisational structures for business.

Matthias Kipping is currently a visiting professor at the Universitat Pompeu Fabra in Barcelona where he teaches business history and business strategy. He is also associated with the University of Reading in the UK, where he was a reader in European Management and Director of the Centre for International Business History (CIBH) until 2001. He has written and published extensively on the evolution of different carriers of management knowledge, namely business education and management consultancy. An edited volume (with Lars Engwall) and a monograph on the management consulting business will soon be published by Oxford University Press.

Tomas Korseman is a manager for edgecom. His primarily focus is electronic/mobile business and CRM. He has experience working with projects that encompass business planning, strategy articulation, and revenue enhancement, mainly from industries such as financial services, telecom, and manufacturing.

Gregg Li is president of the Institute of Management Consultants in Hong Kong.

C. Paul Lynch is a past president of IMC, UK and currently works closely with Integrated Strategies Group Llc (ISG) based in Houston, assisting major global companies with the integrity of their strategic messages to various stakeholder audiences.

Eduardo de Macedo Rocha is chairman of IMC-Brazil and has been director of dsg Consulting and T&D, a firm focusing on change management and organisational development, since 1989. He is a professor of management consulting for specialist postgraduate courses.

Matsui Shigeki is Secretary-General of Zen-Noh-Ren.

Dr Liz Mellish (info@mellish.com.au, www.mellish.com.au) lives in Australia and is a certified management consultant working with government, business, higher education and community organisations in change.

John Mills is a Fellow of the Chartered Institute of Personnel and Development and a managing partner of MPD Aviation Management Consultants. He has extensive experience of airport management and privatisation and advises airport proprietors, operators and financial institutions on the performance, ownership and management of airports worldwide. He was formerly group personnel director of BAA plc for thirteen years and played a leading role in the privatisation of the former British Airports Authority, having previously worked in airport planning and terminal management and operations.

Peter Nolan is emerging business support centre director of Deloitte & Touche.

Heather Osler is president of the Canadian Association of Management Consultants.

Bruce Petter is executive director of the Management Consultancies Association.

József Poór is general manager of Hay Group Management Consultants in Budapest and a part-time professor associated with the University of Pecs. He is a former president and an executive board member of FEACO.

Flemming Poulfelt is a research professor in the Department of Management, Politics & Philosophy at Copenhagen Business School in Denmark.

Anne Radford is an organisational consultant working with businesses, public agencies and communities. She coaches managers and consultants in their use of Appreciative Inquiry, is editor of the quarterly e-mail newsletter dedicated to AI, and a founding partner of Appreciative Inquiry Consulting. Email: annelondon@aol.com, website: www.aradford.co.uk

Dr Michael Reddy is a chartered accountant and clinical psychologist and chairman of the ICAS Group, international market leaders in the provision of employee assistance programmes (EAPs), stress management and counselling for disasters and major incidents. ICAS operates in seventeen countries.

Klaus Reiners is public relations manager of the BDU (Federal Association of German Management Consultants)

E. Michael Shays is president of EMS Consultants and EMS Learning and president of the Institute of Management Consultants, Inc. in the USA. He is also a past chairman and currently Executive Director of ICMCI.

Daniel Shepherd is a consultant for edgecom. His main focus is the mobile Internet and its application to the telecom and banking & finance sectors. He also works with organisational design and process issues.

Hans de Sonnaville set up a management consultancy firm 20 years ago, specialising in HRM and change management issues in all types of large-scale organisations. He lectures at the Free University of Amsterdam. Since 1985 he has been active in the IMC in The Netherlands and is responsible for its professional strategy. In the early 1990s he became a member of the Executive Committee of the ICMCI and was its president from 1999 to 2001.

Daniel Summerfield is a member of the IOD's Corporate Governance Executive.

Sarah Taylor is deputy director of the Management Consultancies Association (MCA) which represents the leading UK based consultancy firms. Sarah has been working in the consultancy industry for six years, providing PR and marketing services to the Institute of Management Consultancy (IMC), Partners for Change and the MCA. She frequently represents the industry to the media, government, academia and other organisations.

Walter E. Vieira is a principal of the Market Advisory Services Group, Bombay. He is also the immediate past president of ICMCI and a past president of the Executive Committee of the Institute of Management Consultant of India.

Martin Whitehill is chairman of the Strategic Planning Society in the UK, vice chairman of the European Strategic Planning Federation (umbrella for strategic management organisations throughout Europe). He is also chairman of the Strategy World Congress in March 2002 at Said Business School, University of Oxford. Martin teaches strategic business development and consultancy as well as consulting and advising blue-chip organisations around the world. Email Martin at *m.whitehill@tesco.net*

Allan P.O. Williams is professor of Occupational Psychology at the City University Business School, London. A founder member of CUBS in 1963, he has held the posts of Pro-Vice Chancellor, Director of the Centre for Personnel Research and Enterprise and Deputy Dean of the Business School, where he has also headed the Business Studies Department. He is a fellow of the British Psychological Society and Chartered Occupational Psychologist and has been a member of the Court of Assistants of the City of London Company of Management Consultants and its education committee since its inception.

André Wohlgemuth is chairman of ASCO, the Swiss Association of Management Consultants.

Sally Woodward is a research fellow in the Centre for Personnel Research and Enterprise Development at City University Business School, London which she joined in 1978 after a period of teaching in Australia and the UK. Jointly with Allan Williams, she conducted the research into what consultants actually do with their clients that identified the 1+7 model of consultancy roles and was published in the book *The Competitive Consultant – a client orientated approach for achieving superior perfomance* (1994, Macmillan). She is a chartered occupational psychologist and apart from her interest in consultancy has also researched fields such as career aspirations, recruitment and retention and future information technology skills.

Li Yong (lycmtd@public3.bta.net.cn) is now the deputy secretary general of China Association of International Trade (CAIT). He worked in Hong Kong from 1988–1993 with particular responsibility for marketing services. Before he joined CAIT, he had been the head of the Centre for Market and Trade Development for seven years. He has extensive experiences in market research in China and most of the research and services he has provided have been for foreign companies.

Foreword

Comparable to the global and national economies, and to all the organisations within these economies, the management consultancy sector has undergone enormous changes. Important trends like globalisation, IC technologies, mergers and acquisitions constantly influence the management consulting industry.

The products and services offered by management consultancy firms are wide-ranging and diverse. Clients, therefore, increasingly insist on more transparency with regard to what the management consulting industry actually involves and how management consultants work. As chairman of the International Council of Management Consulting Institutes, I am very pleased with the initiative to publish this international guide to management consultancy, especially intended for clients. Because of the huge variation in the services being offered, clients feel hesitant about making the right choice.

When deciding to call in the assistance of a management consultant, clients have to deal with certain paradoxes: for example, they want an experienced consultant but at the same time they expect fresh ideas. They want a consultant who can really give added value by a total commitment to the organisation and its management; however he must also be independent and able to keep a professional distance. Clients expect support for specific changes in their organisations but will have doubts and questions about the whole process of the assignment.

This book intends to give clients assistance in choosing the right management consultant who fits the specific situation of the organisation. This guide is supposed to make 'better' clients who, together with their consultants, will be able to achieve better results. Successful management consultancy is always based on two aspects. First of all, a consultant must always have the knowledge and experience to serve the client's needs. Secondly, the relationship between consultant and client should be based on mutual trust. Clarity in the way management consultants work, and how the process of consultancy develops, can lead to a successful outcome.

This guide comprises contributions from a number of experienced management consultants from all over the world. I am convinced that the editors have filled a need for the purchasers of management consultancy services and for the management consultancy profession.

Hans de Sonnaville
President, ICMCI
July 2001

Foreword

It is a great pleasure to learn that Kogan Page, the UK's leading independent publisher of business and management books, is publishing the new *International Guide to Management Consultancy* under the joint editorship of Barry Curnow and Jonathan Reuvid. I believe this is a very timely and proactive project that will greatly assist management consultants successfully to carry out consulting services in these times of accelerating globalisation.

The main theme at the World Management Consultants Convention, held in Berlin last year under the sponsorship of FEACO and the joint auspices of AMCF, ICMCI and Zen-Noh-Ren, was 'Management Consultancy in a Single World'. Mr. Kienbaum, the chairman of the convention organising committee and chairman of the BDU, made these impressive remarks in his opening speech:

> *Rapid progress in IT is revolutionising society, and the structure of the economy. It is enabling us to make business transactions wherever we may be, and the structure of the market is continuing to change with increasing speed. In this age, management consultants throughout the world are recognising that human contact is becoming more and more important in sharing information, especially now that the exchange of information is accelerating on a global scale. Those who use information, ie we management consultants, are facing a new challenge and need to ask ourselves how we should respond to it.*

At the same time as the Berlin Convention, Zen-Noh-Ren, commissioned by the Japanese government, conducted research into corporations and consulting firms – both in Japan and overseas – in order to formulate a vision of the management consulting industry in the 21st century. This research was undertaken as part of an effort to create a base of competitive power in

Japan to help it to cope with change in the business environment here and abroad.

The survey results showed that borderless market competition is the key factor affecting Japanese companies in these times of globalisation, and that the competitive advantage of Japanese industry in terms of quality and cost has diminished. This has given rise to a new need for the services of management consultants.

As Mr. Kienbaum points out, the shift towards globalisation has confronted management consulting industry in Japan with a significant challenge. Therefore, I am sure that *The International Guide to Management Consultancy* will be an essential read for management consultants and for those who aspire to be management consultants, and that it will be an indispensable handbook for everyone who aims to contribute to the peace and prosperity of the world through their profession.

Finally, I would like to express my hearty congratulations on this publication as well as my sincere respect to both esteemed gentlemen for their commitment to the edition.

Akira Hattori
Chairman, Zen-Noh-Ren
May 2001

Foreword

Since the beginning of the 1990s, the world economy has been converging at a breathtaking speed, there has been an increase of regional product flows and national markets are converting to a single global market. These developments are *the* essential characteristics of a globalisation trend in which a liberalisation of trade and investments are linked to a revolution in information and communication technologies.

These developments force the different players – companies, consumers and administrations – to extend their view beyond local and regional borders and to face the challenges and possibilities of the global markets. Borders are losing their importance; tradition is often questioned and frequently has to be waived. Europe in particular must face up and adapt to these changes.

In these times, when enterprises are increasingly multinational and small, and medium-sized companies compete internationally via the Internet and e-commerce, politicians are also forced to think globally. In this context, last year in Lisbon, the heads of state and government of the European Union set the goal that Europe needs to become the most competitive internal trade market in the world within the next decade. The planned establishment of the American free trade area is also a result of these processes.

The question arises of what effect these developments will have on the global consultancy market. The expectations of clients are changing rapidly: they demand not only 'traditional' consultancy services, such as advice, but also practical results, for instance implemented operational solutions that secure a market position through the use of IT or e-business. The new market is global, which means that local particularities (legal, social, cultural etc) need to be taken into account, together with the global perspective. Today, consultancy is much more comprehensive and requires a wide range of skills and disciplines to be successful.

These changes also require a global perspective. Consultancies need to serve clients in multiple countries in different continents. Equally, the frameworks within which the economy operates are rapidly changing; the effect of these changes often reaches beyond continental borders – for instance the EU Takeover Directive, the OECD-Declarations with relation to the tax code and the GATS agreement. In addition, the accession to the EU of Eastern European countries will lead to new dynamics.

In view of these developments, it is clear that only a few consultancies are able to cover the whole breadth of knowledge and services. Consultants will increasingly have to revert to joint ventures and other forms of cooperation in order to serve clients in the global economy.

Many opportunities and challenges arise in the future of consultancy. This guide, covering wide areas of consultancy, will assist consultants whether in larger or smaller firms, to keep abreast of these developments. It identifies national, continental and global developments and trends. It does not limit itself – and in this it distinguishes itself from other works – to technical and economical aspects of successful consultancy as historical developments and professional principles are also covered.

I hope readers will find it interesting and helpful.

Gil Gidron
FEACO Chairman
July 2001

Introduction

We have prepared this book for a specific international readership of buyers and users of management consultancy in both the private and public sectors. We hope that *The International Guide to Management Consultancy* will provide readers with fresh insight into the practice of management consultancy and its key activities, as well as a deeper understanding of the professional standards which local Institutes are establishing worldwide and, most importantly, of best practice in client-consultant relationships.

The book has two distinct but linked themes: the developing professionalism in consulting, to which the International Council of Management Consulting Institutes (ICMCI) and all its member countries are dedicated; and the nature of an effective, interactive relationship between client and consultant as an essential ingredient of all successful consultancy engagements. Although primarily addressing users and potential clients, we believe that the contents of this Guide will also be of more than passing interest to professional consultants themselves, to students of consultancy in the burgeoning postgraduate programmes around the world and to the ever-broadening practitioners of consulting skills and competencies. This audience forms a strong and growing community of allied professionals, ranging from lawyers through executive coaches to corporate change managers, who deploy consulting skills as essential survival skills in advisory work and helping client change efforts in the post-employment labour markets of the international e-economy.

Part One sets out to identify the parameters and definitions of management consultancy. It then presents overviews of the industry's origins and evolution, the present status of the leading multinational management consultancies and some of the global forces shaping the development of management consultancy.

A range of alternative scenarios for the consulting market in 2010 is presented in the final chapter of this section, drawn from a recent study commissioned by the City of London Company of Management Consultants.

Part Two is devoted to ethics and best practice in management consultancy from a number of perspectives. Central to these discussions, and referred to in several chapters, is the international development of the Certified Management Consultant (CMC) qualification, pioneered by ICMCI members and now with academic accreditation in a number of countries and adopted by all ICMCI Institutes worldwide.

Part Three, which forms the core of the book, scrutinises the life of the client-consultant relationship from setting the guidelines for an assignment, selecting and appointing a consultancy, through to closing off on completion and any subsequent engagement. In describing this 'soup to nuts' process (including post-prandial digestion) the authors focus on what clients can do to make the consultant's role effective and their working relationship productive. The emphasis on client involvement throughout the engagement reflects a shift away from the era of top-down management (when companies commissioned consultancy, then sat back and waited for the delivery of a final report) to today's more participatory styles of management.

Part Four comprises snapshots by leading practitioners of thirteen key consultancy fields ranging from strategy and marketing through change management, process re-engineering, management development, communications and customer relations to the newer disciplines of information and knowledge management, m-commerce, ERP and e-business.

Each chapter is intended to give a sufficient understanding of the topic for the client to formulate a consultancy requirement and to manage the consultant appointed.

Part Five consists of a general account of consulting in developing countries, followed by profiles of 26 country-by-country management consultancy markets. In addition, we are indebted to Jozsef Poor, Professor Flemming Poulfelt and Walter Vieira for their respective overviews of Central and Eastern Europe, Scandinavia and the emerging South-East Asian consultancy markets.

A number of books about management consultancy are referred to in the authors' text. These have been written mostly for the general instruction of practising and aspiring consultants, as textbooks for students engaged in academic programmes or as handbooks to specific consultancy techniques and activities. For further reading by users of consultancy we commend Philip Sadler's *Management Consultancy: a handbook for best practice* (Kogan Page1998, 2001), now in its second edition, which is addressed both to consultants and students of consultancy and is endorsed by the UK's two industry bodies, the Institute of Management Consultancy (IMC) and the Management Consultancies' Association (MCA) – both contributors to this book and strong supporters of the task of the joint consulting editors.

For the editors of *The International Guide to Management Consultancy,* working on this book has been both educational and enjoyable. To single out any of the 28 authors of complete chapters for particular thanks would be invidious. They are all busy practitioners or academics in the broad field of management consultancy and, in several cases, are used to performing the client rather than the consultant role. Individually, their contributions carry the weight of experience which ensures a rich blend of theory and practice. Collectively, their work represents a unique body of knowledge. We offer our grateful thanks to each of them for the insight which they have shared in their specific interests and specialisations within the consulting field.

In conclusion, our thanks go to Hans de Sonnaville, Chairman of ICMCI, Gil Gidron, Chairman of FEACO and Akira Attori, Chairman of Zen-Noh-Ren, the All Japan Federation of Management Organisations, for their supportive Forewords. (The memberships of all three organisations are shown in the appendices). Endorsement by these bodies is testimony to the excellent co-operation between management consultancy's leading international organisations, as well as the truly international scope of this book.

Barry Curnow and Jonathan Reuvid
London, September 2001

1

The evolution and practice of management consultancy globally

1.1

The international consulting industry today

Barry Curnow and Jonathan Reuvid

This Handbook aims to help clients make the most of their management consulting advice and services through understanding consultants and consultancy better. There are five different perspectives or lenses through which clients can usefully examine their consulting people, relationships and prospects, five windows on the world of the global consulting community. Each window gives a deep insight into one of the major driving forces that make consultancy tick. It is therefore instructive to consider each viewpoint before major consulting appointments are made or decisions taken. The five perspectives are as follows:

- Consulting as a significant, competitive growing global *industry* with its economic scale and impact, markets, segments, brands and players – both firms and individuals who are salaried employees and self employed
- Consulting as an international *professional* community with its standards, ethics, education, training, qualifications, codes of conduct and professional institutes and trade associations

- Consulting as the *products and services* that consultants provide, their *activities* and what they actually do in partnership with their clients
- Consulting as the perceptions of the role that *consultants* play, their image and reputation in the different cultures and communities on the world stage
- Consulting as the universal skill of the professional adviser, the personal coach or the counsellor who gives guidance to people and companies. The art and craft of tendering consulting advice which recognises consulting as a *life-skill and necessary competency* in the post-employment labour-markets of the digital economy

Aspects of consulting as a professional community are debated in Part Two – Ethics and Best Practice. Consultancy products and services are featured in Part Four, while Part Three examines the roles that clients play in terms of client-consultancy relationships.

Consulting is both very old and very new. States and citizens have sought wise counsel throughout history, often depending literally for their survival on its skill and integrity. Yet the digital economy is revolutionising consulting delivery and underpinning explosive growth in the consulting networks of international business. E-consultancies have been amongst the most rapid growth stories and the most spectacular failures of the dotcom episode in the electronic revolution.

The global consulting industry

The global consulting industry is estimated to be worth between US$100 billion and £100 billion in total fee revenues, depending on the definitions used. Until recently it has been a predominantly North Atlantic phenomenon with the UK and US combined accounting for more than half the world market and together with Western Europe a full two thirds of the total world-wide industry.

However, these are mature markets. The fastest growing consulting economies are those described as 'the rest of the world'

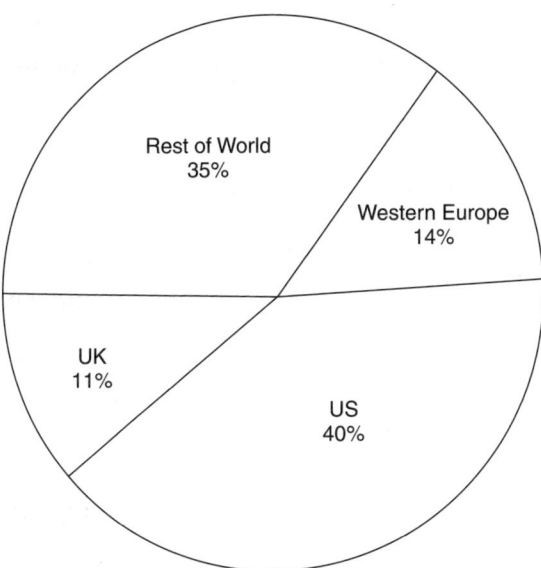

Figure 1.1.1 Geographical share of world market
Source: Calvert Markham CST

including Central and Eastern Europe, Asia Pacific, Latin America and Africa.

This is big business in any economic analysis and the giant brand name consultancies account for up to half of this revenue while representing approximately one third of the employment. Yet the majority of consultancy firms are small, with nearly two-thirds of consultants working in consultancies with fewer than ten employees. Consequently there are the few big brand name firms employing up to 10,000 employees each worldwide and then hundreds of thousands of consultants working from small units, often as sole practitioners.

There are between 250,000 and 500,000 management consultants in the world at the present time, depending on the definition used. The lower figure would approximate to the qualifiable group of potential certified management consultants eligible to put themselves forward for the competence based CMC professional qualification, awarded in the 35 member countries of the ICMCI to a single global standard.

The higher figure would embrace a much wider catchment of professional advisers and sub-contractors and would include: technical specialists in IT who were using consulting skills as described above; consultants in professional areas such as public relations and communications and in non-managerial recruitment and training, where the management component of the advice was modest or the service provided is more of an outsourced facility (ICMCI 2001 estimates).

The growth of consultancy as an industry

At the 2001 IMC Consultancy Forum in London, Calvert Markham of Consultancy Skills Training Limited said

It seems hard to remember a time when the large firms of accountants were not also major providers of consultancy. But 25 years ago, we debated whether the accounting firms would ever be serious players. And 10 years ago, the same question might have been asked of major IT companies.

The current status of the multinational management consultancies and their recent development is discussed in Chapter 1.3.

Markham went on to explain the growth of consultancy as follows:

Providing consultancy services is the result of a natural process of evolution [as shown in Figure 1.1.2]. Product enhancement requires increasing involvement with the customer; the reward is that the customer sees the provider as being of increasing value. So an IT supplier might start by providing a computer (level 1) but then help the customer to maintain and use it (level 2). They go on to help the customer use the computer to automate their existing systems (level 3). Finally – and of most value – they suggest some applications for the computer the customer hasn't thought of, which will give competitive advantage (level 4).

THE INTERNATIONAL CONSULTING INDUSTRY TODAY 11

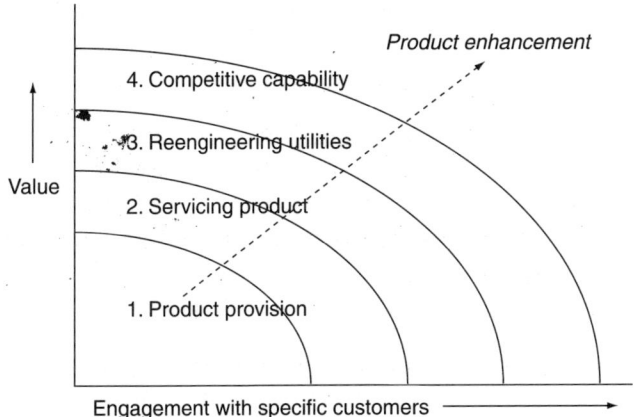

Figure 1.1.2 Product evolution
Source: Calvert Markham CST

Markham recognises that there are plenty of businesses that will not follow this evolutionary progression, but suggests that there are two drivers that have prompted many consultancies to adopt this growth path:

- if a business is set up on the basis of having a differentiated and high value product, it is difficult for them to make the transition to become a low cost organisation where they can compete on price alone. So they look to the evolution as a means of continued differentiation.
- many businesses see consultancy as a way of going higher up the client hierarchy towards the boardroom where higher value projects are authorised.

So the typical transition they want to make is that shown in Figure 1.1.3

The enlarging definition of 'consultancy'

Do these emergent consultancies represent the competition for the future? Markham says that the term 'consultancy' covers a far wider range of activities than it ever did in the past. The situation is now

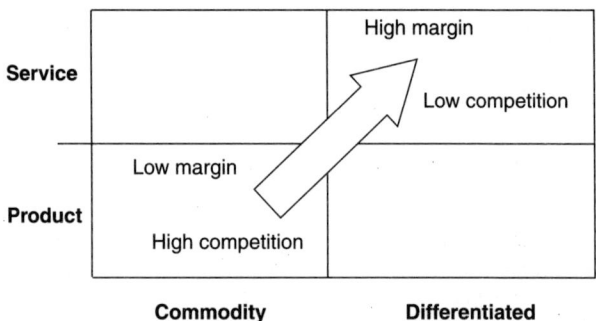

Figure 1.1.3 Towards the Promised Land: Consultancy activities are a means of differentiation and increasing customer intimacy
Source: Calvert Markham CST

further complicated by the work that many firms take on – particularly larger projects. His impression of it is shown in Figure 1.1.4.

Process outsourcing clearly involves people undertaking different work from mainstream consultancy; *new projects* many involve consultancies taking on far more implementation work than they might have done 20 years ago. However, the job of the consultant in many circumstances has fewer degrees of freedom than it had previously – hence Markham uses the term 'sub-contractor'.

He positions the various products in consultancy on a spectrum as shown in Figure 1.1.5.

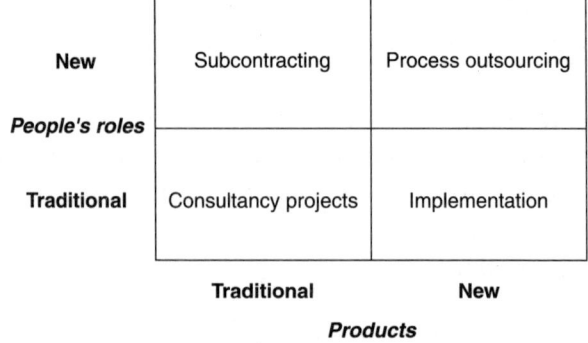

Figure 1.1.4 An increasing product range
Source: Calvert Markham CST

Problem We work with you to define the problem in the first place	High value: customer intimate strategy	Value pricing
Knowledge We can provide the answers to your problems	Medium value: technical excellence strategy	Fees
Commodity We are better placed than you to provide the solutions needed	Low value: operational excellence strategy	Low costs

Figure 1.1.5 Product Domains
Source: Calvert Markham CST

Three domains are shown, with the highest value at the top. In the problem domain the client has a high trust of the consultancy; in the knowledge domain, the consultants have knowledge and abilities that the client doesn't have, while in the commodity domain, the client has elected to sub-contract the work to an outsider. The dominant strategy for each domain shows the area in which the business has to perform superlatively to compete effectively. The preferred pricing policy in each domain is a function of the perceived value.

This analysis illuminates consultancy competition. While many traditional consultancies have been extending their product range down the value ladder, emergent consultancies have been extending their product range in the opposite direction as shown in Figure 1.1.6.

This illustrates both the drive to standardisation that comes with growth as consultancies mature, as well as the development of emergent consultancies wishing to diversify from providing standard products and services into higher added value, more tailored general management consultancy.

Emergent consultancies are to be found among the professional and business service providers who use consultancy skills to provide additional help and value in implementing solutions (see below).

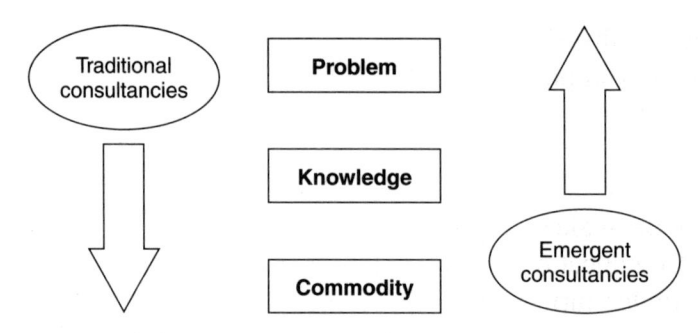

```
Traditional          Problem
consultancies
    ↓
                     Knowledge
                                    ↑
                                 Emergent
                     Commodity   consultancies
```

Figure 1.1.6 Modes of expansion
Source: Calvert Markham CST

Consulting in developing and transition economies

The playing field (or perhaps the goal posts) for consultants may differ in the developing countries referred to in Chapter 5.1, or in those countries in transition where command economies are transforming to open markets. Both types of market pose special challenges for consultants.

In the latter, management mindsets appear to lag behind the changing conditions and more sophisticated business environment. Sometimes this is because the transformation is by decree from the same regime as before or from a para-democratic authoritarian government under which entrepreneurial values are espoused by edict.

More significantly, managers in transition economies find it especially difficult to change their approaches to HR and to take on board 'non-command' activities, such as marketing, product design and customer service where the customer has metamorphosed from vassal to king. There is a temptation to bolt new tools and techniques on to their established organisation structures and management systems, turn on the switch and expect miracle improvements to flow through.

As a consequence of the IT revolution, the awareness of advanced technology and the focus of universities and technical colleges in absorbing the latest first world techniques and equipment, companies in transition economies – particularly state-owned enterprises – insist on taking quantum leaps rather than making incremental improvements. The transformation gap is wider than in developed economies and the consultant needs to recognise the scale of the task.

Finally, education is not enough. While universities and technical institutes turn out streams of graduates – highly qualified academically and technically – they have no practical field or shop-floor experience. Consultants must learn to address the problem of highly educated management teams which are dyslexic in the language and experience of practical business management. This is the opportunity for international professional management consultants in the 'rest of the world' sector of this global industry – the segment where the greatest future growth and opportunity to make a difference is to be found.

Management consultancy as an international profession

The Institutes of Management Consultancy around the world that are member organisations of the International Council of Management Consulting Institutes (ICMCI) recognise the following fields of management activity:

- corporate policy and corporate development
- financial management
- administration
- marketing and selling
- production
- distribution and transport
- information technology
- economic planning
- environmental planning
- human resource management

- management sciences
- technology management

Simply put, management consultants give guidance to those holding management accountability in the above fields of activity within business and not-for-profit organisations. A consultant is somebody, usually from outside the organisation, often with special knowledge, who helps the client to achieve something that moves the business forward which could not be achieved if the consultant were not present.

The fields recognised by the ICMCI as management consultancy are:

- business administration and company organisation
- capital projects, economic planning and finance
- operational research, industrial engineering and production
- marketing distribution and transport
- personnel management training and environmental planning
- systems and data processing.

The ICMCI's formal definition of management consultancy is:

> *The service provided to business public and other undertakings by an independent and qualified person or persons in identifying and investigating problems concerned with policy, organisation, procedures and methods, recommending appropriate action and helping to implement those recommendations.*

It follows therefore that a management consultant is an independent and qualified person who provides a professional service to business, the public and other undertakings by:

- identifying and investigating problems concerned with strategy, policy, markets, organisation, procedures and methods
- formulating recommendations for appropriate action by factual investigation and analysis, with due regard for broader management and business implications

- discussing and agreeing with the client the most appropriate course of action
- providing assistance where required by the client to implement these recommendations.

The international management consultancy profession is organised by its professional institutes who work closely with its trade associations in each country and region. In many countries the professional institute and the trade association are part of the same organisation with Chinese walls to ring fence the independence of the standard-setting, qualification awarding professional institute activity from the business winning, commercial representation role of the associations.

ICMCI, as the umbrella organisation for professional standards works closely with its sister bodies such as FEACO, AMCF, Zen Noh Ren.

What consultants actually do

This view of consulting studies what consultants actually do and the goods and services they provide. It seeks to understand consulting activity by appreciating the client-consultant relationship and the joint work that they do together

There are also clearly discernible roles that the consultant undertakes. Research by Williams and Woodward (1994) identified the '1 + 7' model whereby the consultant is primarily recognised as being an 'expert' in a particular field. This role as 'expert' is central to the consultant but of equal importance to and dependent upon the other seven roles identified by the authors; this is what they actually do, the roles they perform for clients with the expertise that they have:

- *Executive*: the managerial role a consultant must assume when carrying out a project for a client
- *Researcher*: demands a high level of skill in communication, presentation, interviewing, recording and interpreting quantitative and qualitative data

- *Tutor*: in the role of counsellor a consultant helps a client to explore and understand a problem by skilfully questioning, answering, listening and understanding
- *Educator*: the educator/trainer enables individuals to acquire new knowledge or skills through clear learning objectives to use in solving an immediate work problem
- *Powerbroker*: sometimes in order to achieve objectives a consultant must facilitate change by mobilising and harnessing sources of power in the client structure
- *Conciliator*: getting people to work together effectively who have not done so previously
- *Synergist*: enabling individuals to work together and use their talents in new ways

The consulting idea, image and reputation

The idea of the consultant is a powerful and evocative one in the media. Perceptions of what people think consultants do and represent in different cultures and communities, create a strong image of the sort of work and thinking that consultants are associated with in the press and on television and the internet. This is often an evocative image but sometimes misleading. A recent UK television programme referred to management consultants as 'Masters of the Universe' and this, together with books entitled *Dangerous Company* and *The Witch Doctors* fuelled a popular view of consultants as influential, powerful and somewhat shadowy figures exerting far reaching influence over companies. The leaders of some of the more fashionable consultancies have even been quoted by social scientists and opinion pollsters as among the most influential people in different societies and within the international business community.

Yet the advisory role makes the management consultant an easy target for scapegoating. Professor Colin Coulson-Thomas (1992) found in his research that consultants are the necessary evil that company leaders love to hate. He reported a dilemma that *en masse*, the collectivity of consultants and business schools were regarded as parasites, whereas the individual consultants whom Chief Executives used as advisers were seen as facilitators and trusted helpers: the image and idea of the consultant attracting opprobrium but the individual people being recognised for their skill and consulting competency.

Consulting skills

And it is consulting skill and competency that drive the global consulting networks of the international community. Consultancy is still (after the dotcom bubble burst) a first choice employment for the brightest business graduates from the leading business schools of the world. The brand name consultancies still compete fiercely for the intellectual horsepower that is the raw material of the consultancy process. However, there is an important sense in which we are all consultants now, that consulting competency is no longer the magical secret of the chosen few in the top firms but an efficient management housekeeping skill necessary for the support of making everyday business operate effectively.

References

Williams, Allan and Woodward, Sally (1994), *The Competitive Consultant*, Palgrave (formerly Macmillan Press)

Coulson-Thomas, Colin (1992), *Transforming the Company*, Kogan Page

1.2

The evolution of management consultancy: its origins and global development

Matthias Kipping

Introduction

Today, management consulting is a multi-billion-dollar business. Some of the largest service providers have more employees and higher revenues than many of their clients. Others, while of a smaller size, enjoy a considerable amount of influence with decision-makers – not only in the economy, but also in politics and society. The object of this chapter is to trace the evolution of the industry from its modest origins around the end of the 19th century up to today. It will try to show that there were several major waves of development in terms both of the focus of consultancy work and of the major service providers and their features. It will also examine the international expansion of the major consultancies, most of them of American origin, during each of these waves and their influence on the development of the industry outside the United States. While describing evolution and change, it will also attempt to identify a number of characteristics of the consultancy business that remained constant during much of the 20th century.

In a long-term perspective, the evolution of the consulting industry and of its pre-eminent firms is closely linked to the development of management practice and ideology. Consultancy can therefore be understood as a reflection of prevailing managerial problems and definitions. Thus, when there was a major shift in the role of managers and in the focus of their attention, the kind of consultancy they used also changed. This means that consultancies are ultimately dependent on the evolution of management. However, since not all companies everywhere changed at the same moment, the related changes in the consulting industry were not clear-cut and radical. Consultancies with a different focus often co-existed for a considerable time. Examining the life spans and growth rates of the pre-eminent service providers nevertheless makes it possible to distinguish three different – albeit overlapping – waves in the evolution of management consulting since the beginning of the 20th century.

Scientific management and the emergence of a consulting industry

The large-scale managerial enterprise originated with the second industrial revolution in the last half of the 19th century. This meant that in many industries the 'visible hand' of management took over part of the economic co-ordination function from the 'invisible hand' of the market. Almost from the outset, top managers in these enterprises asked for outside advice. A number of different agents, including bankers, advertising agents, auditors and engineers, provided such services – initially on an *ad hoc* basis. Consulting to managers became a clearly recognisable business activity, carried out for financial gain, with the development of scientific management.

At the end of the 19th century, the engineer Frederick W. Taylor (1856–1915) developed a new approach towards the management of workers on the shop floor – later extended by others to office work – based on systematic observation, optimum organisation and stimulation of individual activities. He presented his ideas in meetings with colleagues in the engineering profession and in a number of publications, including his well-known book, *The Principles of Scientific Management*, first published in 1911. He also installed his system for a fee in a number of companies. Some of those who developed similar but competing approaches became much more involved in consulting activities. Harrington Emerson developed his own method of payment-by-results and established a consultancy in 1899, which had offices in New York, Pittsburgh, Chicago, Philadelphia and Tacoma less than 20 years later.

These early management consultants were known as industrial engineers or efficiency experts. Probably the most successful among them was the consultancy established in the American Midwest by the French immigrant Charles E. Bedaux (1886–1944) in 1916. According to a survey carried out by the National Industrial Conference Board in 1930, the Bedaux System had become the most widely used method of payment-by-results in the United States. At that time, Bedaux had offices in New York, Boston, Chicago, Cleveland and Portland. Among his American clients were a large number of well-known firms such as Eastman Kodak, B. F. Goodrich, Du Pont and General Electric. The consultancy also expanded to Europe and other parts of the world from 1926 onwards, when it opened its first foreign office in London. Expansion was particularly rapid during the 1930s and the 1940s, in part prompted by the need for rapid efficiency improvements during the Second World War.

The human relations consultants, most of which originated during the 1930s or 1940s, are in some ways an extension to this wave because they evaluate performance at the managerial level.

Today, the leading service providers such as the Hay Group, Watson Wyatt Worldwide and William H. Mercer have reached a considerable size, with the latter, for example, employing around 12,500 consultants in 2000. However, none of these consultancies ever achieved the same prominence as Bedaux or, subsequently, McKinsey. This might be due to their focus on benefits, compensation and remuneration consulting, which makes them a kind of niche player. Most of their efforts to diversify into other areas have so far had only limited success.

In the UK, Bedaux became the progenitor of the emerging consulting industry, when some engineers left the consultancy to set up their own firms. These included Production Engineering, Urwick Orr and Partners, both set up in 1934, and Personnel Administration, established in 1943. Together with the original Bedaux consultancy, renamed Associated Industrial Consultants (AIC) in 1938, they became known as the 'Big Four'. In 1956, when they founded the Management Consultants Association (MCA), they together employed over 800 consultants and accounted for more than three-quarters of a total market estimated at £4 million. In its annual report for 1961, the MCA estimated that the revenue of its member firms had increased by more than ten per cent per annum over the previous decade. It should be noted that these consultancies were not successful in all countries. In Germany and Japan for example, scientific management methods were disseminated mainly by associations and the exchange of experiences among firms.

From the 1950s onwards, most of the first generation consultancies diversified their activities, but without losing the central focus on efficiency enhancement. The post-war period also saw the emergence of more sophisticated approaches to measure and reward worker performance. The so-called Methods-Time Measurement (MTM) system became particularly prominent and widely used. It allowed managers to establish optimum motions and 'normal' times under laboratory conditions rather than on the shop floor. One of its inventors, Harold B. Maynard, also disseminated it through a consultancy, which expanded rapidly in the

United States and abroad. By the end of the 1960s, it had offices in eight European countries, employing about 330 consultants, making it the largest American service provider in western Europe at the time. However, from the late 1950s onwards these consultancies were increasingly displaced by a new generation of service providers, which focused on issues of corporate organization and strategy.

Consulting top management on organisation and strategy

The second wave of management consultancies first emerged in the United States during the 1930s and came to worldwide prominence from the late 1950s onwards. Its rise benefited from changes in the size and structures of companies as well as from more competitive environments. Following rapid growth, increasing diversification and higher market pressures, a number of US companies, such as General Motors and DuPont, developed more decentralised organisation structures in the 1920s and 1930s with relatively independent divisions, controlled and co-ordinated by a corporate head office. This structure has subsequently been termed the multi-divisional or M-form.

Consultants played an important role in spreading the M-form in the United States and, from the 1950s onward, abroad. They also came to offer all kinds of other advice to the top management of the new corporations. However, it was not the efficiency engineers who took advantage of these new opportunities, but a wide range of new service providers with rather diverse origins, including contract research, psychology and accounting. Among the early movers were Arthur D. Little, Booz Allen & Hamilton, and McKinsey & Company. By the end of the 1960s, Booz Allen had become the largest US service provider with more than 1,200 consultants. But the consultancy, which in a way came to epitomise what some scholars term 'modern' management consulting, was McKinsey.

Its founder, James O. McKinsey, had been teaching accounting at the University of Chicago since 1917 and had published a large number of books and articles on the subject, including an influential volume, *Budgetary Control*, in 1922. In 1926, he established a consulting company based on the idea that budgeting was a way to obtain in-depth insight into the whole organisation and a means of business administration. It was quite successful providing business surveys, initially to financial institutions, but increasingly to large companies such as US Steel. In 1935, McKinsey himself joined one of his clients, the Chicago-based retailer Marshall Fields, as CEO. When he died of pneumonia less than two years later, the consultancy effectively split between the two offices in Chicago and New York, which agreed not to compete with each other. The split was formally recognised in 1946, when the New York office purchased the exclusive right to use the McKinsey name for an undisclosed – but apparently substantial – sum, which also removed any constraints on competition between the two. At that time, Marvin Bower, a Harvard-trained lawyer, was running the New York office. The Chicago office took the name of its senior partner Tom (A T) Kearney.

Under Bower, McKinsey & Co. grew relatively fast and already employed more than 200 consultants by the early 1960s. Subsequently, it surpassed both the scientific management consultancies and the first movers of its own generation, such as Arthur D. Little and Booz Allen, in terms of employees and visibility. McKinsey was particularly successful in its international expansion, opening its first foreign office in London in 1959. By the end of the 1960s, it already had six offices in western Europe, which accounted for more than one-third of its revenue at the time. The success of this new generation sparked a number of spin-offs from the existing consulting firms, namely in the 1960s and 1970s, similar to what had happened with Bedaux and other scientific management consultancies about three decades earlier. Thus, in 1963 Bruce Hendersen left Arthur D. Little to set up the Boston Consulting Group (BCG), which focused on corporate strategy, using a number of innovative tools. Former BCG consultants in turn were at the origin of several other important firms. These included Roland Berger who left in 1967 to set up his own consultancy, which is today the largest service provider of German origin. William Bain started another important BCG spin-off in 1973.

From the 1980s onwards, new challengers emerged to the organisation and strategy consultancies in the form of the large accountancies and some IT firms. Once again this was related to a change in the organisation and management of companies themselves.

A new generation of information and communication consultancies

From the late 1970s onwards, the large diversified corporations came under increasing pressure, notably following the arrival of new competitors with leaner and more focused structures from Japan and other Asian countries. Subsequently, the increasingly global financial markets have continued to force companies to concentrate on their core competencies and adopt leaner management structures. Consequently, the co-ordination of activities both within companies and with suppliers and customers has become a crucial competitive advantage. The role of managers has changed as a result, focusing less on corporate organisation and strategy and more on the management of the value chain as well as internal and external relationships. At the same time, the development of information technology has enabled managers to obtain the necessary data to maintain control over such a networked organisation.

The first to exploit these opportunities for new types of consulting were the large Anglo-American accounting firms. Auditors and accountants had been offering consultancy-type services from the 19th century onwards, for example in cases of restructuring and bankruptcy. Most of the accountancy firms established separate units to provide management advisory services after the Second World War. When the revenues in their main accounting and audit business became more or less stagnant from the late 1970s onwards they responded on the one hand with a series of mergers, which gradually reduced their number to five at the end of the 1990s (Arthur Andersen, Deloitte & Touche, Ernst & Young, KPMG and PriceWaterhouseCoopers). On the other hand, they also expanded their services in other areas including tax, as well as legal advice and consulting to management. Revenues from these activities began to reach significant proportions during the 1980s with an even more rapid growth thereafter, soon exceeding revenues from their more traditional activities.

For these accountancies, much of the growth in consulting services resulted from assignments related to information technology. In this respect, the big accountancy firms had significant competitive advantages. They were among the first to become familiar with large-scale IT systems, because accounting and auditing had increasingly relied on computer hardware and software. In addition, audits, which are a legal requirement and a more or less guaranteed source of income, were a convenient entry for consultancy. But this source of business strength was also at the origin of a conflict of interest. Audit partners were not always happy to introduce colleagues from the consultancy division to their clients. They were concerned that a failed consulting project might lead to the loss of the audit contract and therefore pose a significant risk for future revenue streams. This, in addition to the differences in growth potential, led to increasing strains between the accounting and consulting arms of these large firms. It has prompted some of them to split completely (such as Arthur Andersen and Andersen Consulting, now Accenture) even before pressure from the regulators in the United States accelerated this trend.

Some of the work taken on by this new generation of consultancy firms consisted of IT operations outsourced by companies wanting to concentrate on their core activities. In this particular area, these consultancies competed with other large IT services organizations, such as Electronic Data Systems (EDS) or Computer Sciences Corporation (CSC). Both also expanded into consulting activities through acquisitions. Thus, in 1995 EDS acquired A.T. Kearney, one of the oldest second-generation consultancies. More recently, hardware manufacturers such as IBM have also expanded into consulting because it is seen to offer much higher margins than their traditional business. Another company to enter the outsourcing and consulting business on a very large scale over the last decade was the French computer and software services firm Cap Gemini. It grew almost exclusively through acquisitions. Its merger with the consulting division of Ernst & Young in 2000 propelled it into the top ten worldwide consultancies.

In the last decade of the 20th century, the above mentioned consultancies managed to establish themselves firmly among the largest service providers in the world. In most cases, they displaced or sometimes acquired the larger national firms. American organisation and strategy consultants of the second generation were able to remain among the top ten or twenty firms. However, while still growing in absolute terms, they clearly lost market share to the newcomers.

Summary and outlook

This overview of the evolution of the consulting industry has identified three major generations of management consultancies during the 20th century. They could be characterised tentatively as scientific management, organisation and strategy, and communication and information. The emergence – and the decline – of the different waves of management consultancies were related to major changes in the client companies, in terms of size, organisation and their management (the role and attention of executives). Consultancies of the second and, even more so, of the third generation had been around for some time, but only began to achieve a significant size and prominence when the type of consulting required by companies shifted: from shop floor efficiency improvements to corporate organisation and strategy, and then to IT-based network solutions.

Since these shifts did not occur overnight, consultancies of the different generations usually co-existed for quite some time. The following table summarises the main aspects of the historical overview.

Table 1.2.1 The different waves in the evolution of the consulting industry

Wave	Key Issues	Overall Duration	Major Expansion	Prominent Consultancies
Scientific Management	Efficiency of workers and production	1900s–1980s	1930s–1950s	Emerson, Bedaux, 'Big Four', Maynard
Organisation and Strategy	Decentralisation and portfolio planning	1930s–	1960s–1980s	Booz Allen, McKinsey, A.T. Kearney, BCG
Communication and Information	Internal and external co-ordination	1960s–	1990s–	Big Five, EDS, CSC, Cap Gemini

There is little doubt that information technology has become increasingly central for management and, therefore, for management consulting today. It prompted the rapid expansion of a third wave of consultancy services, dominated by large professional services firms. It seems that this is a shift similar to the move from shop floor efficiency to organization and strategy and that, on the whole, the consultancies of the second generation have already started to decline, albeit only in relative terms.

Some of them have been bought (eg A T Kearney), others are considering merging in order to remain competitive (cf the recent discussions between Arthur D Little and PA). While appearing somewhat far-fetched, the possibility cannot be excluded that even such stalwarts as McKinsey or BCG might eventually decide to give up their independence or, alternatively, continue as niche players.

As mentioned above, many of the consultancies in this third wave have reached an unprecedented size exceeding many of their client firms in terms of revenues and employees. This raises a number of issues (some of which will be addressed in more detail in later parts of this volume), namely regarding market dominance and the governance of these mega-consultancies themselves. It is clear that the large integrated professional services firms exercise a significant degree of market power and cannot always guarantee that their parts act independently if working for the same client. These concerns have prompted pressures from regulators in the United States, which in turn has led most of the Big Five to consider selling or spinning-off their consultancy arms through IPOs. So far, only Arthur Andersen appears to be bucking this trend by rebuilding its consultancy activities following the separation from Andersen Consulting (renamed Accenture from 2001).

Another area of possible market dominance concerns the relationship between the large consultancies and the providers of business software, such as SAP, Oracle or Microsoft. While the consultancies tend to present themselves as independent, they all have close relationships with the software companies who are, in a certain respect, their real clients because it is often they who decide which of the big consultancies is asked to help with the implementation of the new Enterprise Resource Planning or e-business software.

At the same time, the consultancies are likely to push the installation of new IT-based systems as a response to organisational problems. However, their mutually beneficial relationship might come under some strain in the near future, because some of the software providers appear poised to enter the lucrative consultancy market on a larger scale, following a slowdown and the erosion of margins in their core business.

But the repercussions of the recent shifts in the consulting industry go well beyond the clients. They also concern the business schools, which can no longer be assured that the biggest and most prestigious service providers will automatically employ a large share of their MBA graduates. The new mega-consultancies appear to provide most of the necessary training in-house, rather than 'sub-contracting' it to the business schools, like most of the firms in the second wave did and continue to do so today. Finally, the changes are also affecting the organisation and governance of these consultancies themselves. Given their size, it appears increasingly difficult for them to operate as partnerships. Following their IPO, these service providers might adopt more traditional forms of ownership and organisation, which in turn should allow them to react more quickly to changes in the competitive environment and take a longer-term perspective in terms of the necessary investments. It will also make them less dependent on individual partners deciding to leave the firm.

Thus, not only in terms of size, but also recruitment, career patterns, corporate governance, etc, consulting seems to be becoming increasingly similar to other service industries, losing some of the special, almost 'artisanal' nature that it held during much of the 20th century.

Further reading

For a more detailed description and explanation of the different generations see Matthias Kipping (2001), 'Trapped in their wave? The evolution of management consultancies', in T. Clark and R. Fincham (eds.) *Critical Consulting*, Blackwell, Oxford

For the international expansion see Matthias Kipping (1999) 'American management consulting companies in western Europe, 1920 to 1990: Products, reputation and relationships', *Business History Review*, **73**, No. 2, Summer 1999, pp 190–220

For the emergence of the second generation see Christopher D. McKenna (1995), 'The origins of modern management consulting', *Business and Economic History*, **24**, No. 1, Fall 1995, pp 51–58

For the third generation see Roy Suddaby and Roysten Greenwood (2001), 'The quickening cycle of commodification and colonization of management knowledge', in K. Sahlin-Andersson and L. Engwall (eds), *The Expansion of Management Knowledge: Carriers, Ideas and Circulation*, Stanford University Press, Stanford

Details regarding the main service providers of the different generations can be found in: Hal Higdon (1969), *The Business Healers*, Random House, New York

James O'Shea and Charles Madigan (1997), *Dangerous Company: The Consulting Powerhouses and the Businesses they Save and Ruin*, Nicholas Brealey, London

For the developments in the UK see:
Patricia Tisdall (1982), *Agents of Change: The Development and Practice of Management Consultancy*, Heinemann, London

Michael Ferguson (2001), *The Rise of Management Consulting in Britain*, Ashgate, Aldershot

For some of the other countries see the contributions in Matthias Kipping and Lars Engwall eds (2001), *Management Consulting: The Emergence and Dynamics of a Knowledge Industry*, Oxford University Press, Oxford.

1.3

Multinational Management Consultancies: World Market Leaders

Mick James

Introduction

The early years of the 21st century find the global economy in a period of transition: the uninterrupted bull market of the last decade has come to an end, and many young people whose working lives have never been blighted by a negative balance sheet or layoffs must come to terms with the fact that (as a recent newspaper cartoon put it) 'shares can plummet as well as fall'.

For the big multinational consultancies, the past two years have been ones of rapid adjustment after years of rather stately progress in the wake of the bull market: the combination of ever-expanding and cash rich clients with an accelerating dependence of technology fuelled annual growth rates averaging 16 per cent during the 1990s, and it seemed that this would continue indefinitely, or at least until the world ran out of people who wanted to be management consultants. The speed of the e-commerce boom may have caught some of the consultancies off-guard, but it seemed as if the big consultancy firms, with their combination of global reach, technical expertise and delivery capability, were poised for their greatest triumph.

Now things look rather different: the major consultancies may not have suffered (much, yet) from the dotcom collapse, but the world they were preparing for in 2000 has failed to materialise in 2001. Now the multinational consultancies resemble the performers backstage after the first act of a play: some are half in, half out of their costumes, others are dressing up as different characters altogether. Plotlines hang in the air, unresolved: revenge is postponed, marriage contracts are yet to be concluded.

Ownership and identity

The most obvious symptoms of the changes underfoot in multinational consultancy are the changing patterns of ownership: aggregating expressions such as 'the Big Five'- which used to refer to the consulting/audit activities of Andersen Consulting, Ernst & Young, Deloitte & Touche, KPMG, PriceWaterhouseCoopers, and, just for confusion's sake, occasionally Arthur Andersen as well – no longer apply. The disitnction between 'audit-based' and 'IT-based' consultancy has collapsed.

The recent recognition in a survey by the newsletter *Management Consultant International* of IBM Global Services as the world's largest consultancy was a highly symbolic moment. From its position at the top of the tree, IBM looks down on a world in which its main rivals are neither auditors nor 'pure play' strategy consultancies but publicly traded technology and professional services entities.

Andersen Consulting is now just a memory, having completed its long divorce from audit parent Arthur Andersen, if not amicably then with reasonably little damage. Andersen Consulting had long chafed at making 'transfer payments' to a parent firm which was rapidly growing its own consultancy brand.

When it sought formally to separate the firms, Arthur Andersen demanded compensation reflecting the current equity value of the consulting arm. Arbitration ensued, and Andersen Consulting was able to escape with its cash intact but at the cost of its trademarks. So Andersen Consulting rebranded as Accenture, and the accountants absorbed whatever brand equity was left in the Andersen name by dropping the 'Arthur'.

The final split between accountancy and consultancy seemed inevitable when the Securities and Exchange Commission in the US again raised the old chestnut of conflict of interest where audit and advisory services were provided to the same client: an almost unavoidable situation, given the stranglehold the Big Five have over top-level audit. The SEC focused their attention on PriceWaterhouseCoopers, where merger had exacerbated the 'problem'. PwC caved in immediately, announcing their intention to hive off the consultancy operation as soon as possible.

Other bombshells followed: Ernst & Young, having failed to pull off a PwC-style merger with KPMG, sold its consulting services arm to Cap Gemini Sogeti, which swiftly moved to integrate the new acquisition with Gemini Consulting and its IT services group. The merger appears to have gone extremely smoothly, as one would expect from Cap Gemini, itself an agglomeration of 'national champions' in Europe (such as the UK's Hoskyns) and therefore with a fund of post-merger experience to draw on. The move promoted Cap Gemini to the position of Europe's largest consultancy, at the same time giving it a strong foothold across the Atlantic from which to attack the US market.

KPMG, by contrast, having recreated KMPG Consulting as a largely separate entity, took the next logical step and filed for an IPO in the States in 2000. This issue was successful in a difficult market, and although the shares took a hit in April 2001 along with the rest of the technology sector, they have made a respectable recovery. However, the KPMG issue only represents a divestment of part of the US consultancy operation. The rest of the world, including the UK, is not yet a part of this brave new world.

This illustrates the local franchise nature of what are seen as global consultancy brands: during arbitration, Arthur Andersen were able to claim that the global entity known as Andersen Consulting didn't really exist. Deloitte and Touche struggled for years to weld the European and Anglo-American operations together into Deloitte Consulting, while both continued to operate separately under a common banner. Having done so, it shows no sign of wanting to create a further degree of separation. Nor does the reborn Andersen, *pace* the SEC, feel any need to move away (again) from the traditional 'Big Five' model. Creating genuine global corporations behind the façade of the brands will be an ongoing challenge for the big consultancies.

Meanwhile, PwC, whose conflict with the SEC sparked many of these changes, has not yet decided its own future. Talks of purchase by technology giants such as Hewlett Packard or even IBM came to nothing. There is nothing wrong with the logic of such a move, but the pool of potential partners is diminishing. Merger with another consultancy firm is a possibility, but PwC's size militates against it. The other possibility is an IPO, and PwC will spend much of 2001 analysing Accenture's trip to market.

IPOs and capital

The Accenture and KPMG IPOs underline one of the defining trends of recent years: the emergence of consultancy as a capital intensive business. The involvement of the bigger firms in outsourcing, together with rivals such as CSC and the EDS-A T Kearney alignment, had already involved them in the need to raise capital sums: for partnerships, an inelegant operation. The dotcom boom brought consultancies, like many other professional services firms, into the heady world of venture capital. Initially the swapping of services for equity, already a well-established practice in growth consultancy, seemed the ideal way to take on idea-rich and cash-poor dotcom startups. But even when the venture capital was available the opportunities seemed too good to miss. Consultancies came up with a raft of incubators, launch pads and accelerators for start-up dotcoms, all of which would at last expose consultancy partners to the equity benefits of the rising market.

For there was another weakness in the partnership model. Although a consultancy partnership would fulfil most people's wilder dreams of avarice, senior consultancy managers had long resented the more significant gains by their clients' board members in the form of share options. In early 2000, this problem became a crisis. Consultants and partners alike began deserting consultancy firms for the dotcom world (at McKinsey, this became known as 'going e-WOL'). The classic example of this was the sudden departure of George Shaheen from the helm of Andersen Consulting for the online grocery store Webvan, citing a duty to his family to make some serious money. At the same time, the supply of new entrants dried up as even MBA students dropped out of their courses halfway to pursue e-commerce opportunities.

The firms responded in a number of ways: 'virtual' stock opportunities, time off for entrepreneurial adventures, accelerated partnership tracks, the opportunity to move into new entities created as joint ventures. But this was only delaying the inevitable, and in April 2001 Accenture declared it would file for an IPO in the US after a near-unanimous vote of its 2,500 partners. The initial offering of 12 per cent of the company raised about US$ 1.7 billion.

In many ways the marriage of venture capital and consultancy – money and expertise – is long overdue. But public listing brings new challenges to the consultancy world. The need to look over your shoulder at all times to protect shareholder value is an unwelcome distraction. However, as the experience of Proudfoot over the last decade shows, poorly performing stock can affect the perception of your consultancy skills, and vice versa, creating a vicious circle. Whether a 'virtuous' counter effect can be created remains to be seen.

IPOs bring other problems with them, not least the enrichment of the partners who are the key assets of the business. Accenture has tried to resolve this problem by releasing the equity gains to partners in stages, but this provoked a minor pre-IPO exodus in itself, with some restless partners preferring to take a lower sum in redundancy now and try their luck in the outside world rather than be locked into their jobs for a decade or more.

Many consultancy partners are also uncomfortable with the loss of autonomy that comes with an IPO, although it is fair to say that an equal number of staff in consultancies – particularly those outside the partnership track – would welcome the cultural changes that an IPO could bring. These cannot be estimated: firms which have gone by for years releasing cursorily compiled and often heavily massaged gross turnover figures are unlikely to adapt quickly or comfortably to quarterly reporting. The transition from owner-manager to corporate executive may prove a difficult transition for many partners. On the other hand, the imposition of corporate disciplines on organisations which have outgrown the partnership model of governance may be what ultimately ensures their survival.

There only remains the question of what firms will do with all that money, particularly now that some of the allure has gone out of being a venture capitalist. There will probably still be an element of this, but it is more likely to be on the level of joint ventures and partnerships, often with established clients: the creation of partially owned subsidiaries into which consultancy firms can pour money and expertise while minimising risk and maintaining their independence.

In the short-to-medium term however, it is likely that the bulk of the cash raised from markets will be used to fund acquisitions, previously a sporadic and tactical activity for consultancy firms, but now a strategic necessity. At the moment, the consultancy firms are busy hoovering up the e-commerce consultancies, which once appeared to be capable of swallowing the consultancy mid-market on the basis of their paper valuations. Once this distress sale is over, the consolidation of the consultancy market will really get going. Capabilities, market position, technologies and client list will all go to making a niche or boutique firm an attractive buy. However, it is likely that the main item on the shopping list will be staff themselves, still the rarest asset in the consultancy world.

Staff and skills

It is true that in the early part of 2001 the big consultancies added to the general gloom by announcing staff layoffs. Utilisation was down, the dotcom boom was over, and many firms had overinvested in specialised skillsets for which there was now little use. But these layoffs were a mere drop in the ocean compared to overall headcount and the ongoing requirement for staff. It is worth noting, for instance, that Accenture's trimming of 1,400 staff represented mostly the removal of support overheads. The 600 consultants involved were given 'sabbaticals' on 20 per cent of salary, ready to be called back into the fray when needed.

Even by 2000, firms such as PriceWaterhouseCoopers were tacitly acknowledging that they had reached the limits of organic growth. For a consultancy firm employing 50,000 people, the need to achieve growth in the 10–15 per cent range while dealing with a 15–20 per cent churn rate could lead to the requirement to recruit over 1,000 high quality people a month. Not only had recruitment become a mini-industry within consultancy firms, but the post-baby boom demographic time bomb was rapidly drying up the supply. Consultancies have reacted in various ways: Deloitte Consulting has blazed a trail in 'lifestyle' consulting, changing work styles, aggressively promoting women and using diversity recruiting to tap into communities previously excluded from consultancy. But this is only postponing the inevitable: sooner or later the only way to get people will be to buy them. In the future, the manpower challenge for consultancies will not be growth so much as how continually to reconfigure the skillsets they have in the face of changing market conditions.

E-commerce and IT

We only have room here to touch on the effects, and after-effects, of the e-commerce boom, which will be analysed more thoroughly in the following chapter. During the height of the craze, consultancies were rebranding themselves so enthusiastically as e-commerce partners that it appeared they had no thoughts of anything else. Yet the worst effect on them has been a toning down of the hype on the websites. As partnerships, they may have burned off a lot of 'mad money' in dotcom ventures, but were at least prevented by their closely held status from staking the whole farm on the latest South Sea Bubble.

In fact the e-commerce collapse may well have worked in the consultancies' favour: it has eliminated a whole breed of upstart rivals in the 'pure play' e-consultancy, who at one stage threatened to do to the audit firms what they themselves had done before to the old guard of consultancy. In the world at large a similar process has brought 'old economy' brands back into prominence, and these are of course long-standing clients of the multinational consultancies. IT will always be a major component of consultancy work, but it is already segmenting: IT will become a subset of disciplines within an overall consultancy mix, within which firms will have to prove that they can integrate all their activities to offer fully-rounded business solutions.

In this less exciting but less volatile world, the demand for basic consultancy disciplines is re-emerging and, as the number of potential patients multiplies, we are even seeing the reappearance of the old-fashioned 'company doctor' approach to consultancy.

The future

The future of consultancy is difficult to predict: when the multinational firms operate at their best, they mirror and anticipate the client world and so one might as well try and predict the future shape of a cushion without knowing who is about to sit on it. At their worst, the firms occasionally believe they can operate as market-makers in ideas, herding sheep-like clients to a future that only they can fully grasp.

Nevertheless, the consultancy firm of the future will be both a larger and less aloof creature, more closely tied in to clients' fortunes and the economy as a whole by cross-ownership and alliances. Clients will have both the right and the duty to inquire how these relationships affect the delivery capability and objectivity of their advisors. As consultancies are drawn deeper into the mainstream of corporate life, there will be interchanges of staff and capital at all levels. Investors will add a new voice to the mix: will we one day witness the unthinkable spectacle of a consultancy firm having a CEO imposed on it from outside by angry shareholders?

1.4

The impact of the IT revolution and e-business on management consultancy

Fiona Czerniawska

It's hard to think of a factor that has had a greater influence on the development of the consulting industry than technology. The growth of the monolithic, American-style consultancies since the end of the Second World War can largely be attributed to the involvement of firms, like Andersen, in the early application of mainframe computing in business. This was a very different approach to the Taylorism of the first consulting firms. Projects tended to be longer and more homogeneous, making it possible for firms focusing on this area to grow more quickly. The intellectual capital required could be codified more easily into standard methodologies, thus allowing a firm to have a higher consultant-to-partner ratio than was possible in a strategy firm, where the variable nature of the work needed considerable partner-level input. Most importantly, working on technology projects meant that consultants moved beyond their purely advisory role, to help in practical execution.

The first decade of e-business development

Successive waves of technology fuelled this trend, and the task of correctly identifying emerging technologies has become one of the most important strategic challenges facing any consulting firm. But its apotheosis came with the growth of enterprise resource planning (ERP) systems during the 1990s and the preparation for the date change in the year 2000. Dominated by a small number of software vendors, the ERP market created an enormous opportunity for consulting firms: projects lasted years, rather than months, and could easily occupy more than a hundred consultants at any one time. Such large-scale systems work also required process re-design and organisational change: thus ERP projects, valuable in their own right, were also the entry point for a whole host of other consulting services. While less pervasive in scope, Y2K preparations – at their peak – provoked such a level of demand that the traditional consulting firms were unable to handle it by themselves and a new breed of company – the off-shore development company (ODC) – grew up to take their place.

Despite the changing technology, the precepts of success remained constant: quality, consistency and an ability to deliver on time and within budget were what mattered most. Culturally, the consulting firms servicing this sector had to be cohesive and hierarchical: mistakes could be enormously expensive, the potential risks involved were colossal. This was in marked contrast to the culture of non-technology related consultancies, notably the strategic consultancies who continued to stress innovation and diversity. From time to time, technology and non-technology related firms would try to cross the boundary and move into the others' space, but most of these experiments failed, leaving the industry just as polarised as it had always been.

In the late 1990s, several things happened to challenge this status quo. Sudden recognition of the potential of the internet and web-based technologies for business, together with the high levels of returns being earned by internet-based companies on the world's stock markets combined to produce a sudden spike in client demand for consultancy – but this demand was very different from that for ERP-type consultancy. Clients were concerned about time to market: taking several years to implement a system was unacceptable in an environment in which opportunities came and went in a fraction of that time. They were uncertain about what technology to choose: hundreds of new suppliers had entered what had become a much more fragmented market.

Moreover, the incumbent consulting firms were themselves in the same boat: they, too, were having to adapt to a world of almost instant gratification and were poorly-equipped to pick the technology winners from what was now a much wider field. And clients knew this: it's hardly surprising, therefore, that they were more than happy to welcome in a whole new generation of 'e-consultants' who had emerged specifically to fill the gap. Interviewed in 1999, Chris Lochhead, the Chief Marketing Officer of one of these new entrants, Scient, summed up the situation thus: 'We believe that e-business represents the biggest transformation in the economy since the industrial revolution. Two years ago, when we set the company up, we identified a Cisco-like gap in the services market, and one about which existing consulting firms seemed completely oblivious. Traditional service firms had a pig-with-lipstick approach to the internet: they focused on some aspects of strategy and web-site design, but the services they offered were fragmented, reflecting fundamental division in their internal organisations. Rather than offering individual services, we wanted Scient to focus on building complete e-businesses, and we became the first movers into a marketspace which we term "systems innovation"…What Scient does is bring everything together: we don't de-couple strategy from delivery; we don't write a report and walk away. We either build an e-business with a client or we don't work with them: we either engage with the CEO or we walk away. It's the only way we are prepared to work'.

Adapting to market demand

The incumbents had to adapt. According to Tim Mead, the senior vice-president of marketing at Cambridge Technology in 1999: 'our traditional methodologies didn't work well with these clients. We had to develop a framework which was in effect a superset of these methodologies, one that rigorously eliminated all the inessential elements.' But they also came out fighting. Ron Farmer, responsible with several other partners for the launch of @McKinsey, argued that 'our critics claim that our way of working is too analytical for an environment that's constantly shifting, but their solution is to set up a website and see what happens. But you can't defy gravity forever – there has to be something to leverage internally if you're going to gain and keep a competitive edge. E-business has underlying – inescapable – economic rules, just like every other area of business, but people are spending staggering amounts of money acquiring customers from whom they'll never make a return because their life-time value will never exceed the cost of acquiring them.'

The stock markets eventually reached the same conclusion. The latter half of 2000 saw billions of dollars being wiped off the value of the e-specialists and, for most of these firms, retrenchment has become the order of the day. For the incumbent consulting firms, by contrast, the change offered new possibilities: the world was going their way. While dotcom failures dominated the headlines, large corporations – those behemoths of the 'old' economy – had begun to invest millions of dollars in e-business projects. Many were internal (e-procurement projects offered – and continue to offer – enormous savings); most had a very low public profile; all of them offered opportunities for consultants, especially those firms that could demonstrate that they could bring the best of the new and the old together – innovative thinking implemented with 'old' economy discipline. 'People thought that the new economy heralded the death of process', commented one consultant, a beneficiary of this sea change, 'in fact, e-business projects are so complex and the technology involved is so new, that process matters more than ever.'

The future relationship between technology and consultancy

The big question now is: what next? Has the 1998–2000 e-business boom had any lasting impact on the relationship between technology and consultancy? And what form will this relationship take in the future?

It's tempting for the incumbent players to write-off the impact of the e-consultants as a passing fad, but revolutions have a history of devouring their own children, as more than one French revolutionary observed on the scaffold. Philip Evans, a senior vice-president at The Boston Consulting Group and co-author of *Blown to Bits* argues that 'just because we now know that all those kids in garages aren't going to replace large corporations doesn't negate the fact that the pace of technological change is increasing …the recent carnage shouldn't make us underestimate the significance of what's going on.'

Few people deny that e-consultants have had quite a profound effect on the way consulting firms are organised: the integration of strategy, creative and technology consulting skills – something pioneered by the new entrants – is now widely recognised as being key to success in an environment where strategy is becoming increasingly bound up with technology. Moreover, the relationship of a consulting firm to the technology its clients choose to implement is something that will have an impact on its long-term survival. The reason for this lies in the increasing 'technocratisation' of consultancy: for example it's not just that we know that you can't draw up a supply chain strategy without thinking of the systems required to support it, but that we also need complex computer modelling tools to optimise it. Similarly, can you prepare a really credible marketing strategy which isn't based on exhaustive analysis of data on consumer behaviour? Even in the highest echelons of strategy formulation, the software now exists to evaluate scenarios and to calibrate systems thinking diagrams.

But perhaps the most significant change of all is the growing sense of visible, articulated identity among consulting firms. Ten years ago, the majority of consultancy happened behind the scenes: what e-business and e-consultancies have done since 1998 is to bring consultancy out into the open: in books and newspapers, on stock markets, as investors, at the launch parties of new ventures. This is a far cry from the kind of cloak-and-dagger consulting of popular myth and it's something to which consultancy is now committed.

Further reading

Evans, Philip and Wurster, Thomas (1999), *Blown to Bits*, Harvard Business School Press

1.5

Sustainability and management consultancy

Adrian Henriques

Sustainability is a business issue

From outside left field, 'sustainability' seems to have become a significant issue for businesses. Customer demand, new regulations, NGO campaigns and investor pressure have all played a part.

For example, in 2000, MORI (Market and Opinion Research International), on behalf of CSR Europe, interviewed 12,000 consumers across 12 European countries on their attitudes towards the role of businesses in today's society. They found that most people don't think business pays enough attention to its social responsibilities (see Figure 1.5.1 below).

They also found that 70 per cent of European consumers say that a company's commitment to social responsibility is important when buying a product or service, and one in five would be very willing to pay more for products that are socially and environmentally responsible.

Much has been written about the increasing power of civil society groups and NGOs. The history of Shell in relation to the

Industry and commerce do not pay enough attention to their social responsibilities

	Disagree	Agree
European average	16%	58%
Finland	13%	75%
Great Britain	10%	71%
Portugal	4%	66%
Italy	10%	64%
Switzerland	19%	63%
Spain	17%	62%
France	9%	60%
Belgium	25%	57%
Germany	17%	47%
Sweden	19%	46%
Denmark	20%	44%
Netherlands	32%	40%

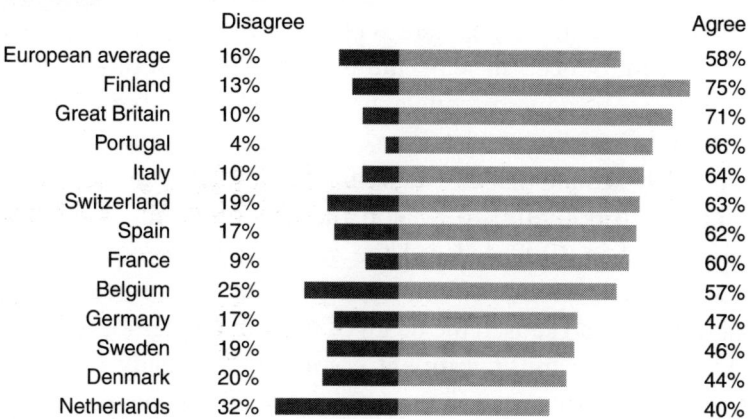

Figure 1.5.1

Brent Spar incident is often quoted. The incident centred on the issue of how to dispose of an oil platform. Shell wished to dispose of it at sea; Greenpeace, a major environmental campaigning group opposed this with dramatic direct action and much media coverage. The result was not only that the company changed its plans for disposal, but that it embarked on a much more energetic change programme to encompass sustainability within its approach to business. More recently, NGOs have challenged governments and the WTO at Seattle and the World Bank at Prague. Other NGOs are engaging with companies in less confrontational ways to achieve change. The lesson from all this is that the pressure is increasing from NGOs and civil society on companies to take more responsibility.

Laws and regulations are also changing. In the UK there have been changes to the Combined Stock Exchange Code, by which all major UK listed companies have to abide. The areas in which change is occurring include directors' remuneration, and the management of risk – including social and environmental impacts. In addition there have been changes to pensions law, requiring pensions schemes to state what their policy is on social and environmental issues in relation to their investments – or whether they have one at all. Clearly, this will feed through to companies, so that all major companies will have to pay greater attention to these issues.

In other countries also, there is pressure from legal change. Bills have been introduced in legislatures from California to Canberra. The courts are also interpreting existing legislation more stringently. For example in the USA, the State of Montana's Supreme Court in a ruling in 1999 found that the State cannot allow activities to continue that have the potential to poison the environment. A Brazilian federal court in 1999 ordered the government to compensate a remote Indian community after it ruled that a road built through tribal territory had caused the death of most of its members.

In relation to the investment community, already over US$2 trillion dollars is invested in the US in ethically managed funds. In the UK, a pension fund executive recently estimated that of the £800 billion under UK pension fund management, from a third to a half would be managed ethically over the next few years. New indices have been developed with which to monitor the performance of companies. The Dow Jones Sustainability World Index is shown below in relation to the general index. It has been shown that for significant periods, those in the DGSI do better. Recently, the International Stock Exchange in London has launched the FTSE4Good index (Figure1.5.2), which uses more rigorous criteria.

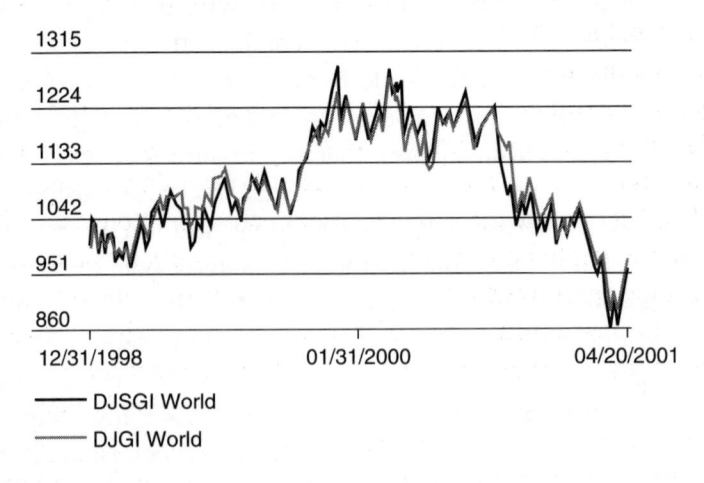

Figure 1.5.2

So what is sustainability?

> *"Good business is all about honesty and fair-dealing – if you can fake that you've got it made!"*
>
> Groucho Marx

Sustainability is a big issue; possibly the biggest there is. It is about whether there are birds singing in the trees, about getting asthma on a sunny day and about rioting in the inner cities. It matters. And yet, while it has caught the attention of some big companies (like Shell, BT and BP-Amoco), it is not something that chief executives tend to lose any sleep over.

So what does 'sustainability' mean? A few years ago someone counted over 140 different definitions of the word; the only thing on which everyone agrees is that, whatever it is, it must be a good thing. Nowadays, everyone shies away from trying to define it. It has become like the elephant in the corner of the room which everyone is too polite to mention. However there are two broad approaches to defining 'sustainability' – one draws on the sense of the word 'sustain', so that sustainability means to be able to continue over time. This understanding, however, doesn't capture the sense of unease or urgency which most people feel over anything labelled 'un-sustainable'. Another type of definition is all about activities which enhance human development in the broadest sense.

A further source of confusion is that the terms 'sustainability' and 'sustainable development' were first used in relation to the natural environment. They are now used to refer, in addition, to the social and economic dimensions of our activities. So we now have a corporate 'triple bottom line', rather than simply a financial one. Perhaps the reason why it only keeps a few people awake at night is that it is very confusing, and so it is hard to see what to do about it; and there is enough to do simply trying to keep the company afloat. Most of us, after all, have a 'too big, switch off' mentality.

It is perhaps obvious that if natural resources run out, as they are doing, and the market does not provide early enough warning for new technologies to be developed in time, there will be big problems for many companies. It is even more obvious that, if economies become too volatile, as they have been in Asia recently, then the impact can be very serious for all companies. What is less obvious is why the social dimension is important and what companies can actually do to help, while sticking with their core businesses.

An important trend in most countries, and certainly in the UK, is that the gap between rich and poor is getting bigger. Apart from any moral aspect, the reason this should concern business is that business requires stable social conditions and a functioning infrastructure (contract law as well as electricity, telephones and roads) if it is to thrive. Now a divided society will become increasingly unstable, and therefore the cost of doing business will rise.

There are other social trends which are impacting adversely on business. These include a declining level of trust coupled with an increasingly powerful media industry. Taken together, this means that any mistake on the part of companies is always a good story. And the exposure can be as global as it is merciless. Corporate misdeeds can be known throughout the world in minutes, thanks to the Internet. Sectors particularly at risk are those with high-street brand names and long supply chains, stretching through the Third World. Under these conditions, confidence in a company can collapse very rapidly, as the cases of Marks & Spencer over the use of child labour in manufacture and, a few years earlier, Shell, in the case of Brent Spar, demonstrate.

Yet social trends are not simply something which happen to a company. It is entirely possible for a company to work with society, rather than in spite of it. One of the practical ways in which this is possible is for a company to work with its stakeholders. Stakeholders may be thought of as all those groups which either affect the company or which it affects.

Managing sustainability

Jim Wolfenson, the president of the World Bank, declared a few years ago that he could tell when a project had been successful by the smile on a child's face. That may be a good indicator, but it is also one which raises the question of how you can systematically understand how well you are doing as a company. Financial accounting has been around for several centuries, yet accountants will tell you that there is no full agreement about the details. Environmental accounting has been around for several decades and it is clearly still under development. 'Social accounting' has only been practised seriously for a few years, and is currently working with its first set of standards. Bringing it all together to look at sustainability performance is tremendously challenging and yet there is one initiative that is attempting an important part of that job – reporting on performance.

The Global Reporting Initiative (GRI) is a network of companies (including BP-Amoco and General Motors), NGOs, academics, and professional organisations such as the Association of Chartered Certified Accountants. In March 1999, the GRI released guidelines for the construction of a sustainability report and a revised set was issued in June 2000. The GRI format will encourage companies systematically to collect information about its main impacts across the three dimensions of sustainability – the environmental, the social and the economic. Currently companies from every continent are working with the guidelines.

As such sustainability reporting formats emerge, it will be important to ensure that the measures and indicators chosen reflect the views of stakeholders as well as reflecting comparisons between different companies. Perhaps most important is to ensure that you are measuring not just the end result of your activities, but also the process by means of which you produced them. So it is vital to measure how you manage pollution, as well as the amount you actually produce. This approach has been incorporated into environmental standards, such as the ISO 14000 series, and is perhaps more important for the social dimension.

What are the success factors of managing for sustainability? One of them is knowing what is happening across all three dimensions of sustainability, the environmental, the social and the economic. However that is only part of the job. It is also necessary to develop:

- tools to support sustainable decision-making
- a culture of making sustainable decisions
- a governance structure to ensure that the overall direction of the organisation is moving towards sustainability.

Currently there are tools, such as NPV analysis, which analyse part of the economic impact of corporate decisions. But how many organisations look at the social impact of their projects in advance of making a decision to proceed? Similarly, environmental assessments are often a poor relation of financial analysis. While companies are now beginning to explore environmental issues in the name of eco-efficiency, how many companies integrate the social considerations into new product development?

Of course, to have the tools is necessary, but not sufficient. It is also vital to have a culture which nurtures sustainable decision-making. Part of this is that sustainability is received wisdom at the top of an organisation – it will not help such a culture if senior executives simply ignore the whole matter. Also, it will be important to establish incentives for all staff to take account of social and environmental issues in their day to day decisions.

And finally, it is central to evolve a governance and management structure which supports movement towards sustainability. It is necessary to ensure that sustainability is embedded in the management processes which maintain the overall direction of the organisation. It is also necessary to ensure that the risks and rewards of pursuing sustainability are built into its fundamental management.

Management consultancy and sustainability

Currently, the major professional services firms and many smaller consultancies are offering services related to sustainability. Examples include:

- environmental management systems advice
- ethical management systems development and training
- assistance with stakeholder dialogue
- PR and reputation management
- social and environmental auditing
- due diligence on the social, environmental aspects of transactions.

While it looks as if the field is well provided for, it should be borne in mind that sustainability is new to consultancies too. Some will be stepping outside their core expertise. Beyond that, sustainability involves working successfully with possibly critical stakeholders. So a key question in a potential buyer's mind should be not only 'what experience does this consultant have?' but also 'what sort of legitimacy will this firm bring to sustainability work?'

Sustainability is obviously a big issue. It is one which it is important to get right. If enough companies get it wrong, it means there will be more asthma, fewer birds and fewer smiles on the faces of children. And perhaps fewer companies too.

1.6

The Delphi Study and Beyond: Scenarios for the Consulting Market in 2010

Mike Jeans

Last year the UK Company of Management Consultants undertook a Delphi study into alternative scenarios for the consultancy market in the year 2010. This study was undertaken with the assistance of Kate Griffiths who is now consulting with PwC. Five possible scenarios emerged. These were:

- High Tech, High Touch Scenario
- Doomsday Scenario
- Hybrid Consultancy
- Commodity Consulting
- Small is Beautiful scenario

The definitions of these scenarios are given below. They are not the only possible scenarios for the European market and there may be other alternatives around the world for both developed and developing markets. Indeed, it is highly unlikely that there will be a homogeneous global management consultancy market by 2010. These alternatives are the crystal ball-gazing of some management consultants whose practices are based in Europe.

A broader and more diverse set of scenarios might emerge from a survey within industry and commerce of buyers and users of consultancy internationally – in other words, the intended readership of this book. Therefore, you are cordially invited to study the alternative scenarios and to contribute your responses, either by mail on the following page or by fax or e-mail to the addresses given.

High Tech, High Touch Scenario

As new technology is introduced, there is a counterbalancing human response. The Tomorrow Company's Report, the Balanced Scorecard approach and the Stakeholder view, will become much more important. Equal emphasis will be given to financial and value based success. Both clients and consultancies will need to take the views of employees and customers into consideration as well as the bottom line. There will be an increase in environmental audits and 'Triple Bottom Line' reporting as businesses are required to report financial, environmental and societal matters. This scenario highlights the increasing significance of reputation management as a priority issue for firms in 2010 and the likelihood that consultancies will develop their value systems as a means of differentiating their product offering. High Tech, High Touch is reputation as a function of client relationship quality and productivity.

Doomsday Scenario

Despite the opening up of new markets in Asia and South America, the consulting industry will not see the same levels of demand in 2010. Large consultancies will increasingly focus on business services provision for global clients and taking equity in start-ups and as such becoming more focused on non-consulting services. The double-digit growth of the 1990s will be a thing of the past as margins become tighter. There will continue to be new entrants in the market but there will be fewer 'second generation' players with the reputation and the client list. The major recession in the early years of this decade started in the USA, spread to Asia-Pacific and Europe and stayed. Of course, there is a cyclical downturn in every decade but historically consulting demand has picked up again in a different form. The doomsday scenario goes beyond the necessary restructuring to allow the consultancy industry to adjust to environmental changes and suggests a future in which consultancy as the archetypal business service industry will be in terminal decline rather as manufacturing was twenty years ago.

Hybrid Consultancy

It is not so much specialisation that will be the key but that as customers become more sophisticated they will expect more and more value for money. Consultancies will need to offer a range and a depth of services. There will be a deepening of the offering to clients. Process consultancy will continue to be in demand. However with transient competitive advantage, clients will also seek the more analytical approach of business schools and strategy houses for new ideas. Outsourcing will continue and interim management comes of age. This would lead to management consultancy losing its identity and becoming just another arm of management. In such a scenario, the distinction between giving consultancy advice, implementation (support/action) and interim management will disappear. Finally it is possible that real breakthroughs in artificial intelligence could automate large chunks of the skill transfer role of consultants. This is really the no change scenario. This is what many consultants think they are doing now whereas the scenario below is what the brand name consultancies are actually doing.

Commodity Consulting

There will be little change in the management consultancy industry in the next ten years. The business environment will continue to become more complex and competitive, as the 24 hour time zone becomes commonplace. Consultancies will continue to be successful, many demanding high fees because they are able to adapt to any change in the environment as the kings – the majority are men – of impression management. SAP may be dead but consultants are already repackaging a solution, which will become the next fad. Managers offer consultants a captive market hungry for the latest recycled idea. Elements of consulting are already a commodity such as parts of IT consulting and outsourcing. Furthermore consultancy will continue to be a people industry, as clients will still want to see a consultant's face. The bedside manner will not be replaced by the e-approach. The drawback of this is that it is not exciting for intelligent people. The key to consultancy is exciting work for bright and curious people.

Small is beautiful scenario

Professional organisations work best with relatively small communities. This would suggest that even the global consultancies would form loose associations and federations of small partnerships. The global brands would still be important, primarily as a measure of quality, but the size of the organisation or unit would be smaller than that offered by the consultancies today. As clients become more sophisticated, and as they understand knowledge-based businesses more, they will look more for communities of competence that are not too large. Of course, working with such communities gives large consultancies a big problem in maintaining efficiency, and potentially reduces their competitive differentiation from medium-sized consultancies. Potentially there will be a situation in which a large consultancy, made up of linked partnerships, will be competing on equal terms with small to medium-sized consultancies that are networked together. This is really glasnost and perestroika through redistributing the power of knowledge; the challenge is that the corporates are trying to go in another direction, ie brand to brand.

In order to assist in evaluating the five alternative scenarios which practising management consultants identified, or to construct your own scenario, you might wish to study the Trigger Thoughts, reproduced below, which were provided to the participants in the original survey with the intention of stimulating their thinking.

The findings of this survey will be based on the self-selected sample of those who read this book. If you do respond you are sure to be interested in the ratings and opinions expressed. The results will be published in mid 2002 and made available on the Company of Management Consultants, ICMCI and Kogan Page websites:

CoMC: www.comc.org.uk
ICMCI: www.icmci.org
Kogan Page: www.kogan-page.co.uk

Trigger Thoughts
The following provide some indicators of the 'current' situation. They are intended to stimulate thinking about the future and to help predict the consulting environment in the year 2010. It is suggested that you add any points that come to mind as you read through the list

Strategic Thrust
Growth
Alliances, merger & take-overs
A move from diversified business activities to focus more on the 'core' business
Globalisation
Lean 'strategic business units' rather than conglomerates with centralised control
Less bureaucracy, fewer levels of management and best practices
Pressure from competition, fewer true USPs and shorter period of competitive advantage (competition mimics quickly)
Decline of manufacturing, increase in service organisations
Privatisation
Effective technological exploitation of natural resources
Corporate Governance

Mainsprings of Performance
Logistics & supply chain
Re-engineering
Quality
Excellence and Corporate Competence
Marketing

Benchmarking, regeneration
Innovation
Suppliers as partners
Entrepreneurship and Intrapreneurship
Customer service/care, loyalty
Learning organisations
The Balanced Scorecard

Ensuring the Fundamentals – Finance
Pressure for greater financial performance of plc companies.
De-regulation in the City and greater competition
Some moves away from 'quoted companies' to private ownership to ensure appropriate valuation
Greater availability of venture capital/private equity funding
More management 'buy-outs'
More active institutional shareholders and also individual (and vociferous) shareholder groups
Strong £; future role of Euro
Employee share participation schemes

Ensuring the Fundamentals – General
Administrative infrastructure – processes, procedures, & methodologies
Physical structures – locations, property, & land
Transportation

Marketing the Message
Branding
Media
Product evolution
Internal and external communication

Organisational Realities
Greater accountability.
Women breaking through the 'glass ceiling'
End of 'careers for life', 'employability', and a return to looking at the retention of talent, career development and succession
From transactional/command and control, to transformational, consensus building, participate type of leadership
Knowledge working and intellectual capital
Increased rate of organisational and other change
Stress
Increased demands for skilled workers especially white collar workers

Wiring the Organisation
Mainframes, PCs, notebooks, networks

Internet, Intranets
Databases
E-commerce
Communications – telephones, video discussions/conferences, mobiles, fax & e-mail
CAD/CAM
Increased productivity through computers, communications and telecommunications
Call centres and databases

Power to the People
Outsourcing
Part-time, full-time working; core and peripheral workers
Supply management
Demand requirements
Utilisation, performance management
'Psychological' contracts
Self-managed learning
'Third age' working
Greater self-employment; also home working

The Social Context
Break down of the family unit; single parent families
More home owners
Increased demand for housing, pressure on the 'green belt'
Greater availability of further education
Greater leisure and overseas travel
Increased crime
Insatiable demands on the NHS, day surgery etc
Ageing population, pensions issues etc
Pop stars

Wider Governmental & World Affairs
Increased influence of European Union through legislation; individual rights through the Court of Human Rights; and workers rights through the 'Social Chapter'
War and 'trouble spots' e.g. Northern Island, Yugoslavia, Middle East, Indonesia, etc
Break down of Communism
Opening of China and Far East economies, difficulties in 'Russia'.
Devolution to Scotland and Wales
'Convergent' politics
Global warming. Environmental and other pressure groups

2

Ethics and Best Practice

2.1

Competition and objectivity: management consultancy, auditing and outsourcing

Bruce Petter

The largest consultancy practices have undergone something of a rollercoaster ride over the last twelve months. The rules introduced by the US Securities and Exchange Commission (SEC) with regard to consultancy services offered by audit firms may have been less stringent than expected, however there is always the possibility of UK or EC regulation to keep some of us awake at night. The Australian Labour Government is considering a crackdown on auditors doing extra service work for clients and may well follow the lead of the SEC. The re-elected Labour government in the UK has a strong productivity agenda which could include closer scrutiny of the professional services sector.

Most of the Big Five audit firms have taken steps to separate their consultancy business from their audit services, partly due to the SEC scrutiny but also to raise capital for investment in technology and staff. Last year KPMG sold a stake in its consulting business to Cisco systems and then floated part of the US business on the stock market; Ernst & Young sold its consulting business to Cap Gemini; earlier this year PricewaterhouseCoopers tried to sell its consulting business to Hewlett-Packard: following its split from Andersen (formerly Arthur Andersen), Accenture (formerly Andersen Consulting) has announced its plans for a partial flotation.

The latest accusation to be thrown at the big firms is that they no longer offer independent advice due to their various alliances with IT vendors. Not only does this fail to show an understanding of the relationship that these firms have with their alliance partners, but is also insulting to the buyers of consultancy services themselves.

What is management consultancy?

The MCA defines management consultancy as 'the rendering of independent advice and assistance on management issues. This typically includes identifying and investigating problems and/or opportunities, recommending appropriate action and helping to implement those recommendations.'

Let's look at one aspect of that definition more closely: the 'rendering of independent advice'. One of the cornerstones of the MCA's Code of Professional Conduct since its inception in 1956, has been the rule that no member firm should 'enter into any arrangement, which would detract from the objectivity and impartiality of the advice given to the client'. In March 2001, the MCA Council went one step further by adopting the following rule within the Code of Conduct:

> *Where a Member is a subsidiary of a parent body, or enters into an alliance with a body, which is not in the public practice of management consultancy, all advice will*

be untied and independent of any influence of that parent body or alliance partner.

The Statement of Best Practice, which the MCA has been developing together with the Institute of Management Consultancy, HM Treasury and now with the Office for Government Commerce (OGC), recommends that consultants should 'explain the pros and cons of various approaches, explaining in broad terms the range of approaches available'.

It is no secret that many of the larger consultancy firms have relationships of varying degrees of formality with a range of technology vendors; KPMG has alliances with Cisco, Siebel, Microsoft, Hewlett Packard, Fedex and Compaq. Accenture has alliances with Microsoft, Nokia, BP, Barclays, Compaq, BT and Baltimore Technologies and has recently announced a joint venture with Hewlett-Packard, aimed at helping clients to migrate more quickly from legacy systems to new business models, while in early 2001 Novell bought Cambridge Technology Partners. Andersen has alliances with IBM amongst others; PricewaterhouseCoopers has recently announced an aviation industry alliance with Hewlett-Packard which will offer business solutions for aviation companies.

Many of the winning entries in last year's MCA Best Management Practice Awards were the results of successful alliances between client, consultant and 'other' partners working on the project. The Open Interactive case study, for example, demonstrated how Cap Gemini Ernst and Young worked as prime contractor to Open, managing a number of advanced technology subcontractors in order to launch a new digital television service. Unisys Ltd worked with a range of IT suppliers to help The Woolwich launch its pioneering Open Plan product.

There are considerable advantages for clients, consultancy firms and IT vendors in establishing formal or informal alliances. The IT vendors see the big consultancy firms as key influencers in client markets. That influence is based on the trust established between the consultancy firm and the organisations it works with. It is therefore in the interests of the technology suppliers to allow those consultancy firms to preserve that trust by maintaining an element of objectivity.

The consultancy firms in turn can pass on economies of scale and speed to their clients by establishing links with world class technology suppliers. They can help the IT vendors to develop their offerings to suit different clients and different sectors. They also have a better understanding of the human and organisational implications of technological change which, if not properly understood, can result in the failure of large IT implementations. The relationship between IT supplier and management consultancy is totally symbiotic and the client should ultimately benefit by receiving better solutions, more quickly and cost-effectively.

So, if consultancy firms are not entirely independent, can their clients be sure that the advice they receive is objective? Or are they simply going to be offered the solutions provided by that firm's alliance partners?

The people buying consultancy are, for the most part highly sophisticated individuals, often with consultancy experience, who have a good understanding of the offerings within the consultancy market. They buy the services of a particular consultancy firm because they expect it to deliver the best solution for their unique set of circumstances. That may well be one of the consultancy's preferred partner solutions and the client may feel that this is the most effective way forward. On the whole leading consultancy firms tend to work with the world's best IT suppliers; it is in their interests and their client's to do so.

There is certainly no evidence to suggest that clients are feeling 'duped' by the big firms. A recent survey by the MCA into the purchasing of management consultancy services showed that 88 per cent of those questioned would use their present consultancy firm again and 79 per cent expect to benefit from the consultancy investment within one year. 84 per cent of those questioned had a preferred list of consultancy firms, compared to only 44 per cent in 1995, suggesting that purchasing practices have improved since 1995 and that clients are more aware of the range of consultancy services on offer.

If, however, the client wishes to know what other solutions are available and how they compare with that of the consultancy firm's alliance partners, that information should be made available to the client who is then free to make an informed decision.

As John Tiner, former head of consulting at Andersen, explained, 'We make a point of transparency about our alliances with our clients. We're very open about it – after all we have nothing to hide.' Why shouldn't an organisation be open about something that is delivering the best results for their client?

Alan Buckle, CEO of KPMG Consulting re-emphasises the point, 'Our clients want solutions from strategy, through implementation of applications, to networks and hardware. They recognise that partnerships of consulting organisations and solutions vendors are essential. Clear and effective partnerships are the key. The client can then choose the right solution.'

Management consultancy is not a regulated industry, nor do we want it to be, but we have to ensure that standards are in place which reassure procurers of consultancy that they can trust an organisation to give transparent and effective advice.

Professionalism in best practice: consultancy and competence in the new e-economy

Barry Curnow

The world of consultancy is undergoing rapid consolidation; Mick James has discussed many of the developments in chapter 1.3. Since the beginning of 2001 KPMG has floated its stock in New York, reducing the shareholding of Cisco Systems in the consultancy, itself a remarkable alliance. The American KPMG LLP looks set to purchase the European operations of KPMG in 2002. As the new millennium dawned, it appeared as though the global accounting industry was selling the global consulting industry to the global IT industry. Ernst and Young was sold to Cap Gemini Sogeti. We saw the long heralded rebirth of the former Andersen Consulting as Accenture on 1 January 2001, and its flotation via an initial public offerng in July, following its divorce from Arthur Andersen in 2000. Arthur D Little has been in on-off merger talks with PA Consulting Group. The planned purchase of PwC by Hewlett Packard collapsed in 2000 when the latter's share price fell, and at the time of going to press, EDS was rumoured as a possible marriage partner for PwC's consulting arm. However, the fact that such alliances have been contemplated seriously underlines the shift in ownership and points to the new centre of gravity of the global consulting business in the new international e-economy. Or does it?

Not so long ago, before the dotcom crash, new economy players raised some challenging questions, such as:

- Would large consulting firms, as we know them, exist in five years' time?
- Given strategic alliances with solution providers, are consultants independent any more?
- What is the future of education and the continued relevance of schools, given the omnipresent world wide web?
- Can the future be predicted when product/life cycles are perhaps less than 2 years?

The City of London Company of Management Consulants' *Delphi Study* provides some alternative scenarios for the future of the consulting market in 2010 discussed in chapter 1.6.

Cisco Systems had become thought leaders in new-economy consulting, with their paperless company and virtual employment around the world. Basically, it is a manufacturing company, making routers that switch data packets on their correct journey around cyberspace, but Cisco has become a role model of inspiration and aspiration for new economy consultants and clients in all industries and sectors. Its chief executive, John Chambers, was featured on the financial pages alongside the chairman of the Federal Reserve Board as a guru making pronouncements about the economic downturn in the USA spreading to Europe. When that downturn came, nobody was immune, including Cisco, but the expected and largely unpredicted outcome was the sheer scale of fallout of the new economy firms, many of which went to the wall. However, at the time of writing it looks as though the established consultancies are weathering the economic downturn with staff reductions – not least in some of the new economy areas of consulting.

It is striking that the brand name consulting firms have all sought to redefine themselves as e-commerce consultants. It is technology that creates and enables the business development opportunities of the new economy but it is people, both consultants and clients, who seize and implement such opportunities.

Increasingly, it has been the large consulting and systems firms – or solutions providers as they increasingly like to be known – who help clients to implement the new technological capabilities. However, it is internal and independent consultants, interim managers and freelancers, who are called upon to train, develop, coach, counsel, support and motivate the people who have to make this potential come true. In other words, client managers are the principal implementers, who make things happen in the call centres, data centres, distributed operating centres, networked units, virtual offices, hotdesks and electronic cottages of the new economy. This new world is a post-employment labour market in which most knowledge workers form what Charles Handy has called the sub-contractual fringe of consultants, portfolio workers, third-agers and techno-mercenaries who freelance their way to where the demand is hottest.

Consultancy is increasingly at the centre of the emerging markets. After the Berlin Wall came down in 1989, consultants, supported by aid agencies, flocked to the new democracies of Eastern and Central Europe. Many of those countries now have impressive social and professional infrastructures, including Institutes of Management Consultants affiliated to the International Council of Management Consulting Institutes (ICMCI), the umbrella body of certifying organisations around the world who administer the Certified Management Consultant qualification worldwide. This qualification reflects a single global standard observed by some thirty member countries of ICMCI, many of whose consultancy industries are profiled in Part 6.

For many years now economists have been predicting the polarisation of the consulting market and the disappearance of medium-sized firms. Already over 70 per cent of consulting firms employ fewer than ten people and 25 per cent employ more than fifty. Arthur D Little predicted that the middle market would disappear, following a study of its own but that has not happened and now seems unlikely. It is true that the population of the middle market is continually changing and renewing itself, as consulting practices move through their life cycles. On average these take seven years for a major shift in ownership, structure, business, products and long-term client relationships to come about and the same time period seems also to apply to consulting careers.

It is highly likely that there will always be a middle market because that is where client relationships are forged and all-round consulting competence is enhanced through learning and development as a joint, collaborative activity between consultants, clients and colleagues. And keeping consultant learning and competence up to date is the key challenge in this fast moving e-world where sole practitioners and giant firms alike have equal access to the marketplace of the Internet.

The fundamental question arises of how consultants keep up to date when know-how becomes obsolescent so rapidly and when even blue chip firms, such as McKinsey, have been criticised for delivering recommendations to clients based on knowledge that is behind the state of the art in the e-world? The answer, of course, must be through continuing professional development that is appropriate to the electronic age. It is no accident that McKinsey, which has invested heavily in consultant training and development throughout its entire history, still goes from strength to strength, while many of the dotcom firms are no more!

There has been an explosion in consulting education and qualifications in the past few years. The Institute of Management Consultancy in the UK now recognises over 25 approved training providers, many of them Universities. The British Academy of Management has set up a consultancy special interest group to discuss the state of the art in consultancy learning and development and, to review the progress of the revolution in consulting studies in higher education. The group has undertaken a survey to map the provision of consulting courses in European universities. This study by Sally Woodward of City University Business School has discovered over thirty substantive postgraduate courses which include consultancy as a major subject. (See chapter 2.4)

Many of these courses award credits for, and give credits towards, the Certified Management Consultant qualification awarded by The Institute of Management Consultancy in the UK, which is recognised in over 30 different countries through ICMCI. The recent European hub meeting in London of seventeen European ICMCI member countries committed to a programme of peer audits to ensure that the highest standards of the CMC qualification, based on a competency model known as the Amsterdam standard, are maintained. This competency model is a completely new method of assessment based on lifelong learning and practical job and client-based development. Individuals may apply and demonstrate their readiness for the CMC qualification by submitting evidence of their competency in the four quadrants of management, functional specialist, consulting and socio-economic know-how.

The two accompanying tables in the sections that follow show the competency tests which consultants applying for the CMC qualification must undergo in order to demonstrate that they meet the required standards.

The Certified Management Consultant (CMC) Standards

Statements of competence

Applicants for the CMC qualification must satisfy IMC of their competence, knowledge, awareness and understanding within four quadrants:

- consultancy competence
- management competence
- professional specialism – prior qualifications and/or prior experiential learning
- socio/technological/economic/political awareness

Some Standards appear in both the Consultancy and Management Competency lists below. This is quite deliberate, and applicants should note that the evidence required to satisfy the Standards within these two contexts is likely to be quite separate.

With particular regard to consultancy competence, applicants should note that if their work does not involve them in management implications or in the interface with client management, they would not qualify for the CMC.

IMC has called on the MCI Management Consultancy Occupational Standards, the MCI Senior Management Standards and Personal Competency Model, and IMC's own Body of Knowledge and Experience as sources for these CMC Standards.

All applicants must agree to abide by the profession's standards and ethics, as embodied in IMC's Code of Professional Conduct and Ethical Guidelines.

Consultancy competence

Candidates are asked to address as many of the statements as they are able to and which are relevant to their consultancy work, and to explain briefly why any standard has not been addressed.

Demonstrate:

- how you market and sell your consultancy services
- how you approach new clients and develop mutual understanding with a potential client
- about the possibilities for an appropriate intervention
- how you assure the client of your integrity and competence as a consultant and define your specialisms
- how you apply appropriate diagnostic tools to determine the current position of the client
- how you ensure that the client shares your perception of their situation
- how you scope the intervention
- how you prepare a proposal for a client
- how you present your proposals to a client
- how you determine the potential of each option with the client, whilst ensuring that you (or your practice) are able to deliver everything suggested within each option
- how you conclude the negotiation with the client and how the details of the agreement are recorded
- how the contractual arrangement and fee basis are agreed with the client
- how you implement the agreed intervention and manage the client's expectations according to the agreed plan
- how you build on the initial rapport created with the client to produce a professional working relationship throughout the term of the assignment (and on-going if appropriate)
- how you identify suitable and accurate sources of information, and the methods of obtaining it
- your ability to make a clear and appropriate analysis of information which is used in the decision making process within a consultancy context

- your ability to select and put into place suitable systems for recording, storage and retrieval of information within a consultancy context
- how you advise, educate and inform colleagues and clients on the basis of your analysis of information within a consultancy context
- the use of appropriate techniques to manage financial resources within a consultancy context
- how you plan the use of physical resources with the client to meet the objectives of your assignment
- how sufficient and appropriate consultancy hours can be made available to fulfil the requirements of the intervention
- how you would ensure sufficient client staff resources with appropriate skills to meet the objectives of your assignment
- how you introduce, plan and control change management with a client
- how you resolve conflicts within the parameters of an assignment
- how you explain, establish and monitor the systems, processes and methods necessary for completion of the intervention
- how you ensure that all of the assignment's objectives have been met in full
- the process by which you enable your client to take ownership of the developments which you have introduced in the intervention
- how you assess your own performance during the assignment
- how you manage your time within the assignment
- how you manage withdrawal from the client

All candidates are asked questions at their Assessment Interview on the IMC Code of Professional Conduct and the IMC Ethical Guidelines.

Introduction to consulting competencies

The Institute asks questions of all candidates for assessment for CMC, and also of existing CMCs wishing to demonstrate they have undertaken the necessary CPD to remain competent; these questions are listed as the (current) twenty-nine competencies. This list is a little daunting and this note provides an overview of the list. It is stressed that competencies are about behaviours, not skills, not knowing what you should do, but actually what the consultant does and can produce evidence of so doing.

The list covers the whole lifecycle of consultancy practice from marketing, selling, scoping the intervention, agreeing the intervention, undertaking and managing the intervention, through to ensuring completion and managing the withdrawal from the client. In order to assist the understanding and navigation through the list of competencies they have been grouped under four key questions, which are listed below. Some of the competencies support more than one of the questions and have been listed only once.

Question 1 How professional are you in your dealings with the business world?

The following competencies cover more than the question. The key issue is what image do you give of the management consulting profession to the outside world. Are you objective and independent in your dealings? (See also the professional code).

Questions asked to elicit:

- how you market and sell your consultancy services
- how you assure the client of your integrity and competence as a consultant and define your specialisms

It should be noted that the Institute is exploring an extra competence under this question to find the extent of cross-cultural awareness of the candidates. This will cover different business cultures, different ethnic cultures and different nationality cultures.

Question 2 How do you successfully manage your relationship with a client?

We all know that a consultant can perform a superb engagement but the client can be left feeling dissatisfied. The question covers relationships with the client throughout the lifecycle of the individual intervention and over the course of the business relationship.

Questions asked to elicit:

- how you approach new clients and develop mutual understanding with a potential client about the possibilities for an appropriate intervention
- how you ensure that the client shares your perception of their situation
- how you present your proposals to a client
- how you conclude the negotiation with the client and how the details of the agreement are recorded
- how the contractual arrangement and fee basis are agreed with the client
- how you build on the initial rapport created with the client to produce a professional working relationship throughout the term of the assignment (and on-going if appropriate)
- how you introduce, plan and control change management with a client
- the process by which you enable your client to take ownership of the developments that you have introduced in the intervention
- how you manage withdrawal from the client

Question 3 How do you successfully undertake an intervention?

The key aspect is: Do you follow due process in your approach to each and every assignment?

Questions asked to elicit:

- how you apply appropriate diagnostic tools to determine the current position of the client
- how you scope the intervention
- how you prepare a proposal for a client
- how you determine the potential of each option with the client, whilst ensuring that you (or your practice) are able to deliver everything suggested within each option
- how you implement the agreed intervention and manage the client's expectations according to the agreed plan

- how you identify suitable and accurate sources of information, and the methods of obtaining it
- your ability to make a clear and appropriate analysis of information which is used in the decision-making process within a consultancy context
- how you plan the use of physical resources with the client to meet the objectives of your assignment
- how you would ensure sufficient client staff resources with appropriate skills to meet the objectives of your assignment
- how you explain, establish and monitor the systems, processes and methods necessary for completion of the intervention
- how you ensure that all of the assignment's objectives have been met in full
- how you assess your own performance during the assignment
- how you manage your time within the assignment

Question 4 How do you make sure you can deliver an assignment?

Having the right ideas, working well with the client and being ethical are not sufficient for a successful engagement. You must also manage your resources so that the assignment is performed to time, cost and quality.

Question asked to elicit:

- how you select and put into place suitable systems for recording, storage and retrieval of information within a consultancy context
- how you advise, educate and inform colleagues and clients on the basis of your analysis of information within a consultancy context
- how you select and use appropriate techniques to manage financial resources within a consultancy context
- how sufficient and appropriate consultancy hours can be made available to fulfil the requirements of the intervention
- how you resolve conflicts within the parameters of an assignment

Certified Practices

This qualification is increasingly being adopted also by Certified Practices who are consultancy firms awarded this designation by the IMC which audits their internal training and development processes and aligns them with the CMC standard. The European countries met in Bonn early in 2001 to review the results of the first audits within Europe and to prepare the European delegates for the biennial Congress of ICMCI in Sydney in September 2001. Major International practices such as those of Shell Services International, IBM Consulting, PWC, KPMG and smaller specialist practices such as Cornwall Associates were represented from Europe at this major decision-making event for policies about consultant learning and development. The Congress adopted policies and standards to secure a single global qualification and flexible local implementation of it in association with national universities and colleges in the member countries.

An earlier version of this chapter first appeared in Effective Consulting, *the international magazine for consultants with a focus on practical skills enhancement. It is bi-monthly and available on subscription. Published by Pentre Publications, Pentre House, Leighton, Welshpool, Powys, SY21 8HL, Wales, UK. Contact details: Tel: +44 1938 553430; fax +44 1938 555355; email: editor@effectiveconsulting.org.uk, website: www.effective consulting.org.uk*

2.3

Ethical norms and guidelines

C. Paul Lynch

Yes! But can you trust them?

Often the easiest part of engaging management consultants is finding those with relevant competence and a demonstrable track record of success with other clients. However, there may still be some questions at the back of your mind, such as:

- Is their previous experience really relevant to my situation?
- Will the management consultants assigned to me (my company) deal with my staff with respect and sensitivity?
- Will they provide impartial, independent advice? If not, will they declare their interest so I can form a valid judgement on the worth of their advice?

The answer may come down to your instinct and observation of their behaviour, supported by personal references from someone you know and whose judgement you trust. However, the million dollar question is 'can you trust them?'

The result of an informal survey of regular clients a few years ago by the head of practice of a small 40-person consultancy revealed that around 70 per cent approached the firm first because they trusted the head's judgement: if his own firm hadn't the competence, he would give the client the name of another firm that could satisfy the client's needs. Clients knew this, and always asked first – even though they knew the firm couldn't carry out the work! So, here are some essential questions that you will need to ask yourself:

- Can you trust them?
- Can you trust them to treat confidential matters securely?
- Can you trust them to report honestly to you the real needs of your organization without fear or favour?
- Can you believe that conflicts of interest are being addressed properly?
- Are you (your company) being treated impartially, objectively and fairly, without regard to the consultant's personal gain, or that of his firm?
- Are the consultants assigned to your organization really experienced in implementing the solution?
- How can you know all these things?

This chapter addresses these concerns and provides a way ahead for any client or potential client.

A short history of management consultancy

Management consultancy originated in North America, and seeds of this new approach to business travelled across the Atlantic in the early years of the last century. Engineers and accountants were the main ambassadors of this wonder of the New World – 'scientific management'. Much of their original work was based on introducing rigour to the process of observation, objective analysis of the alternatives and design of a new 'best' way to carry out tasks. Frequently they were driven by the need to produce more for a burgeoning market, but the Second World War added urgency to the need for greater production from limited resources.

■ 84 ETHICS AND BEST PRACTICE

Management consultancy was used extensively (often discreetly) to achieve greater volumes of output. After the war, those management consultants who had enjoyed the challenge of developing innovative solutions during a time of national crisis turned their skills to peacetime production.

The arrival of large American firms of management consultants in the UK during the 1950s spurred on the development of UK firms, who formed the Management Consultancies Association (MCA) as a trade body to protect their interests. Their backgrounds meant that individuals were often qualified by their original engineering and accountancy institutes. These institutes were rooted in the 19th century, with its concepts of service and trustworthiness. Their rules of conduct were modelled often on the selfless ethic of those engaged in medicine, nursing and teaching. They required their members to observe high standards of personal conduct and behaviour fitting for their public responsibilities.

It was natural, therefore, that when a few of the larger UK firms sponsored the formation of the Management Consultancies Association, they resorted to a model which was familiar to them. The MCA quickly realized that their trade interests did not sit easily with their clients' needs, and in 1962 it sponsored the establishment of a body whose aims included the 'traditional' ideas of high personal standards of behaviour, a culture of service to the client and the avoidance of conflicts of interest.

That body is the Institute of Management Consultancy (IMC), whose name changed from the Institute of Management Consultants in 1998. It was originally modelled on a 19th century exclusive club, but in the ensuing years has evolved into a radical, inclusive 21st century body now playing a leading role in the International Council of Management Consulting Institutes (ICMCI). This helps IMC to provide assurance to clients of the quality and behaviour of its members on a global basis by means of the international qualification Certified Management Consultant (CMC). As an important service, directly for IMC members and indirectly for clients, the IMC established an ethical helpline to complement its legal helpline. This aims to go beyond mere compliance and assists consultants to recognise dilemmas and identify their solutions. Many of the questions phoned in relate to real or imagined conflicts of interest. The legal helpline provides guidance, whereas the ethical helpline helps the member to arrive at his/her own solution.

The MCA itself has grown to represent 38 large UK consultancies at the time of writing (March 2001), and with developments in the marketplace, they have addressed ethical issues more closely. The American and European authorities highlighted their concern regarding the impartiality of advice and the possible conflicts of interest arising from the growth of the large international professional firms. These firms, originally auditors, accountants and tax advisers, had been attracted into the consultancy market. The attraction of enriched fee-income, allied to the respectability and, thus, competitive edge they lent to the service offering, made this an attractive proposition for clients who trusted their auditors, but were unsure about the aggressive selling techniques adopted by the new management consultancies.

With the ever-increasing dependence on technology, the need to have access to the very best solutions became paramount for many, if not most, clients. They were impatient with the traditional consulting approach, which relied on the scientific, objective approach. They wanted their businesses to be the quickest to market with new services and products, and sought the advice of consultancies that had experience of similar implementation exercises. This enabled firms such as Arthur Andersen to post year-on-year growth in double-digit figures for many years. It also encouraged IT companies to enter the market more confidently on the back of standard solutions that worked. Very quickly the distinctions between these firms became blurred. The potential for conflicts of interest also increased, as these firms competed to attract the brightest graduates and to commoditise the consultancy solutions.

To some extent the increasing concern of American and European regulators has had an impact and Ernst & Young responded by selling its consultancy arm to Cap Gemini.

PricewaterhouseCoopers came close to selling its consultancy division to Hewlett Packard, and although that deal fell through, the market appears to expect a similar move to take place in due course. Arthur Andersen has demerged its consultancy and the separate parts are now re-establishing themselves in the marketplace.

Clients have become disenchanted with some large firms of consultancies and their practice of providing armies of young, well-qualified but often inexperienced consultants to provide standard solutions. This may reduce clients' risks, but it may not necessarily provide the solution the client needs. Substantial sums of money have been lost, and the size of projects being aborted is increasing, as the business solutions needed remain elusive. Clients seek independent and informed advice, and need certainty in the implementation phase of any work.

Competency of individual consultants

In an uncertain world, clients seek as much certainty as possible to protect market shares and margins. Obtaining the services of a consultancy firm whose staff can prove they have *current* competency in the services needed is an increasingly important factor in the choice of consultants.

In the United Kingdom, clients can now ask their potential consultancy supplier whether they are registered with the IMC. The client can ask each member of the consultancy team assigned to them whether they are currently competent in the areas the client needs for his company. In order to reply in the affirmative, the individuals must have passed a rigorous assessment of their current capability. This is tested by the IMC on an annual sampling basis. Increasing numbers of firms are registering with the IMC scheme for Certified Practices. This requires the consultancy firm to pass an assessment of their recruitment, training and re-training processes. If the firm succeeds, employees can fast-track to the CMC qualification within three years compared to the more normal five years which other practitioners require to qualify.

The competency of individuals is tested in four areas:
- consultancy competence
- management competence
- professional specialism
- social/technological/economic/political awareness ('step')

The onus for proof of competency is on applicants who must address 29 areas of competence by reference to their work experience. Nine areas must be addressed in the management competencies. A relevant first or higher degree or a relevant professional or vocational qualification is needed for the professional specialisms. Finally, the 'step' criteria must be present in the application, which will contain a professional record, an assignment case study, a presentation and an assessment interview. More details are available from IMC. These processes are validated by Napier University, Edinburgh, whose own quality assurance processes represent leading-edge practice in this area.

When an individual management consultant becomes a member of the IMC, he/she must formally agree to abide by a legally enforceable Professional Code of Conduct, and observe high personal standards of behaviour as expressed in Ethical Guidelines.

International dimension

The ability for clients in other countries to seek confirmation of the qualification of the consultants will become more widespread with the formal adoption of the CMC qualification by the ICMCI, a body which has 33 member bodies from individual countries. Each member is in the process of working towards common practices for qualifying individuals working within their geographical sphere of influence. In some cases, global businesses are forcing the pace by seeking recognition for their global consulting practices (both internal and external consultancies). It is possible that the UK practice certification process will be extended and accepted by ICMCI, so that these global practitioners can give assurance to clients, as well as help to attract the best candidates.

The ICMCI has taken initial steps by adopting a Code of Conduct which focuses on common features; but guidelines for ethical practice have not as yet been adopted.

Legal basis for the work

In order to avoid some of the more alarming results reported in the press, it is always important for buyers to be aware of the potential risks. In any buying situation, the old Roman law adage *caveat emptor* applies. Roughly translated it advises any buyer to be wary – to be wary of unsubstantiated claims and of promises which appear unreasonable. In every case the consultant's proposal will form the basis for sanctions or legal action. It is vital, therefore, when buying a consultant's services to ensure that their proposal clearly states the basis for the work. It should be as specific as possible – in particular it should state:

- their understanding of the client's requirements
- their approach to dealing with the client's requirements
- the number of staff involved and their relevant experience
- their assumptions as to the level of resources they expect from the client
- the estimated time needed to satisfy the client's requirements
- the estimated costs involved.

This provides a sound starting point for any subsequent work, during which it will be important for the client to manage the project along with the consultant. It also provides a fundamental means of measuring the effectiveness of the consultants, and should relations ultimately break down, it will be vital in any legal action.

Sanctions, arbitration and redress

Some management consultancies have been guilty of poor practices, but upon investigation it transpires that the firm in question is not a member of any formal body and thus can escape professional sanction. Even the more normal redress open to a client of requiring the firm to commit resources to the correction of the inadequate work can be unavailable. If a client feels it is necessary, and if the offending firm is a member of the MCA or IMC, then sanctions may be applied for through the appropriate body.

The IMC has moved to introduce a more transparent sanction against errant members by proposing that a prominent individual – not a management consultancy professional – be invited to play a part in the disciplinary procedures. This is seen as a matter of basic human rights as well as a means of protecting the public.

In the rare event that a client suspects that wrongdoing is being committed, contact with the IMC and/or the MCA can help them to determine what redress is open to them. Appeal to the IMC/MCA in UK law will not necessarily prejudice a client's right to damages: it depends on the circumstances. In the event that arbitration is invoked, it would be normal for the terms of the arbitration to bind the parties to the outcome. Otherwise, contract or common law rights could apply.

The position will vary in other countries, and clients should contact their local management consultancy body for guidance.

IMC Ethical Guidelines

In recent years the perceived lack of individual ethical behaviour has received increasing publicity and scrutiny in the media. The public response has been an increased level of expectations of higher standards from public servants, elected representatives and professional advisers. The Institute has published these guidelines to assist members and to provide some tests which can be used to gauge the extent or otherwise of members' ethical behaviour.

The Institute's Code of Conduct is founded on three basic principles, namely:

- high standards of service to the client
- independence, objectivity and integrity
- responsibility to the profession

This guidance describes two additional principles which should attach to an ethical decision, and sets out a number of questions designed to assist individual members to gain an objective insight to their quandary. Having considered these questions, a member may feel the need to discuss the problem with someone else, and the Institute will provide access to a Confidential Ethical Helpline. This service, which is free and without commitment, and which is aimed at assisting the member to develop their own resolution, is described at the conclusion of these guidelines.

Basic Guidelines

A member should consider, with these guidelines, the interests of a wider number and range of 'stakeholders'. 'Stakeholders' has become common usage in ethical circles to refer to those individuals or organisations who have an interest or stake in the situation. Stakeholders may include the general public and the national interest.

Transparency

1. Can you discuss the problem with the client before you make the decision?

The answer to this question indicates to what extent the principles of transparency is present. If there are any circumstances existing which make such a discussion unlikely, you need to consider why this is so. Is it possible that such a discussion could perhaps expose something with which you are uncomfortable or even weaken your legal position?

2. Would you feel comfortable explaining your behaviour to your family? Your friends? Your fellow workers?

The purpose of this question is to explore the degree of comfort you have with your behaviour. If you feel uncomfortable with the answer, you must seriously question your behaviour.

3. Would you feel comfortable if your actions were announced on television or printed in a newspaper?

Although you may feel comfortable with handling your family and friends, you may still be uncomfortable when faced with the possibility of having to explain your actions in the media. Does this have a bearing on your behaviour?

4. Would you feel confident that the action you propose to take (or not to take) would be viewed as proper by your peers?

While you may be confident that you can rationalise and explain your actions to your family, your friends, the stakeholders and to the media, what about your professional peers? They are more likely to understand the issues involved and to be able to provide an informed point of view.

Conclusion

Members are responsible for their own action, and these testing questions are offered as guidance for members to help in forming their own opinion. The questions are not exhaustive or exclusive, and other questions may suggest themselves during the course of working through the process.

For further confidential advice, contact the Chief Executive of the Institute who may refer you to the IMC Confidential Ethical Helpline. If you decide to do so, the Chief Executive will ask you for the following information on a confidential basis:

- the names of the parties involved (to ensure that conflicts of interest are excluded)
- the nature of the work involved, and your role in that work
- an outline of the issue
- the time-scale involved (is it urgent?)
- what sort of guidance you are seeking
- confirmation that you wish the Registrar to approach the Ethical Helpline

The Chief Executive will refer the matter to the Helpline, if it is an ethical problem. An independent panel member will be selected who will contact the member to define the problem and offer assistance – usually by phone. Other panel members will be involved if required and subject to the member's agreement. The panel will aim to help the member come to his/her own resolution of the matter, and under no circumstances can the Institute or panel member accept responsibility for the consequence of members' actions.

IMC Codes of Conduct

Introduction

The Institute has two Codes of Conduct, detailed below:

- the Code of Professional Conduct is binding on all members of the Institute practising as management consultants —including AIMCs, CMCs, FCMCs, Registered Practices, Certified Practices and those Affiliates in practice
- the briefer Code of Conduct is binding on all those members not in practice as management consultants – including Affiliates not in practice and Organisational Affiliates

The objective of the Institute of Management Consultancy is the advancement of the profession of management consultancy through the establishment and maintenance of the highest standards of performance and conduct by all its members, and by the promotion of the knowledge and skills required for that purpose.

Professional Standards

A management consultant is an independent and qualified person who provides a professional service to business, public and other undertakings, by:

- identifying and investigating problems concerned with strategy, policy, markets, organisation, procedures and methods
- formulating recommendations for appropriate action by factual investigation and analysis with due regard for broader management and business implications
- discussing and agreeing with the client the most appropriate course of action
- providing assistance where required by the client to implement the recommendations

In rendering such services to all levels of management, consultants carry a heavy burden of responsibility and an obligation to maintain the highest standards of integrity and competence. Recognising this responsibility, the Institute embodies within its Code of Professional Conduct those duties and obligations required of all members practising as consultants, which will ensure the highest standards of performance, and thereby enhance the reputation and public recognition of the profession, of the Institute and of all its members.

Code of conduct

The Institute has some members not practising as consultants – individual Affiliates and Organisational Affiliates. They are required to adhere to the standards set out in the brief Code of Conduct set out below:

An Affiliate Member:

- will further the objectives of the Institute in as far as they are able
- will not bring the Institute or profession of management consultancy into disrepute
- shall be a fit and proper person to be a member of the Institute of Management Consultancy
- shall at all times be of good reputation and character. Particular matters for concern might include:
   - conviction of a criminal offence or committal under bankruptcy proceedings

- censure of disciplining by a court of regulatory authority
- unethical or improper behaviour towards members or the general public
■ shall not wilfully give the Institute false, inaccurate, misleading or incomplete information.

Qualities of a Management Consultant

The personal qualities required of a person to enable them to carry out these duties effectively and efficiently are:

- objectivity, impartiality and independence
- knowledge of management organisation and techniques
- consulting skills
- practical experience
- technical expertise

Certified Management Consultants (CMC/FCMC) have demonstrated that they possess and are able to apply all these qualities. IMC Associates (AIMC) are required to demonstrate that they are undergoing approved training and development to this end.

Certified Management Consultants and Associates have a basic responsibility to:

- exercise independence of thought and action
- hold affairs of their clients in strict confidence
- deal with management problems in perspective and give well-balanced advice
- strive continuously to improve their professional skills and to maintain a high quality of advice
- advance the professional standards of management consulting
- uphold the honour and dignity of the profession
- maintain high standards of personal conduct.

In recognition of their obligations to clients, to the public at large and to the profession, all members in practice annually agree in writing to comply with the Institute's Code of Professional Conduct, and to undertake relevant Continuing Professional Development activities.

The Code of Professional Conduct

The Institute's Code of Professional Conduct is structured on three basic principles dealing with:

- meeting the client's requirements
- integrity, independence, objectivity
- responsibility to the profession and to the Institute

These principles are underpinned by detailed rules, which are specific injunctions, and practical notes, which either lay down conditions under which certain activities are permitted or indicate good practice and how best to observe the relevant Principle or Rule.

The Council of the Institute may, from time to time, issue further Principles, Rules or Notes which will be promulgated in the Institute's publications before being incorporated into a revised edition of the Code. Members in practice are expected to abide by all such new provisions from the date of their publication.

The Principles, Rules and Notes of the Code apply not only to the members personally but also to acts carried out through a partner, co-director, employee or other agent acting on behalf of, or under the control of, the member.

Definitions used in the Code of Professional Conduct
member: A CMC, FCMC or AIMC
client: The person, firm or organisation with whom the member in practice makes an agreement or contract for the provision of services.
declaration: A written statement referring to and disclosing the facts relevant to the situations covered by particular Rules of the Code.
independent: In a position always to express freely one's own opinion without any control or influence from others outside the (consulting) organisation, and without the need to consider the impact of such opinion on one's own interests.
Institute: The Institute of Management Consultancy.

Disciplinary action
All members are liable to disciplinary action if their conduct is found, by the Disciplinary Committee of the Institute to be in contravention of the Codes, or to bring discredit to the profession or to the Institute.

In accordance with the Bylaws, members may be required to make a declaration in answer to enquiries from the Institute concerning their professional conduct. A member failing to make such a declaration may be found in breach of the Principle to which the Rule or Note relates.

The Principle, Rules and Notes
Principle 1 – Meeting the client's requirements
A member shall regard the client's requirements and interests as paramount at all times.

Rules
Competence
1.1 A member will only accept work that the member is qualified to perform and in which the client can be served effectively; a member will

not make any misleading claims and will provide references from other clients if requested.

Agreement on deliverables and fees
1.2 A member shall agree formally with the client the scope, nature and deliverables of the services to be provided and the basis of remuneration, in advance of commencing work; any subsequent revisions will be subject to prior discussion and agreement with the client.

Sub-contracting
1.3 A member shall sub-contract work only with the prior agreement of the client, and, except where otherwise agreed, will remain responsible for the performance of the work.

Confidentiality
1.4 A member will hold all information concerning the affairs of clients in the strictest confidence and will not disclose proprietary information obtained during the course of assignments.

Non-poaching
1.5 A member will not invite or encourage any employee of a client for whom the member is working to consider alternative employment, unless it is the purpose of the assignment.

Due care
1.6 A member will make certain that advice, solutions and recommendations are based on thorough, impartial consideration and analysis of all available pertinent facts and relevant experience and are realistic, practicable and clearly understood by the client.

Communication
1.7 A member will ensure that the client is kept fully informed about the progress of the assignment.
1.8 A member will encourage and take note of any feedback provided by the client on the performance of the member's services.

Respect
1.9 A member will act with courtesy and consideration toward the individuals contacted in the course of undertaking assignments.

Principle 2 – Integrity, independence, objectivity
A member shall avoid any action or situation inconsistent with the member's professional obligations or which in any way might be seen to impair the member's integrity. In formulating advice and recommendations the member will be guided solely by the member's objective view of the client's best interests.

Rules

Disclosure

2.1 A member will disclose at the earliest opportunity any special relationships, circumstances or business interests which might influence or impair, or could be seen by the client or others to influence or impair, the member's judgement or objectivity on a particular assignment.

2.1.1 *Rule 2.1 requires the prior disclosure of all relevant personal, financial or other business interests which could not be inferred from the description of the services offered. In particular this relates to:*

- *any directorship or controlling interest in any business in competition with the client*
- *any financial interest in goods or services recommended or supplied to the client*
- *any personal relationship with any individual in the client's employ*
- *any personal investment in the client organisation or in its parent or any subsidiary companies*
- *any recent or current engagements in sensitive areas of work with directly competitive clients*
- *any work for a third party on the opposite side of a transaction e.g. bid defence, acquisitions, work for the regulator and the regulated, assessing the products of an existing client.*

Conflicts of Interest

2.2 A member shall not serve a client under circumstances which are inconsistent with the member's professional obligations or which in any way might be seen to impair the member's integrity; wherever a conflict or potential conflict of interest arises, the member shall, as the circumstances require, either withdraw from the assignment, remove the source of conflict or disclose and obtain the agreement of the parties concerned to the performance or continuance of the engagement.

2.2.1 *It should be noted that the Institute may, depending on the circumstances, be one of the 'parties concerned'. For example, if a member is under pressure to act in a way which would bring the member into non-compliance with the Code of Professional Conduct, in addition to any other declaration which it might be appropriate to make, the facts should be declared to the Institute.*

Inducements

2.3 A member shall not accept discounts, hospitality, commissions or gifts as an inducement to show favour to any person or body, nor attempt to obtain advantage by giving financial inducement to clients or client staff.

2.3.1 *Payment for legitimate marketing activity may be made, and national laws should be respected.*

Privacy of information
2.4 A member shall not use any confidential information about a client's affairs, elicited during the course of an assignment for personal benefit or for the benefit of others outside the client organisation; there shall be no insider dealing or trading as legally defined or understood.

2.5 When required or appropriate a member will establish specific methods of working which preserve the privacy of the client's information.

Objectivity
2.6 A member will advise the client of any significant reservations the member may have about the client's expectation of benefits from an engagement.

2.7 A member will not indicate any short-term benefits at the expense of the long-term welfare of the client without advising the client of the implications.

Principle 3 – Responsibility to the Profession and to the Institute
A member's conduct shall at all times endeavour to enhance the standing and public recognition of the profession and the Institute.

Annual Affirmation
3.1 A member will provide the Institute with annual affirmation of adherence to the Code of Professional Conduct.

Continuing Professional Development
3.2 A member will comply with the Institute's requirements on Continuing Professional Development in order to ensure that the knowledge and skills the member offers to clients are kept up to date.

3.3 A member will encourage management consultants for whom the member is responsible to maintain and advance their competence by participating in Continuing Professional Development and to obtain membership of the Institute.

Professional obligations to others
3.4 A member shall have respect for the professional obligations and qualifications of all others with whom the member works.

3.5 A member referring a client to another management consultant will not misrepresent the qualifications of the other management consultants, nor make any commitments for the other management consultant.

3.6 A member accepting an assignment for a client knowing that another management consultant is serving the client will ensure that any potential conflict between assignments is brought to the attention of the client.

3.7 When asked by a client to review the work of another professional, a member will exercise the objectivity, integrity and sensitivity required in all technical and advisory conclusions communicated to the client.

Fees

3.8 A member will negotiate agreements and charges for professional services only in a manner approved as ethical and professional by the Institute.

3.8.1 *Members are referred to the Institute's 'Guidelines on Charging for Management Consulting Services'.*

Publicity

3.9 A member, in publicising work or making representations to a client, shall ensure that the information given:

- is factual and relevant
- is neither misleading nor unfair to others
- is not otherwise discreditable to the profession

3.9.1 *Accepted methods of making experience and/or availability known include:*

- *publication of work (with the consent of the client)*
- *direct approaches to potential clients*
- *entries in any relevant directory*
- *advertisement (in printed publication, or on radio or television)*
- *public speaking engagements.*

Members are referred to the Institute's 'Guidelines on the Promotion of Management Consulting Services'.

Personal Conduct

3.10 A member shall be a fit and proper person to carry on the profession of management consultancy.

3.10.1 *A member shall at all times be of good reputation and character. Particular matters for concern might include:*

- *conviction of a criminal offence or committal under bankruptcy proceedings*
- *censure of disciplining by a court or regulatory authority*
- *unethical or improper behaviour towards employees or the general public.*

3.11 A member shall not wilfully give the Institute false, inaccurate, misleading or incomplete information.

2.4

Higher education opportunities in management consulting

Sally Woodward and Allan P.O. Williams

Introduction

The purchasing of management consultancy services involves significant investments by a corporation to help ensure a successful outcome. Yet, despite these investments, the selection and evaluation of consultancy remains a complex and uncertain process. Traditionally, legally defined entry barriers and quality control mechanisms have not existed in the industry (Kipping, 1999), although the relevant professional bodies are making considerable efforts for change, as demonstrated in this volume. What, therefore, can a corporation look for when selecting a service provider, and how can its management appraise quality and value of consultants and their firms, where quantifiable criteria or indicators are sparse?

In seeking to address these issues and questions, we consider current ways in which higher education (HE) is contributing to management consulting and propose additional avenues for future collaborative exploration by HE institutions, corporations, consulting firms and their professional institutes and associations, at national and international levels.

Quality assurance mechanisms

Since the corporation is purchasing expertise which is difficult to evaluate because of its intangible nature, institutions that can provide a form of quality assurance to client corporations have an important role to play (Gallouj, 1997). Professional institutions alert purchasers to the fact that their members:

- apply skills based on a body of theoretical knowledge
- have undergone an extensive period of education and experience
- have undergone a testing of their competency
- have undergone institutionalised training and/or a period of internship
- are certified practitioners
- follow a code of ethics/rules of professional conduct

This form of 'signalling strategy' demonstrates a move to organise an unregulated market in which individuals can call themselves 'consultants', and to establish management consulting as a profession. It both helps to reduce purchasers' uncertainty and raises the competence and expertise of consultants and thereby raises quality standards within the management consultancy industry, although there are also associated costs (Abbott, 1988; Torstendahl and Burrage, 1990).

Many professional services, such as medicine, accounting and law, have largely succeeded in reducing client risk. This has been achieved through regulating entry to their profession, by the application of compulsory qualifying examinations, and by concurrent developments of HE curricula and qualifications in aspects of theory and practice. Unlike these older professions, however, management consultancy has only recently established a fixed qualification benchmark. This professional qualification, the Certified Management Consultant (CMC), has been adopted in 30 countries and is described in detail in Chapter 2.2. In the UK, the CMC qualification has been recognised by Napier University in Edinburgh, Scotland, which has granted 30 credits for the qualification towards the 120 points needed for a postgraduate diploma and the 180 points required for a master's degree in consultancy. The Institute of Management Consultants (IMC) in the UK is working with a number of other HE providers (University of Glasgow Business School, University of Central England, Leeds Metropolitan University, Aston University) to establish closer links through a proposed Learning/Teaching Partner scheme. Here, the CMC competencies, Code of Conduct and Ethical Guidelines are made explicit in the course material. An alternative model is the inclusion of CMC and ongoing continuing professional development (CPD) activity in the portfolio of the 'Professional Studies' degree programme at the University of Wolverhampton.

Both in the UK and the US, higher education institutions are showing an increasing interest in developing curricula and programmes at postgraduate diploma and master's level in consulting. Similar programmes also exist or are under development in France, Germany and the Netherlands. They can build further on the work of the professional institutes, and on an increasing body of research undertaken by academics and doctoral students. Special Interest Groups (SIG) within both the American and British Academies of Management are yet other communities also driving efforts to codify the practice of consulting and raise standards. There are, therefore, a variety of ways in which higher education can contribute to the professionalisation of management consulting through both teaching and research, which can be of direct benefit to corporate clients. Indeed, since the 1980s, education for the professions has become an increasingly significant aspect of UK higher education (Goodlad, 1984). This is reflected, for example, in City University's mission statement 'to be a university for business and the professions'.

Current provision of higher education to management consultancy

Milan Kubr (1996) has pointed out in various editions of his book, *Management Consulting*, that consulting can be viewed both as a profession and a method which is applied by competent persons whose main occupation is not generally viewed as consultancy. Others have also drawn attention to the heterogeneous activities and organisations included within management consultancy:

> *Its practitioners are large transnational and independent firms, but also certified public accountants, thousands of freelance practitioners, business school professors, in-house consultants, as well as software firms and computer manufacturers.*
>
> (Sauvant, 1993)

Although we acknowledge the debates which question the boundaries of consultancy, by adopting this perspective we can usefully bifurcate the current provision of higher education in management consulting into provision for management consulting professionals and provision for others who use consulting as an aspect of their role. This means that corporates can benefit in a variety of ways from engaging with individuals who are educated and, in some cases, qualified in consulting, and with consultancy firms promoting this.

The academic literature on education and training provision for management consultancy is currently sparse (for an exception see Gregory, 1994). As part of the British Academy of Management's SIG initiatives, one of the authors recently undertook a survey of consulting programmes, which revealed four types of provision in UK higher educational institutions:

- Executive programmes
- MBA electives or modules

- Masters level programmes for specialists, with a strong consulting component
- Masters and postgraduate diploma level programmes focused on consulting

Each of these is elaborated below, drawing out each one's contribution towards corporate development and transformation, in addition to an individual's development.

Executive programmes

These vary in length from short residential weekends, or three to five weekdays, to a number of weeks spread over a period. Examples of providers include ESCP in France with a four-week course in 'management consultancy', offering accreditation towards a professional qualification, and Roffey Park Management Institute in England, with week-long courses in 'consultancy skills for organisational change'. This course has been devised for managers, professional developers and individuals seeking to control their own development. Learning outputs of the Roffey programme include:

- displaying a heightened range of interpersonal skills that will increase participants' ability to influence more effectively as a consultant
- being able to analyse problems and issues more rigorously, and hence develop a clearer and deeper understanding of what is going on at individual, team and organizational levels
- demonstrating increased ability to plan, facilitate and implement change in organisations – their own or others as appropriate

More generally, executive programmes aim to raise awareness of the complexities involved in consulting activities, and introduce participants to the key consulting skills and roles involved. Programmes vary in focus: on either internal or external consultancy, or both. Some include knowledge and skills for managing and developing a consultancy firm. In programmes that take place over a succession of weeks, participants are expected to put into practice the learning they have acquired on the programme, and report back their reflections in dialogue and discussion with other participants and tutors. Obviously, because of time considerations, these programmes operate at a basic level of competence, but through building good foundations, participants can move towards developing their competencies further, where pathways exist. Since corporations must increase and improve their change management capabilities in order to survive in today's competitive marketplace, these types of programmes can make a useful contribution towards building this resource through an 'awareness raising process' for appropriate personnel.

MBA electives

Management consulting is a popular career choice for MBA graduates, and some UK institutions have chosen to offer an elective in consulting (a minority may have it as a compulsory element). Whether an elective will run depends on the number of students showing an interest in taking it. Often, it will be competing with a range of other popular topics such as knowledge management, aspects of strategy, M&As, entrepreneurship, and so on.

Our survey found that eight of the top ten UK business schools offered their students an elective in consulting and, in addition, we identified another 15 schools offering electives. Many varied in focus, with elective titles including, for example: strategy development and consulting skills; management consultancy interventions; consulting skills and consultancy and research methods. Length and approach also varied, with some electives comprising from 14 to 30 taught hours, while others had participants undertaking a live project, with little teaching input. In major electives, students were expected to devote 100 hours plus to the required activities.

MBA electives were designed to meet a diversity of student needs. Some were crafted for existing consultants; others were designed for professionals who were seeking to develop consulting skills as part of their repertoire. In the main, however, courses were focused on MBA students who might move into consulting. A key dimension on which courses varied was the balance of efforts given to developing students' skills or factual knowledge and understanding.

We asked providers about their motivations for offering electives in consulting and, in addition to that of meeting student demand, we found two key drivers: academics with research interests in consulting; and networking and collaboration between academics and practitioners resulting in electives. In a few cases, electives existed because MBA programme directors felt that consulting should be part of the curriculum for credibility purposes.

Large consultancy firms tend to attach little importance to such elective programmes, as they have traditionally preferred to train consultants within their own mould. Students value electives for a variety of reasons. For example, by gaining insight into consultancy, they can make better career decisions. Several of them will decide to utilise existing competencies and start their own consultancy; others will join consultancy firms, while many will decide the lifestyle is not for them. Corporates can benefit as MBA graduates move into management positions and utilise consulting knowledge and skills in their managerial role. MBA graduates can also add value when their corporation needs to select and manage outside consultants, since their experience is likely to make them a better-informed client.

Masters level programmes for specialists, with a strong consulting component

We found several institutions currently offering programmes with a strong consulting component. These are particularly suited to Kubr's (1996) second cluster described above – consulting as a method applied by competent persons whose main occupation is not generally viewed as consultancy.

Included amongst these are programmes developed for human resource specialists, such as an MA in Human Resources

(Consulting) offered by South Bank University, and an MSc in Human Resources Management with a specialism in consultancy from UMIST (University of Manchester Institute of Technology). South Bank has run master's degrees in consulting for nearly a decade. The consulting specialism has been developed in recognition of the changing nature of the human resources profession. The qualification is seen as particularly relevant for HR professionals, human resources and organisational development consultants, and senior managers who have responsibility for organisational change and a desire to deepen their strategic consulting skills.

For accountancy specialists, the University of Reading has recently developed an MA in International Consulting and Accounting, and Northampton Business School also offers an MA in Accounting and Consultancy. The University of Reading's programme covers topics such as the structure and conduct of the industry, its evolution, the role of a consultant in the diffusion of new management know-how and patterns of consultancy work. This is followed by a case-based course on consulting practice, focusing upon consultancy firms and their services. The course is for young people doing a master's degree following upon a first degree and is designed to introduce them to various career options, as well as reflecting the evolution of the consultancy arms of accountancy firms.

These examples illustrate that master's programmes can be designed to meet the needs of people with fairly extensive or little experience of working. In the former, the aim is to meet the needs of those already working in, or providing services to, a corporation. This can mean specialists educated in consulting can add value to a corporation through their ability to adopt a more informed strategic role, and through deeper level inquiry skills gained by undertaking the project work required for a dissertation. In the accountancy example, an entry level qualification into the profession meets the student's need within a context to be determined in the future. Yet, even here, corporations receive value when students make better informed career choices.

Master's and postgraduate diploma level programmes focused on consulting

There are programmes, both well-established and more recent, devoted entirely to consulting. Examples of the former include Sheffield Hallam's MSc in Organisational Development and Consultancy, Ashridge's Master's in Organisational Consulting, and the Tavistock Institute's qualification in Advanced Organisational Consultation. A more recent offering is Sheffield Hallam's MSc in Knowledge Management and Consultancy.

The main themes of the Ashridge Master's in Organisation Consulting programme have been described by the director, Dr Bill Critchley, as threefold: organisations as complex processes; inquiry; and a participative/constructivist world view, with reflexivity as a stance. This is offered as a part-time programme, following the trend in higher education to enable professionals to learn 'on the job' and concurrently apply what they have learned. It has a taught element lasting eighteen months and a six-month period for research and writing up of a dissertation. Each of the three taught modules has a series of three-day workshops, and participation in one-day meetings between workshops in a 'consulting application group' (CAG). The workshops have an experiential focus looking at 'self in context', a professional focus on developing consulting capabilities, and a theoretical component, focusing on developing complex conceptual frameworks of the processes of organising, learning, changing and consulting. The CAG provides an opportunity to integrate all the elements of learning into practice.

In addition to master's qualifications in consulting, institutions also offer postgraduate certificates (in professional development in management consultancy – Strathclyde Graduate Business School) and diplomas (in consultancy practice – Civil Service College). CMC competencies and standards are now aligned with the CSC diploma.

Formal academic qualifications are important signals of quality at the individual consultant level. Clients will be keen to examine the curriculum vitae of people who will be working on a day-to-day basis in their corporation, and evidence of both academic and professional qualifications in consulting can give a strong assurance of quality.

Yet, corporate clients need to be aware that the higher educational system itself is open to scrutiny and that there are 'league tables' of institutions, which can signal the quality of the qualification attained. For example, the *Financial Times* newspaper publishes an annual MBA ranking of the top 100 business schools around the world. Since management consulting is the career choice of many MBA graduates, and some consulting firms only choose from among the best, such market information is of direct value to employing firms and to purchasers.

The quality of an institution and its qualifications are affected, in the form of a virtuous circle, by the quality of the people it recruits and by their interaction. Strong competition to gain a place in a top business school ensures that a rigorous screening process has taken place. Schools' emphasis on group working means that candidates have experience of working on assignments with internationally qualified people, developing broad cultural and language skills which can complement their business knowledge. Additionally, they have to be experienced managers with industry expertise before they can be accepted on to an accredited MBA programme (eg those accredited by AMBA). Hence, some of the knowledge and skills mix required of consultants is already present.

Given the rising demand for management consultancy services, how can higher education meet the need for more consultancy education in the future?

Future provision

In this section, we look at opportunities for building on the different and complementary strengths of higher education providers and consulting firms, and the role of corporate clients. We start by drawing attention to the fact that the higher education sector is undergoing massive change, with positive outcomes for corporations.

First, there has been a dramatic global move towards increasing universities' economic and vocational roles (Etzkowitz, 1998). The basic requirement of universities today is to provide learners with knowledge and skills necessary to sustain a nation's economy, and to link with industries in contributing towards the development of a knowledge economy. In this context, higher education institutions are already working with important stakeholders to provide knowledge and skills, which will directly meet the needs of new emerging industries, such as biotechnology and ICT. Similar linkages have been proposed for management consultancy, and a few already exist (Czerniawska, 1999).

Second, as Gibbons et al (1994) have claimed, universities' role in traditional knowledge creation (the pursuit of 'scientific truth' by scientists holding a Cartesian world view, labelled Mode 1 knowledge production) has been gradually overtaken by knowledge that is produced in practice (labelled Mode 2). While Mode 1 knowledge provides disciplinary education, Mode 2 knowledge results from its application in group working activities which tend to be trans-disciplinary and often result in the generation of tacit (rather than explicit) knowledge.

University schools catering for business professionals' education are already intentionally positioned at the intersection of theory and practice. They can, therefore, usefully bring together the supply side of knowledge (eg HE institutions) and the demand side (eg corporations, professional institutes and consultancy firms) with the whole system depending on the interaction between theory, research and practice for its effectiveness. This can take a number of forms as the examples below will illustrate:

- Higher education institutions can provide management consultancy education within a structure that allows employees to accommodate their educational activities alongside their work commitments, but their employing firms need to partner such initiatives by acknowledging the additional demands. This type of education can be delivered through various interactive media, in different time packages, in open, customised or consortium programmes. Business and management schools can use

established networks and alliances to provide programmes at post-graduate levels in European or global management consultancy
- Professional institutes, corporates and consultancy firms may be actively involved in higher education provision for consulting. For example, strategic level advisory boards can be established to provide inputs to the design, and curricular requirements for teaching/learning programmes in management consulting
- Corporate universities can collaborate with higher education institutions, perhaps within a virtual partnership, to provide management consulting qualifications that can focus on internal or external consulting (since some large corporates with experienced internal consultancy arms now sell these services externally to other corporations)
- Corporations can collaborate with business schools to produce customised or consortium executive programmes that focus on how corporations can develop structures, skills and knowledge needed for acting as more effective clients
- Corporates, professional institutes, consultancy firms and higher education institutions can collaborate on research proposals. For example, the Economic and Social Science Research Council (ESRC), the UK's primary government funding agency for business and management research, has developed a grant programme for work with significant academic and industry links
- Academic researchers can work collaboratively with corporations and the consultancy firms they engage in inductive, theory-building studies, which apply methodologies such as grounded theory. This would generate relevant and current data on which to build better theories of how to create more effective consulting outcomes

Additionally, over the last twenty years or so, higher education has changed substantially with the move to focus on learning as well as teaching, and on developing active learners. A variety of pedagogical perspectives exist which value action as well as theory and reflection, and traditional divides between academics' body of knowledge and practitioners' knowledge are breaking down with teaching/learning methods that encourage science-practice integration. We consider that higher education institutions, especially business and management schools, can provide a valuable 'site' for the development and accreditation of skills and knowledge needed by consultants in the contemporary context of highly competitive industries engendering increasingly complex corporate problems.

Conclusion

Higher education institutions can play their part, with interested others, in developing education and qualifications in management consulting. In spite of the relatively low importance accorded to external accreditation of consulting qualifications by many large consultancy firms, who rely on their reputation and in-company training (Penn and Holt, 2000), developments in teaching and researching management consultancy should benefit corporate clients both directly and indirectly.

It would enable clients to have an additional assurance of quality. Through collective endeavours, the body of knowledge about the practice of clients in consulting could help improve the activity. More generally, clients would not need to rely largely on reputation and 'track record'. Smaller consultancy firms would be able to recruit consultants who would be more eclectically equipped to cope with working in rapidly changing industries and in delivering the various products as they come into fashion. Additionally, increased provision would also help reduce skill shortages since the pool of people from whom large consultancy firms recruit is quite small. It would also enhance career consultants' prospects.

Bines and Watson (1992) have identified three models of professional education: apprenticeship, technocratic and post-technocratic. In the 'apprenticeship' or pre-technocratic model, professional education mainly took place 'on the job'. 'Technocratic' education was adopted by a large number of professions for many years, and was underpinned by the assumption that professional activities are predominantly rational, technical and morally neutral. The third model, termed 'post-technocratic', is currently evolving, but its key feature is the recognition that people acquire professional competences in practice, and move towards 'professional artistry' through continuous learning. This involves reflection in and on practice, which has been informed and enhanced concurrently by the deployment of perspectives embedded in models and frameworks, theories, methods and arguments. These are most effectively gained by exposure to higher education, and refined by exposure to particular political, moral, interpersonal, cultural and social milieux.

Corporate management, management consultants and academics have different, yet complementary, skills and knowledge. The three constituencies can work together synergistically to meet competitive threats, improve business efficiencies and enhance corporate effectiveness. The fact that clients are co-creators, along with consultants, in the actual delivery of the consulting process, means that clients can play an important role in helping support the professionalisation of management consulting. Indeed, it has been argued that the client is the 'moral centre of the professions' – to exist, the professions need to engender and maintain client trust (Koehr, 1995). We hope we have shown that higher education can prove a valuable resource in this relationship.

References

Abbott, A (1988) *The System of Professions – An Essay on the Division of Expert* Labour, University of Chicago Press, Chicago

Bines, H and Watson, D (1992) *Developing Professional Education*, Open University Press and SRHE, Milton Keynes, Bucks

Czerniawska, F (1999) *Management Consultancy in the 21st Century*, Macmillan Business, Basingstoke, Hants

Etzkowitz, H (1998) 'The Norms of Entrepreneurial Science: Cognitive Effects of the New University-Industry Linkages'. *Research Policy*, **27**, (8), pp 823–833

Gallouj, C (1997) 'Asymmetry of Information and the Service Relationship: selection and evaluation of the service provider', *International Journal of Service Industry Management,* 8, (1), pp 42–64

Gibbons, M, Limoges, C, Nowotny, H *et al* (1994) *The New Production of Knowledge:* The dynamics of science and research in contemporary societies, Sage, London

Goodlad, S (1984) *Education for the Professions,* SRHE/NFER Nelson, Guildford, Surrey

Gregory, M (1994) 'The Education and Development Needs of Sole Practitioner Management Consultants: Current developments in the UK', *Management Research News,* 17, (10/11), pp 39–50

Kipping, M (1999) 'American Management Consulting Companies in Western Europe, 1920 to 1990: Products, Reputation, and Relationships', *Business History Review,* 73, pp 190–220

Koehr, D (1995) 'Expertise and Delegitimation of Professional Authority', *American Behavioral Scientist,* 38, (7), pp 990–1002

Kubr, M (1996) *Management Consulting: A guide to the profession,* 3rd edn, International Labour Office, Geneva

Penn, R and Holt, R (2000) *Skills Issues in Other Business Services – Professional Services,* Skills Task Force Research Paper no. 16, Department for Education and Employment, Sheffield

Sauvant, K (1993) *Management Consulting: A survey of the industry,* United Nations, New York

Torstendahl, R and Burrage, M (Eds) (1990) *The Formation of the Professions – Knowledge, State and Strategy,* Sage, London

2.5

What is the case for regulating management consultants?

Ian Barratt

Self-regulation

Almost the only thing people outside the business know about consultants is that they make good money and get a bad press. They are widely assumed to do little to justify the huge fees they command except offer common sense disguised as expertise (Graef, 1999).

The clamour for professionalisation is years out of date. A profession is a social construct (prestige, status, etc), not a business construct, and it's too late to try and grab for social status (David Maister, quoted in Kubr, 1996)

We have the nucleus of a profession, but it needs another 25 years to mature (Glen Van Doren, quoted in Kubr, 1996).

These three quotes encapsulate the background to the question posed by the title of this chapter. There is no doubt, certainly in the UK, that management consultancy has received a negative press over a number of years.

It is also clear that, amongst management consultants as well as a wider community, there is a debate about whether it is a profession or, more simply, an industry. Indeed, the Inland Revenue in the UK regards management consultancy as a trade, on the basis that there is no all-embracing code of conduct or qualification.

The issue of self-regulation cuts across both issues. How is the negative publicity to be avoided, and how is the client population to be encouraged to see management consultants as an integral part of business life, as opposed to an expensive commodity purchased in times of trouble? Is professionalisation one route or, if this is not seen as practical or even necessary, is self-regulation a sensible option?

There is, of course, the background of change in all sectors of society and the economies of all nations. Globalisation, technology, changes in business models, fluidity in the labour market and the blurring of boundaries within management consultancy between advice and implementation and internal and external consultancies are all impacting on the nature and role of management consultants as individuals. They raise an issue with particular resonance for me as the Chief Executive of a professional body – 'within this environment, the place of the traditional professional institute with permanent values appears anachronistic. Are such bodies now redundant?' (Barratt, 2000)

There may be merit in the argument advanced by David Maister, and quoted above, that professions are a social rather than a business construct and, unsaid but perhaps implied, that they might well wither like the Guilds in London into ceremonial or charitable bodies. Yet I am not sure that this view answers totally the proposition that some form of regulation is needed. Business takes place within a societal framework and the view that the market is the ultimate regulator is, surely, flawed and based on the notion – sound in theory but questionable in practice – that the market is a perfect mechanism. Professional bodies do not seem to be going the way of the Guilds, and the International Labour Organisation (ILO) has put another case persuasively: 'Professional awareness and behaviour come when the early juggling with a little knowledge gives way to skilled application of a generally accepted body of knowledge according to accepted standards of integrity' (Kubr, 1996).

Before discussing the management-consulting context, however, we must also remember that there is a greater air of scepticism about all established institutions. This has been recognised for some time in terms of state and governmental institutions. Trade and professional associations have not been immune from these pressures. Commentators have spoken of '…increasing social and media pressures, sometimes fuelled by politicians, which generally take the form of demands that the "industry puts its house in order", with the trade association expected to be a quasi-regulator' (Trade Association Forum, 2000). In the case of professional associations, the view is similar – 'traditionally the state has awarded associations of professionals the privilege of self-regulation in return for an assurance that members abide by a set of standards and an ethical code of conduct to ensure protection of the public interest "…as increasing levels of education and social awareness give rise to greater expectations…", traditional structures, rules and regulations are challenged and justification for privilege is questioned' (Watkins, Drury and Bray, 1996).

The position of trade and professional bodies is also made more complex by the increasing demand from members for such bodies to defend them from these pressures. This representational role has to be balanced carefully against the responsibility of public protection. The regulatory function itself is not without its pitfalls. These are centred on '…ensuring that everyone in the market is covered, how any regulations are to be enforced and also possibly ensuring that restrictive trade practices legislation is not used against them. All such arrangements are potentially unstable and perhaps are held together predominantly by the fear of more onerous statutory regulation' (Boléat, 1996). These difficulties are compounded in an international environment. Developments within the European Union of a single market mean that '...the developments of rules and regulations concerning two issues – competition amongst professionals and standardisation of qualifications – are of particular concern' (Watkins, Drury and Bray, 1996). But the profession is global in nature and regulation has also to be seen against a shifting pattern of international trading and political structures. One driver for change is seen as 'deregulation and privatisation, combined with a gradual shifting of policy-making to the European, global or sub-national level' (Trade Association Forum, 2000).

The view of the Department of Trade and Industry (DTI) is that good self-regulation coupled with high industry and people standards help companies compete in this global marketplace. As service sector companies of all sizes become increasingly global, the development of high industry standards and competencies for individuals that are recognised internationally facilitates opportunities. When combined with effective self-regulatory systems and, where appropriate, supporting mechanisms which exist to encourage good practice and resolve cross-border disputes, this development will reduce barriers and realise a single market worldwide. The key questions are whether this assumption would be borne out in reality and whether any regime would only add to the competitive pressures.

The management consultancy profession has seen its reputation for professional, objective advice questioned frequently by the media and others. Events in the USA, where the failure of confidentiality 'firewalls' between the audit and consultancy arms of accountancy practices has prompted a re-examination of current standards, have been watched with interest. The Association of Management Consulting Firms has made it clear to the US Securities and Exchange Commission (SEC) that any proposal to restrict the consulting services offered by accounting firms might have unintended consequences for the strategic alliances and joint ventures required to service the needs of clients in a new economy. In the UK, the Institute of Chartered Accountants in England and Wales, for example, sees the SEC's proposals as counterproductive. It believes that a framework approach, based on ethical principles backed by professional education and firm enforcement, is more rigorous than a prescriptive approach. The dangers of narrow, legalistic interpretations being used to bypass rules is avoided and yet the flexibility of the approach allows for variations in individual circumstances that in practice arise in the business world.

In terms of professional expertise, there are two sides to the management consultancy equation. Many consultants, certainly in the UK, started their careers as specialists in a technical field, eg accountancy or marketing, and are therefore members of another professional body (eg the Institute of Chartered Accountants or the Chartered Institute of Marketing) for their principal professional expertise. Our approach is based on the proposition that this technical specialism is not sufficient and that consulting skills, ie delivering technical expertise in a consulting context, require separate assessment and qualification. This is an important concept in that it does recognise consulting skills as both a separate discipline and as capable of quite specific testing and accreditation mechanisms. This brings with it, however, its own set of challenges. The fact that members of the Institute also belong to another institute for their principal professional expertise, means that any self-regulation for management consultancy needs to sit with the regulatory functions of other bodies. In the event of a complaint, which would take precedence? How would any self-regulatory system sit with any legal action based, say, on contractual issues?

There are also complications introduced by the business need for large practices in particular to form alliances, especially with IT suppliers, in an environment where e-commerce is becoming all-pervasive. Do these alliances inhibit independence and objectivity, seen by many including the UK Institute as central to any coherent definition of management consultancy, or are they best viewed as enabling practices to deliver the best solutions at the pace required by global competition? Similar questions can be asked about the increasing tendency for practices to implement as well as provide solutions and to invest in, even incubate, the businesses with which they deal. While consulting trade associations see escalating fee income as an undiluted measure of success, there is no reason why clients or society should. Like all overheads, expenditure on consulting services is subject to scrutiny as businesses seek to become more competitive. Management consultants must be seen as adding value and providing advice of a consistently high quality within an ethical framework.

But the limitations of purely national approaches are clear. The global nature of consultancy means that the complexities of jurisdiction and applicable law need to be taken into account, and the dangers of regulatory systems being used as restraints on trade or for the furtherance of the interests of trade blocs recognised. Conversely, it is likely to be the case that others, even if introduced for the best of reasons, may see any system of regulation as a restraint of trade. The danger is that the introduction of any self-regulatory system may also require an accompanying increase in bureaucracy and industry overheads and that the perceived failure of any such system may provoke a call for statutory intervention. The reality is that management consultancy, like every other business, is immensely competitive. Any regulatory proposals must take into account the need for the consulting profession to remain flexible enough to adapt to a new global and technology-driven world. In this global marketplace, 'UK plc' must be as competitive as the next nation. While global practices dominate the market, internal consultancies within UK companies are turning to external – and hence foreign – markets, for business and small practices in niche markets are also competing on a European or global stage.

The key is responding to the needs of clients rather than a regulatory regime that will always be behind developments in the marketplace. The potential costs of any regulatory regime, however light its touch, are of concern when the government does not seem to appreciate the costs, whether financial or opportunity costs, that may arise. Additional administration for practices and activity by professional bodies require resourcing and, in many cases, it is practitioners who have to bear the burden. The Certified Practices scheme is only viable because the Institute designed the concept and the Certified Practices themselves bear the burden of developing practices and procedures that demonstrate their compliance with the standard. The Institute believes that its position on self-regulation represents the best balance between the interests of clients and the wider public, and those of the profession.

Any self-regulatory regime must not fetter the ability of UK management consultants to compete for business, with the opportunities for other UK companies to follow in their wake that they may bring. This implies that there should be no formal role for government. The issue is whether the government can lend its support to what the Institute of Management Consultancy (IMC) is trying to achieve. The Institute of Management Consultancy believes that self-regulation is best delivered through a modern, professional approach, ie through standards backed by disciplinary arrangements. We currently deliver this approach through our Certified Management Consultant qualification (CMC), which is backed up by external validation and a Code of Professional Conduct and Ethical Guidelines. The Institute, through the IMC Consultants Register, actively encourages potential clients to discuss possible engagements with practices that are fully behind the CMC qualification. If the CMC (an international qualification) is to mean anything it must satisfy the needs of consultants for commercial advantage and those of clients for tested expertise, backed by disciplinary arrangements.

The Institute continues to support the aims of the International Council of Management Consulting Institutes (ICMCI) that encourage the spread and development of the CMC worldwide. This places our work in the UK firmly within an international context. The Certified Practices route, by which practices are able to propose individuals directly for the CMC after a full audit by the Institute, has required the Institute to pursue bilaterally the issue of reciprocity of recognition in other countries of those

CMC-qualified individuals who have achieved the qualification by means of a Certified Practice. The increasingly multinational and global nature of consultancy has only served to increase the need for an international, portable qualification for the profession, as represented by the CMC itself.

A partnership approach with other representative bodies in the field, other professional institutes, government and the ICMCI will encourage and support stakeholders in management consultancy, including clients and other institutes, to develop a system that protects users and enables the UK profession to compete in a global market.

This chapter is drawn heavily from the Institute's position paper on self-regulation, published in November 2000 in response to suggestions from the UK Department of Trade and Industry that self-regulation should be considered as an option.

References

Barratt, Ian (2000), Inside Careers, available from www.insidecareers.co.uk

Boléat (1996: 128), Trade Association Strategy and Management, Association of British Insurers

Graef, Roger (1999), *Management Today*

Kubr, Milan ed. (1996) *Management Consulting, A Guide to the Profession*, ILO

Trade Association Forum (2000) *Models of Trade Association Co-operation*

Watkins, Drury and Bray (1996: 7) *The Future of the UK Professional Associations*

2.6

Developments in management consultancy – from stagnation to evaporation or condensation?

Hans de Sonnaville

Introduction

Over the last two decades the management consulting industry has grown considerably and developed into big business.

In 1988 about 100,000 people worldwide were estimated to work full-time as management consultants (*The Economist*, 1988). By 1998, there were more than 100,000 people employed in just the top three consultancy firms (*Financial Times*, 1999) and the total revenue of the top twenty consultancies had reached 43.5 billion dollars. In Europe the industry has an annual growth of 15 per cent and FEACO foresees this trend continuing in the coming years (FEACO, 1999).

Simultaneously with this growth, the management consultancy business has become more heterogeneous. All kinds of specialities and other professions are now defining themselves as management consultants. The 'Big Five' have brought about enormous changes in the consultancy world and it seems that the IT companies, eg IBM, Cap Gemini and Hewlett Packard, will play an even bigger role in the consultancy sector in the coming years.

At the same time, we see an increasing growth of sole practitioners and small firms, while the medium sized firms seem to be in decline. All kinds of different services are now offered by the consultancy firms. Naturally, the more traditional services like corporate strategy, operations management and human resource management are included. However, during the last decade ICT services have become a very important new product and in the last three years consultancy firms have not only offered advice but have also advertised themselves as venture capitalists by participating financially in client organisations.

With the growth of the management consulting industry there is increasing criticism of the quality and sometimes also of the consultant's integrity. Criticisms such as 'too little added value', 'too expensive', 'too superficial', but also 'too much power' and 'too much business' are common from clients and commentators.

The question of what the professionals calling themselves management consultants actually do arises more and more frequently and forcibly. Is it possible to give a clear-cut definition of management consultancy? What can be expected from this professional group with regard to knowledge, skills, content, and ethics?

Some years ago, *The Economist* wrote that 'activities of management advice givers are little understood', claiming that the management consultancy business is a fairytale of mystery and illusion, and that they suspected the consultancy sector of deliberately keeping this fairytale up. There is a growing need for clarity about what can be expected from a management consultant. It is becoming more and more obvious that the growth of management consulting as an industry is far outrunning the developing perception of management consultancy as a profession.

Some believe this is a logical consequence of economic and financial success. If a group of professional workers is successful they automatically turn into an industry with standard solutions for diverse problems. Others believe that expansion into an industry also implies growth as a profession. This would involve agreements on a Body of Knowledge based on scientific theories and conceptions, along with generally accepted quality criteria and codes of conduct which should be communicated to clients.

We do not know a great deal about the management consultant as a professional. For years a number of individual management consultants together with the Institute of Management Consultants (IMC) and many clients, have pleaded for more transparency of this booming industry sector. Is management consultancy a method or a trade, or is it a profession, albeit a 'young profession'? Or is it simply a real business, an industry with products, standard solutions, commoditisation, advertising campaigns, and leverage? Or does it have elements of all of these and should the sector split up into well-defined groups of different kinds of professionals, each with their own view of the profession? There are many questions and few answers about the development of the management consultancy profession, even after so many years of discussion. It would be interesting to know why these questions are being asked and why it has proven so difficult to give answers. The same themes keep returning and conclusions are rarely drawn. The debate has reached a stalemate. In management change this phenomenon is called 'stagnation', in cycling it is called 'sur place'. It costs enormous energy but there is no movement. This chapter will try to contribute to the debate.

Management consultancy on its way towards becoming a profession?

A management consultant can be seen as an example of a professional. A professional possesses a comparatively high status level among all employees in an organisational setting. This high status is rooted in his or her extensive formal education, degree of expertise, altruistic orientation and autonomy. A group of professional workers that has become such an important part of our social and economical market and is still expanding in that market is, from time to time, called to account about the content of its discipline and the role it fulfils for its clients. These clients, and not only they but also other professional workers such as accountants and lawyers, and those who develop knowledge – the universities – ask the group of professional workers calling themselves management consultants for clarification. There is a process of social legitimisation of a group of professionals, in this case the management consultants.

But the process of legitimisation is a difficult one for management consultants. As previously noted, the more fundamental question has been put whether management consultancy is indeed a profession, and whether professionalisation of this group is at all possible; what professionalisation would mean for management consultancy and whether this could contribute to social legitimisation. The status of management consultancy is weak. There are several reasons for this: first of all, the discipline of management consultancy does not have a well-defined, generally accepted basis in academic knowledge. However, there is a huge variety of university educated people working successfully as management consultants.

Recently *The New York Times* published an interesting article about professionals who were being retrained as management consultants in a 20-day programme. The title of the article was 'A Matter of Degree? Not for Consultants', by David Leonhardt. He states that currently more than half of the consultants working with the big consultancy firms like McKinsey or Boston

Consulting Group are not MBAs but derive from a totally different discipline. In a period of three weeks, lawyers, philosophers, physicists, and astronauts were instructed in the basic consulting techniques and in practice appeared to function no better or worse than their colleagues with MBA backgrounds.

Besides the fact that there is no uniform academic basis for management consultants and there is no well-defined and generally accepted academic programme for those who want to become a management consultant, there are more reasons why – in comparison with professions such as law, accountancy and psychotherapy – the status of the profession is not very strong:

- There is no unequivocal basis for the group, no Body of Knowledge
- It is estimated that the greater part (75 per cent) of management consultancy work consists of implementation advice, bordering on temporary employment work
- The client is not dependent on the consultant's unique knowledge, he can make use of various disciplines and often he himself is just as knowledgeable
- There is no exclusivity for management consultants with regard to specific problems and issues. Many other professions and/or disciplines, eg accountants, IT consultants, PR agencies, attempt to draw management consultancy work into their own field, more or less successfully
- There is no culture among management consultants to carry out or publish research into developments in their own speciality; only a very few are involved in discussions about the development of the profession
- Less than 20 per cent of the individual management consultants in the world are members of a professional institute

Many people describe themselves as management consultants. But they will not accept each others' status. *The Economist* wrote in 1988 that defining consultancy is rather like defining the upper class: every possible candidate draws the line just below himself.

So the big strategy advisors rule out the accountants; both groups exclude executive recruiters and headhunters; all three dismiss computer-software houses as glorified salespeople in poor public relations agencies. Yet all are offering advice to managers.

In daily practice we see many descriptions of the management consultant: confidante, process guide, change agent, coach, support, trainer, knowledge worker, external expert, director, arbitrator, conscience, extension of the management, problem solver, etc. There seem to be as many definitions as there are consultants.

The definitions of consulting can be distinguished by two different approaches. The first approach considers consultancy as an activity in which a person attempts to change or improve a situation, although this person does not have any direct control over this activity. In this definition of consultancy everything is in fact 'consulting' as long as there are no direct competencies involved. According to this view, any person can be a kind of adviser in a certain position or role. For instance, a manager coaches his staff, and this could then be called consulting.

Peter Block (1981) adheres to this philosophy: 'An advisor is someone who is in a position to have influence on an individual, a group or an organisation, but who has no direct influence to carry out changes or implement programmes.' As soon as direct influence is exerted someone acts as a manager.

If consulting is directed specifically at organisations and management, a second approach can be distinguished. Consulting is seen as a special professional service with certain requirements that this service must meet. Greiner and Metzger (1983) provide an example:

Management consultancy is an advisory service, contracted for and provided to organisations by specially trained and qualified persons who, in an objective and independent manner, assist the client organisation to identify management problems, analyse such problems, recommend solutions to these problems and help, when requested, in the implementation of solutions.

A much quoted and widely accepted definition is Kubr's (1996):

Management consulting is an independent professional advisory service assisting managers and organisations in achieving organisations' purposes and objectives by solving management and business problems, identifying and seizing new opportunities, enhancing learning and implementing changes.

The International Council of Management Consulting Institutes (ICMCI), the global umbrella body of more than 35 national IMCs, has adopted the following definition:

Management consulting is the rendering of independent advice and assistance about the process of management to clients with management responsibilities.

Therefore, the conclusion must be that, apart from the fact that there is no uniform definition of management consulting, there is also no consensus on the question of whether management consulting is a method or a profession and whether it can reach the status of a profession comparable to that of doctors, lawyers, accountants or civil law notaries.

Stagnation in the debate

The management consultancy world is very diffuse and, many believe, not transparent. For years not only individual consultants and firms but also institutes and associations have been at work to create a recognisable identity along with professional recognition. However, in spite of these efforts there has been little progress towards a generally accepted full professional status. Up to now discussions have been too introspective between the professionals themselves, mostly organised within the IMCs and/or the associations of management consulting firms. After many years of discussion it seems that the arguments, analyses, assumptions, routines, role conceptions and so on have remained more or less unchanged. This has caused stagnation in discussions about the profession.

A well-known statement in change management literature is: 'Organisations fight like hell to stay the same'. The same could be said for management consultants. During the last two decades this professional group has been highly successful, considering the enormous growth it has undergone. But as success increases, the 'comfort zone' tends to become greater.

Many professional sociologists (Abbott, 1988, Whitley, 1992, and Kubr, 1996) maintain that this insight is indispensable for management consultants to carry on the debate. Historically, professional workers (doctors, lawyers, the clergy, professors, etc.) have always developed themselves towards a certain level of general acceptance, and groups of professional workers are always focused on defining the characteristics of their work in order to become a profession and to obtain status. Management consultants do the same. But the new modern sociology of professions is not only focused on defining the profession but concentrates more on the differences between professions.

Some theories about professions

In order to get a better understanding of what goes on in such a pluriform group of management consultants, it may be interesting to find the underlying reasons why an individual worker strives after a more mature level of professionalisation and how he achieves that goal. Once again it is useful to look at the history of those established professions which have already reached a generally accepted level of professional status: the medical and legal professions.

Abbott (1988) studied the rise, growth and fall of several professions and he classifies four different visions on the development of professions:

- *The functional vision*: The profession is a means to control the asymmetry between client and professional worker who is an expert in a certain domain. The fact that there is a gap between the client's knowledge and that of the professional makes it necessary to bridge that gap. The way the professional 'protects'

the client is by defining values and norms which are an important part of the relationship between client and expert.
- *The structural vision*: The second view on professions and professionalisation is based on a structural view: professional workers want to control their own work and want to develop standard solutions for specific problems. This view emphasises the need for a body of knowledge and for a standardised education programme to become a professional. The traditional professions are examples of this.
- *The monopoly vision* – the reason one puts effort into professionalisation is because the individual professional is proud of his/her work and knowledge, and wants to get recognition in the world. This reason is based on a desire for dominance and authority. Abbott calls this vision 'the monopoly school' because status and power become important drives of the professional worker.
- *The cultural vision*: professionals want to give added value to the market and society and they consider themselves unique in their way of working. A profession is a specific group of professionals with their own norms and values who hope to give a contribution to society.

It seems that all these visions of professions and professionalisation argue that there is a general concept in professionalisation. There are five basic assumptions:

- The development and change of professions are unidirectional. The assumption is that there is one given ideal structural and cultural form
- The development of a profession can be treated case by case: the evolution of an individual profession, independent of the other professions
- The social structure is more important than the work professions do
- Professions are homogenous units
- Professionalisation as a process does not change with time

The debate in the world of the management consultant is frequently characterised by these assumptions. If we conclude that the discussions about professionalisation show repetition and have become stagnated, we must investigate the validity of these assumptions. Abbott (1988) shows in his research that these assumptions are not always correct:

- There are varieties in directions for development: strong control is but one of them
- Professions are interdependent of each other; there are many interprofessional relations
- Work must be the focus of a concept of professions, because it has an enormous influence on the way the profession is structured
- The development of internal differences is bound directly to the development of professionalism
- The increasing or decreasing influence of the government reshaped professionalisation. So it is not a general process without a history of its own.

The nature of the debate about professionalisation in the management consulting industry can only be understood by analysing the different assumptions or approaches which influence the debate. We need another framework that can help our strategic thinking in the development of the profession of the management consultant, because the old, traditional model of the 'ideal' profession is not sufficient and does not seem to be supported by research.

Four different views on professionalisation of the management consultant

As noted above, the professional group cannot agree on a uniform description of the content of the profession. Looking at the theory and practice with regard to the development of professions, I distinguish two dimensions as to how professions can be regarded.

self-interest |—————————————————————————| society's interest

The first key dimension is interest: the strategic orientation of a profession is to protect the self-interest by gaining status, power and influence and, in doing so, to protect its own position and income. Professionalisation is a condition of staying in business. The opposite of this key dimension is the assumption that a profession has to give added value to society. This is called the interest of society. A profession has to play a role in society by developing solutions for important problems or issues. This is a more idealistic motivation.

The second dimension concerns the way control is gained.

```
        market control
              ┬
              │
              │
              │
              ┴
         inside control
```

The more traditional view of professions is that of 'inside control', which assumes that a profession is an orderly, well-controlled group organised by the professionals themselves. The crucial concepts are unity and consensus. The strategy is to define and control the profession by standardisation. The assumption is that there is an ideal phase or form of professionalism and the group of professional workers have to bring order into the group by setting rules, codes and standards. The assumption is that a profession is an objective, definable institute and is more or less static and stable. In this sense it is a somewhat mechanistic view of organising the profession.

The other extreme of the axis is 'market control'. A group of professionals is seen as a collection of several kinds of professionals, and development and movement from the market are considered more important than a mechanism coming from inside the professional group. Here the assumption is that a profession is an evolving social construct strongly influenced by what clients expect from the profession. It is impossible to define the profession and ambiguity is the norm. The definition of the group of professionals by Abbott (1988) is a good example of this view: 'Professions are exclusive occupational groups applying somewhat abstract knowledge to particular cases'. A profession is an ever evolving system and in order to understand what a profession is, one has to focus on the work the profession does.

When both dimensions are combined four ideal types of professions appear:

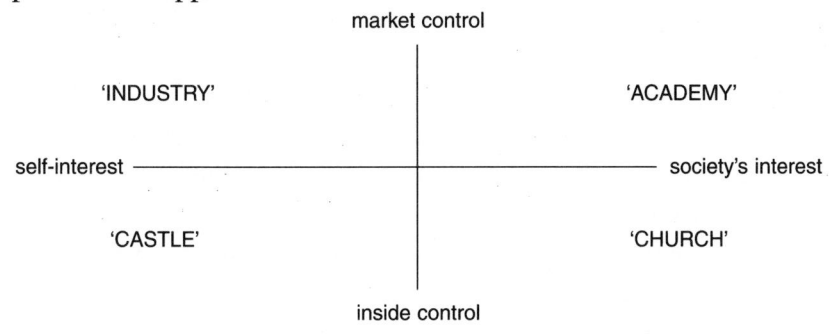

```
                    market control
                         |
       'INDUSTRY'        |        'ACADEMY'
                         |
self-interest ───────────┼─────────── society's interest
                         |
        'CASTLE'         |        'CHURCH'
                         |
                    inside control
```

These four ideal types of profession can be characterised as the 'castle', the 'church', the 'industry' and the 'academy'. It is important to realise that these types are different views of the reality and their function is that it can help us to understand the complex reality better. These types are not concepts and this is not a model, but it may help to explain the movement and discussions in management consultancy.

There are management consultants who view a profession as:

- **a castle**: an elite group of like-minded professionals who have situated themselves on a hilltop and defend themselves against those who are not professionals. A good definition of the profession is very important. This concept of a profession uses 'entry barriers' and wants 'to be seen as an elite'. Certification of the professional is crucial for establishing status and a good position. If a professional does not meet the standards he/she has to leave. Legal legitimation is the ultimate goal to be reached.
- **a church**: a group of like-minded professionals who try to give added value to clients by means of standardisation of the work in case of specific problems. Independence is a key word in this

view of the profession. A code of conduct and a uniform body of knowledge must protect the weak position of the client. These professionals are keen on the ritualisation of their work and they often work with protocols. Legal legitimacy is also important to them.

- **an industry**: these professionals consider themselves to be commercial service providers, who have to work hard to get a position in a very competitive market. They work with a variety of standard products and standard solutions which have proved to be successful in daily practice. They do not work with a code of conduct but with terms of delivery and they have a results agreement with their clients. To stay in business, one must be qualified instead of certified.
- **an academy**: these professionals see themselves as a community interested particularly in the 'professional encounter'. Unity and meeting other colleagues are essential. The concept of the learning organisation is a characteristic of this view. Competition does not exist and there is an open exchange of knowledge, insights and experiences between each other. Continuous personal development and interpersonal consultation are important methods for professionalisation.

These four 'ideal type' concepts play an important role in discussions among management consultants. It follows that the large commercial firms view management consultancy more as an industry than a profession although there are also consultants in these firms who consider their professional group an 'academy' or a 'church'. It is remarkable that boards of management consulting institutes tend to organise the profession as a 'castle' and/or 'church'. But even within the institutes there are numerous members who think these discussions are not expedient because they would define the profession more as an 'academy' or as an 'industry'.

Conclusion

Within the management consultancy sector there are many perceptions about what the profession is or should be. There is no uniformity in definitions, standards or codes of conduct. There are occasional discussions between the boards of professional institutes and/or associations about professionalisation. Consultants of large firms often hold essentially different views on the profession from sole practitioners. Discussions like these are characteristic for the management consultancy sector but these are devoid of meaning because, as confirmed by consultants involved in the discussions, there seems to be no change in the manner of arguing or arguments. Without any insights into the different assumptions about the concept of a profession, or definitions about standards and codes of conduct, discussions like these may be futile.

It may be preferable to maintain that the profession of management consultancy does not exist or, to say that 'a profession is a body of thought thought by thinking thinkers' adapted from Weick (in Choo, 1998). The focus should be on what consultants do instead of what they are. It is more effective to discuss the different ways of professionalisation instead of what a profession stands for or should be (see also Weick and Quinn (1999)).

If we refer to the diagram of the four 'ideal types' of profession previously outlined, we have to realise that professionalisation has an entirely different meaning in each of the four dimensions. In 'industry' it would mean the development of new products and/or effective dispersal of skills, whereas in the 'church' dimension it is the process towards a codification of professional requirements and the fulfilment of obligations in agreement with those requirements. Professionalisation in a 'castle' concerns the process towards accreditation of organisations and/or persons connected with designations like CMC. In an 'academy' setting it would mean philosophising about different ways of continuous learning.

The time has come for management consultants to realise and admit that uniform definitions in this area do not exist and that it is useless to compare this sector with classical professions like the medical or legal profession – the sector has to differentiate itself from them. The quartet of definitions described in this article may be helpful in this respect.

The consequences of this framework are that we will have to abandon the idea that a profession is an institute with: 'traditional and collective patterns of behaviour (of acting, thinking and feeling) which "existed" before we were born, and in all probability will continue to "exist" after we have died' (Zijderveld, 2000). The profession as an institution is not a goal in itself. As we have seen there are different views on the concept of a profession. An important competence of management consultancy is change management. It makes sense to use the theories and concepts of change management to formulate a new way of organising the profession. In the new economy we see a reduction of the classic vertical integrated concept of organisation. Also among clients we see a process of de-institutionalisation of the organisation into a network of specialised companies. The profession of management consultancy should be organised more as a network with all kinds of different views on the profession. Management consultants actively involved in professionalisation processes (the board members of the bigger firms, of the IMCs, and of the associations, and the management of the management consultant schools), and therefore those directing the further development of the profession have to be more aware of this.

The basis of every profession lies in the fact that a person is dependent on certain expertise for essential issues in his life and that person does not have access to that expertise. The person is dependent on the professional who possesses the expertise. The profession of management consultancy should not lose itself in discussions about the content and regulation of the profession because this leads to evaporation. The development of the profession is a process. It is a permanent contest between all kinds of other collegiate professions (Abbott, 1988). The profession has to develop a more intellectual tradition through which we can find all the different views on the profession, together with a strong link to the world of academic knowledge.

After all, in seeking solutions for his problems the client requires assistance and support which should be based on, among other things, academic and abstract knowledge.

References

Abbott, A.D. (1988): *The system of professions*, The University of Chicago Press.

Ashford, A. (1988): *'Con Tricks: The shadowy world of management consultancy and how to make it work for you*, Simon & Schuster Ltd, London.

Block, P. (1981): *Flawless consulting: a guide to getting your expertise used*, Pfeiffer & company, Johannesburg.

Choo, C.W. (1998), *The knowing organization. How organizations use information to construct meaning, create knowledge, and make decisions.* Oxford University Press, New York.

Greiner, L. & R. Metzger (1983): *Consulting to management.* Prentice Hall, Englewood Cliffs, NJ

Kipping, M. (1999): *American Management Consulting Companies in Western Europe: Products, Reputation and Relationship.* Business History Review, 73, Summer p. 190–220.

Kubr, M. (1996): *Management Consulting, A guide to the profession.* International Labour Office, Geneva.

Morgan, G. (1986): *Images of organizations.* Sage Publications, Beverly Hills CA

Strikwerda, H. (2000): 'De onafhankelijkheid van de management consultant' in *Management Consultant*, 3.

Strikwerda, H. (2000): 'Management-consultancy in de nieuwe economie' in *Management en Organisatie*, 54e jaargang, nr 5/6, blz. 174–197.

Weick, K. & R. Quinn (1999): *Organizational Change and Development.* Annual Review of Psychology, 50: 361–386.

Whitley, R. (1992): *Formal Knowledge and Management Education.* Manchester: MBS, October Working Paper No 236.

Zijderveld, Anton (2000): *The Institutional Imperative*, Amsterdam University Press.

Corporate Governance – structures, processes and functions

Dr Daniel Summerfield

The country's economy depends on the drive and efficiency of its companies. Thus the effectiveness with which their boards discharge their responsibilities determines Britain's competitive position. They must be free to drive their companies forward, but exercise that freedom within a framework of effective accountability. This is the essence of any system of good corporate governance (Cadbury Report, 1992).

What is corporate governance?

Corporate governance is a relatively new term to describe a process which has been practised for as long as there have been corporate entities. Before the 1980s, the term was not in popular use and serious study and research on the subject has only flourished over the last few years.

Although the use of the term corporate governance is now commonplace, both in media coverage of corporate activity and in specialist journals, it is still difficult to find a clear, universally accepted definition of what is meant by corporate governance.

A basic definition of corporate governance in the UK context was provided in the first of the major UK governance reports – the Cadbury Report in 1992 (and endorsed by the Hampel report of January 1998). It said:

Corporate governance is the system by which companies are directed and controlled (Hampel report, 1998)

The term 'corporate governance' has been used in a variety of contexts in recent years, particularly in relation to the boards of companies listed on a stock exchange. Many of the issues involved can have implications for boards of privately owned companies too. Indeed, governance is at the heart of the role that all boards of directors play, so an understanding of what it is about and the issues involved can provide useful insight for management consultants.

UK corporate governance model

In the UK corporate governance model, with its unitary board structure, directors owe their fiduciary duties to the company. This means that they are required to act in good faith in the best interests of the company, exercise their powers for the proper purposes for which they were conferred and not place themselves in a position where there is conflict (actual or potential) between their duties to the company and their personal interests or duties to third parties. Their duties are owed to the company, not the shareholders or stakeholders – though they are accountable to the shareholders for the stewardship of the company. The statutory duties of directors towards other parties beside the company are minimal. Indeed there is no explicit duty (in a solvent company) to stakeholders such as employees, customers, suppliers and the wider community.

In Continental Europe, the situation is somewhat different. In Germany, for example, which has a two-tier board structure – a supervisory board and a management board – the duty of directors to the company is more widely expressed than in Britain to include employees and the public interest. In France, split boards with employee participation have been introduced as an optional alternative to the traditional single board.

The effective board of directors

Every listed company should be headed by an effective board which should lead and control the company
(Combined Code, 1999)

The IoD's *Standards for the Board* states that the key purpose of companies is to maximise the efficient creation of wealth, while observing the law and seeking to minimise the negative impacts of corporate activity on participants and society generally. It follows therefore that the key purpose of the board of directors is to seek to ensure the prosperity of the company by collectively directing the company's affairs, while meeting the appropriate interests of its shareholders and relevant stakeholders and taking into account the law, relevant regulations and commercial considerations.

In pursuing this key purpose, a board of directors faces a uniquely demanding set of responsibilities and challenges. It also faces a range of objectives that can sometimes seem contradictory. The board:

- must simultaneously be entrepreneurial and drive the business forward while keeping it under prudent control
- is required to be sufficiently knowledgeable about the workings of the company to be answerable for its actions, yet able to stand back from the day-to-day management of the company and retain an objective, longer-term view
- must be sensitive to the pressures of short-term issues and yet take account of broader, longer-term trends

- must be knowledgeable about 'local' issues and yet be aware of wider competitive influences
- is expected to be focused on the commercial needs of its business while acting responsibly towards its employees, business partners and society as a whole

Each board member is expected to recognise these challenges and ensure that they personally contribute to finding the right balance between these various competing pressures.

Tasks of the board

It is of course impossible to list every task that each individual board of directors has to carry out. Each board has to consider its own situation and circumstances. For example, small privately owned companies might not be concerned with many of the issues that preoccupy large listed companies.

However, *Standards for the Board* does attempt to highlight the broad tasks that are pertinent to every board and also the indicators of good practice that can help boards of directors reflect on how they are fulfilling those tasks. Hence, it is argued, boards can be helped greatly by focusing on four key areas:

- establishing vision, mission and values
- setting strategy and structure
- delegating to management
- exercising accountability to shareholders and being responsible to relevant stakeholders

Each board should decide what it needs to do in order to achieve its overall purpose and identify any gaps or deficiencies in what it is already doing. The board is also encouraged to focus on those tasks that it must – or wishes to – undertake itself and to decide which should more properly be carried out by senior management. Many boards of larger companies devise a schedule of reserved powers that explicitly distinguishes between those tasks that are to be the sole responsibility of the board and those than can legitimately be devolved to senior managers.

The effective board

Within a company, the board of directors is the principal agent of risk tasking and enterprise, the principal maker of commercial and other judgements. Discharging these responsibilities means thinking not only about particular tasks but also about ways of working as a board, and ensuring individual directors can be fully equipped to play their part. Again, there are four particular areas worthy of time and energy:

- determining board composition and organisation
- clarifying board and management responsibilities
- planning and managing board and board committee meetings
- developing the effectiveness of the board.

These activities are normally undertaken by the chairman of the board, part of whose role is to manage the board's business and act as its facilitator and guide.

Where the managing director is also the chairman, it is important that these two distinct roles are properly separated and that sufficient attention is given to carrying out the chairman's role effectively. The board should not be just an executive team.

The non-executive directors play an important part in assisting the chairman to fulfil his role by regularly and rigorously assessing the effectiveness of the board's processes and activities. Given their outside perspective, they are sometimes best placed to ensure that the board focuses its energies effectively on meeting the demands described earlier.

The context for the non-executive director

Each board of directors is faced with unique problems and circumstances that must be addressed for the company to be truly successful. There are, however, some universal challenges that are faced by all boards and a number of strategic tasks that any board must perform if its central purpose is to be achieved.

Legally speaking, there is no distinction between an executive and non-executive director. UK company law does not see the roles as distinct and therefore does not distinguish between their responsibilities. Yet there is inescapably a sense in which the non-executive director's role can be seen as balancing that of the executive director, so as to ensure the board as a whole functions effectively.

Where the executive director has an intimate knowledge of the company, the non-executive director may be expected to have a wider perspective of the world at large. Where the executive director may be better equipped to provide an entrepreneurial spur to the company, the non-executive director may have more to say about ensuring prudent control.

All directors should be capable of seeing company and business issues in a broad perspective. Nonetheless, non-executive directors are usually chosen because they have a breadth of experience, are of relatively high calibre and have particular personal qualities. They may also have some specialist knowledge that will help provide the board with valuable insights or, perhaps, key contacts in related industries or the City. Of the utmost importance is their independence of the management of the company and any of its 'interested parties'. This means they can bring a degree of objectivity to the board's deliberations, playing a valuable role in its task of monitoring executive management.

While much of the comment and discussion on non-executive directors tends to focus on listed companies, it is important to note that they can also make a valuable, albeit somewhat different contribution to private companies. Indeed, there is a growing number of private companies, including relatively small ones, that are now actively searching for the 'right' non-executive director.

The functions of non-executive directors

Essentially, the non-executive director's role is to provide a creative contribution to the board by providing objective criticism. Non-executive directors are expected to focus on board matters and not stray into 'executive direction', providing an independent view of the company that is removed from its day-to-day running. Non-executive directors, then, are appointed to bring to the board:

- independence
- impartiality
- wide experience
- special knowledge
- personal qualities

The non-executive director's key responsibilities

Many chairmen use their non-executive directors to provide general counsel – and a different perspective – on matters of concern. They also seek their guidance on particular issues before they are raised at board meetings. Indeed, some of the main specialist roles of a non-executive director will be carried out in a board sub-committee, especially in listed companies. The board's ability to operate efficiently is often increased by the establishment of sub-committees to give more detailed and objective consideration to major issues before they are formally discussed at the board. While the number of sub-committees varies from company to company, the key responsibilities of non-executive directors remain constant. They lie in:

Strategic direction

As an 'outsider', the non-executive director should have a clearer or wider view of external factors affecting the company and its business environment than the executive directors. The normal role of the non-executive director in strategy formation is therefore to provide a creative and informed contribution and to act as a constructive critic in looking at the objectives and plans devised by the chief executive and his or her executive team.

Troubleshooting

In times of crisis, occasions can arise when only the non-executive director is capable of acting on behalf of the company. This is especially true if a business has been badly managed and the chief executive or managing director needs to be replaced. It would be very difficult for the executive directors to take a lead at board level in these circumstances; non-executive directors have to take the initiative for them.

Communication

The company's and board's effectiveness can benefit from outside contacts and opinions. An important function for non-executive directors, therefore, can be to help connect the business and board with networks of potentially useful people and organisations. In some cases, the non-executive director will be called upon to represent the company externally.

Audit

It is the duty of the whole board to ensure that the company accounts properly to its shareholders by presenting a true and fair reflection of its actions and financial performance and that the necessary internal control systems are put into place and monitored regularly and rigorously. A non-executive director has an important part to play in fulfilling this responsibility, whether or not a formal audit committee (composed of non-executive directors) of the board has been constituted.

Remuneration of executive directors

Devising the appropriate remuneration packages for the executive directors can be one of the most contentious issues a board faces – not least because of the publicity executive pay has attracted in recent years. It is vital that decisions on executive remuneration, benefits and bonuses are seen to be made by those who do not stand to benefit directly from them. In listed companies and some larger private companies, therefore, policy on executive remuneration is usually decided by a committee of non-executive directors.

Appointing directors

One of the board's most crucial functions is to decide on new appointments to the board and to other senior positions in the company. Again, in some cases, this is done within a committee, composed of executive and non-executive directors, whose task it is to ensure that appointments are made according to agreed specifications. Where implemented, the appraisal of directors is often tied directly into the selection and nomination process.

Conclusion

Common to many boards of directors and shareholders is a growing acceptance that non-executive directors have a valued and necessary role to play in maximising board effectiveness. The introduction of truly independent judgement to the board's activities provides all interested parties with greater assurance that the correct strategies and decisions are likely to be chosen.

The contribution of non-executive directors can usually raise the level of discussion and improve the quality of decision-making on the board. This increases the chances of the company acting in the best interests of its long-term security and prosperity.

Nevertheless, it is important to be clear that the challenges and tasks discussed above are those of the board, not of individual directors. While each individual may have a distinct contribution to make, it is the collective responsibility of the board to ensure the company's successful operation.

For further information on non-executive directors, please visit our website at www.independentdirector.co.uk – part of the IoD and Ernst & Young's Independent Director initiative.

References

Cadbury, Sir Adrian (1992), *The Financial Aspects of Corporate Governance*, Gee & Co, London.

Hampel, Sir Ronald (1998), *Committee on Corporate Governance: Final Report*, Gee & Co, London.

London Stock Exchange (1999), *The Combined Code: Principles of Good Governance and Code of Best Practice*, Gee & Co, London.

Renton, Tony (1999), *Standards for the Board: Improving the effectiveness of your board*, Institute of Directors, London.

3

A client's guide to management consultancy

3.1

The client-consultant relationship: setting the guidelines

Barry Curnow

The existence of such a large number and variety of consultants to choose from (between a quarter and half a million worldwide according to the definitions used in this Handbook, but many more if a wider definition is used such as China's own which identifies 800,000 in China alone!) necessitates clear guidelines on how to engage with, choose and use them. The market is very fragmented and studies by Colin Coulson-Thomas of Adaptation Ltd and Philip Abbott of Industry Research Group have revealed a mixed picture of client expectations and experience. Expectations of the brand name consultancies are both broad and modest, as is satisfaction with the results. Yet clients continue to commission major assignments from the brand name consultancies. Indeed it is often the desire for a brand endorsement that is influential in the decision.

It is helpful for clients to be clear about a number of matters before setting their own criteria for a particular consulting engagement. Consulting projects have certain generic stages that the client and the consultant need to go through together in order to achieve an effective working relationship.

Generic stages in a consulting project

There are six generic stages in a consulting project:

- understanding the problem
- understanding the constraints
- understanding the opportunities
- developing alternative approaches
- generating potential solutions
- assessing and reconciling the power, politics and personalities

Achieving a shared understanding of these steps requires the development of a working partnership between client and consultant, supported by developing trust and understanding of each other and what each side brings to the table.

Against these generic steps it is necessary to take into account the specific purpose of the proposed consulting engagement – why the discussions are taking place at all.

The reasons for selecting consultants

- work overload
- development projects
- specialist expertise
- change management
- crisis or critical incident management
- counselling or process consultation
- outsourcing or facilities management

Guidelines on getting the most from your management consultants

Having clarified the type of consulting contribution required, there are ten guidelines that can be applied. These may be regarded as axes along which to consider getting the most from your management consultants.

- select from at least three possible consultants, carefully
- select on the basis of being able to establish a relationship
- establish a common ground of shared understanding and values
- identify potential for learning and growth in the relationship
- agree a mutual, participative, joint approach
- achieve agreement on objectives of the project/work
- ask yourself honestly if you are ready for change
- identify obstacles and barriers to change
- strike an acceptable balance of power in the relationship
- balance theoretical models and practical approaches

Good consultants use models to help their clients learn, understand and solve problems jointly with them. It is important for the models to be shared and valued by both client and consultant. When used correctly, consulting models can be extremely powerful tools of explanation, argument and reasoning. Their use is made easier through identifying and adopting a suitable style of consultant, and by creating a relationship of the appropriate character. The different styles of consulting are discussed below.

Consulting styles and the client-consultant relationship

Teacher-Pupil

The teacher-pupil style of the client-consultant relationship involves instruction and learning, but with the experienced consultant in a teaching mode, imparting expert knowledge of the subject area and of comparative practice data and information elsewhere.

Doctor-Patient

The doctor-patient style involves diagnosis and prescription, with the consultant in an expert mode based on the medical model. The client asks the consultant to diagnose what is wrong and to prescribe how to fix it.

Engineer

The engineering style involves the designing and building of an agreed plan with the consultant as architect and contractor, and the client as client.

Coach-Mentor

The coach-mentor model based on sports and skill-based endeavour implies a client-consultant relationship whereby the consultant has expert knowledge, perhaps as much as the teacher, but uses a coaching style to train and develop self-sustaining skills in the athlete-manager, who borrows the coach-mentor's wisdom until such time as he or she becomes sufficiently their own man or woman to compete alone. Interestingly, in this model the relationship often continues but transforms, the coach becoming a mentor and in time a trusted advisor and guide. If the client-consultant relationship is good, then coach-mentors continue for a long time. In the original Greiner-Metzer (1983) model this role was known as friendly co-pilot.

Counsellor-Therapist

The counsellor-therapist model is content-free. The consultant does not give advice. He or she listens and heals but does not tell the client what to do. The consultant is just there when needed, continuing for as long as is needed (albeit for fixed times and consultations) and for whatever purpose he is needed. However, he or she is often there for a very long time until it stops.

This is how to get the most from your consultants, by working on the client-consultant relationship, building it, developing it and transforming it, often for a very long period of time. And it goes on. And it works. Until it stops. The phases of the client-consultant relationship are described in Chapter 3.5 and the business of ending what may be a long, difficult, important and dependent relationship is covered in Chapter 3.9.

Appointing a consultant should follow the basic common sense principles of choosing any personal or professional service.

Margerrison (1996) points out that citizens who will judge a builder, motor mechanic or hairdresser with skill and discernment and an often sophisticated decision-making matrix, sometimes seem uncertain about how to select a professional management consultant. Yet similar principles apply. When conducting training courses at Maresfield Curnow for client companies in how to choose and use management consultants effectively, we have achieved significant results by asking participants to role-play such everyday transactions before addressing client-consultant relationships. The parallels are striking.

Perhaps surprisingly, a lack of client confidence in choosing consultants may also help to explain the popularity of brand-buying from the large consultancy firms. The brand name consultancies are clearly reassuring – a well-known consulting firm name implies comfort, certainty of delivery, reputation, and the resources and structure to deal with any difficulties along the way. Clients will typically pay a higher fee for this brand value.

References

Greiner, L and Metzer, R (1983) *Consulting to Management*, Prentice Hall
Margerrison, Charles J (1988, 1996) *Managerial Consulting Skills – a practical guide*, Gower Press, Aldershot, Hants and Brookfield, Vermont

3.2

Selecting and appointing a management consultant

Barry Curnow

When choosing a consulting firm, the personality of the consultant and the relationship between the lead consultants and the client are highly influential in the final choice. Clients will tend to shortlist the firms according to brand names and reputation. However, in choosing from a shortlist it is the impact of the consultant who does the presentation that will significantly determine which firm is chosen, regardless of the brand name. The name gets the consultant in the door, but it doesn't necessarily get him the assignment. In pre-selecting big brand names, those who are hiring the consulting firms are putting an established reputation on the shortlist as a benchmark from which they can then feel free to deviate if the individual consultants impress.

Personal introductions and competitive pitches

Most consulting projects are still commissioned following personal introductions, even if a competitive element is introduced before the final selection. However, despite the importance of personal introductions there is an increasing use of 'beauty parades' involving pitching for consulting assignments. Some clients appear to go through the process despite having already decided whom they are going to appoint, and there is a danger that such processes can squeeze out the very creativity and individual differences that a good consultant can bring to the client business.

Nevertheless, the pitch does give clients the opportunity to change their first impressions about who is to do it. Sometimes, people approach pitches as a kind of corporate filter or safety net, and even though they go into the process believing they know who they want, they may sometimes change their minds and end up awarding it to another firm because they were very impressed with their presentation.

So far as large corporate purchasers are concerned, a good presentation by a consultant can rescue a poor proposal but the reverse is not the case. A mediocre presentation cannot be rescued by an outstanding proposal.

Large and small consultancies

However, there are disadvantages to formal beauty parades. The costs are high for everybody and that may exclude some good firms and inflate the costs of all the bidders. Some small consultancies often feel disadvantaged. There is no point in merely filling up the numbers for a pitch as it is time-consuming, wasteful and may lead to a bad reputation for the client. Certain parts of the public sector in some countries have become no-go areas for many consultants – despite greatly needing consulting help – because they have consistently treated consultants badly. So bad consultant-client relationships can be bad for the stakeholders of a client organisation.

Pitching can prove so expensive that many firms now review closely whether they want to pitch for a given tender. It is not unknown for the total costs incurred by all firms making a pitch to exceed the value of the assignment itself. Now, consulting firms are trying to become more strategic in how they decide what to pitch for. By concentrating on one or two jobs rather than five or six, the firms feel that they may have more chance of success.

Offering a value-added pitch

Some consultants will put a great deal of thought into a competitive pitch and try to offer an added-value service package beyond the client's expectations. Clients will often appreciate this, but it tends to work only after the basic engagement objectives have clearly been met, and only then in the context of a long relationship with a particular client. The client may be reassured by the brand name of the large firm and by some knowledge of their processes, so they can conveniently avoid thinking about some of the wider issues.

Brief preparation and shortlisting

A client may find it appropriate to use this section to establish which consultants to approach and how to deal with them, in order to arrive at a shortlist of those to be invited to make proposals. The path to follow is indicated in the steps below.

Create a field of possible consultants to use

For example, by:

- word of mouth introductions from other organisations, colleagues and contacts including those from industries and sectors other than your own
- approaching individual consultancies for their brochures
- contacting trade or industry associations and asking for referrals, especially from those with a consultant database

- contacting the Institute of Management Consultants (IMC) or the Consulting Trade Association in the country concerned
- approaching one of the government-assisted schemes designed to help small businesses – many countries now provide state help for consulting fees for small enterprises

It is recommended that prospective clients should aim to assemble from their preliminary field an initial long-list of no more than five consultants or consulting practices. The next step is to communicate with them.

Communicate with the long-listed consultants

Send them the following information:

- A preliminary brief covering the present problem or objective as it is currently seen by the client, together with some initial explanation of who the client is, the nature of the work required and its prime focus. This can cover, for example, the organisation structure and principal systems surrounding the problem area and the boundaries of the work, including any specific constraints, the timescale and any fundamental conditions such as non-negotiable contractual requirements
- A background information pack containing, depending on the scale and the nature of the work, the history and context of the organisation; essential background papers, for example, an organisation chart, the annual report and accounts, any technical papers such as the current salary structure; and policies in the case of a prospective remuneration review or the information technology architecture in the case of a prospective systems review. The information pack should also include details about the availability of internal resources and the roles of people likely to be involved
- Request for a Proposal (RFP) – a covering letter asking the consultants to state their competence and specific experience, quoting similar work in other organisations in similar industries, and citing referees who are prepared to speak up for their

specific capability to field appropriate people to carry out the work within the prescribed timescale. Using certified management consultants (CMC), who are members of their local IMC, and member firms of the recognised trade association, avoids the need for formal references as these are taken and covered by the strict membership and qualification requirements of the Institute or the Association, but it may still be sensible to speak to one or two previous clients to get a feel for how they worked together
- They should also be asked to indicate their willingness to meet and discuss the situation without obligation in the first instance, and to summarise their initial reaction to the RFP and their general philosophy and approach to such assignments. It is helpful for the client to see how a firm might approach a particular project

In some cases, where a significant amount of technical briefing is required, it may be appropriate to hold a preliminary general session for all prospective consultancies so that they can be briefed on a common basis prior to the issue of the RFP, which in some tender situations can become a formal document in the contract process. In any event, all consultants approached must be given the opportunity to meet the client representatives before making their formal submissions. Indeed, a professional firm might well refuse to make any indication of interest in the absence of a personal meeting, although a consultant's willingness to do so does not imply any lack of professionalism. Their response would depend on the circumstances and in particular their prior knowledge of the client, the firm or the industry. In any case the client should then:

- Meet each consultancy separately for their questions, to receive their preliminary views on the draft brief, to ascertain any issues they see as needing to be addressed during the commissioning process and to agree what may be properly expected of the client organisation
- Use commonly agreed criteria to decide which consultants to shortlist

Do not indicate a budget at this stage. Give as long a lead time as possible to allow preparation and availability from consultants. The consultant will be able to demonstrate his own methods of working and be able to question you in order to interpret the objectives, so it will be a learning experience for both parties.

Tendering and appointment procedure

The appointment process is a project in its own right. How it is set up by the client tells the consultants much about the organisation and its character, and those of the principal players involved. The personal style of the individual client will inevitably condition the impression given. It is important that the client is aware of this and keeps a reasonable balance, demonstrating a concern for focus and discipline (the 'telling' part) while at the same time being flexible and receptive (the 'listening' part).

Messages are also conveyed internally to employees by the way a consultancy exercise is set up. By this stage, the decision to bring in consultants may already be known within the organization and it must be communicated purposefully and sensitively to the variety of audiences. This will help with gaining commitment and eliminate the possibility of misconceptions and unrealistic expectations. Internal protocols and standards are then easier to observe with regard to the contracting process, equal opportunities, agreements on consultation, etc.

In deciding upon the appointment process, ensure that it is appropriate to the scale and nature of the work. What is appropriate for a £100,000 project is not so for one of £10,000. To expect a number of consultants to engage in long discussion and to draft detailed programmes for a short assignment is unrealistic and may result in a good firm being put off. By contrast, if a contract were to be let for over a million pounds, it would usually pay the client first to commission a paid diagnostic survey from one or more firms to ascertain how they would view, approach and deal with the problem. The time and money invested would invariably be recovered through greater understanding and a tighter, tidier commissioning and control of the major project.

Educating the consultants

Develop a steering group so that a variety of people are brought together in order to consider the process – both of hiring the consultants and, subsequently, of how the whole consultancy assignment should be handled. The group should consist of executives who can provide dispassionate advice and guidance on the course of the consulting engagement, as opposed to making any decisions about recommendations that need to go through the formal machinery of the Board. The latter must be taken as part of the ordinary management housekeeping procedures of the company.

Provide each consultancy firm with the same opportunity for informal questioning and discussion with the commissioning client alone, with the commissioning client together with other key people, and with individuals separately as arranged.

Where the later involvement of other executives in the actual project will be important, a short informal meeting with them can be arranged at this stage; otherwise the consultants will have no feel for the character and concern of the company as a whole.

Written proposals

The client should require a written proposal to be submitted by the consultants. They should then review the proposal and take stock of the personal impressions formed of the consultants during the face-to-face meetings, and, if necessary, they may then contact specific consultants individually on any major questions of clarification or to correct any mistaken assumptions they have made.

The proposal should, where appropriate, cover the following:

- The consultants' perceptions of the problem, suggested objectives and other considerations bearing on a successful outcome to the engagement
- Their general approach and proposed style of working
- A programme of work specifying the individual technical components of the programme and how they fit together
  - the distinct phases of the programme with proposed milestones for review and adjustment

- what will be delivered at each stage and what the desired outcome will be
- their assumptions as to the use of and demands upon the client's internal resources
- how the programme will be project managed and through what suggested means of liaison with the client
- the form of reporting
- The total cost of the programme, broken down by event and activity
- Details of who will manage the project, the consulting team, their roles, their relative proportion of time devoted to the work and their CVs
- Relevant past experience of the consultancy
- Terms of business
- A short summary of the key points of the proposal

Presentations

Provide for oral presentation, questions and discussion by the consultants before an agreed panel of a small number of key people chaired by the commissioning client. Time should be divided equally between presentation and discussion. A review should follow immediately by the appointing panel but adjudication should occur only after all the consultancy firms have departed.

The questions put to the consultants should aim to clarify their programme and approach and stimulate discussion of the issues. This time is an ideal opportunity to gain value from all the consultants irrespective of which firm is chosen. New and different insights should be obtained.

Decision

Select the firm whose general competence, methodology and style are most appropriate and who have the credibility to deliver what is asked of them. Once that decision is made the parties can get down to detailed design and tactics. Finally, tell the consultants the result as soon as possible. Add any qualifying points or assumptions and follow up with a confirmatory letter.

Be prepared to respond to requests from the unsuccessful firms for feedback as to the client's reaction to them. This is good professional practice and will help the consultants learn from the process.

Contracting

If the stages thus far have been properly documented (written brief, written proposal and costed work programme, plus any correspondence in amplification, qualification, or recording of any important assumptions) then the client is ready to be entered into a contract. Typically this will be by an exchange of letters, formally incorporating the above as terms, together with any standard conditions which it is appropriate to apply. Considerations to bear in mind will be any advice from professional bodies, industry associations or other sources, and not least the views of the consultants. It must be remembered that this is a two-way professional relationship and the nature of the contract documentation should reflect that.

Furthermore, attempts to tie down the consultants to very specific activities will invariably work against the client's best interests. It is through rigour in the planning of the project and its outcomes, and through commissioning their achievement, that control can be exercised best.

Consultants should seek to make it easy for the client to see precisely what is proposed in the programme: each element, phase and milestone. The proposal which 'speaks' clearly and purposefully to the client and makes it easier to be 'bought' is likely to be seen as a token of a similar clarity of purposefulness in joint working between them in the future.

This chapter assumes assignments of the range and depth to justify full client involvement, competitive presentation and so forth. However, the underlying discipline of the process should be borne in mind, whatever the scale or nature of the work. The effort you ask people to make in getting work must be proportionate to the size of the job.

Making the overall choice

Clients can use this section as a checklist to help them to make an overall choice, to come to decisions to review them, and to agree an appropriate form of contract with the chosen consultants.

When the contract is being drawn up, the following should be in place:

- a clear purpose and specific objectives, tested internally and with the various consultants
- an awareness on the part of the client and the consultants of the issues bearing on the design of the project
- a framework for detailed project design and management
- an orderly and rigorous appointment procedure within which a decision can be made

The client will have had the opportunity of seeing the different shortlisted consultants and receiving their proposals. Given clear and comprehensive guidance by the client, both in their written and oral briefings, each consultancy should have covered all the key elements of the work. But there will be different shades of interpretation, ideas for dealing with them and styles of doing so. From the client's point of view, it is ideal to have reached the position where all the shortlisted consultants are capable of doing the job with realistic programmes. This will leave the client with a choice of which one they prefer to work with rather than rejecting any outright on grounds of fundamental unsuitability.

If the process up to the point of selection is well conducted (a mark of this will be whether the competing consultants have been able to make a useful contribution already), then the client's thinking should have been developed in the process. This may lead to a redefinition of both the purpose and the nature of the work required. A careful balance has to be struck between sharing that thinking progressively with all the consultants, while ensuring that the consultants who have made the most contribution are acknowledged and permitted to build further on the thinking. The client must draw his or her own ethical boundaries in the matter of using 'free work and ideas' provided by one consultancy as part of its presentation in order to brief another. A useful rule of thumb here is that the client can properly use a revised understanding of what the assignment is about, but should stop short of revealing proprietary knowledge, techniques and approaches, or specific original thinking that the other consultant may have done on the client's behalf.

At the oral presentation, other things will impress: the personality of the people, the way in which they capture attention and focus the appointing panel on key issues, the way they engage in worthwhile discussion, the way they demonstrate an alignment with the values of the organisation, what it is trying to achieve – and so forth.

The client must weigh this multitude of impressions against their assessment of needs in the first checklist they drew up containing their initial perceptions. Priorities should be set according to needs, wants, personalities and results. Are they looking at a predominantly technical problem that requires a reliable technical solution from a respected consultancy who are authoritative in that area? Does the work demand a radical and creative spark, combined with diplomacy and persuasiveness to push along the client's thinking and resolve? Are there intractable problems to deal with which need a rigorous and professionally uncompromising stance in order to help the client lever obstacles out of the way?

The personal confidence of the commissioning client and those in the organisation who work with the consultants is crucial. To a surprisingly high degree this depends on the right chemistry between the characters from both the client organisation and the consultancy firm. If your instinct is that there will be a good working relationship then, providing the consultant is capable of delivering, this instinct should be followed.

Costs and contracting

When examining the management of the consulting process, the security of the 'contract' between people, what is to be done, how it should be carried out and who the relationships are to be between must be clarified and agreed in order to secure a successful outcome. Once agreement is reached regarding what needs to be done, each consultancy works out the number of days required, and the cost is calculated according to their fee rates. The importance of defining their outcomes at each stage in the assignment is vital because the whole assignment should be managed by reference to the planned outputs rather than the actual inputs of the consultancy.

Some projects are capable of being broken down into separate phases to which the client need not commit themselves at the outset; for example, a diagnostic phase followed by other phases of option generation, decision and implementation. While this will enable the client to reserve their position, it may be a false economy – not only because it may not be so keenly priced, but because the depth to which the consultants are likely to develop their relationships with the organisation will be proportionate to the depth of involvement they expect to have in later stages. Consultants may 'invest' now for future work.

If the consultants are invited to propose a 'work plan' of what needs to be in place by each stage of the project, together with a statement of their assumptions as to their role, the client's role and the methodology by which that is to be achieved, then it will be possible to decide whether those are the appropriate means or whether some aspect can be dealt with in a different way. For example, if the first stage of the assignment is to gather data and opinion in order to take stock of the key issues there are a number of variables such as:

- the range of people and issues to be surveyed
- the design of any survey instrument, the details of the information sought, the necessary analysis and the appropriate interpretation of it. (Does it need to be statistically accurate or an impressionistic sample?)

- the respective roles of the consultants and the client in that process: the consultant could do it all, or alternatively help with the design of a questionnaire which is administered and analysed by the client (assuming that course would be acceptable from the point of view of internal confidentiality and credibility)

The amount of work required in order to achieve the desired outcome can be explored in this way. A thorough discussion may result in a rescaling of the work, up or down.

Although some consultancies are reluctant to quote daily rates, it is only reasonable to ask what they are, together with an indication of how much will be provided by what level or specialisation of consultant. However, if using information about daily rates to compare consultants on price, it is important to compare like with like: a training consultant charging £3,000 per training day (including preparation time) may be no more expensive than a management consultant quoting £1,000 per day but charging actual time spent on training design, which can be a very time consuming process if – as there should be – there is a high degree of client participation.

The cost of the individual consultants proposed for the project will usually vary. Clients may feel they are getting better value from ten days of a project consultant's time as compared with five days from a partner, yet the determining question is what is required by the nature of the work. A consultancy which provides for an important board-level discussion to be handled by a junior may be able to keep its costs down, but if the experience and 'weight' offered by a partner is more appropriate, then that is a benefit. The value provided by one day of their time may exceed that of ten days' time of an inexperienced person. Circumstances will dictate requirements.

It is important that the client is aware of the differences of approach between the consultancies. A difficult 'political' project may require senior consultant time, and some technical support, but the balance might be the other way for a more technically biased project. By asking the consultants to break down the costs of major parts of their work, it makes it easier to be selective and cut out work according to its perceived importance. The client must be prepared to be advised that certain contributions by the consultants are critical. That is the subject of the next chapter on how to get value from a management consultant.

3.3

How to get value from a management consultant

E. Michael Shays

Unlike many other outside services, management consulting is distinguished by qualities that appear less tangible and are therefore more difficult to assess up-front. Usually the fee must be set before the consultant's assignment begins. So how can a value-conscious manager make sure the company gets the consulting service, support and results that it is paying for?

First, make sure you are using a management consultant for the right reasons: to formulate an objective; to receive an informed opinion; to find a way to solve a tenacious or complex problem; to get something acted upon in a hurry; or to work your way through an implementation. Try not to use a consultant merely to 'shake things up', support a preconceived point of view or do the decision-making for your firm.

Second, before you meet with a consultant, attempt to define your problem thoroughly, clearly and candidly. Determine what you would like the consultant to do and to what degree you would like your own staff involved.

Finally, ask yourself during your first meeting, does the consultant:

- listen well?
- understand the key issues involved?
- know about your industry?
- focus questions on your problem?
- challenge your assumptions?
- offer a relevant approach?
- project a sense of empathy?
- appear trustworthy?
- seem enjoyable to work with?

What to expect from the consulting process

Consulting represents a personal process between individuals working together to solve a problem. By conducting a preliminary, confidential interview with you (usually without cost), the consultant will attempt to understand your perception of the problem, agree on the scope of the assignment and verify your expectations.

Following this interview, the consultant should send you a letter of agreement stating:

- the objective, scope and nature of the assignment
- a summary of your situation
- the suggested consulting strategy
- the potential products and benefits to be generated from the work
- the names and qualifications of the consulting staff
- the nature and extent of your employees' participation
- the proposed start and end dates of the assignment
- an estimate of fees and expenses

After reviewing the letter of agreement, decide whether its terms are complete and clearly stated. Are you satisfied with the staffing plan and schedule? Are you prepared to provide the required support? Is the fee reasonable?

Once the assignment is underway

Inform your organisation about the consultant's role and assignment. Tell your employees who the consultant is, why this person has been selected, when the process will begin and how you expect them to assist in the effort. As for yourself, establish an effective working relationship with the consultant. It is important to be straightforward in relating your concerns, expectations and working style. Appoint someone on your staff as the liaison on the project. Make sure this individual understands the consultant's work plan in order to provide any necessary introductions or resources.

When the consultant comes back with interim findings, listen carefully even if you don't like what you hear. If any conclusion is not well-founded, direct the consultant to an internal source that may provide additional information.

In getting to the heart of a problem, the consultant will frequently uncover other issues that need to be resolved. Some may be prerequisites, but many will not. It's always tempting to add all of these issues to the project. But if meeting your original schedule and budget is important, don't ask the consultant to include them in the current assignment. Where it is necessary to expand the scope of an assignment, be sure the consultant tells you what impact it will have on the schedule and fee.

What if the fee seems too high?

If the fee seems too high you may be able to reduce it by narrowing the scope of the assignment, giving more leeway in scheduling the work or having your own people assume some of the tasks in the project. The fee can also be temporarily reduced by segmenting the assignment into phased projects. Remember, a good job is worth its cost; a poor one is a loss no matter how attractive its price may be.

Research, results and feedback

After the start date is set, the management consultant will want to meet again with you, your key associates and anyone else who will be involved with the assignment. The consultant should use this meeting to introduce the consulting staff and describe the approach and plan of action. After the meeting the consultant will begin the process of generating as much useful information as possible in a limited period of time. This will entail:

- one or more methods of data collection and review
- analysis of the findings
- testing of assumptions
- development of alternative solutions
- more testing of viability and practicality
- drawing conclusions

Throughout this process the consultant should provide you with continuous, informal feedback so that you understand what is being done and why. You also should receive and review the findings and conclusions before the consultant delivers his or her recommendations. After the recommendations are in your hands, the consultant should provide you with a clear direction for proceeding either with or without further assistance.

How to evaluate the consultant's advice

When the consultant presents the recommendations, ask yourself these questions:

- has the consultant delivered the product promised earlier?
- have the real issues been addressed?
- are the recommendations logical and will they work in your organisation?
- are the next steps clear?
- if there are potential savings involved, do you know how to achieve them?

- have your employees learned how to find and solve problems on their own?
- will your company be stronger as a result?
- when will the consultant return to check on the success of the project?

If you are not satisfied with the answers to any of these questions, ask the consultant to give you the additional information you need. A good consultant would rather put in additional effort than leave a client less than satisfied.

Act immediately on the recommendations

To make sure you get value for the fees paid, put the consultant's recommendations into effect before they are lost in the organisational inertia of your company. Tell your staff to come back to you in one month with the status of the progress they are making towards installing or implementing the consultant's recommendations, and call for regular reports until the work is complete. You can expect the consultant to take an equal interest in seeing his or her recommendations result in benefits to you.

3.4

Managing the consultancy assignment in progress

Barry Curnow

with John Downs who contributed to many of the seminars at Maresfield Curnow School of Management Consulting on which this chapter is based.

Consulting engagements need to be managed for results, outcomes and overall benefits to the client. This may seem to be obvious common sense and good management housekeeping. Yet most consulting failures are not those of design and conception, or even of implementation plans and execution. Typically, these are done tolerably well. What makes all the difference is how well the engagement, the project and above all the relationship between client and consultant are actually managed. The reasons why this relationship is paramount were touched upon in chapter 3.1 and are discussed in chapter 3.5 in more detail.

Managing, enabling and influencing the consultant's contribution

At first glance it may appear paradoxical that a client calls in a consultant to rely upon his/her expertise (and all consulting relationships involve an exchange of expertise, whatever else may or may not occur) and yet at the same time as depending on the consultants, the client also has to manage them. This can come as something of a surprise to new clients, or to those in sectors where there is no history of consulting involvement, but it is fundamental to the consulting process. *Clients must actively manage their consulting relationships.*

It is only by managing the entire intervention, from engagement through enabling the consultants to start work, by influencing the (joint) work as it proceeds and extracting and consolidating the final contribution from the consultants that success is assured. In short, this is because technical credentials are necessary, but they are not sufficient. The atmosphere, relationship and chemistry of the client-consultant relationship must also be worked at. Client-consultant interactions obey the general laws of all relationships, whether between husband and wife, parent and child, or old school friends. A relationship's potential is a function of how hard the parties work at it and what each puts in determines what both take out.

So, the client-consultant relationship has to be managed. The client must manage their side of the relationship in a way that will enable the consultant to be effective and secure the desired contribution. This need not be a highly specified result that has been identified before the event. Consulting projects are dynamic and part of what the client pays for is consultant help to define the real need as they go along. Accurate diagnosis and definition of the real client situation is part of the output itself, so it has to be a joint exercise.

Project design and management

The consulting process is built around some common disciplines:
- thinking about the brief at the outset
- checking the consultants' project proposals at each stage
- working together in managing the project

A successful outcome depends on the professional contribution of the consultants, a corresponding contribution by the client, and supportive action within the organisation.

Client and consultants should check that each stage is addressed and these important questions asked at each point: 'Have we prepared for how we are going to handle the process, the communication and people issues?' and 'Are we actively managing the process – or are unfolding events going to manage us?'

The content of a project may take various forms, and the work plan and project may often require change during its course. Clearly, provision should be made for such eventualities.

Managing the assignment

Being clear about each phase and its intended result is fundamentally important. The nature and scope of the assignment will dictate the emphasis and timescale of each phase and its overall shape. Certain basic phases have to be covered as a matter of discipline. Showing the work in phases is a useful way of managing the assignment. If each phase clearly describes the planned outcome, who is to be involved and by when, it will make it much easier for the consultant assignment manager and the client assignment manager to review progress, plan the next stage ahead and also decide how best to report to the client.

Manage for planned results (not just activities)

At each stage, it is necessary to manage not just the activities, the interviews, specification writing, work design or other technical tasks that the consultant is performing but also to identify the results expected both from the client organisation and from the consultants.

Being clear about the client/consultant planning and review machinery is also very important. Client/consultant review meetings should be built in at regular intervals. These can range from informal, weekly 'how is it going?' conversations, to more structured reviews against the work plan at project milestones.

Meetings will be required to share information as well as make decisions and the different purposes will require different processes.

Being clear about roles and expected contribution is vital. Individual meetings need to be 'project managed' to the same discipline as advocated for the whole assignment.

Manage the characters

Individual personalities within the client organisation each have a part to play and will play a particular part, and it is best to acknowledge that they need to be actively orchestrated and related-to – not in a Machiavellian and manipulative sense but rather engaged with and involved in dialogue and appropriate conversations.

The enthusiast, the sceptic, the champion, the gatekeeper, the monitor-evaluator, the hard man and the soft man, the 'not invented here' merchant and the management expert, the practical man of affairs and the Young Turk – each of these stereotypes is to be found in every client organisation; each has a stance and a voice and all of the voices must be heard before the consulting project can lead to implementation.

The role of the client-consultant steering group should therefore be to explore the best ways of managing the process in a purposeful and sensitive way, not least how to prepare the ground and the people for the more formal set-piece decision-making required at board-level. In short, the group should ensure that all of the necessary conversations take place between those who need to have them.

Managing the reporting process

If the client and consultant work together in partnership, the nature of 'reporting' should be to record and discuss progress rather than to focus on the presentation of a document (least of all one which is a surprise to the client). Most important of all is the need not just to anticipate the effect but also actively to plan how to make the process itself a success, so that the very way it is handled adds value beyond the content.

Some projects will have a number of elements which are very clear and for which estimates can be given, but with later stages left contingent upon the outcome of the former. For these, it is reasonable for the consultant to offer a possible order, or range, of cost. They may suggest a contingency budget to be agreed in discussion or they may point to areas where extra work could be required at a daily fee rate.

Obviously, crude comparisons of total price are inadequate. The heart of the matter is what has to be done using the respective resources of consultant and client, the levels of resource most appropriate, with various options of methodology and different levels of risk on the part of the client. These can only be judgements, so the client should check carefully whether the issues in question have been fully addressed.

Different levels of relationship

It is advisable for clients to be clear about who is responsible for maintaining the client-consultant relationship at the different levels. Consulting firms are practised at this but clients should think carefully about it too. There are at least three substantive levels, director level, not involved in the project, a middle or project manager level – and a project worker junior management or professional basic level. At each level there should be at least one person who is clearly accountable for understanding and developing the firm-to-firm relationship with the consultants

Manage the influencers within the client organisation

The 'client' can in fact be a whole range of people. There are at least four different roles to be performed in order for the client to be an effective client and these have been taken (after Leavitt) to mean

- the commissioning client, that is, the individual who is leading the process from within the organisation

- The ultimate client or end user is the organisation or part of the company itself to whom the consultants must owe an over-riding duty. Unless they become alerted otherwise the consultants will assume that the commissioning client fully represents the interests of the organisation or company. This is a significant part of the commissioning client's role. However, there is also
- the economic client, the budget approver who secures value for money and may be the Finance director
- the technical specifier who is the functional director and takes professional responsibility for the quality of the consultant's work eg the marketing or human resources director

Often, the consultant will have someone who is accountable for the day-to-day leadership of their team and management of the project. Maintaining the distinction between those levels of accountability is beneficial because the progress of the work, and whether it is effective, may have implications both for the overall relationship and for the contract. It makes it easier to do this if informal, explicit conversations are held from time to time at the top level, away from the heat of daily project management. Project managers also need to have similar conversations so that the consulting process really can be managed.

Getting the most from your management consultants

The management consultant is now an everyday necessity in running modern business. He or she has become an indispensable resource in most organisations and therefore needs to be managed, just like any other resource. The business imperative puts a premium on choosing and using management consultants appropriately. It involves selecting suitable consultants who are fit for the purposes of the consulting engagement, and these purposes must have been established by clear agreement with all relevant parties, internally and externally, and expressed in clearly-defined terms of reference. The business imperative also involves managing the consultants appropriately to obtain maximum value and return from their contribution.

Manage the expectations

It is common for clients to have unrealistic expectations of consultants and for all manner of hopes and frustrations to be placed optimistically in the lucky bag of the consulting engagement, raising hopes that are unlikely ever to be met.

It is therefore worthwhile to address how the client players see the purpose of consultants. Management of the consultant-client relationship is therefore central to turning the consultants' potential contribution into actual added value that will be reflected in the performance of the business.

Client-consultant relationships are key. They must be productive and of high quality. They are the conduits through which know-how is transferred from consultant to client, through which joint problem solving and imaginative solutions can be created, and planned change programmes implemented effectively. The relationship should be managed as a business project for both parties. Indeed project management skills can be critical to obtaining the most from the personal and professional relationships between clients and consultants.

Manage and develop the relationship

We have already referred in Chapter 3.1 to the different styles of consultant – engineer, teacher, coach and so on. These styles call for different sorts of relationship that are both expected and required between client and consultant. A teaching style of consulting will require the client to be in a learning mode of relationship to the consultant. However, the industry and company culture will also determine how to relate to colleagues and suppliers, including outside advisers and consultants.

Getting the most from your management consultants therefore involves optimising and fine-tuning the client-consultant relationship. This implies achieving mutual trust, honesty and openness that have to be built up, usually over a period. If time is of the essence this period can be short, but the relationship needs to go through a number of phases, and generally speaking it is unwise to skip steps in this process. In one sense, building an effective client-consultant relationship is no different from any other business relationship. The general theory of relationships applies, particularly those aspects to do with the introduction of an external stranger into the midst of an already more or less cohesively-established and functioning group. In another sense a consultant-client relationship is often a so-called special relationship, and even if its special nature is restricted to the sensitivity and confidentiality of the material being worked with, time is needed to form the relationship, to explore, establish, manage and then transform it into the full range of its potential. We should also remember that, while working on the relationship, the parties are frequently solving a business problem at the same time.

Manage the potential relationships in partnership with your consultants

What the parties put into the client-consultant relationship will generally determine the scope, quality and value of what comes out of it, the scale and value of the business problems solved and the significance of the business opportunities taken up. The relationship will flourish if it is established on a clear mutual understanding. The client must understand the consultants' values and vice versa. The surest way of achieving such mutual understanding is through agreeing to write an explicit statement of the expectations that client and consultant have of each other. The discipline of writing down and sharing expectations often helps to clarify as well as to share them. The written statement will act as a guide and point of reference throughout the consulting engagement as the relationship unfolds.

These understandings of mutual expectations, whether written or oral, must be established prior to discussing the objectives that the client starts out with. The objectives of the assignment are of course one benchmark against which consulting success will subsequently be measured. However, since one of the first and frequently the most important tasks of the consultant is to 're-frame' the client problem and objectives, there must already be the basis of mutual understanding and trust in the relationship if that re-framing is to be undertaken successfully. This is because it frequently involves the consultant in helping the client to understand that the client's opening expectations may be unrealistic, imprecise, conflicting, contradictory, or simply unattainable within the time-scale and resources available.

Manage the campaign

The occupational title 'Management Consultant' covers a multitude of activities and services, but from the point of view of the client's business a useful working definition is that 'the management consultant is an independent outsider with relevant knowledge and skills, who enables the business to do something specific that it wants to do and which it could not do alone without the involvement of the outsider'. That role is frequently catalytic and may be as much to do with helping the process of management within the business as the content of what is done.

While the expectations of the client and the initial objectives of the proposed assignment are the starting point for getting the most from management consultants, they are certainly not the end point. There are a number of ingredients in measuring the success of management consulting, all to do with the well-being of the client organisation, but the very definition of those expectations and objectives and what is meant by well-being will typically change as a result of an effective consulting engagement. In fact one measure of success may be regarded as whether the consultant has added value to the client understanding by helping to 're-frame' those starting perceptions. The client-consultant relationship must be strong enough to support such a transformation process.

Often the problem that the client first thought they had is not the real problem at all. This process needs to be carefully managed by both the client and the consultant, rather than by either party alone. It is a process that requires constant questioning and periodical review, preferably in a systematic way, although this cannot be a mechanical process. Rather like a good marriage, the relationship itself will tell both parties the time, place and form of review that are relevant, provided both parties are open to that awareness.

The management consultant will gather information from all sources and then test it, both within the client business and by using comparative experience from elsewhere. Gradually, they will develop a common understanding that the perception of the problem needs to evolve into a new understanding. Problems are seldom what they seem and the solutions seldom rest where one first looked for an answer. The client-consultant interaction will lead, through re-framing, to a redefinition of the problem into a format from which it can be solved.

Manage your own contracts inside your organisation

The success of consulting work depends not just upon the quality and productivity of the client-consultant relationships but also on the health and robustness of the relationships between the consultants themselves and colleagues within the client organisation.

Implementation can only be as good as the relationships are geared up to withstand, and if colleagues are lukewarm or sceptical then a consulting project will have a sub-optimal impact.

This is why it is important to establish an appropriate way of working between insiders and outsiders. It is also why those organisations with internal consulting units often use them to work effectively with outside consultants. The internal consultants understand the power system and they have tacit local knowledge; they 'know where the bodies are buried' and how to get things implemented within the prevailing culture; on the other hand they are part of and dependent upon the existing culture and authority structure for continued employment. Outside consultants on the other hand should be independent and able to take a detached view and to say the unthinkable without fear or favour, to address taboos and undiscussable topics.

So, the insiders and outsiders are complementary. Sometimes the insider provides continuity and the outsider provides ideas. Sometimes the roles are reversed, with the consultant providing continuity while the internal managers move between jobs and companies. Whatever the exact configuration of the roles and relationships, they will typically be complementary and compensatory. The relationship should be close but not too close, achieving a working synergy and creativity through interdependence, while avoiding undue dependence and maintaining independence on each side.

In fact, the secret of managing a consultancy engagement successfully is to strike the right balance between dependence and independence at the different stages of the client relationship management life cycle. This is discussed further in chapter 3.5.

3.5

Phases of the client-consultant relationship

Barry Curnow

Introduction

We referred in previous chapters in this section to the importance of the client-consultant relationship and of the natural phases of its life cycle. The client-consultant relationship is the foundation on which all professional and business success in management consultancy engagements is built – both for the client organisation and for the consultants. It provides the overarching framework within which management consultancy can create added value for clients. No amount of technical expertise or functional experience can make up for a deficiency in relationship capability. A good client-consultant relationship is therefore essential.

Wherever writers describe their experience of client-consultant relationships, they reveal a natural sequence or life cycle to the interaction. At its simplest this may be described as a beginning, a middle and an end but we can explain the stages more helpfully as follows:

- establishing the client-consultant relationship
- managing the relationship
- transforming the relationship

Phases of the client-consultant relationship

These stages can be illustrated as shown in Figure 3.5.1 below. Each phase is not distinct from the next – rather, they overlap with each other.

The overlapping cycles of the client consultant relationship

Establishing — Managing — Transforming

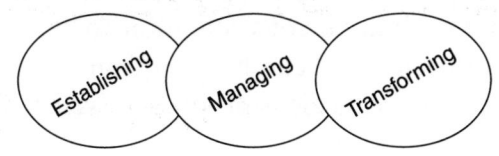

Figure 3.5.1

There are discernible steps and stages in each overlapping cycle of the client-consultant relationship. The simple linear version of the model above illustrates the sequential logic but not the practical reality. In practice, the cycles are dynamic and have to be attended to simultaneously, or even out of order. This feature is shown in Figure 3.5.2 below:

The overlapping cycles of the client consultant relationship

Managing / Establishing / Transforming

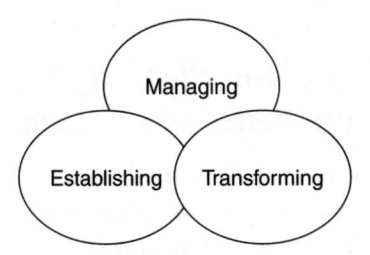

Figure 3.5.2

A client-consultant relationship may need to be managed before it is fully established or it may need to undergo elements of transformation in order to become manageable at all. Certainly, it is a process of continuous review and renewal, rather than a 'once and for all' exercise.

Clients and consultants need to pay constant attention to all three phases – how well the relationship is established in different quarters (phase1); is it sufficiently managed or even overmanaged in some areas? (phase 2) and what types of change are necessary to optimise the firm-to-firm relationship for each stage of the work together? (phase 3)

This need for simultaneous attention to the overlapping requirements of each cycle can be seen from appreciating the dynamic nature of the main elements of each cycle as follows:

Establishing the client-consultant relationship

This engagement phase deals with considerations of consultant understanding of the organisation and its industry and client issues of credibility and acceptance in establishing successful client-consultant relationships. There are three steps in this phase:

- Understanding the client organisation and earning the confidence of key people
- Designing, developing and agreeing viable terms of engagement
- Agreeing and communicating mutual expectations for the consulting relationship

Understanding of the client organisation and earning the confidence of key people

Key personnel in the client company must be convinced that the consultants have a working appreciation of the industry and business, sufficient to understand the key issues, people, economic context, operating parameters, pressures and inter-relationships. Clients do not expect consultants to know as much about the operating conditions of the enterprise as they do themselves but enough to make a difference and to be relevant and helpful. Consultants need to know things – quite a lot of things – about a business in order to consult effectively with that business. This is because unless key managers in the business believe that they are understood, they will not invest the consultants with the necessary confidence for them to be effective.

Designing, developing and agreeing viable terms of engagement

It is a common fallacy that a client writes a specification against which several consultants pitch for the business and that the successful firm implements the project specification and is measured by criteria established at the outset. This very rarely applies to true general management consulting work although it can be an oversimplified approximation of certain types of sub-contracting work. This 'engineering' model of aim, objective and results is only one strand of a truly professional terms of engagement model for consulting as illustrated in Figure 3.5.3 below:

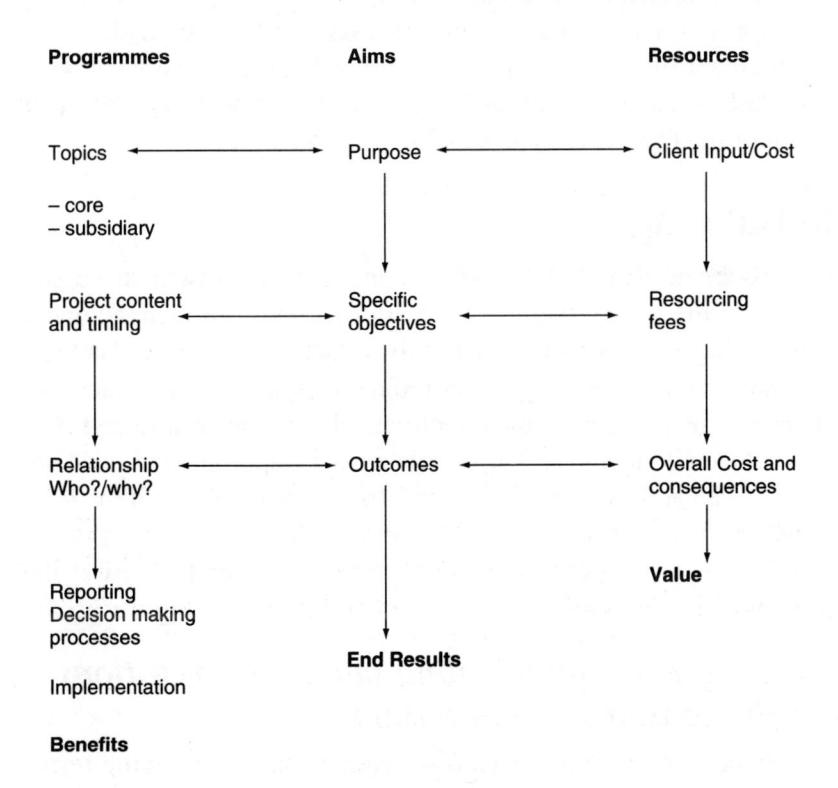

Programmes	**Aims**	**Resources**
Topics ⟷	Purpose ⟵	Client Input/Cost
– core		
– subsidiary	↓	↓
Project content and timing ⟷	Specific objectives ⟷	Resourcing fees
↓	↓	↓
Relationship Who?/why? ⟵	Outcomes ⟵	Overall Cost and consequences
↓	↓	↓
Reporting Decision making processes		Value
Implementation	**End Results**	
Benefits		

Figure 3.5.3

The central strand in the middle column above shows aims, purposes, specific objectives, outcomes, benefits and end results. This is a narrow approach to keeping track of certain central tasks and it is a necessary structural framework for the more important work of planning and evaluation. This is covered in the columns to the left and right of this central strand labelled Programmes and Resources. These illustrate the really powerful choices that need to be made when designing viable terms of engagement for a consulting project: those of determining the nature and scope of the activities and tasks contained in the various programmes of work in the left-hand column – who does what, where and when – and the resource decisions contained in the right hand column. Naturally these two columns affect and are affected by each other and relate to the central strand that describes the aims to which the activities and resources are applied.

Again, these steps are not necessarily linear within the engagement life cycle of the relationship but they must have been attended to satisfactorily, at least in an initial way, for the next phase of the life cycle to be satisfactorily negotiated.

Initial diagnosis

It will become clear that the essential matters that must be discussed as part of the initial diagnosis preceding a consulting engagement can only be acceptably resolved if the relationship itself is made an agenda item in its own right. Far too many consulting contracts are silent on the question of the client-consultant relationship and how the parties will handle it. The details are not important and need not be specified at the outset but it is key for the psychology of the relationships between the parties to be recognised as a significant matter in its own right, just as worthy of attention and review as the progress with dates and events of the work itself (see Figure 3.5.4).

Agreeing & communicating mutual expectations for the consulting relationship

When these topics have been discussed as part of agreeing terms of engagement, there is a basis for agreeing and communicating

> **Initial Diagnosis**
>
> Think about:
> • Needs
> • Time
> • Scope
> • Fees
> • Terms of business
> • Psychological relationship

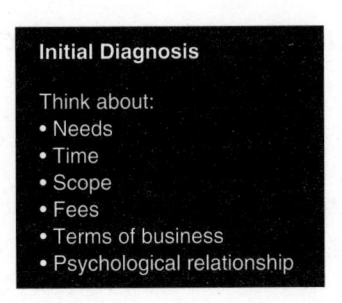

Figure 3.5.4

the mutual expectations that client and consultancy have of each other for that relationship. The way in which they will work together, resolve any disagreements, communicate progress, consult interested parties and so on would be communicated in the appropriate level of detail to all parties. This should not be done just on a need-to-know basis but in a way that engages the energy, curiosity, enthusiasm and commitment of the whole organisational community.

Common principles must be shared with all constituencies, but there is scope for more tailored communications in different branches and divisions according to their involvement and the likely implications for both participation and outcome.

It may come as a surprise to clients that consultants have expectations of and for the relationship between them and that these need to be considered for success to be assured.

Managing the client-consultant relationship

This is the phase of actually doing the work together – joint work between client and consultants, each understanding and relating to the clear expectations of the other.

- establishing issues, managing projects, achieving synergy
- managing interrelationships in the organisation's culture
- know-how transfer & skills development

Establishing issues, managing projects, achieving synergy

In a sense, it is only when the legal, financial and psychological business of establishing the relationship is underway and achieving some of the clarity and mutual understanding that are the outcome of the first cycle, that the serious work of the consulting project itself can start. This helps to explain why it may appear surprising for the task of establishing issues to appear in phase two rather than phase one. The reason for this is that the client issues set out in the early stages of the relationship may tend to be provisional or just restricted to the explicit business terms of reference rather than what is really exercising people under the surface. These implicit issues of people, personalities and power must be made explicit in a suitable manner as part of the main work of phase two, determining what is really going on and what are the substantive challenges to be resolved in the project. Only when these are aired and discussed in the open can the consultants act effectively as catalysts to induce synergy in the client organisation. Synergy is defined here as getting more from the same or less. Synergy is typically achieved between ideas, teams, client and consultant, colleagues within the organisation. Achieving synergy may be regarded as the heart of any consulting relationship – enabling the client to make more of what he already had and to achieve more with less.

Managing interrelationships in the organisation's culture

Synergy is about interaction, about concerted, purposeful action in harmony between people or divisions and business units. This is not to suggest that departments never disagree or fall out. On the contrary, constructive conflict is typically a necessary part of the synergy that consultants seek to help their clients to achieve. Orchestration of the interrelationships within the client's culture, together with the provision of coaching and counselling in new skills and behaviours are characteristic work of this central phase.

Know-how transfer & skills development

These softer skills of coaching, counselling and mentoring prepare the organisational ground for the changes in working practices and behaviours that significant consulting projects typically envisage and require. Some emotional and interpersonal shifts need to take place before true learning can occur, before know-how about effective business and management repertoires can be transferred from consultants to the client and new skills developed through joint work and practice together.

Transforming the client relationship

This is about managing endings and moving on. Transformation means that there is an irreversible change in the relationship. The initial dependency of the client on the consultant ends and gives way to independence and autonomy, allowing and requiring a new type of relationship which evolves into a new phase with new cycles of its own. The identifiable steps of the transformation phase are:

- building the implementation team
- obtaining the necessary implementation support
- securing professional implementation & client independence

Building the implementation team

All consulting engagements should begin with implementation in mind, with an image of what success might look like when it is achieved and with an eye to who will make the future operations work. The implementation team should include consultant and client personnel working together and with a range of personality types to cover the different team roles and functions.

Obtaining the necessary implementation support

We mentioned above the place of coaching, counselling and mentoring in preparing the organisational ground for change.

These helping or supporting processes are just as critical during implementation to reinforce learning and establish new routines and working practices in the client organisation. In new situations, client staff will not necessarily know what they do not know so the support needs to be signposted, made available in user friendly packages such as implementation packs for managers appointed to new jobs as a result of re-organisation or new systems.

Securing professional implementation & client independence

The last stage of the final phase in this model occurs when the client personnel take full accountability for operating the new organisational processes and the consultants withdraw, with as much or as little ceremony as necessary to symbolise the importance of the transition from consultant dependency to client independence and full responsibility.

So, client-consultant relationships have a life of their own. If left unattended they are born, they develop and they decay. But if properly attended to with respect and understanding by all parties, strong, productive, high quality client-consultant relationships will transform themselves, leaving the client organisation with enhanced value and capability and the consultancy personnel with worthwhile experience and a changed relationship that will be appropriate to the next phase – in which the business of establishing a new, post engagement relationship starts all over again.

This important business of ending is examined in more depth in Chapter 3.9.

3.6

Evaluating advice and recommendations

Jonathan Reuvid and John Mills

This chapter follows on directly from the five preceding chapters and, like them, is focused on providing guidelines for the client to manage the client-consultant relationship effectively and on how to extract the maximum benefit from each consultancy assignment experience. From the foregoing, it has been established that the commissioning and management of consultancy assignments demand clarity of thought and self-discipline, as much from the client as from the consultant.

Restating the obvious – and setting aside those assignments for which the commissioning is motivated by corporate politics or the wish of one senior manager or management faction to utilise the consultant's report instrumentally for subjective ends – the client's aim is to receive objective conclusions, advice and recommendations from its consultants which, when put into effect, will add value to the company's business and ultimately its shareholders. Having authorised the commissioning of the assignment, the board's expectation may be that no further involvement is required until the consultants' report is presented, when a clinical evaluation should be possible. However, if this evaluation of the consultants' advice and recommendations is undertaken in a vacuum, it is unlikely to be a satisfying process or add value to the company.

Directors not participating themselves in the management of an external consultants project have an important role to perform in objective assessment and evaluation – not just of the recommendations but of the parameters and conditions under which the project is commissioned. This chapter, then, is intended as much for board members as for the corporate management involved directly in the continuous monitoring and management of the assignment.

Forewarned is forearmed

In parallel with the routines and disciplines set out in Chapter 3.2 and perhaps as an appendix to the letter of appointment containing the list of specific items identified in chapter 3.3, the client should deliberate and determine its evaluation processes and the evaluation criteria that they will apply to interim and final reports.

Too often, clients commission consultancy assignments with reasonably clear expectations of what they expect at the end of the day, hopefully communicated to the consultant at the outset, but without a template of the evaluation criteria and processes they will apply to the advice given and recommendations made. This lack of 'upfront' definition exposes the client to the risk that the consultant's interim and final conclusions will be deliberated and evaluated by individuals subjectively or, in committee, by reference to criteria that are only then established *ad hoc*. Worse still, if the need to set criteria is recognised after the consultant's report is read, the criteria may be influenced by the advice and recommendations – both by the report's contents and its omissions. At this point, objective assessment by the client company may become impossible.

These risks can be avoided if the client takes the time and trouble to set down clearly the evaluation process throughout the project and at its conclusion, and the evaluation criteria which will be applied both by the project management team and by the board before endorsing the assignment's action fall-out.

There is a strong case for revealing these specifications to the consultant, either at the 'educating the consultants' stage or the 'contracting' stage (see Chapter 3.2) or in the 'Agreeing and communicating mutual expectations for the consulting relationship' phase (see Chapter 3.5). In this way, if the client disagrees with or rejects, wholly or in part, the consultant's advice and recommendations, there can be no grounds for the consultant to complain that the evaluation process was inapplicable to the assignment or otherwise 'unfair' – provided that the client sticks to their own guidelines. Forewarned is indeed forearmed.

The board's role in the evaluation process

The client board's involvement in a consultancy project will depend on both on the size of the company and the size and nature of the project. For a large corporation, an assignment to select and install the most suitable order processing system may demand no more than prior approval of the project and acceptance of the recommendations endorsed by its client project management team. For a much smaller company, such projects may require a more detailed involvement with regular board progress reviews and the engagement of the financial or IT director as a project team member.

At the minimum, for projects that will have a significant organisational impact on management and staff, the board will need to define closely the objectives of the consultancy and appoint the internal project team assigned to manage the project. A fuller definition of board responsibility would be the requirement to sign off the:

- formal brief to be given to short-listed consultants
- consultant selection process
- project management duties and responsibilities
- monitoring and review process
- evaluation process throughout the project and at its conclusion
- evaluation criteria which the company will apply
- board members involvement at each stage

The depth of director involvement is a matter for the board to decide and will depend much on the degree to which management responsibility is delegated within the company, the importance attached to the consultancy project and the management style, collectively and individually, of the executive directors. The consultant selection process is addressed fully in Chapter 3.2 and board involvement in the final selection may not be necessary if the selection process has received sufficient attention. However, the selection of the project leader (whether a director or a senior manager) and the monitoring and the review process are the two operational issues to which the board is wise to pay attention.

Selection of the project leader

The selection of the project leader should be endorsed by the board. Although commitment to the project and its timely completion are prerequisites in the choice of leader, it is important to avoid the risks of 'ownership' by a single project manager, or manipulative control of the assignment to achieve predetermined conclusions which will satisfy internal political factions. Therefore, it makes sense to appoint a balanced project team, which together has some expertise in all key aspects of the project, with the condition that each team member can make a sufficient time commitment throughout the progress of the project. The client may also be well-advised to include in the project team one senior manager who has no responsibility to work alongside the consultants during the progress of the assignment but who sits in on all progress reviews and in effect performs a continuing quality audit function.

The monitoring and review process

The assignment programme agreed with the consultants on appointment will provide for regular progress reports and meetings between the corporate and consultancy teams. At each of these intermediate reviews the project team should carry out a thorough evaluation of the assignment and its execution to date. All review meetings will be fully minuted.

These regular reviews are important for a number of reasons:

- there are opportunities through regular review to trap surprises early on, to refine the scope of the project, its parameters and its execution, and to reappraise whether the needs of the corporation as a whole are being satisfied (any recommended changes to the definition of the assignment must, of course, be referred back to the board or other approval body)
- if the consultancy assignment is 'off the rails' with no hope of returning it on track, the project team should not hesitate to recommend abortion, even if there are cost penalties
- if the investigation phase indicates that the scope of the consultancy assignment could be extended with advantage into new territories, the client should think very carefully before agreeing to any extension at additional cost

During the phase of 'establishing the client-consultant relationship' (see Chapter 3.5), the client will make initial value judgements about the calibre and capability of the consultancy team which is being fielded and its responsiveness to client needs. Through the review process it may become apparent, for example, that in arriving at intermediate conclusions, members of the consultancy team are relying on their firm's database of case studies rather than on first hand experience. Alternatively, defects may emerge in the performance of the consultancy or project teams or in their relationship which cause the client (or the consultant) to seek changes in the composition of either team.

The board needs to satisfy itself that there are review routines in place at sufficiently frequent intervals to throw up all issues of this kind which can then be addressed before serious damage is done.

Evaluating the final report

If regular review routines are followed, the consultant's final report containing advice and recommendations should contain few, if any, surprises. Typically, the report will first be delivered in draft form to the project team. As a first step, it is recommended that each member of the team should read and make his or her individual assessment in writing. The project team will then share and debate the individual assessments in order to arrive at a collective evaluation against the prescribed criteria. Clarification from the consultant may be sought at this stage before the project team prepares its appraisal to accompany the consultant's report which it will submit to the board.

Project team appraisal

In its appraisal, the project team will examine the integrity of the report in terms of its thoroughness and credibility and the logic of its analysis. If report conclusions or recommendations are inconsistent with the conclusions reached at intermediate reviews, the team will need to question the consultant closely.

The team will want to benchmark the findings against industry experience and best practice and to verify that recommendations are linked to specific outcomes that can be integrated into a business plan if the report is accepted.

Management will want to apply sensitivity tests to the findings and to keep separate the consultancy recommendations from any service offering from third party providers which the consultants may include in their recommendations. In particular, where the services of an associated company are recommended (as in IT solutions) the client will want to examine thoroughly alternative offerings from arm's length suppliers (see Chapter 2.1 – *Competition and objectivity, auditing and outsourcing*).

Finally, the team's responsibility should extend to examining whether the company has the resources to implement recommendations and, if not, advise the board as to the additional temporary or permanent resources which would be needed.

Board evaluation

Without becoming immersed in the detail of the consultant's report, the directors meeting as a board are likely to ask themselves the following questions:

- Did we get what we signed up for?
- Is this report the result of objective investigative inquiry and rigorous analysis (not an off-the-peg stereotype solution)?
- Would the recommendations make a favourable impact on our business plans?
- If applied, do the recommendations give us a sustainable competitive advantage?
- What added value would the implemented recommendation give to shareholders?

In the case of uncertainty or disagreement about the validity of the report, its conclusions or its implementation, the board may call for an independent second opinion.

A virtuous circle in the use of consultancy

The client management of consultancy programmes demands as much rigour as the consultant's executions. For companies inexperienced in the engagement of management consultants, the use of consulting is an exercise in self-education.

In Chapter 3.9, Barry Curnow examines how the client-consultant relationship moves into its final phase and how the nature of the relationship changes and matures. But the relationship may not 'grow old gracefully', even if the commissioned assignment is completed on time within the letter of the contract. Chapter 3.9 examines why recommendations are often not carried out but there are other reasons why the client may be left with a feeling of dissatisfaction.

One of these is assuredly lack of engagement on the client's part by senior management or the board. Advice and recommendations are only as good as their evaluation; and evaluation is only as good as the client's involvement in setting the guidelines and rules of engagement.

Appreciative inquiry: Building on strengths in your organisation

Anne Radford and Liz Mellish

Appreciative inquiry (AI) is a powerful option for an organisation that wishes to engage all its stakeholders in planning and implementing organisational change and at the same time to build commitment and innovation.

Appreciative inquiry: A constructive approach to organisational change

Appreciative inquiry looks for the positive core in an organisation to begin the discussion on organisational change. It invites people to discuss what is working in a system, to envisage a future that builds on that success, to look at all the structures and procedures that would support such a future, and to develop a way forward.

This approach was developed by Dr David Cooperrider and his colleagues at Case Western Reserve University, Ohio, as they became increasingly dissatisfied with the organisational change processes prevalent in the 1980s. Not only did the processes focus on the short term, but they enjoyed very limited success. Cooperrider and others began asking different questions about the organisation, such as 'what was right with it?' rather than 'what was wrong with it?' They noticed that people responded very differently to the different questions. People became enthusiastic about their work and their organisation. Change was no longer a fearful threat – it was an opportunity to build on earlier successes.

This discovery led Dr. Cooperrider and others to carry out research into people's attitudes towards change and how this affected their behaviour. This took them to medical, social and behavioural research. As they became more aware of the impact of this research in an organisational context, they developed the appreciative inquiry approach to organisational change.

Many organisations have chosen this approach although others have not. An organisation's views about leadership, employee participation, organisational innovation and individual self-esteem determines the level of interest and willingness to engage in this type of systematic inquiry.

And the results of using this approach? The benefits include improvements in financial and productivity ratios, in recruitment and retention, and in internal standards.

This chapter will help you learn more about this approach, its principles and process, how it has been used in different sectors in Europe, North and South America, and Australasia, and its impact and results. It also has a set of questions to help you decide whether this approach could be used to good effect in your organisation.

Five core principles and the AI 4D cycle
The power of dialogue
Appreciative inquiry is grounded in the theory of social constructionism. Ken Gergen (1995), working extensively in this area, describes language as being the creator of reality:

> *Social constructionist dialogues concern the processes by which humans generate meaning together. We recognize*

that as people create meaning together, so do they sow seeds of action. Meaning and action are entwined. As we generate meaning together, we create the future.

Instead of decisions about an organisation's future being sent down through the layers of management for implementation, the assumption here is that the future of the organisation is created through discussion and dialogue.

The power of image

Also important is the power of image. Much has been written about this in many different fields such as the power of the inner game in sports, the powerful impact of positive inner dialogue and the power of thought in medicine.

Golfers and tennis players are now trained to focus on where they want the shots to go rather than what to avoid. Being told to 'avoid the woods' is the same as telling the brain to focus on 'the woods' rather than the fairway.

The power of image – its impact on a person's behaviour – was a key part of the foundations that David Cooperrider (1990) set down for appreciative inquiry. When he and his colleagues began to apply this approach to organisations, they found that organisations were heliotropic; they moved, like plants, towards whatever gave them life and energy.

Appreciative inquiry in organisational change can be said to be a combination of dialogue and the power of a compelling image (Watkins and Mohr, 2001).

The five core principles of AI

The following five principles are central to the theory of appreciative inquiry:

- **The constructionist principle:** Information about an organisation and the future of that organisation are interwoven. Organisations are living entities where the power of language creates the present and the future. Whatever leaders or change agents take to be true about an organisation will affect the way people act and the way they approach change. Thus, the way we know is fateful (Gergen, 1995).

- **The principle of simultaneity:** Inquiry and change are not separate moments. They are simultaneous. Inquiry, therefore, becomes an intervention.

  The seeds of change are implicit in the very first questions we ask. One of the most crucial things a change agent or an organisation development (OD) practitioner does is to articulate questions at the beginning of an organisational change process. This directs what people think and talk about, what they discover and learn, and the images they begin to build about the future.

- **The poetic principle:** Organisations are like an open book whose story is constantly being co-authored. The pasts, presents or futures are endless sources of learning, inspiration or interpretation – like, for example, the many interpretations of a good piece of poetry.

The important point is that we have a choice about what we study in an organisation. We could study moments of creativity and innovation or debilitating bureaucratic stress. It could be about teams working well to launch a new product or where they have failed. People's energy will follow the topic of inquiry.

- **The anticipatory principle:** The shared image of an organisation drives change. This image can be positive or negative. Positive images of the future lead an organisation to positive actions. Much like a film projector on a screen, people project ahead of themselves and it is this image that keeps them moving forward.

  The talk in hallways, the metaphors and language bring the future powerfully into the present. Creating positive images together may be the most important aspect of any inquiry (Cooperrider and Whitney, 1999).

- **The positive principle:** The more positive the questions used to guide a group or an organisational change initiative, the more effective and longer lasting the change effort (Bushe and Coetzer, March 1995).

In addition, the momentum for change requires large amounts of positive effect and constructive interaction. Large group methods such as the Appreciative Inquiry Summit, which has emerged from Appreciative Inquiry and Future Search, enable the people involved to experience hope, inspiration and sheer joy in creating with one another.

The appreciative inquiry 4D cycle

The 4D cycle is one way to use appreciative inquiry in organisational change work.

Choosing the topic

Since the energy of the inquiry will follow the topic, it is crucial to choose a topic that will generate the energy for change.

Figure 3.7.1 Appreciative inquiry 4D cycle

Here are three examples: an American company in Mexico; a professional practice in London; and two regions in Eastern Europe.

- Marge Schiller, a consultant based in the United States, helped a part of the Avon cosmetics corporation to re-frame the topic of sexual harassment. The emphasis at first was on reducing the number of sexual harassment cases. By re-framing the inquiry, she and the company began an inquiry into exemplary teams. They asked for men and women to nominate themselves if they thought they worked effectively together. The company was greatly surprised with the large number that came forward. The company went on to study these successful teams so that they could develop more such teams, thus addressing the issue of sexual harassment differently.
- With a set of barristers in London, I was brought in initially to look at why their marketing activities were not working. The focus was to be on studying the mistakes and correcting them. After we talked about the implications of that focus, they decided that it would be better to look at what they wanted from the practice and their marketing activities.

    This topic translated into questions about the times when the work had been satisfying for the barrister, had given greater visibility to the practice and been financially sound.
- In two communities in Eastern Europe, businesses, community groups, teachers and mayors wanted to resolve a regional conflict so that they could start living a more normal life. Since resolving the conflict was in the hands of the politicians, we asked what people would be doing if they were living a more normal life. With this change of focus, people realised that there were many ways they could develop their communities, thus improving the situation for everyone.

Discovering what gives life to an organisation

This discovery phase discovers the 'life-giving' forces of an organisation.

In the United States, British Airways North America looked at the exceptional handling of a flight's arrival and baggage.

In Denmark, members of the HK Union, a union for professionals, highlighted the times when they were most involved in shaping the Union.

In the UK, BP has been discovering their examples of passionate leadership which led on to revising HR systems and improving productivity.

The discovery phase involves people telling stories of special situations in their organisations in interviews with their colleagues. Using a set of questions developed in the organisation, one person asks the other positive questions and inquires into the significance of the story. It becomes a mutual learning process. Colleagues then come together in small groups to hear about each other's stories and highlight the affirmative themes in them.

Dreaming or envisioning phase

In the dream phase, participants take these themes and co-create a shared image or vision of the future.

This phase is an opportunity for people to be very creative in how they generate their vision or image of their organisation. For an organisation in Northern Germany, drawing the future helped each part of the organisation to communicate in a way that was successful for all of them.

For consultants at a workshop in Austria, taking part in a guided visualisation on the future of their work helped them describe the core of their work and how that would influence the future.

For a senior manager in a City of London bank, writing about the ideal day helped him highlight the significant parts of his new role.

Design phase

In the design phase, participants translate that image or vision into a macro statement – a possibility statement or provocative proposition for the whole organisation. This statement is written in the present tense as though it is the current situation.

With this compelling image and statement, the question is then 'what would the organisation and its systems look like if they supported that shared vision?' People then develop micro statements for these systems, processes or roles. This process becomes an opportunity to see what systems already support that image and statement and which ones would need to change.

This part of the 4D cycle of appreciative inquiry is also an opportunity to use many different frameworks to aid the discussion such as open space, future search or the balanced scorecard.

In two communities in England, the professional, managerial and administrative staff in the health service and social services are now developing all their systems to deliver an integrated mental health service for patients in two localities. They are building on the best of the two agencies and creating new systems where necessary. The design phase is taking place as a dialogue: ideas are developed, presented to the wider team, further modified and finalised. People on the various working teams will present their work to the wider community such as local groups, hospitals and medical practitioners.

The senior managers are providing full support and are only getting involved in the detail where necessary to ensure there is appropriate co-ordination with county-wide bodies.

Destiny

There are two parts to this next phase: delivering the systems and sustaining the appreciative learning culture.

Some parts of the organisation want to ensure that the practical steps are taken and others want to continue to look for ways to sustain the appreciative learning approach that is so evident in the phases of the appreciative inquiry cycle (Barrett, 1995). Both are important and mutually reinforcing for organisational change.

The outcomes

The impact or result of using AI to effect organisational change has been measured in different ways.

In the Bank of Scotland, the stories from ten workshops led to people developing common standards for communication practice. 'The stories were regarded as being true so that they represented the nearest equivalent to the equally unarguable hard data so beloved of bankers', comments Ruth Findlay (2001), internal communications manager in Corporate Finance.

Dex, a billion-dollar subsidiary of a Fortune 100 company in the United States, decided to collect some data during six months of using the principles and processes of AI. The return on investment (ROI) was $15.62 for every dollar invested; product quality improved 51 per cent; cycle times improved over 400 per cent and employee morale improved 245 per cent. They were very pleased with the data! (Chandler, 2001)

In the health and social services situation, there is a significant difference in attitude towards the government-mandated changes in these teams compared with others in the area. A person in contact with the many different teams in the area observed that 'the teams are feeling positive about the change and are looking forward to it. They feel valued, have shared knowledge about each other's roles in delivering mental health services and are open to constructing the future together'.

This attitude may be surprising since people have been developing the new systems while carrying out their regular heavy workload.

The AI process has also been helpful in other situations such as:
- a downturn in the electricity and coal mining sector in Germany where morale was very low
- a city in southern England that wanted businesses, voluntary organisations and government agencies to participate in developing a vision of the city's future
- a food manufacturer in Brazil that needed to take a hard look at their future given the increased competition in the sector

Is AI right for your organisation?

The appreciative inquiry process is very effective in some, but not all, organisations. Dr. Liz Mellish's research in Australia (Mellish,

2000) indicates some key questions that an organisation needs to ask itself before using appreciative inquiry in addressing organisational change. These questions are:

- Are we in transition? Is there a need for something better?
- Does achieving a new direction and way of operating depend on our people?
- Does creating and sustaining the change demand a participatory process?
- Is questioning organisational life vital to sustaining it?
- Is our meta-strategic management cycle best driven by diversity and participatory decision-making?
- Do we want to articulate a shared vision and the means of achieving it?

Mellish's study also indicates that a cluster of three organisational conditions predispose organisations effectively to select appreciative inquiry as a method for organisational change. They are (a) being in transition; (b) a willingness to work with diversity; and (c) searching for shared vision and social sustainability.

The consultant's role in AI

The consultant's role in AI is that of an agent of inquiry and includes four aspects:

- to view organisations as living social systems, mysteries of creation to be nurtured and affirmed, not as mechanistic or scientific operations with problems to be solved.
- to work in the affirmative, continually seeking to discover what gives life to the organisation and its members.
- to be facilitators of possibilities, hope and inspired action.
- to continually seek ways to give the process away, to support organisation members in making it their own (Cooperrider and Whitney, 1999).

With this kind of participative approach to organisational change, the steering group, core group or project team co-creates the activities with the consultant.

The benefits of using AI

Dr. Mellish's research also shows that the benefits for organisations using appreciative inquiry include:

- achieving widespread engagement and ownership of staff and stakeholders in large scale-strategic change initiatives
- building commitment to organisational change through the process and sustaining the commitment (and the process) for use in future changes
- achieving high impact, low cost implementation of promotional and public education programmes by engaging the end user in the process
- implementing major organisational re-positioning and restructuring activities in a participatory manner and with no industrial disputes
- launching a successful virtual company that is global and continues to grow and outperform its competitors

Appreciative inquiry is a vital process and way of thinking that is being used throughout the world to effect change. If the conditions are appropriate, your organisation or the ones you work with could begin to address change more positively and with greater inclusivity.

For further information on appreciative inquiry resources, consultants in Europe and links to other websites, go to the AI Resource E-Centre at www.aradford.co.uk.

Anne Radford would like to give special thanks to Dr Liz Mellish in Australia (info@mellish.com.au, www.mellish.com.au) for the use of her research on appreciative inquiry and her special contribution to the final three sections of this chapter. Liz Mellish is a certified management consultant working with government, business, higher education and community organisations in change.

References

Barrett, F J (1995) Creating Appreciative Learning Cultures, *Organisational Dynamics*, (2), pp 36—49

Bushe, G and Coetzer, G (March 1995) Appreciative Inquiry as a Team-development Intervention: A Controlled Experiment, *Journal of Applied Behavioural Science*, **31**

Cooperrider, D L (1990) Positive image, positive action: The affirmative basis of organizing, in Chandler, David (February 2001) 'AI Improves For-profit Companies', *Appreciative Inquiry* e-mail newsletter, (12), Anne Radford, www.aradford.co.uk/Ainesletter.htm

Appreciative Management and Leadership: The Power of Positive Thought and Action in Organisations, eds S. Srivastva, D.L Cooperrider & Associates, JosseyBass, San Fransisco

Cooperrider, D L and Whitney, D (1999) *Appreciative Inquiry*, Berrett-Koehler Communications, Inc

Gergen, Kenneth (1995) *Realities and Relationships*, Harvard University Press

Harben, Johnny and Findlay, Ruth (February 2001) 100 Voices Making Change in the Bank of Scotland, *Appreciative Inquiry* e-mail newsletter, (12)

Mellish, E E (2000) Appreciative Inquiry at Work, EdD dissertation, Queensland University of Technology

Watkins, J M and Mohr, B J (2001) *Appreciative Inquiry: Change at the Speed of Imagination,* Jossey-Bass/Pfeiffer

Further reading

Gergen, Ken (1991) *The Saturated Self: Dilemmas of Identity in Contemporary Life*, Basic Books

Gergen, Ken (1999) *An Invitation to Social Construction*, Sage, Thousand Oaks, CA

Other work by Ken Gergen can be found on the Taos Institute's website: www.taosinstitute.org.

3.8

The consultant's role in managing change

E. Michael Shays

Since 1994, managing change has remained a hot topic in consulting. Almost every major accounting or consulting firm has some group dedicated to marketing and delivering change programmes. It's a big-ticket item. Most of these firms have developed good systematic methods for their change practices. Yet both consultants and clients report too many change programmes fail. Some programmes may fail outright and be aborted. Most fail to achieve the benefits expected, or find that achieving them was a greater struggle than it should have been – resulting in excess costs and expended energies.

If asked what went wrong, consultants describe how the client was unable to manage the change process, particularly the part implementing change. If asked what as consultants they would do differently next time, some say they would be more assertive about the human resources involved. But their bottom line is that it's up to the client to make managing change a success. This is only partly true. Consultants bear a greater responsibility for the success of managing change than their clients.

How far does the responsibility of the consultant extend? A consultant, who was about to visit Norway north of the Arctic Circle during July where the sun never set, wanted to know what the weather would be like. The answer came back: 'In Norway there is no bad weather. Only bad clothes'. In consulting, there are no bad clients. Only bad consulting. If a client really is incapable of following the consultant's advice, the consultant shouldn't take the engagement, or having taken it, should withdraw.

But most clients can follow their consultant's advice, if it's right, timely and presented effectively. This is the role of the consultant in managing change: to pilot clients through the rough waters of change and not to lose them in the tides. Here are ten channel markers to help with this navigation.

Match expectations

To start with, it's important for everyone involved to understand that wholesale redesign of business processes requires people to change old habits. This is hard to accomplish if stakeholders – people who have a vested interest in the results – expect to confine the programme to immediate operational improvements or to a single functional department. An analogy might be the room-by-room redesign of a home. The individual rooms may look brighter and newer, but overall the house won't be much different. To change the house the architect needs to understand the functions the *home* must perform, and remodel individual rooms to best achieve these functions.

A client who *talks* change but expects the consultant to produce immediate benefits or to work only in restricted areas of the organisation isn't ready to embark on a change programme. The consultant must avoid the temptation to humour the client in the hope that after the engagement has been awarded he can broaden the client's outlook. This rarely works. Educate the client before starting the engagement or run the risk of one of the two greatest causes of managing change failures: mismatched expectations.

Improve processes, not organisations

Improve processes, not organisational functions. Organisational units are arbitrary divisions of labour and lead the consultant to in-the-box-thinking traps. The consultant must understand the processes that the *business* must perform and redesign individual organisational functions to best achieve them. A manufacturer of consumer goods identified the cause of frequently damaged goods as poor handling at the loading dock. A natural response was to re-engineer the loading dock function resulting in a recommendation to install automated equipment. If the solution worked at this one loading dock as well as expected, the company would install similar equipment at its 23 other warehouses across the country.

Instead the company took a business process view. The loading dock function was part of the warehousing process, which was part of the distribution process. The best way to get products to dealers, the company concluded, was to re-engineer their distribution system. Instead of adding equipment at all 24 locations, it eliminated the loading dock in question – with its warehouse – along with twenty other warehouses in the system. The handling problem went away and so did many other problems. More significantly, inventory costs went down, the product moved through the system faster, and distribution to customers improved.

We know that every system can be divided into sub-systems. It's also true that every system is part of a larger one. Look for breakthroughs in re-engineering by identifying the larger system of which your engagement is a part, then explore with the client opportunities to eliminate or radically reduce the function you were originally asked to improve.

Identify and expand purposes

Identify and expand the purpose of the process being improved. The operative word here is *expand*. We identify the purpose of any activity to ensure we work on the right problem or opportunity. We *expand* the purpose to give us enlarged solution space. The purpose of the loading dock was 'to move product into the trucks'. If you were to ask the purpose of moving products into the trucks, the answer would be a larger, higher-level purpose such as 'to consolidate shipments to dealers'. Expanding this to an even higher level, the company discovered the purpose of its loading dock was 'to deliver products to dealers' in order 'to distribute products to customers'.

In their book, *Breakthrough Thinking*, Gerald Nadler and Shozo Hibino explain that by creating a purpose 'hierarchy' this way, the consultant expands choices for solutions and is more likely to achieve breakthroughs. A solution to consolidate shipments to dealers would differ from one to load trucks, and as the company found, the solution to distribute products to customers yielded a stunning result.

In addition, the purpose hierarchy will confirm that the consultant is working on the right problem or opportunity. A regional service company determined it must expand to survive and was already in negotiations to acquire another company. But when the consultant led management through a purpose expansion, they identified diversification as the real purpose. As the other company was just like itself, management aborted the acquisition before making a serious mistake.

The consultant will find that the purpose hierarchy will also build commitment. By focusing on expanded purposes, not the perceived problems, stakeholders will eventually settle on a purpose level on which all can agree. Two sister hospitals struggled for years to determine how to allocate limited funds for expansion between the two properties. After working with architects on different solutions, they finally developed a purpose hierarchy that led to a unanimous decision: close one facility and expand the other. Where stakeholders will disagree on solutions, they'll come together on purposes, and having done that will find a solution that works for all interests.

Use goals to measure, not to design

The consultant shouldn't confuse goals with purposes. The purpose of the process being improved is a business purpose, not to decrease costs or increase customer satisfaction. These are goals. One could decrease costs by shutting down the business, but that wouldn't achieve the business purpose. Goals are arbitrary measures and they don't necessarily measure the achievement of the purpose. Sometimes they're even wrong.

One major corporation started each of several re-engineering programmes with a session to establish objectives for the programme. While these objectives gave urgency to the programme and justified the resources that would be provided, the project teams frequently found themselves trying to re-engineer to meet an arbitrary goal instead of doing it to achieve the more important business purpose. An aircraft manufacturer gave one team the goal of redesigning the tool cribs to reduce space by 30 per cent. Trying to solve the space problem missed the point and got the team nowhere. When it put the goal aside and focused instead on solving the business purpose of the tool cribs, the team discovered that the higher purpose of getting the right tool to the right place at the right time was more important than storing the tools in 30 per cent less space – even if it took 30 per cent *more* space to do this. The result was a concept of mobile tool carts placed strategically around the plant acreage. It reduced floor space, and labour as well.

Useful as they are as drivers, goals tend to suggest preconceived solutions and limit innovation. The consultant must keep the client focused on the purpose of the business process and provide a solution to achieve that purpose in the most effective way. If the new process is a breakthrough for the business and the right one for all the critical success factors, the goal has either been met or it no longer matters.

Focus on the customer

The centre of all business processes is to satisfy customers. Without customers, the consultant's client has no business. Some improvement programmes focus on making a more 'efficient' company operations process while ignoring how difficult or inflexible the process remains for the customer. The consultant should get client agreement on who is the customer or beneficiary of the process to be improved. Internal customers count, but if these internal customers don't serve external customers, the consultant might ask whether the process adds any value to the revenue customer. If not, should the process be eliminated instead of re-designed?

When the customers have been identified, what do they want? One team put itself in the customers' shoes and concluded that its customers wanted to have new releases of the product instantly when the need was discovered. It was like answering the phone before it rings. The old paradigm was 'Customer orders, company delivers'. Instead of trying to find ways to shorten the order processing-delivery cycle, the consulting team found a way to implement a new paradigm: 'Company delivers, customer orders'. The company makes its product immediately accessible to the customer (company delivers) before the customer knows it's available. When the customer decides it needs the product, the customer activates it (customer orders) and that triggers a payment due. It was a remarkable breakthrough in the customers' interest that radically changes the way the company will do business in the future. It also promises to reduce costs and increase market share.

Involve stakeholders

Involve those who are going to be affected by a change process in its design and implementation. This requires understanding who are or will be the stakeholders of the process and reaching out to them for input. Far more people have a vested interest in the programme than would at first appear. But too often the consulting team relies on middle management, or worse, on people from headquarters instead of from the field. Some of these are really out of touch with what is or should be happening in the business process to be changed.

Many middle managers are also gatekeepers in the information flow. A division of one multinational company orchestrated a major presentation of its change programme to ninety managers from around the world in an off-site meeting. It was considered a success until three months later when the team found that none of its message had reached anyone outside of that meeting. One wag suggested the mistake lay in not telling the managers the programme was a deep secret. That would have ensured everyone would have got the word. The point is that the consultant must follow up to see that communications reach those who need to know.

The consultant knows the reasons for involving others. They include tapping the real knowledge from those closest to the process, and getting buy-in. Involving others also helps dispel anxieties and cool rumours. But effective involvement comes with participation based on an understanding of the change process. Therefore the consultant needs to provide broad training in the principles or methods of the improvement programme. Otherwise, client participants will use the only tools and methods they know and that may be counterproductive to what the consultant and the team are trying to achieve.

Not everyone can be a participant, but everyone should be afforded the opportunity to contribute. One team set up a voice-response-unit hotline that anyone can call for information or to leave questions and comments about the programme. The hotline handles more than 600 calls a month.

Finally, the process of involving others includes the important step of validation. First comes the validation of purpose. Will management support it? Next comes validation of the vision. Will customers like it, use it, buy it? Last comes validation of the process and technology. Can it be done? Will it work in the company's environment? Validation is a continuing, iterative process and involves employees at all levels, technical and non-technical specialists, customers and vendors.

Sustain sponsorship

Sponsorship must come from the top down. Although managers agree in principle to this and say the right words, the actions of some of them don't demonstrate their commitment. The problem is, sponsors don't always know what to do. It's often up to the consultant to write the script and produce the play. Sponsorship is more than showing the flag, although that's often neglected too. It's involvement at the right time and place.

There are three levels of sponsorship, the first two of which aren't mutually exclusive: *sponsor*, the one who provides the resources and stands behind the commitment; *protector*, the one who keeps the corporate immune system from killing the programme; and *mentor*, the one who coaches the team but has no line authority to sponsor or protect it. Without the sponsor, the team has no franchise, no funding, no resources, no management commitment, no change programme. Without the protector, the team will get pushed off course, get boxed into a narrow scope, and be pressured to go for short-term 'hits' in lieu of long-term payoffs. It may lose funding, have to shelve its visionary ideas, and become a process improvement activity – another change failure. Without the mentor, the team will struggle to get advance warning of risks and other problems, someone to open doors for it, sage advice.

One problem the consultant may encounter is discovering that designated sponsors have too many initiatives to sponsor. In this case the consultant might draft a relationship chart between the various initiatives and try to consolidate them wherever possible.

The Seven Principles of Breakthrough Thinking®
1. *Uniqueness Principle*: Whatever the apparent similarities, each problem is unique and requires an approach that dwells on its own contextual needs.
2. *Purposes Principle*: Focusing on purposes helps strip away nonessential aspects to avoid working on the wrong problem.
3. *Solution-After-Next Principle*: Innovation can be stimulated and solutions made more effective by working backward from an ideal target solution. Having a target solution in the future gives direction to near-term solutions and infuses them with larger purposes.
4. *Systems Principle*: Every problem is part of a larger system of problems and solving one problem inevitably leads to another. Having a clear framework of what elements and dimensions comprise a solution ensures its workability and implementation.

> 5. *Limited Information Collecting Principle*: Excessive data-gathering may create an expert in the problem area, but knowing too much about it will probably prevent the discovery of some excellent alternatives.
> 6. *People Design Principle*: Those who carry out and use the solution should be intimately and continuously involved in its development. Also, in designing for other people, the solution should include only the critical details to allow flexibility to those who must apply the solution.
> 7. *Betterment Timeline Principle*: The only way to preserve the vitality of a solution is to build in and then monitor a programme of continual change.
>
> *Source:* Nadler and Hibino, 1994

Think forward, innovate backward

The conventional way to redesign starts with an analysis of the present system, segments it into sub-functions, and pieces together improvements segment by segment. It starts with what is done today and moves directly to something else that can be done today. This approach rarely results in significant change or improvement.

Change improvement, using the Nadler/Hibino approach called Breakthrough Thinking® (see box), starts at the opposite end of the spectrum. It starts with an idea – or better yet, several ideas – that probably could never come to pass physically, then moves progressively to a target solution or process that's still a 'reach' in today's environment. Here's a summary of the approach:

From the purpose hierarchy the team selects a 'focus purpose'. The consultant then facilitates the generation of a number of ideas that could achieve this focus purpose. The ideas must be from the realm of vivid imagination; mental illusion going to capriciousness; something from the land of fantasy; 'whacko' in Michael Hammer's terms. In this way, the short tether to reality is broken and the team is free to think without inhibitions.

Next, the consultant asks the team to select a few ideas from the fantasy list and 'invent' technology or other enablers to *approximate* the whacko processes. Think of these as science fiction. This approach will generate one or more ideal processes in their absolute perfection, not necessarily achievable now, but possibly achievable someday. Finally, the team selects one of the ideal processes as a target for re-engineering.

As the team analyses the target, the consultant presses for an implementation that will stay as close to the target as possible, sending team members out to test hypotheses and validate concepts. They will be surprised by how much of what they thought was not achievable can be implemented. Technology and knowledge are advancing so quickly that if the team bases a design on what it knows today, its design will be approaching obsolescence by the time it can be implemented. On the other hand, if the team *fictionalises* technology to implement the target and then does some basic research to find out how soon its fiction will be reality, it will discover much more is available or coming off the drawing boards than it knew.

A CEO of a manufacturer of dynamometers, a device to diagnose truck engine performance, was intrigued but not convinced when a group that had never before heard of dynamometers developed a vision for the company that included telling truckers on the road of engine problems before they happened. Although no one in the group had any special technical knowledge, the consultant asked the group to 'invent' or fictionalise technology that would accomplish the vision. Again the CEO was intrigued but said such technology was too far in the future to have any immediate practical value. The CEO was wrong. Not only was the technology available, but some engine makers were already preparing for the vision the group had imagined.

Yet some barriers to implementation will arise. The consultant's role here is to list them and have the team continue as if the barriers don't exist. When all the hypotheses have been tested, the concepts validated and the core design roughed out, the consultant brings out the list of barriers. Some of the barriers will have vaporised or been solved in the core design. For those that remain, the consultant leads the team in barrier 'work-arounds' to preserve as much of the integrity of the target as practical. By deferring discussion of barriers until after the core design exercise, the target isn't killed off by the first couple of negative perceptions.

Prepare people for change

Change programmes involve at least eight system design elements: Purpose, Output, Input, Process, People, Technology, Information and Environment. A design that ignores any one of these elements will have implementation problems. Ignoring the people element is the second greatest cause of change failure. Preparing people for change isn't the same as involving them in the design. In addition to their participation or the team's open communications with them, those affected by the change need to be prepared for it. The consultant's role is critical here.

First, the human interventions in the improvement processes must be as carefully and thoroughly designed as any technological or information interventions, and then clearly documented. Second, the nature of the changes from the current processes – and the timetables when these changes will be phased in – need to be understood. Third, the people who will be affected should be identified by name. If they are to be reassigned, or the nature of their work will change, some retraining may be necessary. This should be provided in the implementation.

The consultant must recognise that change, even what the team might consider *good* change, is traumatic. People have great anxieties and insecurities about change. It almost always involves giving something up. William Bridges (1991), author of *Managing Transitions*, says we must compensate for losses. To paraphrase him, the consultant must ask: 'What can we give back to balance what has been taken away? Is it status, turf, team membership or recognition? If people feel that the change has robbed them of control over their futures, can we find some way to give them back a feeling of control? If the feeling of competence has been taken away when their job as they knew it disappeared, can we give them new feelings of competence in other functions with timely training?'

A consultant working on an acquisition for a client discovered the president of the acquisition candidate was getting cold feet at the eleventh hour. The consultant advised his client to provide the retiring president with office space in the new company. His client resisted; he wanted a clean break. But when the consultant pointed out that the president, although eager to sell his business, was paralysed by the prospect of having no place to go to in the mornings, the client relented. The retiring president got his office space and the acquisition went through. In a few months the president found a new business venture and vacated the office space. The consultant rightly diagnosed the president's cold feet as fear of giving up something that had nothing to do with the sale of the business. The correct compensation to balance the loss was simply providing a place for him to go to in the mornings.

Monitor and control risk

No amount of planning or systematic methods will cover all the risks that could scuttle an otherwise seaworthy improvement programme. The consultant needs to monitor, control and manage risks of failure. This must be done by frequent visits to stakeholders across all parts of the programme. Otherwise the consultant will be listening only to his or her own press, or the press of the team. It's an easy way to get blind-sided.

A consultant discovered in one such visit that management really didn't believe in the vision of a change effort and didn't expect it to succeed. Yet the team was allowed to continue in ignorance pending the arrival of a new manager in the functional area. A visit with the new manager found that he had no confidence in the programme and was planning to proceed independently with a programme he had started in his previous position. When the new manager described his programme, it was so much like the existing solution that the consultant was able to put both together and keep the existing project afloat.

On another series of visits two consultants learned of six competing or conflicting initiatives in the company that were proceeding on independent courses even though the leaders of these initiatives participated in the project improvement meetings. The consultants were able to consolidate these initiatives, and in one case, to bridge a potentially serious gap between the field and company headquarters.

Conclusion

Managing change requires a broad range of skills, constant monitoring and many course corrections to achieve success. The client needs to understand this. At the height of the Total Quality Management (TQM) surge, a CEO called his managers and told them he had been reading about this TQM business. 'Get us one of those', he said. The CEO didn't understand one doesn't plug in a quality programme and expect it to run without incident. Neither are re-engineering or other improvement programmes the kind of engagements where the consultant can simply walk his client through some proprietary method and expect everything to work. Too many things can go wrong. The consultant must be alert and aware of everything that's happening (or not happening) with the programme. He must be an inventive programme manager because if the programme fails he can't blame the client.

References

Bridges, William (1991) *Managing Transitions: Making the Most of Change*, Addison Wesley, Reading, Mass

Nadler, Gerald and Shozo, Hibino (1994) *Breakthrough Thinking: The Seven Principles of Creative Problem Solving*, Prima Publishing, Rocklin, Calif.

3.9

Closing off the consultancy assignment

Barry Curnow

Endings don't just happen

It will have been seen from the discussion in earlier chapters that consulting relationships and projects have lives of their own, with specific stages of growth and development that they must go through. This means that 'you cannot skip steps' because there is a natural organic pattern to how events unfold. It is counterproductive to rush a stage prematurely before the preceding stages have been completed satisfactorily or to omit it altogether.

This means that the ending of an assignment or project and the commissioning or 'signing off' of the work that it has comprised needs to be done properly and at the proper time if the benefits of implementation envisaged in the Terms of Engagement model in Chapter 3.5 are to be realised.

The well-known personal development guru Steven Covey, author of the best-selling *The Seven Habits of Highly Effective People* enunciates as one of his seven principles, *Begin with the End in Mind* and this is nowhere more true than with consulting engagements.

In Chapter 3.5 we described the third of the overlapping cycles as being that of transforming the client relationship. Transformation is used here in the sense of moving through a state of irreversible change to a point beyond which things will never be the same again. Once the chrysalis has turned into a butterfly it can never be a chrysalis again and so it is with endings. They may, and indeed invariably do, presage new beginnings and opportunity for change but inevitably and unavoidably, they signal the end, forever, of the state that went before. And so it should be, since consultants who stay beyond their time are a sign of failure, not success.

A serious business

So closing off a consulting assignment is a serious matter and not to be undertaken lightly. However good or rocky the course of the relationship that has led to that point, the client-consultant interaction will inevitably be very different in future. The final stage of the third cycle is called Professional Implementation and Client Independence. Implementation of the consultant's advice or joint work is both the aim and the outcome of the consulting engagement. It is the essence of what consulting is all about: building the implementation team, getting the right mix of people, styles and skills, between hard and soft, between people and systems, between old and new ideas and ways of working, and so forth. The client and the consultant need to engage in the implementation stage with a joint effort. Experts agree that both the terms of implementation and the expected/desired results have to be clearly defined from the early planning stages to ensure this collective understanding (see Kubr, 1996).

The inter-relationship of responsibility for the ending

Of course, the client is ultimately responsible for implementation and executive action before, during and after the implementation phase. However, in order to be certain of securing the desired benefits from the project, it is not a straightforward question of the consultants gradually withdrawing and the client personnel taking over. Rather a proper closing down of an assignment involves a planned handing over of the different operational batons and responsibility for seeing that certain things happen. Some years ago, the typical modus operandi was for consultants to write an expert report, give advice and then walk away. Implementation rates were low in those days and the consulting report was seen as the final product. Many of them ended up gathering dust on shelves, not because they were necessarily bad reports but because the business of implementation and managing the ending had not been adequately handled. Neither clients nor consultants understand as much as we think we do nowadays about change management and the need to prepare the conditions in which it can take place. This is what a proper ending is for – to prepare the conditions in which change can take place in the client system and the consultants may safely withdraw to other assignments and a new role and relationship with the client under review. Increasingly nowadays, clients have required consultants to be part of and accountable for the success of implementing the changes that their work together defines and prescribes. This requires very careful attention to be paid to the allocation of roles and responsibilities during implementation. On the one hand, the client must become self-sufficient without depending on the consultants; on the other, the consultants must secure effective know-how transfer at the point of hand-over.

Consultant involvement and client activity in the transformation phase

Sometimes for financial reasons (to save fees – often a false economy) or because of a feeling that the consultant has outstayed their welcome, clients seek to exclude consultants from the implementation phase. This is sensible if the task is straightforward and/or if the client has demonstrable management capacity available to ensure that the implementation plan happens in line with the intentions of the project. However, an unthinking project management discipline at this stage can be destructive and inhibit success.

- there should be open and frank discussion with the consultants about different possible avenues to implementation
- the number of consultants on site should be diminishing in number, but regular visits by specialist advisers and trainers could be increased.
- the client should be left with the bulk of the responsibility for the work and just get the consultants to do what only they can do!
- the consultants should be consulted regularly for guidance on progress, but only actually undertake implementation work that is properly the province of executives if expressly asked to do so by the accountable executive – and for a good reason (eg further training) rather than a doubtful reason (client fear of rehearsal, practice or making mistakes)
- key client personnel should have grown and developed as a result of the consulting engagement and clients may properly become increasingly challenging of the consultants when it is time to close down an assignment
- clients will have internalised what the particular consulting firm has to offer and may be hungry for new ideas and new experience.
- clients may start to do surprising things – that is, things that surprise the consultants

All of these are signs that the client is moving ahead and no longer needs the consultants for what they did before, which is to help the client with what to do and how to do it. Now, during the ending phase and the stage that follows, clients still need the consultant but in order to monitor, review and reflect together on the joint work that has been done and on how the client is faring in their approach to implementation. This shift signifies that the client is exhibiting organisational growth and not just struggling for independence from the consultant.

Marking the ending

Different styles of consulting suggest different ways of dealing with the business of ending and closing down the assignment.

Some projects, such as large scale IT or Information Engineering projects, behave according to the engineering mode: there was design and build and then commissioning day comes with a formal, contractual, ritual handing over of the 'car keys' or the entry code to the computer room or the licensed operators pass to the petrochemical plant, as the case may be.

In the doctor-patient model of consulting, client and consultant will have moved beyond diagnosis and prescription to self-medication.

Learning assignments according to the teacher-pupil or training model often attract a formal certificate of competence or licence to operate, traditionally in safety conscious industries like aviation or hazardous materials storage but now in relation to IT systems and protocols. One global consulting firm has a fail-safe procedure whereby no new recruit, however senior, can receive their first pay cheque until they have been signed off as having successfully attended the half-day workshop on how to operate the company's desktop computer protocols!

In the coaching model, the emphasis will continue to be on enabling the client. But if you feel the need to change your coach after working successfully with them for some time, then that is often a sign of having reached an advanced stage in the transformation phase. Whether or not to give in to that temptation is another matter that requires careful reflection and, ideally, a discussion with the coach/consultant themselves. Of course coaches and consultants have feelings too and are not immune to sensitivity to rejection and loss, so these discussions need mature handling and thoughtful consideration.

A most sensitive and delicate relationship negotiation

In our seminars at Maresfield Curnow for consultants and clients we always ask one question of both populations that elicits a near universal answer. We ask seminar groups to consider how a consultant should act when in their professional judgement a major cause of the client organisation problem is that the client representative who brought them in needs to be removed from their current job for the good of the organisation. The consistent response across many different groups, industries and backgrounds is that a good consultant is one who can tell the client who hired him or her that they should go, and for the client to think not only that it is a good idea but that it was their idea! The point here is that the consultant is expected to risk both possible future work and the relationship in order to help the client see and do what is right for the organisation as a whole. And, assuming that the consulting firm has been properly remunerated at prevailing professional rates for the work to date – no special deals or unduly pressurised or awkward compromises on present fees against the promise of future work – then a professional consultant should be in a position to give such difficult advice without fear or favour. This is where external consultants can, and sometimes must, do and say things that deal with sacred cows and taboos, the undiscussables, in a way that internal consultants would find much more difficult without losing the jobs.

Happily, the occasions when a consultant feels ethically compelled to tell his or her principal client contact that they should make an early exit from their job, are few and far between. But what is striking is the consistency of the view as revealed at the Maresfield Curnow seminars of the expectations that both clients and consultants have about what behaving professionally means in such limiting cases.

And similar expectations apply to the business of endings and closing down the assignment. Human nature being what it is, consultants have to trade-off their commercial responsibilities to their firm against their professional responsibilities to their clients. The only way to deal with this is to have serious and repeated (ie not just once in the corridor) client-consultant conversations about how to handle the ending.

A good consultant should have an informed professional view of when a particular engagement is ready to end and the client has a right for that view to be openly discussed.

Similarly, a good client who has really benefited from joint work with a consultant who is having difficulty in letting go will be able to re-frame the relationship into one appropriate for the next stage, one that works for both parties and for the consultant to feel that it is right and proper.

Final thoughts

- the transition of the ending should be marked in some way that celebrates the place and pertinence of the work and how it will be remembered and worked with after the consultants have gone
- internal consultants can be helpful for developing post-implementation proposals
- the nature of the continuing client-consultant relationship should be discussed and not left hanging
- the arrangement for recording, writing up the lessons and communicating the end of an engagement should aim to bequeath a shared understanding of what happened and due recognition of the contribution and progress of all parties

Recognise that the client is going from the known to the unknown and that this causes anxiety. One of the main benefits of working with consultants is that they have done similar projects beforehand and therefore can signal what the client is likely to expect along the way. After the ending, the consultants will not be there in the same way, but before leaving they can and should help the client to anticipate future milestones and put into practice lessons from their joint work about learning and learning how to learn. In other words the consultants will not be on site or on tap in quite the same way in future – although electronic communications make accessibility relatively painless – but hopefully as a result of the assignment client personnel will have learned from and with the consultants about *how to learn* in future. In other words, to have absorbed principles, understanding and experience that will equip them to solve unknown and unanticipated contingencies with relative equanimity.

Above all, endings are about providing the opportunity to build new beginnings.

References

Milan Kubr, *Management Consultancy – a guide to the profession*, 3rd edition, ILO Geneva 1996

4

Key consultancy activities

4.1

Strategy

Martin Whitehill

Two aspects immediately leap to mind when people hear the title strategy consultant. One thought is of a team of 'experts' who sit down with management and help them develop a corporate strategy for the organisation. The other is a vision of 'men of mystery' working secretly upon a merger or acquisition. These may be true but most often strategy consulting work is brought about because an organisation is not performing as it needs to be and an external perspective is required to help define the problem and possible solutions. Strategy consultants are foremost creative problem solvers.

Strategy consulting: a different way of thinking

Creativity is one of the key differences between true strategy consultants and other types of consultants. The majority of strategy consulting work is comprised of performing mostly economic and financial analysis of industries and organisations to define the problem. However, the frameworks and methodologies are to the most part available to all leading business school MBA graduates. Individual consultants or consultancies frequently customise tools and processes to be able to offer a 'unique' value proposition to their clients. Have you ever wondered why strategies of different organisations are so similar? The strategies are put together by staff schooled in similar analytical methodologies.

If you educate thousands of the brightest individuals in leading business schools around the world based upon 'best practice' strategy analysis tools and methodologies, then they are going to go out and come up with similar strategies. The academics even came up with a tool to analyse the similarity of thinking and strategy within the same industry. They call it strategic group analysis!

The analysis may make up 80 per cent of the work but the crucial value lies in the other 20 per cent. That 20 per cent is creativity. Having analysed the problem, a creative strategy consultant can help their client imagine what could be and then ask the question 'well, why not?' A competitive strategy is different from that of rival organisations, not just better.

Most individuals tend to favour specific approaches to thinking. So, some may be analytical. They are often referred to as 'left-brain' thinkers. Some individuals are more creative thinkers than analytical and they are often referred to as 'right-brain' thinkers. Strategy consulting is 'whole-brain' thinking. It is both analytical and creative. It requires individuals who excel at both. That is why, as a rule, the best strategy consultants are not found in those organisations specialising in 'off-the-shelf' solutions. Original problems require original solutions and that requires original thinkers, not automatons. Very few individuals are 'whole-brain' thinkers.

Part of strategic thinking is being able to see the big picture in the future. It is being able to imagine the economic, social and political operating environment in, say, five years time and the position of the key industry players, suppliers and customers in the same time frame. At the same time, the strategic thinker must be able to understand and see the detail at the level of individual functions within the organisation. The strategic thinker must be able to see both the big picture and the functional detail for the organisation in the future and today. They must have their heads in the clouds but their feet firmly on the ground.

More importantly, they must be able continually to swap back and forward between today, the future, the big picture and the detailed function. This is often referred to as 'chunking' up or down, forward or backward. Only a minority of individuals find this easy to do. Most individuals quickly travel to that level at which they feel most comfortable, ie the current functional operation, and stay there. Most individuals are operational thinkers and do not find it easy to think strategically for long periods of time.

In problem solving, there are two types of problem. There are those that are convergent in nature. The solution converges upon a single right answer. These are the type of problem at which 'left-brain' thinkers excel. The other type of problem is divergent. The more information and time available, the more possible solutions can be found. There is no single right answer. Strategic management is full of divergent problems.

This is the nub of strategic management problems. They often deal with variables that are in the future and the wider operating environment. As such, the problems tend to be complex and the data uncertain and ambiguous. Complexity, uncertainty and ambiguity are the three types of variables that most managers discount or avoid because they are the most difficult within which to operate. However, this is the real world and they are not avoidable.

Problem resolution is based upon identifying the cause and effect. If I drop a china cup on to a concrete floor, the effect is that the cup smashes. A clearly visible cause and effect. However, most strategic management problems have causes and effects that are not so closely linked in location or time. If I reorganise an order-processing system in London, it may have a major impact in three months time in Sydney, Australia when they come to print out their performance reports. Most organisational changes have causes and effects not closely linked in space or time.

Fatter caterpillars or butterflies

It is important to understand fully this distinction between operational thinking and strategic thinking. Many solutions have been sold to organisations as strategic necessities when in fact they have only been operational improvements. Operational thinking delivers increased efficiency. Strategic thinking delivers an effective solution. Operational efficiency will deliver ever-fatter caterpillars. Conversely, a strategic solution will metamorphose the entity into a butterfly – a more effective solution that is not just fatter or better.

Operational efficiency is about adopting 'best practice' for each function and process. This requires continuous organisational improvement. By its nature it tends to be continuous incremental change and improvement – more of the same but 'better'. Typical operational solutions in the 1990s were benchmarking, total quality management (TQM), business process re-engineering (BPR) and change management. They became industry standards that every organisation needed to adopt to stay competitive. They were the 'hygiene' level that everybody adopted. Each adoption did raise the bar for new industry entrants but everybody in the industry adopted the standard.

Strategic solutions place the organisation in a *unique* competitive position. The strategic solution enables the organisation to compete in a different way from rivals. The strategic solution creates a unique and sustainable competitive advantage for the organisation.

Sustainable competitive advantage

This is where we reveal the big differences between being different or only better than the rivals. When we contemplate strategic business development, there are two principal approaches. We can try to take existing market share away from our rivals or we can try to grow by expanding the entire market.

Take the yoghurt market. It is a commodity market. One plain yoghurt is the same as another. If it is not possible to compete by differentiating a product from the rest of the market, the choice is to compete based upon lower price. That is why there are rarely high margins in commodity markets. This was the position in the yoghurt market many years ago.

One day, somebody decided to take the cream out of the milk for the yoghurt to sell separately and to sell the low fat yoghurt as a healthy life-style product. Overnight, the market size was doubled as new customers purchased this new healthy yoghurt. They had increased the size of the market 'pie' and not just tried to re-divide the existing pie by cutting price or by marketing spend. But nothing is forever. Very soon others copied and entered this new market and took market share away from the first mover. It is not creatively easy to come up with a solution that expands the total market but the rewards are enormous. The alternative is continually declining margins and overall profitability.

Sustainable competitive advantage requires an organisation to focus upon a distinctively different market offering, delivered to a distinctly different market segment by an organisation optimised to best serve that offering to that market segment. Higher profitability is mostly evidenced by those organisations which adopt a focused strategy. It would require a competitor to duplicate not just the market offering but the whole organisational structure to capture all of the relational points with the customer.

From this, it is clear that strategy is as much about defining what an organisation won't do, so as to stay focused, as well as stating what it will do. The organisation chooses to serve a specific market segment so that they can provide a better product/service tailored to the specific requirements of that sector. The organisation must therefore define the other market segments as ones they will not serve. Equally, the same applies to the product/service portfolio. They focus upon those market offerings which can uniquely add value which will be appreciated by their market segment.

Let's look at the opposite of this strategy. Take most large organisations that have evolved over the decades, if not generations. Over the years they have sought to grow in size by adding to their product/service portfolio and to move into additional market segments. In order to please this wider market with a wider selection of products, the organisations have compromised their unique sustainable competitive position. Their products are less customer-specific and more generic, unless complete new product portfolios are added for each additional market segment entered. The organisational structures, functions and processes have also lost their tight, lean focus. The organisation must service a large portfolio over a wide-ranging mixture of market segments.

So, the organisation has become bloated. It has become a fat caterpillar. Quite often, financial analysis of these companies makes frightening reading. Let's arbitrarily accept the 80/20 rule which will not be far wrong for our analysis. It is common to find that in these organisations about 80 per cent of the profit comes from only 20 per cent of the products. Only 20 per cent of the customers provide about 80 per cent of the profit. First thoughts are: are those 20 per cent most profitable customers, who deliver 80 per cent of the profits, buying those 20 per cent of the products that provide 80 per cent of the profits?

When we graph these phenomena, they show a curve with a steep decline past the profitable 20 per cent followed by a long tail of questionable profitable transactions. Most large organisations have a high volume of unprofitable transaction – unprofitable products to unprofitable customers. The punishment for losing strategic focus. There are other common phenomena as well. It is not unusual to find that 90 per cent of the sales are delivered by only 50 per cent of the sales force.

Major industry players are then surprised when other lean organisations enter the market and focus upon delivering a service tailored to the specific requirements of the most profitable market segments. The bloated caterpillars accuse the new butterflies of 'cherry-picking'.

So, sustainable competitive advantage is as much about what you will not supply, who you will not serve and how you will not serve. It is not only about what you will sell, to whom and by which methods. By deliberately focusing upon the specific needs of a discrete market segment, the organisation will be able to provide a product/service that offers greater value to that market segment in a way that best suits the specific customer. A rival will be forced to copy not just the product but the whole delivery system and organisational structure, as well as capture the customer relationship. The only way to do this is to change the rules.

Changing the rules is the challenge for strategists in order to capture significant market share from an entrenched incumbent. Demographic and, to a lesser extent, lifestyle changes are easily foreseen. To change the rules, an organisation must take advantage of a change that the rival has not seen coming or has underestimated.

The most likely possibility is the use of new technology. By quickly adopting new technology and tailoring their complete business model to take advantage of its benefits over the old or existing technology, an organisation can change the industry rules. The new entrant may be able to capture significant market share away from the industry incumbent before they are able to reconfigure their long-established organisation and its way of working.

There are possibilities other than technology. One may at first appear to be almost impossible: an organisation could influence those with power to change the regulations or industry standards to a set that favours themselves more and not the existing actors. We are all aware of different technology standards that have competed. From a regulation point of view, Chiquita managed to influence the US government to take a case on their behalf before the World Trade Organisation (WTO) to end preferential treatment given by the European Union to Caribbean banana growers. Chiquita won. They changed the rules.

There are other technology rule changers of which many (older) readers will be aware. Bic is a French company that hit the international headlines decades ago with a disposable ballpoint pen. Until they entered the market with their technology for forming plastic, pens were a relatively major consumer investment. It was a durable good. When its ink ran out, a replacement refill was purchased. Bic entered the market with a cheap, disposable plastic pen. Once the ink inside the transparent plastic 'stick' pen was used up, it was thrown away and a new replacement pen purchased. Bic changed the rules so that pens became disposable consumables.

Having captured the writing implements market, they looked for another market in which their competence could be used to change the rules. They came up with the disposable cigarette lighter. Again, the existing product was an expensive metal durable product. They changed the rules. Next, they brought out the disposable razor. Previously, metal razors had been used with replacement blades. Now they produced razors very cheaply in huge volumes that were cheap enough to be thrown away when blunt. Bic looked at how they could use their unique competences in different product markets to change the rules from expensive durable products to cheap disposable products.

The questions are the answer

From this brief overview, it becomes apparent that yesterday's answers are not the solution for a strategy that will deliver a sustainable competitive advantage. Being better is not sufficient. An organisation must also be different from its rivals. So packaged solutions are operational efficiency that everybody will adopt. Original thinkers are required to help organisations develop unique business models.

It is worrying that consultants are accused of learning from an assignment with one organisation and then going on to sell similar solutions to everybody else in the industry. It is worrying because clients can cause this. They demand a consultancy team that knows the industry at least as well as the client themselves. They demand to be served by consultants who have served, and probably will continue to serve, that one industry. In effect, organisations are buying benchmarked best practice. They are buying operational efficiency, not strategy consultancy.

Not only are consultants obviously going to sell a similar solution to maximize their profits to all of your rivals, but how good, how different is your solution going to be? One way of looking at the assignment is that the organisation's management should already be experts upon their own industry. If the organisation has a technical problem, not a strategy problem, then technical experts could be employed by the organisation. If the organisation needs to review its business model and to develop a new strategy, then could they learn quickly from strategy consultants with broad experience across industries?

Many industries face similar problems that may take years to learn and solve independently. For example, there are many similarities between oil, gas, and electricity transmission line companies as well as train companies, telephone companies and transport companies. Airlines have branded separate classes and fares on the same plane and charge different rates according to the time of day and time of year.

Similar strategies have been adopted by the other industries. So, for aeroplane or route, substitute telephone line. They can all learn from each other. On the subject of airlines, why did it take so many years before the frequent flyer club card concept was copied by the supermarkets to reward customer loyalty? Could it be that they were all using industry specialist consultants?

Ask your consultants what they bring to the party in addition to industry knowledge. Many industries are experiencing ever-faster, shortening product and strategy life cycles. Somebody who arrives with a solution to yesterday's problem is not going to be as valuable to you as a consultant who knows which questions to ask to identify tomorrow's problems and solutions. The questions are the answer – not the other way around.

4.2

Marketing

David Hussey

Introduction

Most companies have marketing departments, and the majority of these are staffed by competent people. Depending on the nature of the product, companies may already be using other types of professional service companies, like advertising, public relations and marketing research. So why should there be any need for consultancy help? There is, of course, the very obvious situation of those organisations where there is too little attention paid to marketing, with the resultant effect on the quality of the marketing department; but to assume that this is the only situation where a management consultant can improve performance is to ignore the very wide range of skills and experience which a good marketing consultant can offer.

The client is primarily interested in the value that a consultant can bring in relation to the cost of providing it. Sometimes value can be measured in positive gains, sometimes in the avoidance of profit reducing situations, and sometimes because the cost equation shows that it is cheaper to outsource a short-term task rather than hire in extra people to do it internally.

Marketing can be described as detecting and satisfying customers' needs at a profit but, although accurate, this definition does not reflect the dynamism of markets, the turbulence of the business environment, and the fact that companies themselves change their visions and overall strategies. The approaches, methods and techniques which help companies to analyse market situations reflect these changes. These dynamics are one reason why even those companies with excellent marketing capability can benefit from the objectivity, different experience and up-to-the minute knowledge that management consultants bring to a marketing assignment.

There are situations where companies retain consultants to work on a general basis at board level, or at senior level within the marketing department. Usually such advisory roles are broad, continue for some time, and although the consultant has the resources of his or her firm to tap into, these advisory roles are usually person-specific, going to a person of seniority and standing.

More frequently, the assignment is a definable task, which can be defined both in content and duration. Frequently, the consultancy will deploy a team – the size of which will depend on the scale of the work, the client's deadline and the mix of competencies needed to ensure success. There is also a need to match the seniority, and therefore cost, of the different members of the consulting team to the tasks within the assignment. Sometimes it is appropriate to use a mixed consultant/company team, which may be a way of expanding the knowledge and experience of key employees, and transferring skills to the company.

The following list shows some of the areas where management consultants can provide value to a company. This is followed by a brief description of some of the tools and techniques which may be appropriate to a specific situation. Neither list is meant to be definitive, and the aim is to give some idea of how what consultancies offer can benefit companies with different needs and internal marketing resources.

Some specific areas where consultants can help

Marketing 'audit' of all aspects of marketing activity

One of the problems that besets many companies is that things change, but the activities that take place in the company do not always change to reflect the situation. Things grow up around company policies, and are then seen as immutable when a different understanding would perhaps show that they should be changed. All managers take decisions within the boundaries of their perception, and sometimes what they believe to be a fact is not necessarily true. Even the market research undertaken, and other information which is seen as important, may be decided within this predetermined perception; thus excluding things which are critical. Sometimes, there may be problems of effectiveness, but more often the issue is one of being very effective at something which is no longer as appropriate as it once was.

One way in which consultants can help is by undertaking a complete audit of all aspects of the company's marketing activity. 'The marketing audit is a comprehensive and structured examination of the firm's market and the forces impacting the market, the firm's activities and performance, as well as the processes by which marketing decisions are made. The outcome of a marketing audit should highlight the opportunities and challenges for the firm's marketing and suggest recommendations for improvement, and a plan to achieve superior performance' (Jenster & Hussey, 2001). The sort of problems which I have uncovered through such an audit include:

- several companies which had not recognised that the industry they sold to had begun changing technologically, which meant that the market was disappearing
- a life insurance company that concentrated on segments which had been the most profitable when the general management had served their management apprenticeships, and which had not seen that market changes had opened up some segments with even better prospects
- companies which had once been market leaders believed that they still were, and were blaming reductions in sales on recession when in fact the major cause was market share erosion

Companies can sometimes undertake such an audit themselves (Jenster and Hussey, 2001), but as a minimum, at least one outsider should be attached to the team that carries out the audit to ask the unthinkable questions. An internal audit can only be justified when appropriate people can be detached for long enough to undertake the audit as their sole task, who are strong enough to challenge the conventional wisdom, and have enough standing in the company to ensure that their analysis is acted upon.

Specific investigations

Examples of specific investigations might be the long-term prospects for an existing product; product prospects for a new market; new product evaluation; or the effects of external changes on marketing (such as changing from being a supplier to being a preferred partner in an outsourcing situation).

A typical situation might be an oil company whose research and development people have a prototype product which would reduce emissions from internal combustion engines. Before they can decide whether this is a viable product, either to market or to license, they need to undertake an assessment of the market. Knowledge of the global automotive markets, the industry and its organisation are basic essentials for such a study, supported by knowledge of environmental legislation in key countries. Management consultants are the logical answer to the need to assemble a team with the necessary skills and knowledge.

Another example, with some similarities, is the desire of a company to extend the marketing of its products to a different country. Here again, investigative work is needed before strategies can be formulated, combining knowledge of the target country, the nature of the markets and an understanding of the capabilities of the company commissioning the assignment. Such studies can sometimes be handled internally, but again questions need to be answered about whether the people are available to undertake it, and whether they have those extra skills needed (which may include language capabilities) which make the difference between a good or poor study.

Economic evaluation of marketing driven projects

Not all marketing investigations relate only to marketing capabilities. Any of the examples given above could have major capital investment implications to obtain the physical elements of a distribution capability, IT investment and/or manufacturing facilities. Most consulting firms are able to undertake a full economic and financial appraisal, comparing options and assessing risks. This can greatly reduce the risks of making a poor decision or of moving into a situation where the salami principle has applied: serving the sausage slice by slice, instead of looking at the whole, so that the full shape is never seen.

Marketing aspects of e-business

With e-business the world has moved into a field where there is little experience, but which requires a combination of very specific IT skills and marketing capability in equal measure. The best IT solution will not produce orders unless the customer trusts the site: the best image building exercise will be to no avail if the site is insecure, or if there is difficulty in managing the delivery of the orders to the customer. Some major customers have chosen to implement their e-business strategies in alliance with a firm of consultants, so that the missing skills can be applied in an integrated way.

Outsourcing marketing activities

Outsourcing is a way of gaining flexibility and focus, and it can apply to marketing as well as to most other units within an organisation. It has long been traditional for certain basic services, like retail audits and much other market research, to be outsourced. Modern thinking is that the outsourcing should move beyond such definable task related services to many other aspects of the marketing function. But this usually calls for structural and cultural change, and management consultants can often help to identify what is sensible, and to make it all work.

Marketing plans

Sometimes there is a need to take stock of what the company is trying to achieve, and one way this may be tackled is through the development of a marketing plan. This is rarely something a management consultant should do for a client, but it is something the client can often do a better job of with the help and support of a consultancy. This may be in the structure and process of the plan, in specific investigations to support it, or to provide an objective critique of the plan.

Implementation of projects and plans

Implementation is the forgotten side of strategic marketing management, and may involve planning, project management and change management skills, particularly if the strategies set the organisation on a new path. There is often an in-built assumption that managers will make sure that a marketing plan or new project is implemented, and this may well be a valid assumption for incremental situations. However, all the evidence suggests that implementation is a black hole which gobbles up many otherwise first-class decisions, and this is an area where consultants can help.

Here is one piece of evidence that supports this statement. In 1999, KPMG found that only 17 per cent of mergers and acquisitions increased shareholder value, 30 per cent left it unaffected and 53 per cent reduced it. It would be naïve to suggest that all the problems are caused by a failure to attend to implementation after purchase, but this is the area of greatest weakness. A marketing strategy may not necessarily involve acquisition, but it often does include other difficult change situations and, here too, the general body of evidence is one of neglect.

Application of specific tools and techniques (examples)

There are specific tools and techniques which apply to marketing. Consultants may have more recent knowledge of applying these than a company's own employees because of the larger number of situations in which they work. In addition, many consultants have developed their own approaches, which often make it easier and more productive to apply academic concepts in practical situations. Some idea of the type of tools and techniques in popular use can be obtained from the annual survey by consultants Bain & Co (see Rigby and Gilles, 2000, for an accessible description of the 1999 survey).

Market segmentation analysis

Most companies already look at their markets in terms of segments, but there are increasingly more sophisticated ways of looking at segmentation. Companies that are already using these will not need consultancy help, but there are many who are missing out on new thinking where consultants could bring real benefit.

Customer segmentation analysis

The Bain survey points to the emergence of a variant of market segmentation. This groups customers on various criteria in an attempt to identify unfulfilled customer needs. It involves measuring the profitability of individual customers, and their potential, and finding solutions which enable the organisation to concentrate on gaining leadership in the most profitable areas.

Product portfolio analysis

Not all techniques are new and portfolio analysis has been around for a very long time. It is mainly used to compare the strategic outlook for the various discrete business units within a multi-business company. Typically it is a matrix, which has market prospects on one axis and market position on another. It is also capable of being used at the product level in some circumstances. The concept is easy to understand (see Hussey 1998, pp.309—350), but more difficult to apply and interpret. Good information is needed to plot the positions on the matrix, and someone must have worked out how to use numerous facts to produce a position on each axis. Consultants can advise whether this is an appropriate technique for a given situation, and help in its application and interpretation.

Market migration analysis

Some analytical methods are data heavy, and require a lot of work to collect the necessary information and to make sense of it. This is a spin-off from Porter's five forces (see Porter, 1980 or Hussey and Jenster, 1999). The aim is to analyse the competitors in an industry, particularly those which have been gaining ground and those losing it, and from this to establish the most successful business models, the lessons from which can then be related to one's own company. As with so many of these techniques, consultants can save a company time and wasted effort in undertaking such an exercise, or can help the company establish it as a normal, ongoing procedure.

Competitor analysis

In theory, anyone can undertake competitor analysis, and indeed should do so. My own experience as a consultant is that the outsider brings a methodology which is better for analysis and communication, and I have often been invited into situations where the company's managers considered they did a good job. The methodology forced a logical examination of the quality of much of the information being used (for example if a competitor has annual sales that are greater than its annual capacity, is one of the figures wrong, or is it doing something of which we are unaware?), but also forces a proper consideration of all the important points.

Consultants can be used to help obtain missing information, and are sometimes in a better position to do this than the clients. They can also help set up an ongoing competitor analysis system so that the whole process becomes more dynamic.

Summary

This list could be extended to include many other tools and techniques, like: benchmarking the marketing function; scenario planning in relation to markets; numerous matrix methods of analysis; value chain analysis; and market modelling. However, the need is not to demonstrate everything that might be done, but to make the point that management consultants can help successful organisations as well as those that are ailing. Often consultants should be considered as providing preventive maintenance in order to help the organisation to more profitable growth. If they have to come in for emergency repairs, it may already be too late.

References

Hussey, D (1998) *Strategic Management: From Theory to Implementation*, 4th edn, Butterworth-Heinemann, Oxford

Hussey, D and Jenster, P (1999) *Competitor Intelligence: Turning Analysis into Success*, Wiley, Chichester

Jenster, P and Hussey, D (2001) *Company Analysis: Determining Strategic Capability*, Wiley, Chichester

KPMG (1999) Mergers and acquisitions, a global report, *Unlocking Shareholder Value: The Keys to Success,* KPMG, London

Porter, M E (1980), *Competitive Strategy*, Free Press, New York

Rigby, D and Gilles, C (2000), 'Making the most of management tools and techniques: a survey from Bain & Co', *Strategic Change*, 9.5.

4.3

Organisational change

Colin J Coulson-Thomas

Organisational change is assumed to be desirable and beneficial. Its necessity is taken for granted and many of us uncritically assume that change is invariably advantageous. 'Change management' has become a lucrative area of consultancy. Many managers are assessed and rewarded in relation to the amount and nature of change they bring about.

Anticipating the impact of organisational change

However, expectations of the benefits of change can rise faster than its achievement. Also, many organisational changes are not met with universal approval. Change can be stressful and destructive if mismanaged. There may be both winners and losers – the satisfied may favour the status quo while the frustrated, ambitious and blocked may desire a new regime. Debates may occur in the boardroom between those who are for or against particular changes.

The impacts of change are not always immediately apparent. Some people who advocate particular actions may be ignorant of their consequences. In contrast, the disadvantaged may be very aware of adverse effects. When benefits are widely spread their recipients may not even be conscious of them, or they may lack the motivation to prevent the blocking action of sectional interests. The indifferent or ambivalent may simply 'go with the flow'.

Much will depend upon the purposes of change and the capacity of the people involved to adapt. Directors can make a valuable contribution by questioning the rationale and justification for proposed changes, and asking whether an impact analysis has been undertaken of the likely implications. Are the potential consequences of proposed changes for employees, customers, suppliers, business partners and investors adequately assessed? Are harmful results and implications usually foreseen?

The 'tide of events' can be hard on minorities and tough on the atypical. Over time, once those adopting an innovation reach a critical mass, the provision of alternatives may be stopped. Supplies and spare parts may no longer be made available. For example, since most people have acquired CD players, many albums are no longer available in vinyl or magnetic tape formats. Arrangements should be made to identify and protect the interests of significant, important and disadvantaged minorities.

Introducing changes without thought as to their costs or consequences can do great harm. Many managers lack an 'end-to-end' perspective. Altering a task at one point in a process, or introducing a new activity, may cause problems for those operating elsewhere, either within the same process or in a related or dependent one.

One way of spreading responsibility for determining how much of particular forms of change should occur is to create new markets for the areas in question. Entrepreneurs will set up and launch a multiplicity of them. Early adopters will be able to go ahead without having to wait for an organisational or board consensus to form in favour of a proposal or development first.

Implications of change can be consciously made explicit or surreptitiously concealed. The cynical influence opinions by emphasising the advantages of proposals while playing down their drawbacks. Opposition may be bought-off and neutralised, or even eliminated, by those who are determined to bring about particular changes.

Change can also be disorienting and disruptive, even when beneficial. It may be that people can only take so much of it. Without some variety they may go to sleep, but subject them to too much that is new or unfamiliar and they may suffer stress and become unable to cope. The last change 'initiative' might break the manager's back.

Assessing the impact and contribution of subordinates and colleagues by the amount of change they introduce can sometimes encourage change for change's sake. In reality, the preservation of an existing reputation and core values may be what is required. However, preventing unnecessary activity in order to protect what is important and prevent compromise of beliefs is less glamorous and may be more difficult to evaluate.

The balance between change and continuity

An organisation might benefit from the establishment of new 'guardian' roles. Wise and respected individuals who 'hold true' might be able to protect us from ourselves. Independent directors should perform this duty in boardrooms. Particular attention should be paid to whether changes are resulting in the loss of strategically important knowledge and understanding and whether sufficient effort is devoted to building longer-term relationships with customers, suppliers, investors and business partners.

The board of an organisation needs to achieve an optimum balance between change and continuity. A degree of continuity is desirable for those who crave for something to hang onto in an uncertain world. Companies sometimes attempt to change too much. Is there sufficient continuity for people to have a sense of identity, belonging, direction and purpose? Are conscious efforts made to provide enough continuity for people not to feel threatened and insecure?

The visions and rationales for change that are offered by many boards are excessively general. People should only be expected to make demanding changes for a good reason. Effort should be concentrated where it is most likely to make a difference.

Justifiable changes are those which focus upon the critical success factors for achieving key corporate objectives and delivering greater customer and shareholder value (Perrin, 2000). For example, the key factors for winning competitive bids and building successful key and strategic account relationships in various commercial sectors and professions have been identified in a series of practical reports produced by the Winning Business Research Programme team (Kennedy, O'Connor, Hurcomb, James et al, 1997—2001).

Change may have its opponents and saboteurs so the board needs to be politically astute. Are the directors aware of those who are slowing down, undermining, blocking or campaigning against what it is seeking to achieve? How adequate are arrangements to deal with vociferous and vested interests, and determined but unrepresentative minorities?

Another key area for the board to address is whether people are being equipped to achieve the changes they are expected to bring about. A recent survey of corporate learning strategies and activities reveals that while general 'change' programmes are becoming more common, specific and bespoke initiatives and tools to help individuals bring about particular changes are few and far between. In general, our perceptions and individual and collective actions will determine whether certain changes are beneficial or harmful.

Problems experienced by some can represent business opportunities for others. Thus professionals and those offering specialist services could work on a flexible basis to provide support and outsourced help to start up and transform companies and e-business ventures. The nature of the assistance required can alter significantly as an enterprise changes, grows and develops. Hence, companies that supply people with distinct skills and interim executives are likely to face a growing demand for their services.

Both individuals and organisations will have to distinguish between goals, values, objectives, policies and activities that need to be changed and those that should be continued and perhaps cherished. Some people will 'follow the herd' without thinking or fear being left behind. Whenever a clear majority appears to favour a particular course of action, there is a tendency for the uncommitted to climb aboard the bandwagon.

Members of the majority may be naïve or mistaken in relation to what is in their best long-term interests. The respective merits of different options can also become confused amidst competing advertising and marketing claims. In the case of the battle between video formats, technologies that many considered superior to $V_H S$ (which became the *de facto* standard) were abandoned, simply because they came to command a minority market share.

Views, preferences and priorities can alter as situations evolve, circumstances change and fashions come and go. Nothing is more frustrating than to find that certain options have been forgone because a selected course of action cannot be reversed. After it has been cut down, the rainforest may not re-generate itself. Because their habitat is destroyed, particular species may also cease to exist.

In the age of mass markets and long production runs of identical goods, those who were on the 'receiving end' of 'adverse trends' had every reason to feel abandoned and unloved. With suppliers clambering to get out of declining markets, minority consumers would find themselves under pressure to switch. In many cases, manufacturers would simply discontinue the provision of 'old models' or stop holding spare parts.

An exodus of mainstream suppliers from a marketplace creates opportunities for niche suppliers to fill gaps and exploit 'tail ends'. Some of these will be enthusiasts for the products and services in question. Perhaps there will be enough of them to form owners clubs, open swap shops, establish steam railways or re-stage historic battles. Some companies discover when it is too late that their customers may have more regard for their offerings than most senior managers.

Changes are occurring all around us and may or may not represent challenges or opportunities. Boards and management teams should identify significant trends and developments, consider who are likely to be 'gainers' and 'losers' and assess whether there are alternative offerings which would mitigate undesirable impacts and enable people to take fuller advantage of whatever is likely to occur. Those affected might be sufficiently numerous and motivated to represent a potential target market for products and services tailored to their particular interests.

Sometimes consistently rapid development can be easier to handle than sudden discontinuities in growth rates. Those who ride the crest of a technological wave may feel confident that they are 'in the right place at the right time'. They may come to assume they will have plenty of time in which to accumulate stock options and cash them in before the tide turns. Small setbacks may be masked by a generally favourable trend of events. However, even corporate stars like Cisco Systems that expand at a frantic pace sometimes find themselves facing adverse market conditions and the need to retrench.

Addressing minorities affected by change

Those employed in smokestack industries may become reconciled to change for the worst and accustomed to a succession of bad news. Yet there will be some individuals who stubbornly refuse to give up. So long as actual or potential customers exist, there is hope.

Certain trends continue for longer than others. Some lose momentum, stop and eventually go into reverse. A small minority of like-minded people may be sufficient to safeguard what remains or cause a renaissance. Communities of enthusiasts can be assembled via websites that issue 'calls to arms'. They also enable supporters to co-ordinate responses and allow other interested parties to monitor the progress being made.

On occasion, advance may result from regression to desirable aspects of past periods. Addicts and the ardent may finally determine that 'enough is enough'. The vision of a replica of a steam engine or fully rigged tall ship in sail may stir emotions that could never be reached by anaemic 'corporate communications', a fancy new job title or the latest restructuring.

Astute entrepreneurs look for preoccupations and interests of previous ages that met deep-seated needs and which could be reborn. It will become progressively cheaper and easier to make direct contact with those who share our enthusiasms. With the dramatic growth of the Internet, like-minded people will be able to contact each other and initiate collective action.

Conditions have never been more favourable for minority interests to flourish. Traditional barriers to entry are falling. Systems and processes are becoming more flexible. Many people in developed countries are more prosperous. Because they are healthier and are living longer, they will have more time for further careers, additional causes, new enthusiasms and fresh obsessions. And they will be able to enjoy the results of lifestyle changes.

The future is likely to be characterised by greater diversity, as those who are against certain combinations of changes take positive steps to safeguard what is threatened and re-create what has been lost. Rather than meekly resign themselves to marginalisation, they will actively set out to find locations and establish arenas in which they will be able to live life on their terms. Recognising opportunities to cater for minorities will be a more important skill than the ability to replicate me-too provision.

Corporate leaders will be unable to become directly involved with the many and varied activities that more bespoke and imaginative responses to a greater variety of requirements will require. Corporations need to transform themselves into incubators of enterprise and communities of entrepreneurs. Different venture teams will be empowered and enabled to determine and bring about whatever changes are required to enable them to achieve their objectives and deliver value to their customers.

References

Kennedy, Carol, O'Connor, Matthew, Hurcomb, John, James, Mick et al (1997–2001) 'Winning Business, The Critical Success Factors' series of reports, Policy Publications, Bedford

Perrin, Sarah (2000) *Managing Intellectual Capital to Grow Shareholder Value*, Policy Publications, Bedford

Further reading

Coulson-Thomas, Colin (1997/1998) *The Future of the Organisation, Achieving Excellence through Business Transformation*, Kogan Page, London

Coulson-Thomas, Colin (1999a) *Developing a Corporate Learning Strategy*, Policy Publications, Bedford

Coulson-Thomas, Colin (1999b) *Individuals and Enterprise: Creating Entrepreneurs for the New Millennium through Personal Transformation*, Blackhall Publishing, Dublin

Coulson-Thomas, Colin (2001) *Shaping Things to Come, Strategies for Creating Alternative Enterprises*, Blackhall Publishing, Dublin

Brochures describing the Winning Business series of reports are available from Policy Publications, 4 The Crescent, Bedford MK40 2RU, Tel: 01234 328448, Fax: 01234 357231, E-mail: policypubs@kbnet.co.uk, website: www.ntwkfirm.com/bookshop. All the publications cited can be ordered via the website.

4.4

Organisation and culture change in post-merger integration

Geoffrey Kitt

The immediate post-merger environment in large, complex organisations is a fascinating area of practice for experienced organisation change consultants. It can be likened to being the geologist who finds himself on the rim of the crater when the volcano erupts – it's exciting, but you can get hurt!

Although enterprises have increasingly favoured mergers as a route to enhanced success – however measured – the experiences of many organisations during the past ten years have consistently warned us that merging businesses is a risky occupation. Some risks arise early in the life of the merger – for example, the wrong partner may have been selected, the due-diligence exercise may have failed to reflect the true financial position or too high a price may have been paid. All of these will have an impact on the likely success of the merged undertaking. However, in other cases, even if the merger is founded upon realistic and seemingly achievable goals, the post-integration business will often fail to match the vision upon which the merger was founded and the performance characteristics against which it was justified.

Success or failure in post-merger integration will ultimately be determined by the ability of the merger partners to weld their separate organisations into one. Research has shown that mergers will encounter a range of problems in completing this task. The following are perhaps most common:

- insufficient pace in transition planning and execution
- inability to evaluate realistic synergies
- lack of recognition of challenges to be surmounted in delivering synergies
- ineffective merger and acquisition management
- cultural incompatibilities
- mismanagement of people issues
- divergent management philosophies
- incompatible information technology

Most of these issues can, however, be dealt with, provided that the following basic requirements are dealt with as part of the integration process:

- achieving appropriate pace
- stabilising the organisation
- setting realistic goals for the integration process

Achieving appropriate pace

Merger announcements give rise to expectations, doubt and uncertainty. Decisions must be made and key strategies put in place quickly in order to limit the disruption to all parties to the merger. Amongst the questions requiring urgent consideration, you will need to decide:

- What resources will be needed to plan and execute the integration programme?

- Are there quick wins which will provide early payback and demonstrate a sense of purpose to stakeholders?
- How should we communicate with key stakeholder groups during the integration process?
- How will the impact of change and disruption on customers be minimised and what steps need to be taken to reduce the risk of their loss to competitors less preoccupied with joining two organisations together?
- What technology is required to support the business strategy?
- How much will the integration effort cost?
- How can the desired level of savings be secured within the required time-frame?
- How long will it take to achieve a fully integrated, stable organisation?
- What needs to be done to retain key talent?

Strong resolve is needed to accelerate the decision-making process. There will be a strong temptation to engage in over-lengthy analysis. Decisions within a merger context can be more than usually uncomfortable – they often affect people's jobs. However, there is a lot of evidence that an imperfect but timely integration strategy achieves more than a perfect strategy implemented after delay.

Stabilising the organisation

Mergers are an intensely destabilising influence on their constituent organisations and the people who work within them. Fear of loss of one's job is, to an extent, inevitable and it is therefore unsurprising that productivity and quality tend to deteriorate quite quickly within merging organisations following the announcement of the deal. The effects of these concerns can last a considerable time if the integration process is not well managed.

A number of measures will help to mitigate the impact of this loss of focus. Perhaps the most important factor is frequent, clear and honest communication to employees throughout the integration programme. This communications exercise is non-routine and it is unlikely that normal communications channels will suffice to provide the updates and reassurance which will be needed to:

- get attention focused on ensuring that business activities carry on as smoothly as possible during the transition period
- release capable and willing resources from within the workforce to ensure that integration planning and execution can be carried out to the target timescale

Immediately after the merger, there will be much speculation about the future organisation structure and who will get jobs in it. Appointments therefore need to be made quickly to reduce the distracting impact of this speculation. We often see the impact of lengthy delay. Although the most senior appointments are usually announced quickly, those at second, third and lower tiers are often delayed as a consequence of political infighting and damaging turf-warfare. This has an immensely de-motivating impact and usually leads to the departure of talented and experienced personnel who would have had a place in the integrated organisation and whose skills and experience will be greatly missed.

Differences in organisation culture and the leadership style of the senior management team often cause confusion in the immediate post merger time-frame. Different and often contradictory messages may be communicated inadvertently – usually through behaviour rather than any more formal and explicit means of communication. Though the design of organisation culture is often neglected in the post-merger situation due to a perceived need to focus on more concrete issues, this often has a major influence on the eventual success of the merger.

Setting realistic targets

Notwithstanding the need for pace in driving the integration process, it is as important in this arena, as in any other, to ensure that achievable targets are set and met.

Interested third parties and external stakeholders will be watching progress and will not be slow to give their views on the effectiveness of the integration process – whilst it is still incomplete – if it appears that milestones and interim targets are not being achieved. Loudly voiced opinion will have an impact inside the organisation – potentially damaging the integration process – so it is important to set realistic targets based on a careful assessment of potential rather than simply accept a heroic, yet unattainable, goal. Management of relations with key stakeholders, including shareholders and market analysts, will be of great importance.

Features of successful integration

Successful integration programmes have a number of features in common. These include:

- strong and effective programme management
- a thorough integration process
- careful attention to organisation change issues
- prioritisation of objectives and supporting activities
- a sound business case
- a target model which is designed to enable value creation – not just the achievement of cost savings

Strong and effective programme management

It is arguable that the integration of similar organisations is more difficult than that of dissimilar organisations. Put simply, the latter task consists of the aggregation of two (or more) organisation structures and the elimination of overlapping processes and responsibilities – usually within central services – where these occur. When integrating similar organisations, however, overlaps occur everywhere and the task of rationalisation is therefore much larger.

In order to plan this work successfully and steer it through to completion, strong and effective programme management is of great importance. The corporate programme director will face the task of co-ordinating a large number of projects with a high level of interdependency between them. Teams of employees involved in the work will often be unfamiliar with each other and with key aspects of the processes and structures of the combining organisations. As has been observed earlier, productivity is likely to be much lower than that usually achieved. And, in the early stages of the work at least, there is the likelihood of a low level of trust and, perhaps, limited co-operation and information sharing.

These latter factors in particular distinguish merger integration programmes from more conventional programme management situations. Yet, because in most organisations merger activity is a rare occurrence, it is difficult to find leadership of the integration process with significant relevant experience to draw upon.

A thorough integration process

Successful management of merger integration programmes involves:

- a careful assessment of each predecessor organisation involving all aspects of its business, processes, infrastructure and operations. Once this is complete initial comparisons can be made of the features of each organisation
- this information provides input to the process of developing a target model – a blueprint for the merged organisation. This needs to be completed in considerable detail and, again, will cover all aspects of the business, processes, infrastructure and operations. Once this is complete and agreed then it will be possible to develop the transition plan – a roadmap to take us from our current separate organisations into a single merged entity
- there then follows the task of implementing the plan. Each part of the overall plan is carefully co-ordinated and executed with progress monitored through to completion
- having engineered a single organisation the task is not yet complete, further effort will be required to leverage the anticipated advantages and secure the objectives of the merger

In order to minimise risks, the above steps need to be carried out at the maximum pace consistent with the required level of detail and thoroughness.

Attention to organisation change issues

We have already observed that the human aspects of mergers are not limited to deciding who will go and who will stay. However, it is common for other aspects of organisational change to be neglected in a merger situation. In order to eliminate serious risk of failure of the overall integration programme a comprehensive organisational change programme is required covering five key areas:

- communications and stakeholder management
- organisation culture integration
- carrying out an assessment of readiness to change and intervening where necessary to improve the likelihood of success
- organisation and job design
- re-recruitment of leadership, managers and staff for the integrated organisation from the employee pool of the constituent organisations. This will obviously also involve dealing with those people who will not have a role in the new organisation

The likelihood of a successful transition can be improved dramatically by properly resourcing and prioritising all of these activities within the overall integration programme.

Prioritisation of objectives and supporting issues

Clarity around the strategic intent underlying a merger is of great importance because ultimately this will be what drives the integration process. There is often an explicit need to respond to cost savings targets which may have been made public.

It is rare that any merger will not have, as one of its key goals, the building of a lower-cost organisation. This will not only enable targets for the reduction of operating costs to be met, but it will help to provide products and services to customers at prices which will make it more difficult for competitors to take them away from the newly-merged organisation.

To succeed in the objective of retaining customers, the merged organisation must be able to offer more than just low prices. It will also need to maintain – and perhaps in some areas improve – customer service levels. By continuously reaffirming the overall priorities and outcomes needed from the merger it is possible to ensure that achieving low costs does not by itself – or with the aid of organisational disruption brought about by the integration programme – ultimately sabotage attempts to achieve these objectives.

The development and deployment of a merger scorecard will be an important means of measuring progress against all key and supporting goals throughout the integration process.

The business case

Each component of the transition plan will naturally have costs associated – hopefully to be exchanged for benefits aligned with the achievement of merger objectives. Notwithstanding the scope and scale of the transition, the level of risk inherent in the programme can be reduced by exposing individual projects within the overall programme to careful assessment through the development and validation of a robust business case.

The target model

All too often post-merger organisation structures ultimately reflect the relative weight and political adroitness of predecessor organisations and their leadership. Others look like victims of an ill-considered quota system – some even having joint management in key roles. This rarely works well and is usually the result of over-zealous application of the concept of 'a merger of equals'. But perhaps because of the far reaching changes which they bring, mergers can offer an unrivalled opportunity to review the assumptions underlying the prevailing organisation and business model. To achieve this, most merging organisations will wish to identify and validate the implications of a number of alternative scenarios before selecting a new organisation model. This requires the establishment of:

- a clear, coherent and agreed understanding of the merger strategy, vision and objectives
- baseline information with which to build alternative models
- decision criteria against which to test alternative models

Use of this approach to target model selection will reduce the risk of misalignment between the merged organisation and its objectives.

The role of a strong and resourceful integration partner

Merger integration cannot be treated as 'business as usual'. Leadership must focus intently on delivering commitments, managing risks and limiting organisational disruption. But merger goals cannot be achieved by the leadership team alone. In many cases the resources and experience of a strong and resourceful integration partner can improve the likelihood of successfully transforming the merging organisations into a new entity, capable of achieving lower operating cost targets and, at the same time, creating new value which will enable it to win in a more competitive market place.

In identifying suitable integration partners, merging organisations are likely to value the following attributes:

- *Experience*. Merger is an extremely risky occupation if you don't know what you're doing so you will want a partner who has lots of experience in helping clients – and probably themselves – to achieve the goals of their mergers
- *A strong team*. You will need the advice of professionals for whom the turmoil and ambiguity of a merger is their everyday environment rather than a once in a lifetime experience
- *Access to a proven methodology and underlying toolset*. The need to achieve a fast pace during merger integration doesn't

■ 272 KEY CONSULTANCY ACTIVITIES

allow sufficient time to work everything out from first principles, so you will want access to a proven methodology, templates and toolset to enable you to stay focused on resolving issues rather than designing an integration process
- *Deep programme management skills.* Merger integration is a complex set of tasks so you will want a partner who can successfully manage large, multi-stranded programmes to a demanding timescale
- *A profound understanding of organisational change issues.* Merger leads to loss of performance, personal insecurity and widespread behaviour change within organisations. Whilst this is happening, you're trying to ensure that existing business carries on and, at the same time, persuade your employees to transform the organisation within which they work. Achieving this requires a very deep understanding of the change process itself, the impact of change on people and the means of avoiding or mitigating negative impact where it occurs
- *Breadth and flexibility.* Mergers put a big strain on organisational resources. There are many tasks to complete and much of the work must be carried out to demanding timescales. Because mergers require more, not less, manpower in the short term it's common to find that you are resource constrained. Having access to a partner who can step into the breach, wherever it occurs, helps to ensure that delays don't occur
- *IT skills and resources.* The impact of IT in a merger is immense. Data conversion and infrastructure consolidation often hold the key to realising a high percentage of merger cost savings. As such, the importance of finding a partner who can advise on IT as well as business integration will be an important element in achieving your merger goals.

Many large consulting practices now have M&A integration experience; some even maintain dedicated teams. M&A integration work is demanding, even by the standards of other types of organisational transformation work. Practitioners must be able to maintain pace and focus in an environment which will inevitably be full of ambiguity and confusion. Integration projects sometimes have to survive more than one change of sponsor and, in the immediate post-merger situation, it is sometimes difficult to know who is responsible for what. Individual behaviour is much less predictable than would be the case in a more stable environment; most employees will be more concerned with their future than with their job in the weeks following a merger. Key employees may be tempted away by competitors leaving a knowledge or experience gap which can cause considerable problems, both in sustaining 'business as usual' and in building the integrated organisation.

These factors are a good test of the depth of skill of an individual consultant and of the strength and effectiveness of the consulting team of which he or she is a member. But remember, like the rim of a volcano, merging organisations are a dangerous environment for the slow, inexperienced or unwary.

4.5

Leadership in Corporate Transformations

Philip Channer and Jonathan Reuvid

The old command-and-control corporate hierarchies and 'scientific' management models have given way to new, devolved and empowered ways of running a business. According to consultants Gouillart and Kelly (1995), the transformation of a business, which is now the central management challenge and the primary, if not the sole task of business leaders' is 'the orchestrated redesign of the genetic architecture of the corporation'.

The transformational leader's task – in effect, a dramatic rearrangement of the DNA of the whole system – is the regeneration, over time, of all aspects of a business. Not all transformation programmes are of the same intensity or scale, but they can involve every aspect from redefining the vision, through restructuring where necessary, to the creation of new businesses, and the putting in place of the people, organisation structures, processes and systems to make it work out.

At an individual business unit level, a transformation programme is likely to have an impact, directly or indirectly, on 60 to 80 per cent of employees: redesigning the way they work through process re-engineering; removing layers of management and making them more viable and accountable; providing better information flows or improving teamwork, within and across departments.

The heading-up and direction of a corporate transformation programme, of managing a series of operational and staff functions involved in the planning and execution of the overall project, might once have been perceived as a chief executive's responsibility but are now recognised as a an exercise in leadership, demanding a quite different range of qualities and set of skills.

Often, the scale of change requires a huge, sustained effort, and requires many people to let go of things they held near and dear. In this context, transformational leadership is described by Seltzer and Bass (1990) as 'the process of fostering dramatic changes in an organisation by building commitment to the organisation and its mission'.

Defining leadership

Before examining in detail the leadership role in transformational change, we should take a step back to the established body of leadership theories in order to understand why there is so much interest in what it takes to be an effective leader and how to differentiate between leadership and management.

Few would disagree with the observation of Levinson (1996) that 'leadership is like beauty: it's hard to define, but you know it when you see it'. By the mid-1990s Manfred Kets de Vries (1995) had already identified 70 published definitions of leadership; by now there are undoubtedly many more. Kets de Vries suggests that the current emphasis on leadership reflects the need for 'a beacon in an era of change' and this corresponds to many recorded experiences of corporate transformation in which a leader's ability to articulate a compelling, high-order, utopian vision at the outset of the programme, emphasising the contribution of the individual, was evidently crucial to the successful outcome.

A favourite way of looking at leadership used to be to list all the desirable traits of a leader. This approach dates back to the era when the first large-scale industrial organisations were being created, and the emphasis was on designing, operating and managing these new businesses in a quasi-engineering sense. This 'scientific management' approach required managers, who had an entirely rational set of abilities, to plan and budget, organise and staff, control and problem-solve. The quest for a list of leadership traits was therefore focused on what are now seen as basic skills.

As the distinction between leadership and management was accepted, it was recognised that the emotions were clearly one dimension in which they might differ. For Zaleznik (1992), leaders relate to people in a way that is more intuitive and emotional, and convey a more personal vision through images that excite and inspire. Seeking to contrast the roles of manager and leader, John Kotter (1990) draws the following distinctions:

- where the manager plans and budgets, the leader establishes direction
- where the manager organises and staffs, the leader aligns people
- where the manager controls and problem-solves, the leader motivates and inspires

Defining effective leadership further, Kets de Vries reflects that we would really like our leaders to perform both charismatic and instrumental roles, both perceived as necessary. 'Leaders need to envision the future and empower, energise and motivate their followers. But leaders also have to structure, design, control and reward behaviour'.

Fulfilling both roles is a difficult challenge and one that has to be met at a profound, personal level. As Zaleznik points out, 'a crucial difference between managers and leaders lies in the conceptions they hold, deep in their psyches, of chaos and order. Leaders tolerate chaos and lack of orderManagers seek order and control'.

The role of the leader during transformation

Selzer and Bass describe transformational leadership as 'the process of fostering dramatic changes in an organisation by building commitment to the organisation and its mission'. As a working definition, this will serve well enough but it gives no flavour of the passion and emotional risk-taking involved in delivering effective leadership.

The following are the key elements of the transformation leader's role:

Planning

The prior development of a planned programme using the familiar, comfortable planning tools of mega-project management may give the leader some degree of confidence but is a non-starter in terms of inspiring the organisation. More important is the development of a communicable vision and the strategy and tactics for mobilising the organisation, sustaining the momentum of the transformational journey and handling the pressures and anxieties which will inevitably develop en route.

Mobilising the organisation

So great is our in-built aversion to change that the first challenge a leader generally faces is how to get the organisation out of this state of denial and mobilised in a new direction. To do this the leader usually has to create a 'burning platform', to make it more dangerous to stay put than to move. The leader has to prepare him/herself to play a highly visible role in signalling the danger of standing still, communicating the need for change and personalising the urgency.

Building the vision

A key way to mobilise the organisation is to start building a picture of what the upside might look like. It matters not that the picture is at first woolly and based on intangibles; one task of the leadership group is to evolve the vision statement over time. The challenge for the leader is to gain commitment from a critical mass of those in power to embark on this voyage of discovery.

Personal risk

The mobilising process may be an emotionally draining experience for the leader who may have to take personal risks, as well as accepting accountability to those whom he addresses, in order to set an example for others to follow. In a hierarchical organisation this may involve introducing an openness in discussion and consultation in decision-making not formerly present; sometimes, the leader may need to make a public admission of 'having done things wrong' in the past.

Sending the right signals

Organisations are highly sensitive even to the smallest unintended signal from their leaders. Often, leaders will be called upon to maintain confidence levels by demonstrating personal confidence, although they themselves may feel anything but confident that things are on track.

Holding course

After the initial excitement that accompanies the start of the new initiative, the warm fuzziness may evaporate and exactly how you are going to make that goal is revealed as being decidedly unclear. As the first milestone slips a bit and the benefits case starts to show holes, the leader has to suppress that feeling of panic.

Making the tough calls

Leaders cannot afford to flinch from making the tough calls when they are needed; typically firing those who continue to resist change, usually covertly; even colleagues who have become close friends.

Asserting themselves

For some leaders, the hardest thing is to assert themselves in face-to-face confrontations with colleagues, even when they are hierarchically superior.

Handling anxiety

Leaders have to be able to live comfortably with the risk of not being certain, whether it is making investment decisions on incomplete data, supervising functions they don't understand or betting on the success of key appointments.

Coping with overload

Whatever your energy level, the higher you rise the more certain it becomes that it is impossible to do everything that needs to be done. Given the culture of most organisations, it is easier to progress by compulsive 'workaholic' behaviour than by adhering to an unstressed lifestyle. Feeling 'OK' when leaving something undone is often hard to do.

In summary, leaders have a tremendous impact on change. They can prepare the organisation to step off the edge of a precipice by defining the future, and shaping the emerging vision. They have a critical importance in defining the new culture and role modelling how it needs to be different. Often the leader is required personally to do something different, and therefore the ability and commitment to change oneself can be a critical success factor in moving the organisation along. While a strong intellect and technical ability may be necessary to deliver change, many of the demands are to do with character and 'human strength'.

The changing challenges of leadership

Leaders in the 21st century will need, more than ever before, to be capable of:

- creating and communicating a vision
- providing a binding and compelling sense of purpose
- holding together loose and shifting networks and alliances
- making change happen

Warren Bennis (1996) draws attention to the chameleon-like properties of leaders who have to 'keep recomposing and reinventing their leadership' which presupposes that they 'have enough self-awareness and self-esteem to sense when a different repertoire of competencies will be needed, without being threatened by the need to change'.

The stresses of the leadership role have been identified by Sadler (1997):

- loneliness
- status anxiety (wanting to be simultaneously respected and popular)
- the difficulty of maintaining a personal identity
- the problem of achieving a balance between work and home.

Emotional needs

Change leaders depend on being able to engage the hearts as well as the minds of the organisation. This achievement is greatly helped by an ability to empathise with what people at all levels are feeling, or as Cooper and Sawaf (1997) have put it: 'effective leaders put words into the formless feelings and deeply felt needs of others'.

If a leader needs to engage the emotions of others, they need first to engage their own. It is unlikely that you will arouse strong feelings in others about a change programme, without feeling strongly about it yourself.

Fear of change is the strongest barrier to the acceptance of the need for change; we are conditioned to react to any change as a potential threat and our instinct is to opt for the *status quo*, which seems safer.

For leaders themselves

The leader has to develop or strengthen a raft of personal capabilities to perform his role effectively:

- *Being able to change him- or herself*

    Real change on the organisational level has to begin with real change inside the leader.

- *Surviving turbulence*

  The self-confidence and resilience which enables change leaders to stay on an even keel, whatever the circumstances, is a key success factor.

- *Protecting themselves against stress*

  The ability to put a clear dividing line between oneself and the business when needed is crucial to maintaining balance.

- *Avoiding derailment*

  Avoid psychological risks such as being isolated, or being idealised by the organisation. It is essential to seek mechanisms for keeping in touch with reality.

And for the organisation

- *Role modelling personal change for others*

  Before people at all levels make the necessary change, many will look to the leader as a role model.

- *Forming a fulfilling and creative work culture*

  There will be increasing expectations of personal fulfilment from the workplace (independent of the need to adapt to change); for example, an improved balance between work and relaxation.

Being an effective coach and developer

The future leader's ability to achieve results through coaching will probably become more important. In addition to 'core skills' (such as listening and observation) and 'technical skills' (ability to adapt coaching to the preferred learning style), an effective coach needs several 'personal' skills, according to Eric Parsloe (1995). They include the ability to:

- display sensitivity and empathy and understand the need for appropriate feedback
- establish rapport and good communications channels

- encourage the learners to take responsibility for their own development
- support and build confidence in the learner

Practical steps towards developing the human side

Possibly there is a need to build your and your organisation's emotional capability.

There are a number of steps to achieve that goal, but first we need to clarify what is meant by 'emotional competence or capability'. Our levels of emotional competence are defined by two distinct capabilities:

- how we manage our own emotional capability
- how we use our own capability to increase the effectiveness of our interaction with others

The former depends on a heightened awareness of our own feelings, and enables us to control or limit the impact of our negative emotions. For the latter, empathy is the basic building block for increased effectiveness in working with those around us.

Potential areas of benefit to the leader

There are three levels in the hierarchy of emotional leverage, which may reward a leader who makes greater emotional competence a priority.

- *Greater emotional literacy*

    in an organisation is likely to promote greater emotional well-being through the avoidance of emotional negatives, such as stress and derailment.

- *The level of change*

    The importance of the emotional dimension during change (e.g. overcoming resistance, tapping into deeply held values, harnessing latent energy).

- *At the highest level*

    The potential for maximising the upside of putting in place a culture of co-operation and interpersonal capability, which satisfies both the company's need for creative collaboration and the individual's need for fulfilment in work.

For the business leader, there are always two dimensions: the personal and the organisational. The first relates to the leader's own growth, renewal and development; the second to what they can do for their organisation as a whole. But the two dimensions are interrelated. As a survivor of the transformation of General Electric (GE) under Jack Welch noted, 'if that change agent had not been able to change himself, how could you trust him to change the company?'

The personal dimension of self-change

The good news is that we can change ourselves. As Daniel Goleman (1998) says, 'All emotional competencies can be cultivated with the right practice'. At a more challenging level, because such learning is experiential, not only does it take time, but also a number of conditions have to be right for it to succeed.

Much has been written about self-change, and there are many approaches; however, whatever route is taken, the components are broadly the same:

- take stock and begin to build self-awareness
- identify change needs and set goals
- practice
- ask for feedback
- make sure you have coaching support throughout

The organisational dimension: an emotionally healthy culture

As Claude Steiner (1997) testifies, the power plays, subtle and otherwise, and secrets present in most organisations can turn the workplace into a 'minefield of emotionally illiterate, toxic transaction'. Once again, the biggest barrier is 'fear, a pervasive emotion in organisations today'.

At the very least, a leader should care enough to prevent emotional ill-health in their organisation and to create, as far as possible, a culture which recognises and manages the downsides of stress, or of dysfunctional, internal conflict. The influence of personal example is extremely powerful, for good or bad. How a leader conducts him- or herself will have the biggest single influence on whether the organisation takes the subject seriously.

This chapter is a linked series of extracts from "Emotional Impact" by Philip Channer and Tina Hope, first published by 2001 Palgrave, Basingstoke, Hampshire, to whom the Editors offer their grateful thanks.

References

Bennis, Warren (1996), 'The leader as storyteller', *Harvard Business Review*, January/February

Cooper, Robert and Sawaf, Ayman (1997), *Executive EQ*, Orion

Goleman, Daniel (1998), *Working with Emotional Intelligence*, Bloomsbury

Gouillart, Francis J, and Kelly, James N (1995), *Transforming the Organisation*, McGraw-Hill

Kets de Vries, Manfred (1995), *Life and Death in the Executive Fast Lane*, Jossey-Bass

Kotter, John P (1990), *A Force for Change: How Management Differs from Leadership*, Free Press

Levinson, Harry (1996), 'The leader as analyser', *Harvard Business Review*, January/February

Parsloe, Eric (1995), *Coaching, Mentoring and Assessing*, Kogan Page

Sadler, Philip (1997), *Leadership*, Kogan Page

Seltzer, J and Bass, BM (1990), Transformational leadership beyond initiation and consideration, *Journal of Management,* 16: 693–703. Cited in Ashford and Humphrey, 1995

Steiner, Claude (1997), *Achieving Emotional Literacy*, Bloomsbury

Zaleznik, A (1992), 'Managers and leaders: are they different?' *Harvard Business Review,* March/April, pp. 126–35

4.6

Coaching in management development

Myles Downey

Over the past ten years, coaching has found its place in the business lexicon. The business section of almost any bookshop will have at least one book on coaching. An article on various aspects of coaching appears in the press on, it seems, a weekly basis. There have been two international conferences on coaching in Europe in the last year and many smaller local ones. Many people have a coach – in the city of London it has become as obligatory as the Porsche as a status symbol. In many organisations it is no longer enough to be a manager; you must be a coach as well.

There are a number of factors behind the emergence of coaching but this is not the place for that discussion. Suffice to say that the pressures of today's business world have placed a higher demand on individual performance and, increasingly, on learning. Coaching is one way of achieving improvements in these areas.

Coaching occurs in the business world in two forms in particular. The first is known as Executive Coaching, or Performance Coaching. This is typically a one-on-one relationship with a professional from outside the organisation that lasts anything from a few weeks to a year. The second form is as a critical element of the line-manager's role where the manager uses coaching skills to help a subordinate perform, learn and develop. There is a third, less frequent way in which coaching appears in the workplace and this is in the form of a tutorial on a single, specific topic, often for an executive who is 'too busy' to attend a workshop.

This chapter is concerned with Executive or Performance Coaching as it takes its place alongside other more traditional management consulting disciplines. There has been a proliferation of agencies providing these services, either as 'boutique' consultancies, as off-shoots of larger international consultancies and training organisations or as independent coaches. This expansion of coaching is very exciting for the providers but is something of a headache for the buyers. Potential clients are faced with a veritable minefield, splattered with the confusion that might be expected in an emerging discipline. This confusion comes from a number of factors:

- the people offering coaching come from a wide variety of backgrounds; from the psychological and psychotherapeutic disciplines; from training and consultancy; from sport; from 'popular' psychological disciplines and from the business world itself, while some choose to engage in a second career to share their experience
- the offerings vary considerably; from programmes lasting a few weeks to those lasting a year or more; from programmes whose content is driven by the provider's background to those where it is driven by the needs and interests of the participant
- there are no agreed standards, principles, or ethics. There are, for instance, quite differing positions on who the client is; is it the person being coached or their employer who is paying the bill? The answer has a major impact on issues such as confidentiality and information that the employer might want to have access to.

In this scenario it becomes very difficult to choose a coach or even to decide if coaching is the kind of intervention that is needed for the individual or the organisation.

A Definition of Coaching

Not surprisingly, given some of the things that have been said earlier in this chapter, there are many definitions of coaching. One that has some currency is:

Coaching is the art of facilitating the performance, learning and development of another

Coaching in business must ultimately be concerned with *performance*. If the intervention does not impact on the results that the individual achieves then it is a waste of time, money and effort. This may seem a terribly obvious statement but I know of one blue-chip organisation in particular where, after two years and many hundreds of thousands of pounds the organisation could detect no measureable benefit.

A coaching programme must begin with clear performance goals. Such goals may be related to the achievement of business objectives, the execution of a specific project or task or, more generically, greater effectiveness or efficiency. *Learning* is another potential outcome from coaching and is arguably at least as important as the immediate performance because future success is dependent upon it. The distinction between learning and *development* is that while you clearly need to learn in order to develop, learning as used here refers to a broader domain of learning such as learning how to approach a new task or process or learning a new skill, while development refers to personal growth and self awareness.

The word *facilitating* is used in this definition to suggest that the person being coached has the capacity to think, to have an insight or creative idea themselves. The role of the coach is to help them explore, to gain a better understanding, to become more aware and from that state to make a better decision than they would have done otherwise. It is not the role of the coach to do the thinking for the person being coached.

Next, *art*. It is true that there is an emerging 'science', some tried and tested approaches, but the notion of art suggests that the experienced coach can move beyond the rules and fully engage with the person being coached, allowing the intuition and imagination of the coach to play an occasional but useful part.

There is a further distinction that is important to understand and this is the distinction between directive and non-directive coaching. Directive coaching (the equivalent of 'didactive teaching' in academic studies) means just that: to direct or to instruct. It is what we are most familiar with. Teacher, boss or sports coach, the coach is the expert and it is their job to impart this expertise to the person being coached. There are clearly times when the coach does know and when their expertise is of use but there are limitations to this approach. The biggest limitation is of course the coach's knowledge – if they don't know, they cannot help.

Non-directive coaching is again just that; the coach does not direct, instruct or impart their wisdom. The non-directive coach realises that each individual is endowed with an in-built capacity to learn; a learning instinct maybe. For evidence of this look to how you learned to walk. There was no parent there issuing specific instructions and giving directions. The parents rather trust that you will learn for yourself. Unfortunately as the pressure builds (school exams etc) parents forget this and start trying to teach, become more and more judgmental and the inherent pleasure in learning is lost. The non-directive coach trusts in this learning instinct and through careful listening and questioning and the creation of a non-judgemental environment helps the person being coached to think issues though for themselves, come up with new ideas and identify appropriate actions.

Non-directive coaching has huge benefits. Firstly, the process is not limited by the coach's knowledge. I occasionally give golf lessons and these are frequently better than the tennis lessons I also sometimes give. What may be difficult to grasp about this fact is that, while I am a good tennis player and a qualified tennis coach, I have hardly ever hit a golf ball and have no golf teaching accreditation. The capacity of the coach to create an environment in which people can learn allows this phenomenon to occur – usually with remarkable results and a lot of pleasure. A further benefit of the non-directive approach is the confidence that the person being coached gains from the process. They see that they have a capacity to be more effective; that it was their own idea and that ultimately they are not dependent on the coach.

Many people profess to operate in a non-directive manner, also known as a 'client centred' approach, but in reality very few actually do. Either the distinction is not fully appreciated or the coach gets too much satisfaction from solving the problem for others and enjoys the dependency this generates.

Tim Gallwey (1999) talks about coaching as something that 'must be learned mostly from experience. In the Inner Game approach, coaching can be defined as the facilitation of mobility. It is the art of creating an environment, through conversation and a way of being, that facilitates the process by which a person can move towards desired goals in a fulfilling manner. It requires one essential ingredient that cannot be taught: caring not only for the external result but for the person being coached'.

I find the word mobility fascinating. It suggests that the coaching leaves the individual being coached with the capacity to move but makes it clear that the choice to move rests with them.

Before I go on to give some specific example of how coaching can be used in organisation let me say some things about what coaching is not:

- coaching is not the application of psychological or psychotherapeutic disciplines in business. It is true that some of the skills are the same and some of the techniques and methodologies can be applied but the workplace is not the place for these activities
- coaching is not training that is delivered on a One-on-One basis
- coaching is not Neurolinguistic Programming or Transactional Analysis or Transformational Technology or The Inner Game
- coaching is not a philosophy
- coaching is not 'Life Coaching'

While coaching may borrow from and be informed by some of the above it is a skillset in its own right that is focused on performance and learning.

The use of executive coaching within an organisation

The definition of coaching provided above is fairly generic and could be applied in many situations and environments. It is relevant for teachers, sports coaches, managers and Executive Coaches. Some situations in which Executive Coaching is commonly used are outlined below.

One-on-one performance coaching

This is perhaps the most common form of coaching. An individual agrees a number of performance goals with a coach, and they then work together to achieve the goals. The length of the coaching programme is dictated by the time-frame in which the goals are to be achieved. The goals are often drawn from business objectives, projects and other tasks and can include things like improving working relationships and personal effectiveness.

An example

A director of an international pharmaceutical company was charged with re-organising the European distribution network. His goals included:

- delivering the project on time and within budget
- maintaining the performance of the existing system during the change-over
- building a team with representatives from each country involved
- becoming more effective so that he had a better balance between home and work
- learning to work with the various stakeholders so that they became allies not detractors

One-on-one development coaching

This is very similar to the above. Engagements of this nature are concerned with the development of more personal skills and behaviours and may involve gaining a deeper understanding of the individual's beliefs, attitudes and motivation. Many of the practitioners in this field will have a psychological background and will use a variety of assessment methodologies and instruments. Programmes are typically longer than for a performance coaching programme, although I believe this is because in many cases the coaches are stuck in a more clinical or therapeutic model and, in fact, the programme need not be so long.

An example

A partner in a consulting firm who, while being intellectually exceptional, found that other consultants tried to avoid being on his projects. Goals included:

- developing a leadership style that was less aggressive
- becoming more adept at helping/facilitating/coaching
- becoming less obsessive about the need for solutions that were 100% correct

Team coaching

Team coaching involves working with a group of people that share a common purpose, task project or set of goals. An initial part of such an engagement will typically involve building the team itself and then focusing on the performance goals.

An example

A small team of seven was charged by their organisation to create a telephone and internet bank from scratch. Goals included

- building a robust team in which individuals could be open and creative, take risks and be supported
- generating a vision for the new bank
- creating a strategy for the delivery of the vision

The strategic use of coaching

Organisations are increasingly using Executive Coaching to support senior individuals during major change programmes, particularly programmes that involve behavioural change around issues such as leadership, management style etc. This can be a very effective use of coaching as a kind of critical mass can be built up, with a number of people developing in the same direction at the same time.

An example

In a not-for-profit organisation, a new chief executive launched a change initiative to make the staff more outward looking and client focused and to adopt a more facilitative management style. The eight most senior executives engaged in a coaching programme where each individual developed personal goals congruent with the purpose and objectives of the change programme.

Three questions to ask a coach

The following questions are designed to help assess the professionalism of a prospective coach:

- *How do you propose to measure the success of the coaching?*

Answering this question convincingly is one mark of a competent professional coach. It can be difficult to measure success because some of the results are so personal. Having a set of goals that are generated between the coach and the person being coached and include input from a representative of the employer organisation (HR manager or line manager) is one option. Such goals can be reviewed at the end of the programme. Another option is to collect feedback from colleagues before and after the coaching programme. Finally, many organisations have performance management systems that can also be used to measure changes in performance and behaviour.

- *Which party is the client, the person being coached or the employer organisation? How do you serve the interests of both parties?*

Professionals with a background in, say, psychotherapy will tend to view the person being coached as the client. I believe this is not right, in most cases at least. Where the employer organisation is paying the bills and the coaching is designed to help the individual achieve business goals the organisation is the client and has certain 'rights'. A representative of the organisation will want to know what the intended results of the coaching programme are and may want to make some suggestions as to those intended outcomes. At The School of Coaching we typically generate a set of programme goals with the person being coached. Some of these goals are private and are kept between the individual and the coach; others are public and are passed to the individual's manager and a HR representative for input and feedback. The goals are revisited at the end of the programme. This ensures that the best interests of all parties are served.

- *Do you have supervision and if so in what form?*

The notion of supervision is borrowed from the various 'helping' professions from psychology through to counselling and refers to a relationship between the professional and another, usually more experienced, colleague. The purpose of supervision in coaching is to ensure that the best interests of the individual being coached and the client organisation are protected and that the coach is supported and continues learning. Very few coaches have this as a regular feature but it is a key feature of a professional operating as a coach.

- *What training have you had?*

A number of organisations have emerged in the last few years that provide training for coaching. Most of the reputable firms operate a kind of apprenticeship model. The quality and depth of the training (if any) will give a strong indication of competence.

Let me finish with an endorsement of coaching. In a business world, where there is an ever increasing demand for results, higher performance and efficiency and the impact of these demands on the human beings who must deliver on them is to all intents and purposes ignored, coaching is a route to helping people achieve more – but in a fulfilling manner. And perhaps to bringing a little humanity and joy to the workplace.

References

The Line-Manager's Role and *The Place of Coaching*, both available from The School of Coaching
Downey, Myles (1999), *Effective Coaching*, Orion Business
Gallwey, Timothy (1999) *The Inner Game of Work*, Texere Publishing

Supporting employees across the world

Michael Reddy

Introduction

Consultants may take it for granted that levels of support for employees are rising and will continue to rise steadily for the foreseeable future across the world. The thrust behind this growth is three-fold.

The first is a growing appreciation, most evidently among hi-tech and financial companies, of the true value of certain individuals to the business in terms of retention of intellectual capital, to the point where attempts are now being made, for example in Sweden and Japan, to quantify such human capital as part of the company's asset value.

The second is a desire, particularly but not uniquely among American-led multinationals, to match operational quality controls across the world with uniform levels of support. Companies such as Dupont, with a zero-error philosophy, or others wishing to become the employer of choice within their own market, or any organisation which has identified retention as a key component of strategy – all of these will be looking to international market-leaders in the domain of employee support.

The third is the growing army of employees, among them key management and technical personnel, who are involved in cross-border activities. These often entail frequent travel and/or may require them to adjust their domestic work schedule to meet the demands of clients in different time zones. International couriers, press agencies, airlines and transport or distribution companies are only some of the more obvious members of this group who will be looking to international management consultants for guidance.

Two further aspects may be noted with regard to companies in this group, one of them being the threat to employees' work/life balance and the consequent need to provide protection and support to their families as well. The other is the more potent threat of medical and psychological vulnerability for frequent travellers and, indeed, even physical danger.

All of the above has given rise to a requirement to find providers of employee support services with international outreach. One such provider organisation has over the last twelve months dealt with passengers and crew of an airline disaster, terrorist activity including hostage-taking in three different parts of the world (Eastern Europe, Africa and the Far East), a maritime accident in the Gulf of Mexico, an on-site explosion on a Middle East oil installation, a diplomatic incident in one of the former Soviet Republics, and numerous (over a thousand in the course of a year) critical incidents and emergencies on a smaller scale throughout the world.

Such instances are sufficiently frequent to have persuaded some organisations with similar needs to form consortia in order to leverage better rates from providers. The consortia are sometimes formed by organisations from different sectors, but occasionally they are comprised of groups of companies within the same sector on the basis that a single provider will develop a sharper understanding of the special needs of that particular market.

The breakdown of what follows into five segments is somewhat arbitrary but will give the international management consultant a flavour of the kind of services which are now regularly being deployed.

Capitated employee support services

The most basic and all-embracing support mechanism used by many organisations, sometimes carrying the word 'counselling' in its title, is most often packaged as an Employee Assistance Programme (EAP) and boasts a fifty year history. It may carry a similar title in different locations (in Hispano-America, for example, it is usually called *Programa de Apoyo a Los Empleados*). Part of the impetus behind the accelerating growth of this particular approach to employee support is the wish among many American multinationals to harmonise such systems worldwide as a means of gaining assurances that providers work to similar service delivery agreements and standards. Global providers in this area are still relatively few and are likely to be based in the USA, UK or Australia, with working alliances of various strengths between them.

An Employee Assistance Programme usually offers employees a 24-hour telephone helpdesk service with the capacity to provide information and helpful support across a wide range of topics including legal, family, financial, health and consumer matters, as well as offering a number (around three or four) of face-to-face sessions to deal with more personal, emotional and relationship matters. It will also provide support to managers and offer useful statistical data of usage to the employer.

The EAP 'industry' in the USA has until recently kept the developing work/life balance providers at arms length, and vice versa. But this is changing and a UK-based EAP provider will historically have always included work/life balance components. The better providers will have a training and consulting capacity as well. As implied above, such services are usually invoiced on a per capita basis, which for local reasons often varies considerably, eg, US$25.00 in the States, £30.00 in the UK, SF100.00 in Switzerland, etc.

> **Example**
> Kathy is First Class Cabin Crew with a major airline. She comments on the EAP of the airline: 'It's a marvellous service because you can feel terribly isolated on long haul, and pretty helpless at 8,000 miles distance, with a 3-year old at home. The counselling service is a godsend. They don't only help with personal problems, as they did for me and my husband last year, but they have a huge amount of practical information and guidance – on legal and financial matters, and health and consumer stuff and money management, which the whole family can use. They've kept me flying more than once.'

Emergency psychological and human resources services

These may well be offered by the same national and multinational provider companies as for capitated employee support services above, but they are designed to address *ad hoc* situations which arise in any organisation from time to time and may vary from sharply deteriorating performance or behaviour to conflict situations, and from small-scale industrial accidents to full-blown crises. A substantial provider will be anticipating and resourcing between two and three such incidents per day throughout the world, and will be dealing with problems which are either outside the capacity of local human resources, line management and occupational health, or which in-company specialists will prefer to outsource for a variety of reasons – such as transport accidents at some distance from the company offices, armed raids, nightclub and forecourt violence involving employees, and so on, as well as large-scale disasters such as civil unrest, wars and earthquakes.

This kind of *ad hoc* assistance is usually contracted on a retainer plus fee for service basis, and is normally set in motion by referral from a senior executive.

> *Example*
> Keith works for an international distribution company and flies frequently. He was unfortunate enough to be caught up in a hijack and, though released quite quickly, was disturbed by the incident. A global critical incident provider on retainer to his employer got to him almost immediately. Keith's comment was interesting. Not only was he grateful for the direct help which he says enabled him to regain his balance rapidly, but 'that was the first time I knew the company cared. The whole thing was b****y brilliant and I wrote to the boss to say so.'

Expatriate support

There is a growing need for expatriate support in both traditional forms and in more recent adaptations. Conventionally, where an executive is given an overseas appointment for a relatively lengthy stay the family is likely to be relocated as well. It is common wisdom that in these circumstances 'failures' are as often due to the family unit as a whole rather than to the individual executive, despite seminars and a wide range of acclimatisation mechanisms which are usually offered. Such failed assignments are costly and have led many multinationals to look for more robust testing (with titles such as 'cross-cultural adaptation assessment') where individual and family dynamics are taken more fully into account.

Alongside this historical expatriate profile, a new breed of international executive is evolving with no less need of support, who with the increased mobility and ease of travel 'commutes' rather than relocates. The needs of this newer breed of international traveller will be for stability and protection of the home base rather than the establishment of a new one overseas. This is an additional attraction of the Employee Assistance Programme given that it may be extended to, and often already includes, close family members (spouse and dependants living at home) who may turn to the service for help in all sorts of daily and urgent situations. This is a particularly valuable contribution to the travelling executive's peace of mind.

Expatriates have traditionally been the focus of attention from the perspective of the home country as the main source of support and assistance. But with the development of locally provided services, complementary services have appeared, often under the title of '*in*-patriate services', tasked with welcoming the traveller into the host country.

> **Example**
> A senior police officer commented that 'I had to be all over the world on one case, a particularly unpleasant one at that. It had started in the UK and I had already had a couple of sessions with an independent and confidential counsellor paid for by the Force as part of a scheme to support officers under exceptional pressure. I'm as good as anyone at keeping a stiff upper lip but just having someone local to download with in most of the places I had to visit – or by phone and email from time to time – gave me the sense of help close at hand if I needed it. In fact, I needed it very little but the fact of it just being there made all the difference. I told my superior officer afterwards that if it hadn't been for this support I was sure I would have gone off 'sick' at some point or needed to come home or developed a 'back problem'. As it was, I didn't miss a day's work. It was reassuring too that my wife also had access to the service if she needed to while I was away.'

Employee benefits

There has been a parallel shift in the pattern of employee benefits towards more substantial support which, while retaining their normal shape in the form of childcare vouchers, eye vouchers, uniform vouchers and the like, is seeing the rise of 'concierge' services which offer the busy executive, whether an overseas commuter or not, the help of a designated 'Agent' or 'Lifestyle Manager' who will (if the executive wishes) almost 'run his or her life'.

Nothing is too much trouble for the agent of some of these relatively new but fast-growing firms, whether it is booking a holiday, recommending a restaurant or buying a house, having the plumbing upgraded, getting the car serviced, delivering flowers to loved ones or key-holding in the executive's absence. Also, there are special services aimed at *in-* as well as *ex*-patriates. The cost of tailored 'concierge' services ranges from a retainer of £300 to £2,000 per person per annum, with all individual items (eg, attendance of the plumber) charged additionally at cost.

> ***Example***
> Such services are on the whole too new for formal evaluation but many individual executives are enthusiastic about them, and clients come from across a wide spectrum of organisations. Frequent comments are 'I never expected I would ever rely on such help but it's changed my life', or 'I can't tell you the load it takes off my mind. I never know when I'm going to be home, all sorts of important domestic things simply weren't being done...etc., etc'. Such services are at the cutting edge of attempts to offer exceptional add-ons to salary and bonuses, and they are seen as a further inducement to loyalty among staff – professional, financial and hi-tech especially – where competition for key employees is intense.

The addition of psychological help is a natural add-on, through telephone and face-to-face assistance, again as a regularly available service to the agent's customers, as a fall-back in sudden crises and as a further means of support to the whole family. A number of international concierge services now see an Employee Assistance Programme as an integral part of their own service, especially where the provider is well resourced throughout the world.

Specialised services

A number of specialised international services is likely to grow in the wake of steady international development, especially audits of various kinds and under a variety of titles – cross-cultural audits, employee attitude surveys, employee commitment surveys, stress and mental health assessments – particularly where an organisation wants to measure differential impacts of corporate change programmes across countries or regions.

Example

This is true where (for instance) a specialist accountancy or investment firm has re-structured, as many have done recently, in such a way that overall responsibility for one particular global product/service may be located in New York, another in Singapore, London, Brussels, and so on, where previously such services and products were fragmented across the globe in regional silos.

Conclusion

The field of employee support on a global scale is not only growing rapidly, it is also changing in the direction of combining and melding a number of the elements described above. Thus a human resources or employee benefits consultancy may be finding that their professional base is too narrow or too geographically restricted on which to build a self-standing business and are seeking alliances and mergers with – for example – Employee Assistance Providers. And vice-versa. Similarly it has already been noted that there is a synergy with very little overlap between an EAP provider and a 'Concierge' or 'Lifestyle Management' service, with the two companies together in a position to make a joint proposal to a potential client. Whether or not the Employee Assistance Programme emerges as the core 'envelope' for many or all employee support services remains to be seen.

It may certainly be anticipated that the delivery of a wider and wider range of employee support services will develop in the direction of partnerships, interlocking contractual relationships and joint ventures. Employee support is a rapidly expanding corner of corporate life and an additional opening for the international management consultant.

4.8

Communication consultancy

Colette Dorward

The growth and development of communication consulting

Much has changed over the last decade in the consultancy marketplace, but nowhere has that change been more marked than in what is now known as the discipline of organisational communication. Ten years ago there were no specialist firms offering advice or support in this area and few of the big firm 'one-stop-shops' had a dedicated practice within their consulting portfolio. Today a broad spectrum of consultancy offerings is available, from the practical to the strategic, and we have also witnessed a parallel emergence of seasoned communication professionals within client companies. These individuals are typically expert in elevating communication high up the management agenda and in cherry-picking the appropriate advisors to support the strategies and management initiatives of their corporate paymasters.

In fact, in some parts of the world, the quickest way to find your way through the communication consulting maze is just to hire one of these professionals onto your senior management team, sit back and reap the benefits.

Of course, the discipline of corporate communication is not equally developed in all parts of the world. English speaking countries, on the whole, tend to have more specialist offerings. This is partly due to the huge North American influence on the expanding power of consulting firms generally, and partly due to the prevailing social, cultural and regulatory conditions, where traditional methods of collective bargaining and union representation have largely broken down and where the question of who is the 'buyer' and who is the 'seller' in employer-employee relationships is often unclear. Many sectors are experiencing a reversal of the traditional power structure on which large Anglo-Saxon corporates have been able to attract and retain, in effect, whoever they choose.

In these organisations in which a more inventive approach is necessarily being adopted to the attraction, retention and productivity of their people, the communication buzzwords of today are 'employer branding', 'cultural change', 'winning the war for talent' and 'capitalising on diversity'. Because these are largely concerned with what people feel about their employer and their work, they have come to be grouped principally under a communication – rather than a human resources or change management – umbrella.

What kinds of advice and services are available?

This varies hugely by geography and prevailing culture. In both the less developed and the more truly social democratic economies, the service offerings that tend to predominate are:

- *Employee communication support:* the provision of professional services in internal publications, intranets, film, video and event management. Some firms will help you identify your employee communications needs, develop an integrated communication strategy and undertake the requisite resource planning. Others restrict themselves to the provision of the creative, journalistic,

production and project management talents that can enable clients cost effectively to outsource as much as possible
- *Co-development of internal and external communication strategies:* the provision of advice, research and practical development work to ensure that messages communicated to and stances taken with all stakeholders – from regulators and pressure groups, to customers, staff and shareholders – are at least consistent and at best mutually reinforcing
- *Internal marketing initiatives:* advice and practical/creative implementation support for specific corporate/organisation-wide campaigns such as relocations, changes to employee working conditions or quality improvement programmes.

The client for these services is typically the corporate communication or employee relations function.

In the larger and/or more complex economies (and typically in those with an Anglo-Saxon management style), there is a distinct and increasing trend for the deployment of strategic thinking about how an organisation communicates with itself and its key stakeholders as a core part of the process of management and of the ever-present need for organisational change. Here the labels applied to different types of consulting activity are as numerous as the number of firms professing expertise in the area. They typically comprise advisory, facilitation and management development activities for Boards and a range of senior line and functional executives, and can be categorised as:

- leadership development and coaching in the deployment of organisational communication, and how leaders obtain the mandate to lead effectively from their constituent stakeholders
- input to the strategic planning process by helping organisations to ensure that their thinking is based on the properly researched needs, views and opinions of stakeholders, especially customers and employees
- the design of people-centred change processes
- teambuilding at various levels to ensure that leaders and managers are fully equipped to 'live' the corporate values, to

champion change or to create a culture of good communication within their area of management responsibility
- incorporation of communication competence into management skill sets
- culture mapping and advice on cross-cultural communication, including cultural integration (eg following corporate mergers or acquisitions) or cultural change (eg improving the customer service ethic, or raising profits through the generation of more cross selling opportunities)

Getting what you want

In the fast moving – and internationally uneven – world of communication consulting, it is particularly important to make sure that the consultants you select really are capable of adding value to your organisation. General methods for selecting and assessing consulting output are covered elsewhere in this Handbook, but there are a few special aspects of the communication world that are worth singling out.

Track record and expertise

Have your chosen advisors demonstrably got the set of competencies and experiences you think you need? If you really want to take a people-centred approach to the way you manage change in your organisation, has your chosen consultancy got the depth of skill you need in organisational behaviour, applied psychology and business strategy?

Creativity and practical communication knowledge

Many workforces today are either change-weary and therefore highly cynical about management communication and anything that smacks of 'spin', or they are nervous of the personal implications of change in terms of their continuing value to their employer. Is there sufficient evidence of creativity in your advisors that suggests they understand how to engage and involve people in such a way that you will have the best chance of harnessing their energy and motivation to help your organisation to succeed?

Cultural sensitivity

The ability of advisors to understand your organisational culture and the complex overlays of national, sectoral, professional or other cultural differences evident in your employee/stakeholder population is paramount. Challenge your consultants on the validity and transferability of their ideas, and make sure they put enough tracking devices in place to prevent you from shooting yourself in the foot or alienating parts of your audience with insensitive or wrongly targeted communication.

Standards you should expect

A specialist communication management consultancy that has both international experience and exposure (and there are only a handful of these globally!) should be fully equipped to operate across the full range of consulting assignments described below. The consulting staff working in such firms tend to be the highest calibre in the industry by virtue of their commitment to a firm that specialises solely in organisational communication and lives or dies by its success in this area. They are a natural first port of call when you know you have a significant task on your hands.

If your own view of your communication requirement is that it is an integral but secondary part of a larger management consultancy intervention in terms of your structure, strategy or use of technology, then start by looking at the in-house capabilities of your existing business consulting advisors. Here, the success of the communication component of your consulting brief will probably be determined by the degree to which the communication consultants work in a fully integrated fashion with their other consultant colleagues who are covering different parts of your brief.

If, on the other hand, you need a simpler type of tactical or creative support, look for (typically small and often local) specialist firms who really have a specialist technical or creative skill and cherry pick what you need. Expect high quality creative and hi-tech skills – at least of an equivalent standard as the best creative or technical agencies serving your organisation against an advertising, marketing, new product development, design or customer relations brief.

Typical assignments

The following list of typical communication consulting briefs should help you decide whether or not you are shopping in the right sector for the kind of help you need.

- How do we communicate effectively with a large number of employees based in several different countries around the world? How do we help them all to feel 'connected' to the same organisation?
- We realise that our greatest competitive strength lies in the quality of service delivered by our front line staff. How can we motivate our people to provide a consistent customer experience that matches the image we want to project in the marketplace?
- We are merging two organisations together. The management challenges we need help with are:
  - minimising the loss of key specialist staff and star performers
  - keeping market confidence high in the cost benefits that will derive from the merger
  - integrating two strong cultures and trying to keep the best of both
  - engaging employees in the vision and values of the new entity and enabling them to identify their own role in making it successful
- We need to introduce significant changes in working practices. How do we ensure not only that employees are receptive to

change but that we harness the best of their ideas and get them to drive change in their own part of the organisation?
- It is increasingly difficult to attract and retain the high quality of staff we need to maintain our competitive edge and break into new markets/technologies. How do we rapidly generate a reputation as an employer of choice in our sector?
- We've hit a crisis. Misleading allegations in the press are causing our own employees to doubt the integrity of their leaders. How can we turn the situation around?

A communication management consultancy can help you address these and similar problems. Activity will typically centre on:

- facilitating senior teams to come to a shared vision and a set of achievable communication objectives, based on a clear understanding of the different communication needs of different groups of employees in the organisation
- taking full account of the cultural sensitivities and the organisation's readiness – and capability – to change in the way senior management wants it to: qualitative and quantitative research will typically be employed to map culture, employee perceptions and current communication practice
- facilitating and coaching managers to ensure their leadership style and activities are actively championing the organisation's change and communication objectives
- ensuring appropriate temporary and permanent communication media are in place to promote the relevant amount of productive, consultative two-way feedback and participation in relevant decision-making processes
- advising on the way management initiatives and change processes are introduced to the organisation to maximise employee support and involvement
- helping organisations to improve their own measurement activities to make sure they understand how effectively they are communicating and where resources need to be focused.

Money well spent?

Unlike many other forms of strategic consulting or practical implementation management, communication is an area where many feel that all that is required is applied common sense. Even when business leaders admit the need for professional help or external input, few see the value of investment in communication as being as important as, for example, structure, strategy, market analysis or technology – typically in receipt of the substantive consulting budgets. While it is ultimately a pointless exercise to expend too much time on such a comparison, it is clear that organisations that are characterised by a well communicated set of values or principles and/or an engaged workforce, where the flow of ideas and feedback is strong and which are seen as attractive places to work, have many advantages in the competitive marketplace.

> **A sample case**
> Because communication 'problems' typically centre on specific stages of organisational development and culture, it is hard to talk in terms of standard briefs or case studies. The following example, which represents an amalgam of several current client examples, demonstrates a relatively typical brief and consulting output.
>
> **The organisation**
> Several hundred employees, several locations, operating in a traditional service sector; experiencing market deregulation, new forms of competition and significant business opportunities in new technologies.
>
> **The brief**
> How do we engage and involve employees to minimise their resistance to change and so enable us to capitalise on the new market opportunities fast?
>
> **Consulting assignment**
> *First phase: Planning and preparation*
> - Define the values and behaviours needed to sustain the 'new' organisation and determine how the culture will need to shift to support these
> - Optimise the way senior teams work together to demonstrate shared objectives, a united vision and active role-modelling of the changes they want everyone else to make

- Communicate the scope and intent of the changes to all
- Introduce the needed changes to the organisation in a way that motivates and involves all employees, causes them to take forward change on a local and personal basis and raises their enthusiasm

Second phase: Implementation
- Support the change management process with a comprehensive communication strategy for all aspects of the way change will be designed, experienced and embedded in the organisation and its operational processes
- Transfer responsibility for delivering the new values and behaviour to the employee population as a whole
- Build powerful feedback loops at all stages of the process, to facilitate better (and, in problem areas, pre-emptive) management decision-making
- Maintain visibility for the vision and for the leadership throughout
- Measure and track cultural shifts and communication effectiveness

4.9

Customer relations

Clive Bonny

The aim of this chapter is to describe some key processes which a consultancy service applies when assigned to improve customer relations. This will help the buyer of consultancy to quantify the extent to which their service provider follows good practice during assignments.

The international management consultant Stephen Covey described one of the Seven Habits of Successful People as 'starting with the end in mind'. This chapter therefore starts with an analysis of how consultants focus on the needs of the customer at the end of the supply chain. This identifies key results to be achieved. Additional enabling processes which precede results are then examined by using two case studies drawn from actual assignments. This chapter is based on the supposition that the aim of client relations is to achieve customer 'delight' and not just customer 'satisfaction'.

The failure of companies to achieve customer 'delight' can often be attributed to a failure to keep in touch with changing customer needs. The larger the supplier, the greater the difficulty in focusing the workforce to obtain high quality, up-to-date information regarding client wants and needs. There are several challenges: the time taken from product design to market can fall behind changes in consumer requirements; the widening ranges in product and consumer segments are becoming more difficult to match; competitor speed to reproduce similar offerings is faster;

consumers are looking for added value; and suppliers overlook relationship management skills.

The standard management practice of the supplier performing a survey by mail or telephone is unreliable; single sourcing feedback may omit stakeholder input and client contacts may not wish directly to criticise their supplier contacts. Consultants can bring objectivity to the survey questions and the responses, and demonstrate to customers a supplier's commitment for accuracy and integrity of feedback. Questions such as 'How does supplier X compare to suppliers Y & Z?' and 'How responsive do you find Mr X and Mrs Y?' are more likely to obtain frank feedback when asked by an independent third party.

The consultant should prepare before making such contacts by reviewing the client file and checking the account manager's understanding of client needs. The latter can include observing behaviour on the telephone and at meetings or presentations with the customer, to assess the level of rapport and their proficiency in surveying customer requirements. The consultant's role can be described to customers openly so the customer recognises the involvement of a third party as an opportunity to strengthen relations with the supplier. This is particularly effective when there is conflict or mistrust between buyer and supplier. In such circumstances there is even less chance of feedback if undertaken by the supplier. Behavioural assessment of performance at work should be competency-based, ie assess specific and visible actions which help or hinder interpersonal communications. For example, when conducting an initial customer visit, does the account manager prepare by obtaining the most recent relevant company information? When meeting for the first time, does the account manager clarify both parties' roles, objectives, strategies and support networks?

Network mapping of each organisation's people, objectives, values and processes is a prerequisite for understanding the opportunities for co-working between supplier and buyer towards common goals with a shared methodology.

The following case study outlines the challenges, actions and outcomes of a consultancy project undertaken in an environment of restricted market opportunities and internal restructuring to reduce costs.

> **Case study:** *Business partnering – using values to add value*
>
> The purpose of this case study is to demonstrate how an already successful organisation has cost-effectively applied external development resource to build further on success in customer relationship management.
>
> *Background*
> The company has a multi-million pound turnover and contributes to the parent company's triple A rating on the stock market. Specialists in vehicle finance and maintenance, they have been recognised as the fastest growing supplier in their field. The industry's trade association found them to have the highest levels of customer satisfaction and their senior executive team were also recognised as the highest performers in their sector in independent surveys.
>
> *Challenges*
> The market is highly competitive with major international finance companies bidding against each other and against vehicle manufacturers' own in-house finance packages. There is increasing pressure on margins and higher customer expectations of service levels. Consequently, success is dependent upon innovation to maintain differentiation in the eyes of the customer. At the same time the company has to increase profit on assets employed by improving efficiency.
>
> Cost of sales represented a significant overhead and the regional sales team's performance required more consistency. The sales director decided to review the structure of the sales force in consultation with the top performing regional sales manager and with an external qualified consultant.
>
> *Action*
> This review resulted in a restructuring of the sales force, removing the regional management layer to save costs. All sales people nationally reported directly to the sales manager whose first step was to undertake a skills audit with the support of the consultant who had previously undertaken the company's Investors In People (IIP) diagnosis. The audit involved field accompaniment and team workshops in which individuals created their own skills logs and reviewed each others' strengths and weaknesses.

The outcome was the identification of core competencies, the creation of a training plan and agreement on the most appropriate management styles to apply for each individual. The workshops were co-designed and co-facilitated by both the sales manager and the consultant.

They included open sharing and discussion of new goals and processes to ensure the teams understood and committed to a programme of change. One of the core organisation competencies was 'business partnering'. This was driven by the company's explicit promotion as a 'Business Partner' to every customer. The team wanted a more active demonstration to clients of the partnership approach and held a series of short workshops focused on attitudinal and behavioural change in personal communications with customers. This included analysing and linking people's personal styles with the values of the team and those of the customer.

Outcomes
The work on styles and values has shown the team how to adapt and modify their communications, both internally and externally, to build stronger interpersonal relationships. This, in turn, has resulted in more interdependent teamworking and greater trust enabling the manager to switch from a command-control style to one of supporting and facilitating change. Instead of diminishing management effectiveness, the increased number of direct reports has improved it.

More openness between individual territory sales people and improvements in teamworking has led to sales people widening the portfolios offered to their customers. This extra capacity of account managers has encouraged customers to spend more with their primary contacts, increasing loyalty and renewals.

Summary
The translation of this concept of business partnering into active reality perceived by customers has created a unique factor to differentiate the supplier. Starting the process of change by addressing the fundamental values of individuals established a firm foundation and desire for change. Converting sets of values into identifiable behaviours and developing specific skills ensured that new attitudes were reflected by new behaviours. These competencies then became visible to customers whose satisfaction was manifested with more business.

The sales manager commented that 'a planned and structured programme related to winning both hearts and minds has been key to a successful internal restructuring and external repositioning of our sales and customer account managers. Relationship management initiatives must start with the values of Business Partners.' Last year they increased profits by 22 per cent, despite a downturn in their industry. Their strategy of values-based relationship building has won them many new customers with recognised brand names who, like themselves, do business with people they trust.

In this case study the consultant role was to facilitate the strengthening of relations between buyers and suppliers without creating a dependency upon the consultancy. This was achieved by the consultant transferring knowledge of relationship management processes, and by training the supplier in interpersonal skills. In order to accomplish this, the consultancy needed first to ensure that the supplier's internal support staff and managers had a customer focused attitude and an infrastructure of targets, systems and processes which helped the relationship managers in their client-facing work. This requires a more sophisticated consultancy intervention starting with top-level strategy, then addressing operations and activities down the reporting line. The next case study outlines the processes which the consultancy applied in order to support effective client relations at the front line.

Case study: The design and development of customer focused processes

Background

The managers had achieved significant success to date and were now a valued contributor to their corporate and shareholder objectives. In order to maintain and increase this level of contribution, the senior management team wished to establish a stronger infrastructure with customer focused process improvements. A brief initial survey of process strengths and weaknesses identified managers' perceptions of the areas for greatest potential improvement. This showed how issues could be addressed without distracting managers and staff from their necessary day-to-day activities.

Scope

Senior management recognised the fundamental need for their business to become more customer-centered, integrating the internal and external supply chains. They wanted a coherent and integrated strategy to support company-wide goals, measures and accountabilities. This required the creation and communication of a business plan which was flexible enough to meet the fast changing nature of the market, and which was to become a focus for teamworking across the organisation to align the priorities of the organisation as a whole.

Line managers wanted tools and techniques for problem analysis and prevention, and to install processes for managing their teams more effectively. This required their understanding of current and future business priorities and their ability to successfully manage change in order proactively to improve performance. The scope of external consulting support therefore covered two phases:

- Strategic business planning for senior managers
- Customer focused processes, to include design and development of customer processes and problem-solving tools and techniques for team leaders.

Methodology

The consultancy approach was underpinned by consultation around process change. This required:

- *Openness* in sharing the how and why with clients and in explaining risks as well as benefits
- *Teamworking* with all stakeholders supporting company-wide ownership of the clients' objectives

- *Respect* for people when proposing change that affects individuals at work
- *Innovation* to ensure each challenge was examined afresh and solutions are tailored accordingly
- *Achievement* of assignments following agreed outcomes within clear terms of reference.

Each project had clear links to business objectives with measures and milestones to map progress. Ownership was kept internal with the external consultant positioned as facilitator and coach. Each project also followed the principles of the learning cycle: plan, do, review. This ensured active assessment of the business outcomes and benefits during assignments, which subsequently allowed for appropriate mid-term amendments to the programme.

Key activities and results for strategic business planning

A strategic planning workshop was set up to determine organisation-wide business critical issues, key objectives, measures and accountability within the organisation. This was prefaced with a staff survey so that gaps between managers' perceptions and staff were analysed and prioritised. Tactical planning workshops for functional managers converted strategic goals into departmental objectives and measures. This was prefaced with a customer survey to analyse current issues related to customer expectations. This phase required consulting support to:

- assist in the design and rollout of a staff survey
- analyse the survey results and prepare the initial workshop
- facilitate the strategic planning workshop
- review the workshop and recommend the communication of outputs to line managers and staff

Design and development of customer focused processes

This responded to the following key objectives:

- define the customer experience
- identify process improvement or design requirements
- provide process improvement skills to front-line employees
- provide a problem solving methodology
- demonstrate measurement capabilities in the process
- address leadership involvement in the initiative
- create and provide a consistent message to employees and demonstrate how the initiative would be reinforced over time

The consultant recognised the need to create cross-functional improvement teams to minimise deficiencies in core processes. Employees were given the opportunity to master skills and tools for effective teamworking, problem solving and process improvement driven by customer experiences. This transferred knowledge of key skills and tools whilst simultaneously mapping the customer experience and creating new processes.

The following components of the project ensured successful implementation:

- reviews with senior managers;
- implementation planning with process owners
- project management reviews;
- team leader workshops covering front-line issues of process improvement awareness, such as:
  - teamworking skills
  - problem solving tools and methods
  - techniques for measuring process improvement
  - action planning
  - learning with employee and customer feedback
  - training of staff with project reviews which included
    - understanding customer relationship strategy
    - planning with project team members
    - training of process owners

Consultancy resource
The organisation development programme was supported by external consultancy with three components: clear deliverables to track results; aligned methodology with enabling customer processes; qualified advisors with a delivery team of an external consultant to help plan and implement the programme, a support consultant and a programme director to monitor and control quality.

Training workshops
These included awareness of customer relations so that people could:

- identify their role in the improvement of customer relations
- recognise the moments of truth in customer activities
- apply best practice to improve processes that had a high positive impact on customers
- recognise the importance of getting support and involvement across functions

This focused teams on the customer in order to ensure that resultant improvements were relevant to customers.

Teamworking
This was vital so that people could:

- understand the purpose of process improvement teams
- identify what makes teams successful

This gave the knowledge for people to work on process improvement teams and to understand what factors made teams successful.

Identifying cycles of service
This was necessary so that people could:

- identify the moments of truth that customers faced
- analyse processes from the customer's point of view

This linked to the training to improve processes. It showed how to analyse customer experiences and mapped out each step of a customer's experience from a customer's point of view in order to improve a process.

Improving moments of truth
This was in order that people could:

- assess customer expectations in a cycle of service
- identify factors that detracted from the customer relationship
- develop process improvements that could be implemented immediately
- plan how to recover when mistakes were made

This focused on how to improve the customers' experience. Some could be fixed immediately, while other improvements took more time. If a particular process was poor, they could minimise the problem while a longer-term solution was created. Recovery was a method for keeping customers feeling positive despite breakdowns in the core processes.

Customer interviews
These were implemented so that people could:

- determine customer issues
- assess their level of importance
- picture what success looked like
- identify resources needed
- identify potential constraints

Teams started on their process improvement projects and found outcomes the customer wanted in future.

Prioritising and proactively improving moments of truth
This covered choosing the most critical moments to work on so that people could decide which moments of truth to focus on. A danger in process improvement was the desire to do it all at once. Teams needed to assess which fixes had the most impact and the logical starting point so that a quick success could be achieved. People could design points of contact that customers experienced and identify how to build a process to support the new point of contact beyond the reactive fixing of the problem.

Tracking success
So that people were clear about the goals critical to the success of the project, measures were needed for teams to compare the 'before' state with results afterwards. Teams had to choose the most applicable measures for their process improvement project and, where appropriate, create new measures to ensure that their desired results were achieved.

Besides success measures, they created a list of all the tasks involved in the process improvement work, clarifying roles and responsibilities. Teams function best when each person on the team is clear as to what their role and goals are. Team members agreed on their roles and assigned responsibility for the tasks they set in an action plan at team meetings, during which they established project deadlines and deliverables. This allowed the team to plan key dates and milestones as they worked through their process analysis and improvement programmes. Checkpoints were set to monitor progress.

Process tools were applied after being supplied in a pocketbook showing pareto charts, process maps and flowcharts, cause and effect diagrams and force field analysis.

Summary

A consultancy approach which builds customer relationship skills in line with customer service strategy is essential to the success of such projects. Aligning people and processes with external customer needs will ensure success, provided there is active and visible top level support and involvement with all the stakeholders. This requires a planned and structured approach with a high level of communication and training across all levels in an organisation.

In both case studies, the work was spread over six months to enable staff and management consultation to take place, allow change to be embedded and to minimise direct consulting fees. Both projects also ensured that the consultancy transferred ownership and skills to the supplier to allow future programmes to be managed with less external support.

These projects were also delivered with explicit links to the principles of the international benchmark standard of Investors In People. IIP is a framework of good practice for organisation development. It began as a UK-based standard in 1991 and its successful application across thousands of UK employers has led to its acceptance internationally. The IIP standard supports external customer relations by enabling management to assess the effectiveness of their internal supply chains. It identifies blockages in corporate communications and guides employees into self-managed learning to support organisational goals. In both case studies, the companies selected consultants who were accredited Investors in People advisors to ensure alignment between internal back-office and external customer-facing changes.

This chapter shows that consulting interventions in customer relations should consider people and process issues both inside and outside the organisation. Such interventions should be based on proven international standards for managing change. Finally, the consultancy should be adept at transferring skills with explicit processes, which begin with the end in mind: what does the customer want and need?

4.10

Information and knowledge management

Colin J Coulson-Thomas

In many companies, existing knowledge – which may or may not be relevant to current priorities – is being shared, but the new knowledge needed to deliver greater customer and shareholder value is not being created. Contemporary approaches to knowledge management focus excessively upon sharing an existing stock of knowledge and pay inadequate attention to the determination and development of the new knowledge required for achieving priority objectives.

Far too many people access and use corporate know-how without reviewing and updating it and doing very little to replenish the supply. Many companies have difficulty identifying the net contributors. The superstar creators of new knowledge are not necessarily the silver tongued or the best presenters. Sometimes they find themselves the victims of de-layering, headcount reductions and ageism.

Board members need to ask themselves some fundamental questions. What proportion of people are actively creating, packaging and exploiting know-how? Are the various forms of knowledge from designs, websites, patents and copyrights to processes, skills and customer and supplier relationships that exist being fairly valued, fully exploited and converted into profit and ultimate shareholder wealth?

Knowledge creation is becoming increasingly important. Moving up the value chain may depend upon new forms of differentiation and additional ways of adding value. More bespoke responses to the requirements of individual customers might require new attitudes, skills and tools as well as redesigned processes and supporting technology. Efficiency and cost cutting drives need to be complemented by efforts to generate higher margins, for example from improved exploitation of intellectual capital.

The proportion of final value delivered to customers that is represented by 'know-how' continues to increase. This trend may accelerate as emphasis switches from re-engineering and retrenchment to value creation and the generation of incremental revenues. Consequently, people will need to become more effective at creating, packaging, sharing, applying and generally managing and exploiting information, knowledge and understanding.

Developing a corporate learning strategy

Knowledge management should be an end-to-end process from identifying knowledge requirements and gaps, through knowledge creation and the sharing and packaging of knowledge to its application, to doing new things and delivering additional income streams. However, surveys of corporate practice undertaken by the National Centre for Competitiveness suggest many knowledge management initiatives are focused almost exclusively upon the middle or sharing section of the process. This chapter addresses the missing dimensions of knowledge creation and exploitation. They should be addressed when briefing consultants.

Current training activities, development preoccupations and learning priorities could be a significant determinant of tomorrow's attitudes, skills and knowledge. Boards should urgently assess whether training and development inputs are resulting in knowledge and intellectual capital outputs. Maybe data-warehousing software is being bought to help capture existing knowledge, but are people learning and creating new knowledge?

In many companies training and development activities deserve closer scrutiny. Could business development and the processes of value and knowledge creation be better supported? Could particular training activities be made a revenue centre, a separate business or simply outsourced?

A two-year examination of corporate learning plans and priorities has addressed such questions. The investigation included corporate visits and 69 structured interviews with individuals responsible for the training and development of some 460,000 people. The results with case studies, checklists and key action points are summarised in the report *Developing a Corporate Learning Strategy*.

The findings are sobering. Many courses have passed their 'sell by' date, while essential requirements and critical corporate priorities are largely ignored. Millions are being spent on fashionable concepts such as empowerment and general 'teamwork' training, yet only one of the organisations surveyed is equipping its people to be more successful at bringing in new business. People receive standard courses regardless of their individual interests and needs.

While value is increasingly delivered by supply chains rather than individual companies, the organisations examined focus overwhelmingly upon the internal training of employed staff. External development needs of customers, contractors, suppliers, supply chain partners and business associates are being ignored.

Overall, little effort is devoted to business development and relationship building, e-business, or knowledge creation and entrepreneurship. Overwhelmingly, the emphasis is upon squeezing and cutting costs, rather than income generation. Training and development are not perceived as a source of incremental revenues. Nor are they used as a means of building relationships with key decision-makers in strategic customers, suppliers and business partners.

The education, learning, training and updating markets represent exciting contemporary business opportunities. The *Developing a Corporate Learning Strategy* report identifies no fewer than 25 different categories of learning support services that could be offered. Intellectual capital, from simple tools to advanced techniques, can also be licensed or sold. There is enormous potential knowledge entrepreneurship. Yet, despite these opportunities, most trainers are not directly supporting the creation, sharing and application of knowledge and understanding.

Managing current stocks of information, knowledge or understanding might or might not be relevant to individual aspirations, customer requirements or corporate objectives. But new insights, discoveries and breakthroughs, the dynamics of the creation and application of pertinent knowledge, are often the keys to leadership in competitive markets, particularly when knowledge sought or created relates to critical success factors for competitive advantage.

Education, training and development expenditures are still widely regarded as costs rather than vital investments in the creation of knowledge, intellectual capital and value for customers. Switching the emphasis from cost cutting to innovation, business building and value creation would result in both enhanced corporate performance and greater personal fulfilment.

The *Developing a Corporate Learning Strategy* report suggests a way ahead. Boards and managers should actively champion enterprise and learning. Knowledge development should be explicitly rewarded. Pioneers do not play 'me-too' or 'catch-up' according to yesterday's rules. They are energetic creators, imaginative innovators and restless explorers. They devise and set up new games with different rules. When tailoring responses and differentiating, the ability to learn quickly and effectively is a source of both value and competitive advantage.

The most successful enterprises will evolve into communities of knowledge entrepreneurs.

Knowledge creation and the information entrepreneur

Learning processes can be created, improved or re-engineered, and learning support tools acquired. Learning should also be built into work processes, and standard training offerings should be abandoned in favour of specific and tailored interventions to support learning and knowledge entrepreneurship. *The Information Entrepreneur* provides practical checklists which entrepreneurs, investors, managers and individual members of the board can use to create customer and shareholder value by packaging and exploiting knowledge.

Knowledge creation should start with what an organisation is setting out to do. Next, roles and responsibilities, processes, and ways of working and learning to achieve the desired objectives have to be designed and agreed. Role model behaviours and, importantly, the knowledge, experience and understanding likely to be required can then be determined, along with any additional tools, techniques and methodologies that may be needed. Centres of excellence, or panels of experts, could review certain areas of a company's 'body of knowledge' to keep them up to date.

The sale of specialised knowledge, or the licensing of intellectual capital, such as particular approaches or techniques, can contribute additional income streams. However, the report *Managing Intellectual Capital to Grow Shareholder Value* suggests that most of the 51 companies surveyed fail to manage properly and exploit fully the 20 categories of intellectual capital examined (Perrin, 2000). The term 'intellectual capital' encompasses all forms of corporate knowledge that can be converted into profit, including know-how and processes, patents and copyrights, as well as the skills and experience of employees and relationships with customers and suppliers.

'Leaders' already generate significantly more income from intellectual capital than 'laggards'. They also expect the contribution of know-how to product or service value to rise substantially or significantly over the next 5 years, while the 'laggards' expect it to increase only slightly, remain the same or decline. The 'leaders' understand key management of intellectual property issues, while the 'laggards' fail to make 'know-how' an important driver of shareholder value.

'Leaders' are much more motivated than 'laggards' to exploit their intellectual capital. Developing new revenue streams, enhancing profits and growing existing revenues are given a higher priority and they recognize that intellectual capital can be used to create new opportunities and attack and penetrate new markets. 'Leaders' are also more likely to measure their performance at managing and exploiting 'know-how'.

Customer information, design rights and R&D know-how are currently the three most significant income generators. Both 'leaders' and 'laggards' anticipate that all 20 categories of know-how examined in the report will become increasingly important. The 'leaders' expect over 30 per cent revenue growth from five categories of intellectual capital: namely licences, brands, market intelligence, website/internet and management methodologies. However, the majority of companies fail to manage properly most types of intellectual property.

The greatest growth in revenue earnings is expected to result from exploitation of websites and the Internet, management methodologies, customer information, brands, distribution networks, licences, market intelligence and management tools and techniques. The least growth is expected to result from copyrights, goodwill, patents, royalties, design rights, proprietary technologies, software and R&D know-how.

A wide range of executives can contribute to the more effective management of intellectual capital. The three most active groups are Chief Executives, Marketing Directors and Financial Directors. About a third of the annual reports and accounts of the companies surveyed contain some informal reference or a passing mention of the contribution of know-how, but fewer than 10 per cent of the balance sheets show a value for intellectual capital.

Most of the companies fail to report intellectual property developments to the board.

Only just over 11 per cent of respondents thought creating asset registers and similar tools was either important or very important. However, approaching 47 per cent considered better ways of archiving and accessing knowledge to be either important or very important.

Because there are many different forms of intellectual capital, staff responsible for keeping records and protecting knowledge assets increasingly need knowledge management frameworks and repositories that can handle a diversity of formats. The various categories of know-how range from electronic databases, printed documents and slides through designs and other visual images, to audio and video material and animation. One example is K-Frame (www.k-frame.com), winner of the 2000 eBusiness Innovations Award for Knowledge Management.

K-Frame allows intellectual capital from text and spreadsheets to multimedia and information from the Internet to be captured and stored within a single portable framework. Fuzzy searches can be undertaken, including on audio and video material. The search function can cope with spelling mistakes and even look for words in audio files and voice-overs. Knowledge creation tools and report and presentation generators can be included.

Such a knowledge management framework can support other activities that various members of the board are involved with, such as the production of corporate credentials or annual reports. Thus multimedia content could be issued to interested parties by means of a CD-ROM disc. Laptop computer based sales support applications for companies like call centre technology supplier Eyretel to incorporate a pricing engine and proposal generator.

Boards should undertake formal reviews of corporate approaches to the management of intellectual capital, and formulate proactive strategies for harvesting more value from it. Incentives should be put in place to encourage this. The focus should be upon areas where knowledge management activities can have most impact upon the critical success factors for achieving key corporate objectives.

The *Managing Intellectual Capital* research report and *The Information Entrepreneur* guide suggest some key questions to ask:

- How significant is know-how as a source of customer and shareholder value within your company's sector?
- Is its contribution assessed and tracked?
- Is the sharing of information, knowledge and understanding measured?
- Are sufficient resources devoted to thinking, learning and the acquisition, creation, management and exploitation of information, knowledge and understanding?
- Is intellectual capital identified, packaged, badged and protected?
- Is intellectual property valued and re-valued and appropriately treated in the annual report and accounts?
- Is an appropriate knowledge management framework like K-Frame in place?
- Does this allow the company quickly to capture, access, present and exploit intellectual capital?

'Leaders' are far more determined than 'laggards' to exploit corporate know-how, and much more effective at monitoring intellectual capital performance and revenue contribution. They are also more likely to identify know-how as a primary driver of shareholder value; focus on the roles different management functions should play in creating and exploiting intellectual property; and address the relevant people, culture, process and IT factors.

Copying, me-too approaches, benchmarking and accessing and sharing commodity knowledge are not the route to market leadership. The superstars question, challenge, explore and discover. They use the 'know-how' of their superstars and corporate capabilities to craft distinctive offerings that provide customers with new offerings and genuine choice. They regard their knowledge, processes and ways of working as a source of competitive differentiation.

Knowledge exploitation for differentiation

In our confusing and chaotic world, consumers are assailed from all directions with a multitude of similar but conflicting messages. Being noticed is crucial for a business that needs to attract new customers. Differentiation and tailoring to individual requirements can also enable the avoidance of commodity product traps and generate the higher margins needed to fund development.

Developments in manufacturing, process and information technologies give us the potential to reflect our individuality. However, despite multifarious possibilities we find very often, when we strip away advertising claims, that various suppliers offer essentially the same product. Thus, all cars within each price bracket seem to have the same aerodynamic shape. We buy software packages that provide us with the same capabilities as everyone else when bespoke development would enable us to be different and might create additional intellectual capital.

People should strive to provide customers with additional options, genuine choices and better alternatives to those that are currently available. Boards should seek alternatives to bland consensus and middle ways. They should champion reflection, debate and challenge; and instil a desire to innovate and an urge to discover.

Some people may need to be helped to distinguish fundamentals from fads, substance from surface and reality from illusion. Checklists for doing this and questioning contemporary assumptions, and exercises for formulating new marketplace offerings are available. People can be equipped to challenge the relative importance of action and reaction, complexity and simplicity, activity and reflection and change and continuity. Shifting the balance between them can produce genuine alternatives.

Intellectual capital enhancement

We need to keep information technology in perspective and avoid panaceas and single solutions. The top three management issues for participants in the managing intellectual capital survey are people rather than technology related, namely recruiting 'good quality' staff, developing a culture of innovation and providing board leadership Perrin (2000). The 'leaders' outscored the 'laggards' in all three areas.

Over 70 per cent of 'leader' companies felt that improving staff training and learning was either important or very important for building or enhancing intellectual capital compared with less than 60 per cent of the 'laggards' (Perrin 2000). Passive learning needs to be replaced with creativity, active problem solving and innovation.

The tangible consequences of knowledge creation and exploitation include improved employee and customer satisfaction, an enhanced image and an increased share valuation. Those responsible for training and development should consider whether their current activities are contributing to uniformity and resulting in a standard attitudes, knowledge and skills set or stimulating diversity and knowledge creation. Training teams could be tasked with becoming separate and profitable businesses. Individuals could become 'customers' with personal learning accounts.

Targets and measures should reflect these changes. Input indicators such as 'bums on seats' should be replaced by verifiable outcomes. For example, what proportion of turnover is accounted for by new products and services? What value is ascribed to newly packaged intellectual capital?

The emphasis should switch from standard competencies and providing people with a common experience to self-directed learning and creating learning environments, such as a corporate university that can respond to the interests and aspirations of individual members of staff and encourage innovation and knowledge creation. Staff can be seconded for specified periods to work upon strategic knowledge creation and exploitation projects. Think-tank environments can be conducive to 'blue skies' thinking, and the open-minded, systematic and imaginative consideration of alternatives.

References

Coulson-Thomas, Colin (1999) *Developing a Corporate Learning Strategy*, Policy Publications, Bedford

Perrin, Sarah (2000) *Managing Intellectual Capital to Grow Shareholder Value*, Policy Publications, Bedford

Further reading

Coulson-Thomas, Colin (1999) *Individuals and Enterprise: Creating Entrepreneurs for the New Millennium through Personal Transformation*, Blackhall Publishing, Dublin

Coulson-Thomas, Colin (2000) *The Information Entrepreneur*, 3 Com Active Business Unit, Winnersch

Coulson-Thomas, Colin (2001) *Shaping Things to Come, Strategies for Creating Alternative Enterprises*, Blackhall Publishing, Dublin

Further information

Brochures describing *Developing a Corporate Learning Strategy* and *Managing Intellectual Capital to Grow Shareholder Value* are available from Policy Publications, 4 The Crescent, Bedford MK40 2RU, Tel: 01234 328448, Fax: 01234 357231, E-mail: policypubs@kbnet.co.uk, Website: www.ntwkfirm.com/bookshop. All the publications cited can be ordered via the website.

4.11

m-commerce: the next wave of management consulting

Tomas Korseman and Daniel Shepherd

This chapter will explore the emerging m-commerce market and how consultants can assist companies in entering this market. We shall look briefly at the forces that are paving the way for m-commerce and the impact that these forces have on the market and on organisations. The level of its importance to the CEO's agenda will be discussed, given that m-commerce will address and also add another dimension to some of the strategic business issues that a company faces. The chapter will then introduce a consulting model to illustrate the ways in which a company can adopt an m-commerce strategy. We aim to demonstrate that companies can use differing approaches depending on their internal capabilities, asset base and their strategic intent.

Market forces

The convergence of the fixed Internet and mobile communication is set to revolutionise the way people work and communicate with each other, creating one of the fastest growing markets ever.

Capitalising on commerce over a mobile platform (m-commerce) is not restricted to players in the mobile arena. Companies from almost any sector are provided with unforeseen possibilities to apply new business models to acquire, retain and expand customer relationships.

Before the Internet, companies focused on the trade-off between 'richness' – providing customised products and services – and 'reach' – the extent of the customer base. E-commerce redefined this trade-off, enabling companies to sell a rich offering of products and services to a large customer base. M-commerce, enabled by the transformation from second-generation (2G) to third-generation (3G) mobile technologies, is set once again to redefine the boundary of richness and reach to new levels, providing greater richness through personalisation, and more extended reach through portability.

The conversion to 3G technologies is expected to equip everyday mobile users with a wealth of new services and applications over the next five years. Through the combined use of a number of different mobile devices, people will be able to access the *same* content and services wherever, however and whenever. Mobile users will enjoy the convenience of having access to the Internet anytime and anywhere, where services are individually defined and driven by personal choice. Also, because the mobile device will be equipped with location sensitivity intelligence, services can be individually 'pushed' subject to the user location. Thus, m-commerce will work best in areas where its core attributes, convenience and portability will be emphasised.

A new and more complex mobile value chain is emerging and no single person has all the skills needed to exploit the market opportunity. Companies, therefore, tend to look for areas where they can add most value, which might not be at a singular point in the value chain. Rather, they can target several value elements and concentrate on forming long-term strategic relationships with complementary players. This is best described as a value web, which is depicted in Figure 4.11.1 for a particular telecoms business model. The model no longer assumes that you can clearly

■ 336 KEY CONSULTANCY ACTIVITIES

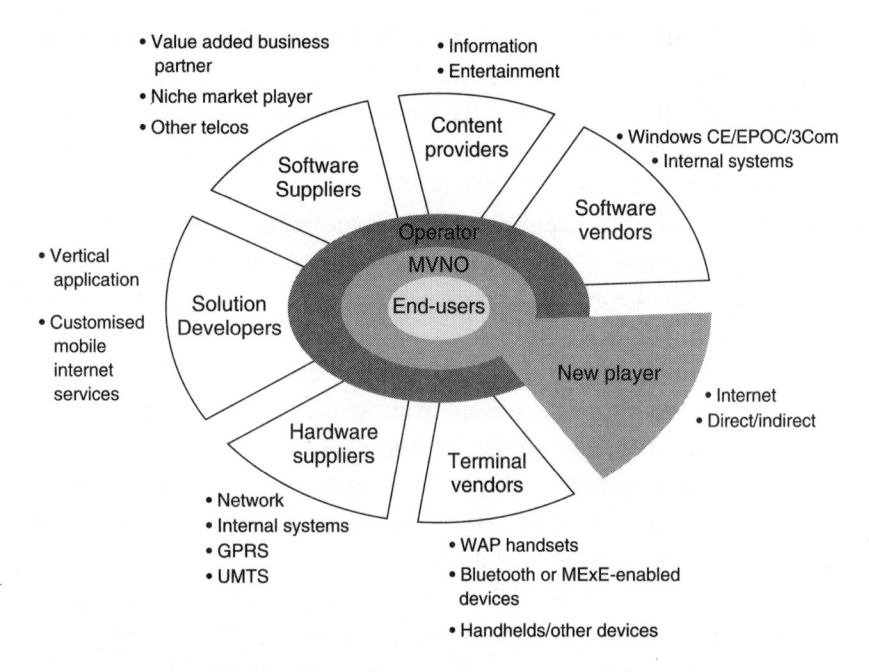

Figure 4.11.1 Example value web in the telecoms sector for mobile virtual network operators
Source: edgecom

define where the value-added of any one particular player begins and ends.

Value in the value web depends on applications and services, and some players are better positioned than others to reap the benefits of m-commerce. Obviously, the customer relationship owner is best positioned to become the m-commerce distribution channel and may be able to receive a commission from each transaction and control the service offering. However, because the battle for ownership of the customer relationship is open, there is a great deal of competition between companies trying to gain control of the customer interface. One method of engaging this interface, which in terms of mobile telephony, once belonged exclusively to the incumbent mobile operators, is the formation of Mobile Virtual Network Operators (MVNOs), who essentially operate a mobile network without actually owning the spectrum.

Virgin Mobile is probably today's most successful and best-known example.

The MVNO business model is just one of many possibilities, while the concept itself has several permutations and levels of involvement in relation to ownership of infrastructure and control of the consumer relationship. Other business models have already begun to feature in the market and include service providers, content providers and content or service aggregators.

Given the impact of technology and communications trends on markets, industries and organisations, it becomes a top priority for the senior management of a company to determine how best to enter the m-commerce arena. Consultants are well placed to assist companies in the identification of trends and in researching and evaluating the specific impact they may have on the client's organisation.

The impact of market forces on the organisation

The main concerns for any CEO continue to circle around the issues of how to remain successful and how to make the business grow, through the pursuit of revenue generation, margin maximisation and competitive advantage. The mobile Internet presents new business opportunities to address these concerns. When adopting an m-commerce strategy, a CEO needs to think about strategic and operational activities from a different point of view. There are many possibilities, including supply chains and distribution networks. Three of the main activities that will be explored below are:

- market-entry strategies
- strategic marketing
- customer relationship management

Market-entry strategies

Entry into the mobile Internet arena can be achieved in many ways. A starting point for considering the alternative ways for a company to tap into the market is to eliminate the traditional view of a company's position within a value chain.

As a result of convergence, increasing market complexities and greater focus on the end-consumer, it is helpful to conceptualise a value web, where players focus more on their core competencies and seek to build synergies through partnership arrangements.

The value web enables companies to position themselves according to the strengths they bring to the market, while never losing their proximity to the customer. The dynamic nature of the value web means that the form in which partnerships develop is also different to traditional M&A or alliance-forming activity. With the dissolved value chain and a fragmented market, companies cannot build an m-commerce empire based on one partner, nor can the company hope for alliances that last forever. Partnerships have to be formed on the basis that there are mutual benefits to be reaped for a significant period of time.

Inevitably, the approval structures for such partnerships will also differ from traditional arrangements based on cross-ownership and financial transactions. These are less dynamic and flexible arrangements compared with alternative forms such as sales agreements and joint ventures, which tend to be preferred for m-commerce market entry strategies.

Strategic marketing

The decision to adopt an m-commerce strategy and the design of a vehicle for market-entry provide opportunities to extend a company's brand, to enhance customer relationships and to drive revenues from previously impossible market offerings. Such opportunities spur the need for a strategic marketing plan which achieves these objectives even over the mobile Internet.

Companies will wish to leverage existing assets as far as possible. Therefore, key areas of analysis will be the extent to which products and services, supply and distribution networks and customers are compatible with mobile applications. This will be driven to a great extent by a top-level decision as to whether the company wishes to utilise m-commerce as a support channel to market, or the primary business model. Either way, a two-pronged approach will be required. On the one hand, mobile Internet opens up a whole new array of possibilities for what can be delivered to the client. Here we are thinking of the integration of localisation and other personalisation technology, where a 'pull' strategy to marketing which stimulates demand from the client can be implemented as effectively as a 'push' strategy.

Conversely, the focus on the consumer should not be lost. Companies will need to look to the market to assess requirements and match these to both their strategies and capabilities. This assessment will provide the foundation for a strategic approach to the development of a value-added services portfolio that will support the core products and services but will add the incentive to utilise the mobile platform.

Customer relationship management (CRM)

The choice of an approach to the m-commerce market needs to be supported by a strong communications strategy. Customers need to understand what the new channel means to them. The value proposition needs to be clear in order to steer customers towards the mobile channel. This communications effort will be the first step to re-defining the relationship with the customer. Customer relationship management (CRM) provides a means to this end, especially given the growing evidence that it can be beneficial, through substantial impact to the bottom-line, for companies to identify those activities that add most value through a CRM strategy.

An m-commerce strategy, though, will flourish in a specific customer context, where mobility and data-based transactions are defining features of the user's requirements. This development will be important because companies will subject themselves to increased customer exposure irrespective of their position in the value web.

CRM is affected by the company's decision to adopt the m-commerce channel as either primary or secondary. As customers will already be accustomed to the established relationship, which may involve value derived from content-rich media of the Internet, an m-CRM strategy should either provide a support mechanism for that channel or target a specific market with specific needs.

Further CRM challenges will surface with the advent of m-commerce. Companies will need to revisit their understanding about the mechanisms and processes through which people carry out transactions over the mobile device. Companies will also have to look at how to develop appropriate levels of service that differentiate between types of customers based on the new understanding of the customer's commercial behaviour.

Clearly, the impact of m-commerce is substantial on these three key activities. The role of the consultant involves working with the senior management of the client organisation to explore to what extent and in what form these factors will play out. Furthermore, the consultant will assist the client to determine how best to redesign a strategy and an organisational model to maximise the impact on the bottom-line of any strategy that is proposed.

M-commerce strategies

We have looked at how and why m-commerce is developing and what it is driving, as well as the impact the underlying trends of technology and communications are having on the structure of the market and the dynamics of companies. We have also looked at the broad impact that m-commerce has on companies' approaches to various key strategic activities, as well as the role that consultants play in assisting their clients through the process of identifying the impact of market trends and the scope of this impact on a number of strategic activities. It is also important to identify the particular ways in which companies can adopt m-commerce strategies and the way in which consultants can help to guide their clients through what is essentially a strategy selection process. Clearly, not all companies will wish to go down the same m-commerce route, given the interests that may be at play, as well as particular product or distribution barriers that prevent companies from exploring certain channels.

Companies will adopt m-commerce strategies for a variety of reasons, amongst which will be: as a competitive weapon (in which case we can probably infer that they are emulating another player's move), as a revenue generator or as a cost reducer, or as an opportunity to extend a strong brand. The list goes on. There are essentially two ways that a company can achieve any of these results to varying degrees; this approach is rooted in the most basic tenets of strategy. In theory, companies can either seek to gain further expansion of their customer base while focusing on existing products and services, or seek to diversify their product and service portfolio within their key markets. As such, we present a model that incorporates these strategic alternatives in Figure 4.11.2.

In practice, there is no absolute trade-off between expansion and diversification strategies. Rather, companies will position themselves somewhere within that matrix and pursue both to varying degrees. Therefore, we have associated high and low levels of focus to each of the axes, giving four quadrants, defined as:

- **m-support:** A company that will utilise the m-commerce channel as secondary to existing channels, which may or may not already involve e-commerce. Apart from strategic or political reasons, companies may pursue this strategy on the

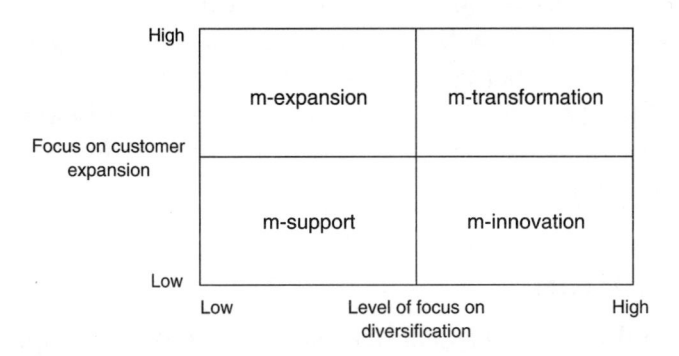

Figure 4.11.2 Models of m-commerce adoption
Source: edgecom

basis that their products, services, distribution networks or customer base lack synergy with the mobile Internet.

- **m-expansion:** A company that wishes further to tie-in existing customers and proactively generate new customer segments through creative use of new distribution strategies that are enabled by m-commerce. The focus will be on delivering additional existing products and services to an expanded marketplace.
- **m-innovation:** A company will utilise the m-commerce channel to explore new products or services that are now possible. The company may wish to enhance the user-experience for the existing customer base. The focus will be on delivering new products and services to existing customers.
- **m-transformation:** A company adopts the m-commerce channel as a primary means for both marketplace expansion and product/service diversification; this is the most advanced m-business model. Not all companies can or should pursue this approach.

To see how these strategies work in practice, we will briefly cover some existing case studies of what companies are already doing in relation to m-commerce. We tackle this approach by selecting four companies that we have recently been involved with and which fall broadly into each one of the quadrants within our matrix. In this respect, what we aim to illustrate is a benchmark model, while in practice, reality will be somewhat less clear. Additionally, bearing in mind that this is a developing market and companies have yet fully to explore new strategies, the positioning of m-commerce strategies may vary for different activities at a given moment in time.

Conclusion

The mobile Internet presents a clear opportunity for companies to position themselves within the m-commerce arena. To do so successfully, companies must develop strategies that leverage their current asset base and internal competencies. Clearly, these internal drivers must be matched with the external demands for products and services from the market and specific consumer groups.

The reasons why a company would wish to enter the mobile arena are many, but can essentially be boiled down to two extreme decisions, namely that of diversification and expansion. These are not 'either/or' strategies that a company is forced to choose between; in reality, companies will elect to pursue both to the degree that they are enabled to do so through synergies with the mobile platform, or the level of their commitment to transforming the business into an m-business.

The role of the consultant within the m-commerce market is distinct from other forms of consultancy, not so much from a process, or relationship perspective, but rather from a competency perspective. From a process perspective, the consultant will carry out many of the traditional tasks such as building business cases, designing business models, providing financial models and defining road maps to implementation. However, when determining a strategy to enter the m-commerce market, there will be a greater emphasis than ever before on uncovering what products and services the consumer will want and designing value-added portfolios around the findings.

However, more importantly than the process will be the emphasis on certain competencies that are required of the consulting firm that will allow it to help a client understand convergence trends and the impact of those trends on organisations. Such competencies will involve experience in those sectors that are driving convergence, telecommunications and media, as well as the underlying facilitator, technology. These competencies will be sure determinants for the design and implementation of a successful strategy to enter the m-commerce market.

4.12

ERP to e-business – the opportunities

Sarah Taylor and Barry Curnow

Introduction

Clients have invested heavily in Enterprise Resource Planning (ERP) and can be forgiven for wondering about the implications of the shift to e-business – much has been written about the opportunities for the consultancy industry but what does it mean for clients? In order to set this in context we will reflect on the development of our industry, its relationship with technology and the implications for the future of consultancy.

History

In recent years the development of management consultancy has been inextricably bound up with that of information technology but we should remember that management consultancy was around long before the first computers – Arthur D. Little was established in 1886, Arthur Andersen in 1913 and McKinsey in 1926. The last ten years have seen phenomenal growth in the sector with global revenues rising from less than US$10 billion to over US$100 billion between 1991 and 2001.

Who would have thought twenty years ago that five of the world's largest IT consulting practices would grow out of traditional audit based firms? Who would have thought that IBM Global Services, and Cap Gemini Ernst & Young would be ranked as global leaders in consultancy?

Over the last ten years IT decisions have moved from the backroom to the boardroom, as technology has become a key business driver. There is no longer such a thing as a pure IT project or a pure strategy project. Clients are demanding 'end-to-end' solutions combining management consultancy and systems integration.

Technology has enabled clients to operate on a global basis and their consultants have had to match their global reach.

The development of ERP

ERP was the first major IT investment for many clients, often a rite of passage that marked a company's transition to the new technological age. The need for Year 2000 compliance provided an extra impetus for ERP as organisations chose to invest in it rather than modify their legacy systems. Consultants had a key role to play here in ensuring that business processes were appropriately 're-engineered' and that those within the organisation supported and implemented the changes. Unfortunately, many implementations were done hurriedly without consultancy input and as a result, failed to deliver the expected benefits. ERP enabled organisations to manage their operations more efficiently and to reduce their costs, but in some cases it has still not delivered real value.

Another phenomenon of the last ten years has been the massive growth in the outsourcing industry, much of it IT related. The US Outsourcing market is estimated to be in excess of $300bn for the year 2001. Here again, management consultants can make the difference between a highly successful outsourcing contract and one that delivers little value.

A recent survey carried out by PMP Research provides this breakdown of consultants' revenues (see Figure 4.12.1). Non-IT related work represents only 12 per cent of revenues for the group questioned.

The statistics for MCA firms in 2000 showed that IT consultancy and systems development represented over 25 per cent of income and outsourcing consultancy over 30 per cent. That's over 50 per cent of consultancy income from predominantly IT-led projects.

Both surveys reflect the fact that as IT moves up the business agenda it is also permeating all areas of management consultancy.

Recent Trends

There are four main recent trends: ERP; SMEs; EAI and e-business.

ERP

Understandably, those who invested heavily in ERP in the 1990s are reluctant to discard it and start again and indeed there is no reason for them to do so. No one disputes that ERP provides a solid foundation for an efficient back office and supply chain.

However, as the focus of client management shifts from cost savings and internal processes to adding value through improved customer management, ERP vendors are now offering a whole new generation of products which enable organisations to be more responsive to customer needs: CRM, e-business, sales-force automation and warehouse management.

Many clients have also learned from their first experience of ERP that consultancy support is needed to get maximum return on investment through effective change management, process re-engineering and communications.

SMEs

Enterprise Application Integration (EAI) is allowing SMEs to purchase affordable off the shelf ERP solutions or to bring together a selection of 'best of breed' solutions. This will provide opportunities for those consultants who work in the middle market and those involved in incubator or Venture Capital activities. For many MCA members, even the largest, the 'middle' market is a new key area of concentration.

Breakdown of consultancy activity

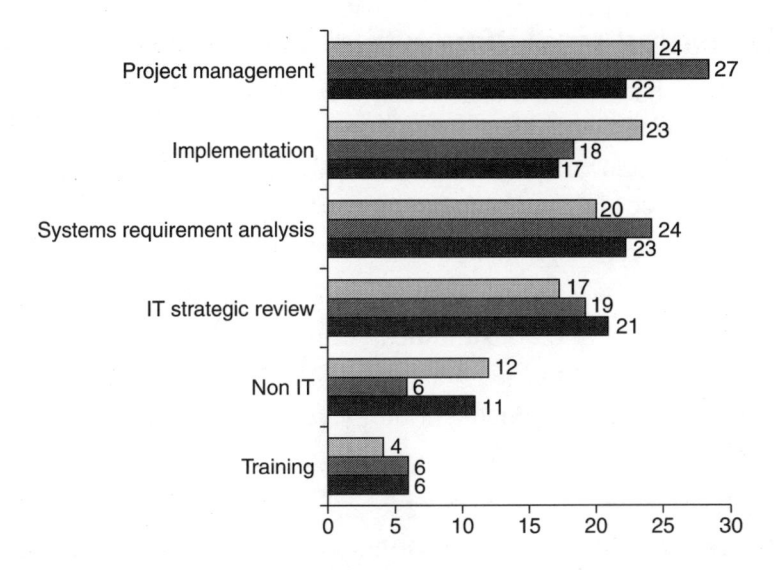

Activity	Values
Project management	24, 27, 22
Implementation	23, 18, 17
Systems requirement analysis	20, 24, 23
IT strategic review	17, 19, 21
Non IT	12, 6, 11
Training	4, 6, 6

Figure 4.12.1 Breakdown of consultancy activity – predominant involvement

EAI

EAI will give customers more choice and will force ERP vendors to unbundle their products and integrate them with best of breed products for CRM, e-business and similar applications. Ultimately, there will be more choice and flexibility for the customer. EAI removes the need for large and costly systems integration projects and enables integration to be more flexible and responsive. The role for consultants here is to ensure that the right products are used for each organisation and that products can be replaced or updated according to changing circumstances.

Knowledge management

Another growth area is the field of Knowledge Management Software, as firms recognise the need to retain the knowledge and skills within the organisation, but in a very different and much more flexible working environment. There are some real cultural problems here and therefore real consulting opportunities as well.

The digital revolution: e-business

And last, but by no means least, e-business or the digital revolution. It is estimated that up to 70 per cent of the fee income for large consultancy firms is now related to e-business work. There are a number of discernible developments:

- technology driving change
- incubators/investment – consultancies as active players
- new entrants – e-consultanies, some of which have suffered from the bursting of the dotcom bubble
- alliances – dotcom and technology vendors
- flotations/stock options – the need for capital
- war for talent

In a recent PMP survey consultants were asked whether they believed the demand for ERP solutions was slowing down. A slowdown in ERP activity has been anticipated for some time, and while consultants were not experiencing it in 1998, by 1999 the softening in the market-place was clearly identifiable.

The MCA statistics showed a drop in IT consultancy revenues in 1999 after an exceptional year in 1998.

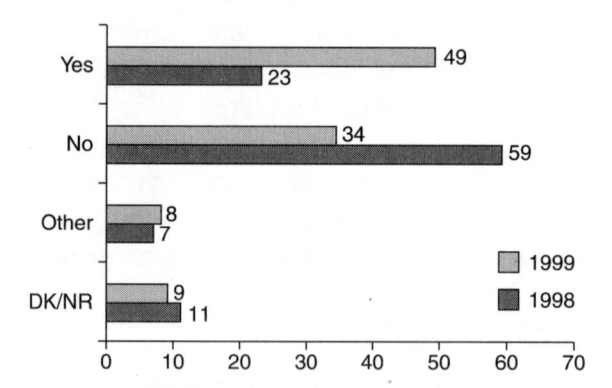

Figure 4.12.2 Is demand for ERP solutions slowing down?

The principal reasons for this slow down have been market saturation and the fact that the Year 2000 had actually arrived, as shown in Figure 4.12.3.

ERP TO E-BUSINESS – THE OPPORTUNITIES 349

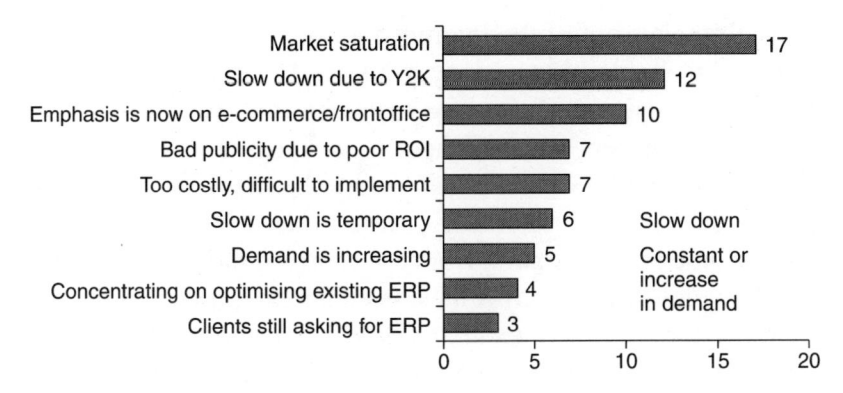

Reason	Value	Category
Market saturation	17	Slow down
Slow down due to Y2K	12	Slow down
Emphasis is now on e-commerce/frontoffice	10	Slow down
Bad publicity due to poor ROI	7	Slow down
Too costly, difficult to implement	7	Slow down
Slow down is temporary	6	Constant or increase in demand
Demand is increasing	5	Constant or increase in demand
Concentrating on optimising existing ERP	4	Constant or increase in demand
Clients still asking for ERP	3	Constant or increase in demand

Figure 4.12.3 Reasons for slowdown or increase in demand for ERP solutions

While some commentators believe that this slowdown is temporary, the underlying reason that might prevent a resumption in take up is that ERP solutions at the top end of the market are no longer seen as leading edge and the emphasis has switched to e-business and CRM development. In other words, the relentless pace of technological change has rendered yesterday's perfectly good functionality less fashionable alongside today's capability-made possible not least by the success of and feedback from the near global adoption of ERP by corporate enterprise.

The range of interpretations for the moderating demand for ERP Solutions is illustrated in the following survey responses.

"Because a lot of organisations already have ERP. But to be competitive it is now critical that they develop areas of functionality such as e-commerce, business to business procurement and supply chain management."

"Because no one has any need to spend three years implementing a financial system. Things can be done more quickly – the web has changed everything."

"Because of 2000, most people have replaced their software and hardware"

"Because of SAP they are extremely aggressive."

"Different ways of implementing systems such as application service provision – rather than implementing in-house."

"For the simple reason that the market has been saturated and also because of the perceived inability of organisations to receive the return on investments for these systems."

"It is changing, there is a new climate – ERP vendors need to shift their value position offering new modular products to clients – it is changing towards a new business climate."

"Superseded or diluted by cheaper middleware solutions – depends on how businesses operate over the next few years."

Figure 4.12.4 Comments on the slowdown in demand for ERP solutions

With the advent of the Internet and the dramatic growth of e-business, technology is no longer just an enabler but a *driver of change*. E-business is forcing organisations to address their customers, partners and suppliers in an integrated way. This in turn in having a fundamental impact on the management consultancy industry. The large firms estimate that up to 70 per cent of their income is now coming from e-business related consultancy.

Many consultancy firms have become key players in the new economy through their *incubator and venture capital activities*. For example, Accenture, McKinsey and Bain all have incubators which develop and launch dotcom start-ups, often providing consultancy in exchange for equity. Accenture's e-units allow staff to share in the wealth created by their venture capital operations around the world.

New Entrants

A number of pure Internet consultancies emerged during 2000, such as Scient, Viant and Sapient, many transferring skills, experience and staff from the States where the e-consultancy market is more mature. Some have suffered from the recent Nasdaq crash and the burst of the dot.com bubble.

Many consultancy firms are entering into alliances with software suppliers, telcos or communications conglomerates in order to provide a broader range of services to their clients and extend their global reach. Cisco still has a 10 per cent stake in KPMG Consulting. In 2000 Cap Gemini purchased the consultancy arm of Ernst & Young and is now launching a global telecoms consultancy firm with Cisco. Deloitte is working with WPP to provide e-marketing solutions through Roundarch.

Flotation

The SEC (Securities and Exchange Commission) is trying to increase controls on the consultancy work provided by audit firms to their clients. One response is to float the consultancy business. KPMG achieved an initial public offering of its US business, PricewaterhouseCoopers is considering a similar move and Accenture's partial IPO has been an initial success. As we go to press the latest rumour is that EDS is interested in PWC's consultancy business. Flotation also provides the opportunity to access money markets for the much-needed capital for expansion and in the war for talent stock options are becoming a powerful weapon. However opinion in the industry is divided on flotations, and a variety of other solutions to the problems of SEC interference and need for capital for expansion will doubtless emerge in time.

Before the economic downturn in the USA of 2000/2001, many consultancy firms experienced high staff turnover as competitors poached their good people or the lure of the dotcom became irresistible before the bubble burst. In response, many of the more traditional firms have to rethink their whole structure. Young high fliers want and expect to become partners sooner and to share in the profits.

Future investment in IT

PMP research into future IT investment shows e-commerce as the most likely area for IT investment. It is seen as a key consultancy opportunity as clients seek to realign their businesses either to capitalise on the opportunities afforded by web technology or to react to the threat of competitors doing so.

The survey showed that ERP as well as business intelligence, data warehousing, sales and marketing would continue to provide consultancy opportunities. In reality, these areas are interrelated and reflect the client's different stages of systems development. Areas of growing significance are cross-enterprise applications (EAI). Consultants revealed that they would be placing greater emphasis on partnering in the future.

Consultants were also asked what they thought were the key factors in a successful vendor partnership. The key driver was identified as e-commerce strategy at 15 per cent, and significantly ERP is down to fourth place at just 8 per cent.

352 KEY CONSULTANCY ACTIVITIES

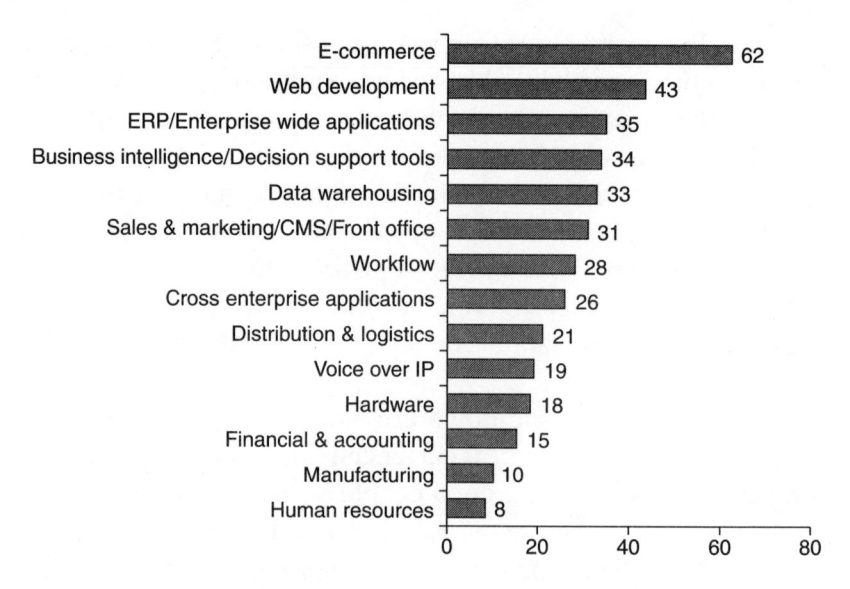

Category	Value
E-commerce	62
Web development	43
ERP/Enterprise wide applications	35
Business intelligence/Decision support tools	34
Data warehousing	33
Sales & marketing/CMS/Front office	31
Workflow	28
Cross enterprise applications	26
Distribution & logistics	21
Voice over IP	19
Hardware	18
Financial & accounting	15
Manufacturing	10
Human resources	8

Figure 4.12.5 Areas in which significant increases in IT investment are anticipated

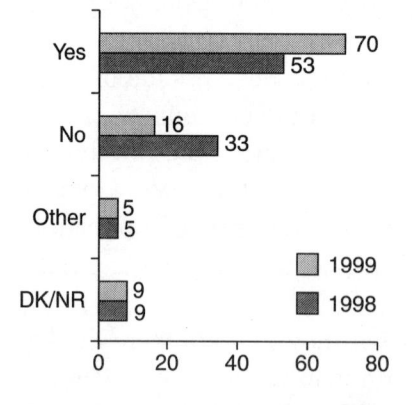

	1999	1998
Yes	70	53
No	16	33
Other	5	5
DK/NR	9	9

Overwhelming opportunities for best of breed vendors lie almost exclusively in the e-commerce/business and customer relationship management spaces

Figure 4.12.6 Whether firms will place greater emphasis on working with 'best of breed' vendors in the coming 12 months

Figure 4.12.7 Views on partnering strategy over the next two years

Strategy	Value
Driven by e-commerce strategy	15
Always client driven/independent	12
More best of breed	10
More enterprise (ERP) solution	8
No change to current strategy	7
Going more global	5
Strong links with smaller number	5
Will follow market leaders	4
ERP at backbone, best of breed frontoffice	4
Integration standards enable both	3
Recruiting more partners	3

The Future

So, following the dotcom re-structuring and the economic downturn, what does the future hold for management consultancy beyond ERP in the new world of e-commerce?

Consultancy firms are becoming directly involved in the new economy rather than simply enabling it to function. Their venture capital, incubator activities and alliances are making them key players and active participants. Their extensive networks across and between industry sectors put them at the heart of the 'next' economy.

The next economy moves much more quickly than the old; this requires consultants to be more flexible and entrepreneurial than their old economy counterparts. Strategy has to be constantly modified and objectives re-evaluated.

The client-consultant relationship is changing and the boundaries are blurring. Consultants can become part of the client organisation for periods of time, may invest in them and ultimately share in their profits. Consultancy firms, which have historically competed, are now working together on client projects.

Consultants will play a key role in e-procurement, digital market places, supply chain, CRM and outsourcing.

Many of the larger firms have launched separate e-business brands e.g. Roundarch (Deloitte/WPP) and Metrius (KPMG Consulting).

Venture consulting will increase as consultancies use their networks and skills to identify and nurture business opportunities. This will also provide those firms with a means of attracting and retaining their best people, allowing them to develop and use entrepreneurial skills in the security of a large firm.

There will be greater convergence within and outside the industry as firms co-operate and merge in order better to service their clients.

The future looks bright, but of course technology alone cannot provide all the answers; however if the right technology with sound business practice and innovative consulting are harnessed, the possibilities are extensive.

The strategists have to understand more about IT and the IT vendors have to understand more about strategy/business. Both have to understand the cultural implications of the rapidly changing work place, which is affecting everyone in this industry.

And we must never forget that the achievement of real business value is paramount. Indeed it is the only reason that clients will continue to value and use the services of management consultancies.

This chapter was prepared from a talk originally given to a consulting audience by Bruce Petter, Executive Director of the Management Consultancies' Association in December 2000.

5

Consulting Internationally

bcb

www.bcb.co.uk

Over 110 Sectors and Disciplines of Professional Services

MAIN AREAS OF ACTIVITY

- Agriculture & Rural Development
- Energy
- Healthcare
- Human Resource Development
- Maritime
- Planning & Infrastructure
- Tourism and Leisure
- Privatisation & Project Finance

The Americas
Europe
Africa
Middle East
South Asia
Asia Pacific

Promoting British Expertise Worldwide

One Westminster Palace Gardens
Artillery Row
London SW1P 1RJ

Telephone +44 (0)20 7222 3651
Facsimile +44 (0)20 7222 3664
E-mail mail@bcb.co.uk
Website www.bcb.co.uk

5.1

Consulting in the developing world

Colin Adams

We are often asked how firms or individuals should go about working internationally rather than at home and this particularly applies to the developing world. There are many misconceptions, ranging from complete ignorance on how even to get started to total overconfidence. At times for example there is what I would call the scattergun mentality: 'we intend to work throughout the world!' An admirable ambition but not generally achievable when starting internationally from scratch.

The perceived wisdom is that working on consultancy projects in the developing world is fraught with problems, so much so that it is a step many firms are reluctant or even refuse to take. This is a great pity – the long-term rewards of working successfully in such countries can be of enormous benefit to the recipients, many of whom are suffering from abject poverty; it is an excellent way for the firm concerned to gain experience and, naturally to enhance their profitability and a useful way for the potential establishment of trading partnerships between the client country and that of the consultants. Inevitably, there are hurdles to be jumped and pitfalls to be avoided, but provided consultants set about doing work internationally in a planned and well-structured manner, there are only marginally more problems to surmount than there would be at home.

In this chapter I would like to discuss the ethos of working in the developing world, the techniques for identifying work, for establishing consortia, and the different potential areas of funding and bidding for projects. It would also be useful to highlight some of the risks involved, and to make some comments about being paid!

Background

In most countries of the world, even the poorest, there is a history of using consultants to assist in both the distribution of aid and economic development. Such consultancy is not of course confined to management and institutional development but encompasses all sectors ranging from agriculture, healthcare, infrastructure, and as economic stability is achieved, to such areas as sport and tourism, cultural development, retail etc. There are however few sectors – irrespective of their technical nature – in the developing world where a large element of management techniques is not required. The provision of advice is not confined to consultants and anyone in this area must be prepared to work in liaison with those in the voluntary sector, the NGOs etc.

Naturally, developing countries have a fierce sense of pride and independence. The result is that a small minority resent the imposition of international consultants, feeling that they are quite capable of doing the job themselves. An even smaller minority do not even understand the concept of consultancy and regard the expenditure involved as a waste of resources. I was, for example, given a hard time by a Minister in the Asia Pacific Region over why his newly graduated engineers should not do the task of a highly experienced international consulting engineering practice. It was only when I gave him my analogy of a patient being given a heart transplant by a newly qualified doctor without experience that he started to get the point!

At the same time those new to international work should beware of making the mistake as many of their predecessors have done, that developing countries have no national consulting capability of their own. It is often difficult to identify appropriate firms but a vital ingredient is to establish local partnerships. However good a consultant may be at his specialist subject, without local advice it is simply not feasible to produce a balanced result. Examples are legion of companies who have gone into developing countries and tried to impose criteria more appropriate to California, London or Rome. Hence the reason why those who win repeat work have local offices where the preponderance of their employees come from the host country. I will return to the topic of choosing partners later.

Identifying target markets and the types of consultancy required

Fifteen to twenty years ago it would have been possible to say that virtually all developing countries required all types of consultancy, but, as already highlighted above, a substantial element of the work can now be bid for and successfully completed (and at a lower price) by local consultants. Indeed there has been a measure of resentment that for too long the International Financing Institutions (IFIs) and bilateral donors have continued to give work to international consultants when an equivalent national capability existed in the recipient country. Those countries borrowing money, for example from the World Bank, resent having to pay international fee rates; at the same time their national consultants resent the fact that they are paid a lower rate for what appears to be the same job. This has led to the IFIs adopting a not unreasonable policy of trying to allocate at least 40% of projects to local consultants or firms resident in the region with local employees. Once again this is a reason for establishing a local office with local staff.

Given this trend, it is clear that anyone wishing to work internationally must be capable of providing a combination of high-tech or state of the art advice, and experience which can enable the recipients to shortcut the development process and avoid the mistakes and pitfalls that others have encountered. This is the most convincing argument why countries should import consulting advice.

The Internet has revolutionised the way projects are advertised. All IFIs such as the World and Asian Development Banks, the European Bank for Reconstruction and Development, the European Commission and many national agencies such as the UK's Department for International Development now advertise projects on their websites (and these incidentally can be accessed through BCB's). Projects are also advertised in the local newspapers of the country or region concerned. While this is potentially a good method of acquiring some types of projects, it is the companies who have done their homework earlier who will get themselves on the fast-track. They will have visited the country of interest, made preliminary contacts, even established partnerships or tentatively appointed agents, and started to sniff-out potential projects. In some cases by the time a project is advertised, the client will have a pretty good idea of some of the firms they would like to short-list and have met the personalities involved. Such a headstart is considered vital by most firms experienced in international work.

In a developing country the potential for identifying work in the private sector is by definition going to be somewhat limited, but again should not be underestimated. The technique is similar to work for government although of course such contracts are not going to be advertised as they are in the public sector. It is therefore even more imperative that those seeking work should get to know the particular market. The resources of effective commercial representatives in Embassies can be key in identifying such potential opportunities. Another method is to establish partnerships with other consulting firms who are more experienced, and the advantages of this are explained more fully below.

Piggy-backing

One of the biggest impediments to a new firm being selected for short-listing is in the eyes of the client or an IFI lack of experience in the country or region concerned, or in working for that specific IFI. I can recall a cousin trying to start an acting career and being told that she could only get a part in a play if she was a member of Equity but she could not become a member of Equity until she had a part! One technique of getting the necessary consulting experience is to become a sub-contractor of someone who has ie, a 'piggy-back technique'. We in BCB are approached by potential government or individual clients from all over the world on a daily basis to find UK consultants, but six times out of ten previous in-country experience is required. Our advice to those wishing to get started is invariably to work for a fellow consulting firm, unless of course the type of consultancy is unique and a client will accept a firm's services irrespective. Such identification of potential partners is one of the roles of international consultancy associations.

Partners

Working together with local consultants is no different from working in partnership with firms in one's own country with one notable exception: there are often cultural differences to be borne in mind but these can too often be exaggerated. However experiencing them can for the most part help international consultants to better adapt their work to the local environment.

The techniques for determining whether a partner of the same nationality is competent, financially sound and reliable needs no explanation from me. For a developing country project however, it is often difficult enough when seeking either international or local partners to identify suitable firms, be they other consultants or contractors, and even more difficult to determine their professional standing. For a long time we have agitated for the IFIs to organise better databases throughout the world of local firms including consultants. Too often unfortunately such information is patchy, seldom complete and not based on professional competence. Limited assistance in identifying firms can be given by the commercial staff in Embassies, consulting organisations and websites. It is money well spent to use the services of professional firms whose role is to give advice on such matters (especially financial), together with more general political and financial risk on the country concerned. Once again fellow consultants – unless they are in direct competition – can also be very helpful. In my organisation alone for example member firms were last year NOT working in only two countries of the world and the level of corporate knowledge is therefore very high.

Funding

One of the greatest 'fears of the dark' is about the ability to get payment for carrying out this type of consultancy. Of course there is a need for prudence but today for the most part anyone working in developing countries can apply the same acid test as they would at home. Inevitably the cases of bad debt are the ones that are highlighted and the vast proportion of satisfactory business transactions never reach the headlines. That said, it is sensible for someone beginning such work for the first time to either be, as stated earlier, a sub-contractor of another firm with experience, or working under an IFI-funded grant or loan. However if for example the World Bank is providing a loan, (and the same goes for many other IFIs), the contract will be with the client country and not with the Bank itself. The Bank however provides a sensible safety net to ensure that payment is made for satisfactory work.

It is however essential (and in some cases compulsory) that some form of consultancy indemnity insurance etc is taken out, and credit guarantee cover (for payment) is sensible. The majority of countries except those with extensive political risk or in major financial difficulty have some form of formal cover provided by such as the Export Credit Guarantee Department (ECGD) in the UK and this can be negotiated for many different types of activity. Where the situation is less secure financially such cover may not be available and consulting firms would be well advised only to do work where payment arrangements are solid, underwritten by the IFIs, or by, for example, a multi-national company. Some private insurance brokers can also arrange cover.

It is also worthwhile checking what the arrangements are in the event of a legal dispute. Even if judgement is awarded, it may be difficult in a small minority of countries to ensure that a judgement is served and enacted.

Taxation and currency

The majority of countries in the world have bilateral personal taxation agreements. Furthermore in the preparation of projects the tax liabilities in terms of Corporation and all manner of other taxes should be made clear, but this is not always the case. It is therefore essential that you are quite clear what your tax liabilities will be in carrying out and being paid for the consultancy. There are well-documented examples of consulting firms who have on the face of it made an excellent profit, only to find that the price they quoted for the project did not include the tax liability.

Another area to be checked is any currency exchange restrictions. Clearly there is no point in doing a project only to find that the currency must by law remain in the country concerned.

And finally, what currency are you being paid in?

Registration, expression of interest, short-listing and project award

Before a firm will even be invited to submit a proposal, many IFIs, national governments etc, require consultants to be permanently registered with them and/or to make an expression of interest for a particular project. Unfortunately virtually all organisations have their own procedures and it is only by careful study of the appropriate websites or attending suitable courses that you will learn who requires what. Oh for worldwide standardisation! Clare Short, the UK's Secretary of State for International Development highlighted the problem in Tanzania where some 43 different IFI and bilateral funding agency procedures were in use. Nevertheless such study will be rewarded; there is plenty of work to go round and careful preparation of proposals will result in short-listing. There are however no short cuts.

Often nationality can be an issue, and a good technique is to have member firms from the client country and where possible from more than one country. It is becoming increasingly evident that those seeking international consultants are much more likely to select a consortium with members from more than one nationality. Take care however! Some organisations, eg the Asian Development Bank, will only accept nationals whose countries are members of the Bank.

Sometimes short-lists may only contain, as they do for the EBRD, only two short-listed firms from any one country.

Winning the project

It may seem a blinding statement of the obvious but a few inexperienced firms put all their efforts into writing and winning a proposal without looking at the practicalities if they actually win – movement of personnel, initial finance, appropriate equipment, accommodation, timing and a host of other details. Being caught on the back foot over such preparation can lead to an indifferent start to the project. It is therefore axiomatic that a sensible degree of outline planning should be done when winning the project looks like becoming a strong possibility.

Project delivery

Carrying out the project can produce no more difficulties than it would if done at home – discounting of course terrain and climate! However there is one significant point that should be underlined: many projects evolve as they go along but should the client, particularly if an IFI is also involved, want extra work performed, this should not be done on a handshake but should be negotiated and agreed in writing. One of the principle causes of payment difficulty is generated by inadequately authorised contract extension.

Getting paid

In a comparable way, nothing should be left out of a written contract. One area that can generate discord is bonus payments for a successful outcome. Again the wording of these must be totally unambiguous and legally enforceable.

Should a firm experience payment difficulties and an IFI is involved it will often be incumbent on that IFI to assist the firm in reaching a satisfactory outcome. Other avenues are to use consultancy trade associations with experience in dealing with recalcitrant clients or again to use the services of an Embassy in the country concerned to put pressure on the client country (if it is a public sector project). It is often better to use a trade association such as BCB to work for you rather than to be deemed a troublemaker and risk the goodwill so valuably needed to obtain future projects. I have had experience of IFIs reluctant to use companies they feel complain too stridently.

The follow-on

Few projects in a developing country should ever be regarded as an end in themselves. Even before winning or carrying out the first project, consultants should be looking at the potential to bid for others. Neither the developing countries themselves, the funding institutions nor potential partners in consortia have time for those who want to do a one-off project except in special circumstances.

Conclusion

In a short chapter such as this, it is all too easy in highlighting problem areas to give the impression that it is all too difficult. I am fortunate in representing well over 300 firms all of whom are working successfully throughout the world. The majority of them win projects in some of the world's most challenging markets. And you can too!

There are four points I would underline:

- Remember, many firms and individuals in developing countries have far more skill than often the developed world give them credit for. It does not therefore pay to be patronising
- Use all sources of advice
- Initially keep your ambitions modest
- Finally, working in developing countries is not as difficult as people would have you believe!

5.2

Selected international institute and market profiles

The EU

AUSTRIA *Herbert Bachmaier*

The Austrian Institute of Management Consultants was founded in 1985 and is an association representing management consulting and information technology consulting companies. Together with more than 130 other professional groups, the Institute is a sub-organisation of the Austrian Chamber of Commerce. It is not an association based on voluntary membership but an organisation under public law, which was created by an Act of Parliament to serve the special interests of the professions it represents.

This special Act of Parliament (the 'Economic Chamber Act') is what primarily distinguishes the Institute from other, private associations on which it is based because it defines membership as compulsory. Therefore, every management consultant in Austria automatically becomes a member of the Institute. This fact explains why the Austrian Institute has so many members compared to the size of the country.

The Institute is an independent body and the government has no jurisdiction concerning the Institute and the Chamber of

Commerce. Activities and policies are decided by the members through democratically elected representatives.

The objective of our Institute is to represent the interests of its members in all types of issues and problems confronting management and IT consultants. Our association has approximately 23,000 members – 2,300 management consultants and more than 20,000 IT consultants.

The Institute is a member of FEACO and ICMCI.

Management consulting and IT disciplines

The members of the Institute normally work in the following disciplines:

- general management consulting
- management practices in information technology
- strategic performance management
- corporate culture
- financial management
- mergers & acquisitions
- controlling
- human resource management and development
- administration
- logistics
- skills transfer and training
- environmental management
- total quality management
- marketing & sales management
- computer applications for management
- innovation and technology management
- system development and introductory support
- software engineering
- IT project management

Management consultancy in Austria

Management consultancy is a relatively young occupational field in Austria. Potential clients only began to develop an awareness of the profession at the beginning of the 1970s and it wasn't until the early 1980s that clients began fully accepting management consultants, making the profession a major success story during the course of the last decade. In 1976 only 700 consultants were licensed to work as management consultants in Austria. By the end of last year the Institute listed 2,300 full time management consultants.

Management consultancy agencies in Austria are mostly individuals or very small organisations. There are hardly any large companies such as can be found in other comparable countries. The largest agencies in Austria rarely have more than 100 employees – rather small by international standards but consistent with the general structure of the Austrian economy, which is composed mostly of small and medium sized enterprises.

The main reason for this positive development is Austria's joining of the EU in 1995. This date is a turning point in the political and economic development of Austria and it came at just the right time. Membership of the EU not only forced the country to hand over legislative rights to the EU, but also kick-started an hitherto unknown process of deregulation and liberalisation in politics, economics and culture, making room for many new liberal business laws. One of many examples is the liberalisation of the telecommunication field, which had an enormous impact on service industries such as management consultancy, the software and information technology industry as well as the advertising and communication industry.

Incite

Incite is an innovative new concept devised by the Austrian Institute of Management Consulting. Incite (Institute for Management Consultants and Information Technology Experts) is the Austrian platform for certification of management and IT consultants. Apart from the CMC certification, Incite is introducing the CITC – certification for IT consultants – as well as the CCT certification for business trainers based on the already established CMC certification process. Furthermore, Incite offers special supplementary courses for consultants in advance of certification.

GERMANY *Klaus Reiners*

BDU

The Federal Association of German Management Consultants BDU e.V. is the industrial and professional association of management consultants and executive search consultants in Germany. It is the biggest association of management consultants in Europe and is a member of FEACO and the ICMCI.

Founded in 1954, the BDU presently represents approximately 16,000 management consultants and executive search consultants, who are currently distributed among 520 member companies. The functions of the association are to increase the performance standard of the business sector; to implement quality standards by means of professional regulations and principles; positively to influence the economic and legal framework conditions of the sector, and finally to support the demand for management consultancy.

Occupational right

The BDU continually lobbies for an adequate occupational right for management consultants, in which among other things the possibility of coalition with, for example, lawyers, qualified auditors and tax advisors as well as consultancy in the 'interfaces' for a tax and legal consultancy is facilitated. In a time, however, in which complex company requirements need interdisciplinary solution approaches the BDU prefers a modern and practical organisation, which supports free competition and which is much closer to the demands of industry and economy for comprehensive consultancy performance. Therefore the liberalisation of all professions in associations would be the up-to-date and most desirable solution. In this context, the BDU has been striving to establish the independent occupation of 'qualified management consultancy employee' with a training requirement since 1999.

Professional structuring

The BDU has responded to the wide range of standards in entrepreneurial, economic and technical consultancy by founding specialised professional structures. Consultancy specialists for controlling, marketing, technology and logistics, quality management, information management, executive search, personnel development etc. find a professional platform here. In these professional structures (professional associations, professional groups, working groups and working circles) individual experts from the member companies regularly meet for professional exchanges of experiences and to gain some further education. From this work new consultancy concepts as well as a network of relationships and know-how are being developed, and they frequently result in strategic alliances – particularly between individual consultants and smaller companies.

The CMC/BDU title

BDU membership is subject to strict requirements and the exclusive award of the internationally acknowledged qualification CMC, support the market transparency and document the special efficiency of the BDU member companies. Interested customer companies have the opportunity to find the ideal consulting company for their needs, by means of a database or a directory (CD-ROM, internet or book version).

Requirements for BDU membership

In order to be admitted to the BDU the management of a business consulting firm must fulfil strict requirements:

- provide proof of professional aptitude
- have five years of professional experience as a management consultant

- have three years experience of independent and self-employed work as a management consultant (applies to company managing directors)
- supply three excellent customer references
- pass two professional and technical interviews with BDU management consultants
- undertake to abide by BDU professional principles
- professional supervision by the five-member BDU honorary council

The BDU structure

The honorary presidency of the BDU (president and three vice presidents) is elected for two years by the general meeting and is regularly advised by the association conference. Members of the association conference are the presidents of all professional and branch organisations. The managing director of the BDU with his 14 staff in Bonn and Berlin is responsible for the implementation of the BDU policy, all current tasks and the support of the work within the professional organisations. The organisations form the centre of the association's work. Here, 20 to 50 professional or branch specialists meet three times per year for further training, to exchange practical experiences and know-how or to discuss questions of management.

Professional organisations

- AK Berlin-Brandenburg
- AK Baden-Württemberg
- Business Consultants International
- eBusiness
- Timber and furniture industry
- Information management
- Insolvency and redevelopment management
- International consultancy companies
- Communication management

- Management and Marketing
- Public customers
- Outplacement
- Executive search
- Personnel development
- Project management
- Quality management consultation
- Technology and logistics
- Company management and controlling
- Company foundation and company development
- Administration manager of consultancy firms

Offices

Zitelmannstraβe 22, D-53113 Bonn
Tel: 0049(0)228/91 61–0, fax: 0228/91 61–26
Kronprinzendamm 1, D-10711 Berlin
Tel: 0049(0)30/893 10 70, fax: 030/893 47 46
info@bdu.de; www.bdu.de

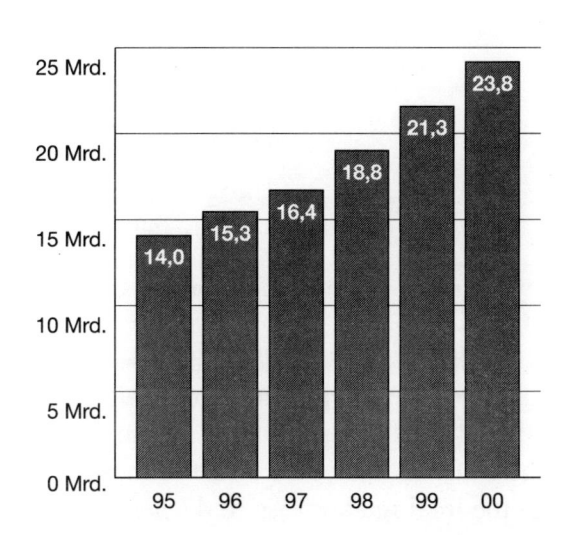

Figure 5.2.1 Development of management consultancy market in Germany 1995–2000 (DM)

The German management consultancy market in 2000

Despite a slight decline in the rates of escalation, the demand for management consultancy remained high in Germany in the year 2000. Compared to the previous year the total sales volume of the sector increased by 11.8 percent to a new high of DM 23.8 billion (1999: DM 21.3 billion). Since activity generated by the introduction of the Euro, as well as changes to standard software and programming systems following the new millennium has abated, management consultants find their business is increasingly required in information and telecommunication technology areas. An indication of this is the expected increase in consultancy projects, which includes at least a share in e-commerce, from 38 per cent in 1999 to 50 per cent in the year 2000.

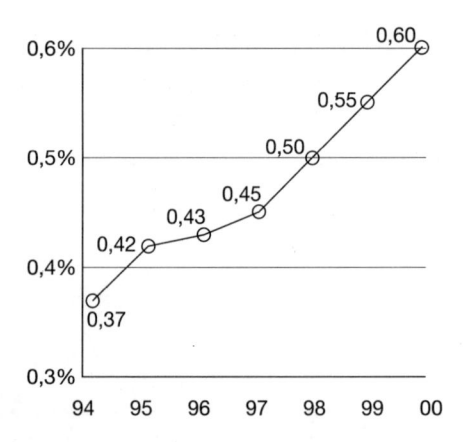

Figure 5.2.2 MC-Turnover as a percentage of the German Gross Domestic Product (GDP)

68,000 management, IT and personnel consultants were working in approximately 14,700 consultancy firms in Germany in 2000. Meanwhile the BDU estimates the share of the 40 biggest consultancy firms in the total market rose to 47 per cent (45 per cent in 1999), corresponding to a sales volume in absolute figures of DM11.2 billion. The market share of the smaller consultancy firms and individual consultants was about 17 per cent with a sales volume of DM4.1 billion. While the top 40 of the industry recorded strong increases in growth, averaging 18 per cent increase, the rates of growth were much lower for medium-sized consultancy firms with an average of nine per cent and at smaller consultancies with 2.5 per cent.

The strongest demand for management consultancy activity in the past year came again from the credit and insurance sector. The share increased from 22 per cent in 1999 to 27 per cent in 2000. Online banking and direct insurance companies have meant that industry has changed drastically and the traditional financial services companies are looking for possible ways to react to the change in competition. The demand for management consultancy from trade and public administration is declining slightly.

Due to the completion of change and readjustment projects at the new millennium and the decreasing intensity in consulting following the introduction of the Euro, the IT consulting/IT services share decreased from 46 per cent in 1999 to 43.4 per cent of sales volume in 2000. However, this sector continued to be the clear top-selling area. The share of strategy consulting was 27.5 per cent (26 per cent in 1999), for organisation consulting the share was 24.5 per cent (23 per cent in 1999) and for human resources management 4.6 per cent (5 per cent in 1999).

GREECE *Yiangos Charalambous*

Introduction

People, especially entrepreneurs, have been trying for centuries to develop a 'perfect world'. Various professions, economic theories, political and polemical strategies are continuously being developed in pursuit of this, each promising means, ways and tools of achieving targeted objectives.

Although the 'management consulting' profession existed centuries ago, especially in Greece, the initiation and development of a scientific approach to the study of management in industry and commerce really began with the industrial revolution in the 19th century. Noted pioneers in the science of management are Charles Babbage, Frederick Winslow Taylor, Henry Fayol, Mary Market Follet and a number of others. In spite of their contribution to this science it was only around 1960 that it was 'branded and marketed' from American universities, academics and professionals, irrespective of nationality. This younger generation of pioneers took the heavy burden of promotion upon their shoulders and within a relatively short period of time made the profession of management consulting one of the most interesting, especially to recipients of MBA degrees. Undoubtedly, Greek management consultants, whether in Greece or abroad, have played an active role in spreading the seed of management consulting.

The profession in Greece

In an Ancient Greek drama, the play usually opens at the end of a dramatic story. This article also adopts this approach. Within the limited space available, I have attempted to cover the contributions of prominent members of the Greek business community, professionals and academics whose work and writings are contributing to the expansion and development of our profession in Greece and internationally.

The structure of the management consultancy market in Greece today is as follows. Most of the major international management consulting firms are already established or represented in Greece. The international companies are competing with a growing number of local consulting firms of various sizes that are offering their services to the government and public corporations, small and medium-sized local companies as well as multinational companies, that are established in Greece. Also, in recent years many of our members have adopted an international approach, bidding for and winning important contracts in the Balkans, former Soviet States, Eastern Europe, Africa and the Far East. The European Union, the World Bank and the European Bank for Reconstruction and Development are among the clients of some of our members.

Our members provide a wide range of consulting services and are continuously developing new products to meet the needs of their clients in the race for competitiveness in a very rapidly changing hi-tech world. The market for consulting services in Greece is growing at a faster rate than in the majority of European countries, with most of the growth coming from the information technology sector. The demand for energy management and environmental management systems is also expected to increase. Many of our members are well positioned technologically to meet this demand.

The Hellenic Association of Management Consulting Firms (SESMA), formed 10 years ago, already has 45 corporate members in its ranks which employ more than 1,200 professionals. This small number of members reflects in part the growth of the consulting market in Greece but also the high standards set by the Association for membership. 16 firms' applications for membership are presently being examined. In addition, there are over 100 firms offering management consulting services but which have not yet applied or do not currently meet the criteria for membership. SESMA is an active member of the European Federation of Management Consulting Associations (FEACO).

The expansion of our profession described above has taken place in the last 20–25 years. Being a partner in one of the first accounting firms that established a consulting department, I can recall the 'scene of loners' when asked by my senior partner to meet with Nikos Embeoglou (still a prominent member of our profession) to discuss the possibility of co-operation on a project for which PA (then the only large international consulting firm established in Greece) was intending to submit a bid. To achieve this co-operation, I departed from Piraeus on a green bus on a hot summer day. I arrived wet with perspiration at Niko's office in Kolonaki, in the centre of Athens and found him behind a desk fully covered with his books, trying to find the information he needed for a matter he was dealing with. Even today this prominent professional is one of the most active members of our profession, always submerged in books and encouraging young people through his work to master this art and/or science. This he does through the Hellenic Society of Management Consultants (EEDE) and Alba University.

EEDE, which now has more than 6,000 professionals as members, plays a leading role both in the education of consultants and in providing facilities for conferences and activities related to the consulting profession. EEDE owes its establishment to the efforts of some of our prominent industrialists amongst whom are Mr. Dimitris Kyriazis, Mr. Georganas and Mr. Marinopoulos

The globalised business world

In the globalised, electronic business world of today, Greek academics and consultants, amongst them Professors Nicolas Negroponte and Michael Deltouzos, are researching and developing new tools and techniques which Greek consultants are studying closely and implementing in an effort continuously to improve the services we can offer to clients.

Conclusion

As far back as 429–347 BC, Socrates was exploring the nature of knowledge itself and its applications. It was Plato who told his pupil Aristotle that, within any organisation, nobody should earn more than five times as much as the lowest worker. The principle of experience in management was also studied by Greek philosophers and this is summarised by the statement 'before you become a helmsman you should serve as a rower'. Finally, quality that adds value to our clients' operations is described in Aristotle's statement – 'excellence is not an act, but a habit'.

In conclusion, I would like to note that the newly elected Board of Directors of SESMA, with its new President Mr Thanos Mavros, is aiming to expand and improve the services that our Association offers to members and young professionals, as well as to our clients in the public and private sectors, to whom we extend our thanks for their continued support.

IRELAND *Peter Nolan*

There was once a time of clarity when the question was whether the glass was half empty or half full. Now the question is whether there is a glass at all. The confusion – if not created by, then certainly augmented by media hyperbole – is threatening to convince us that we are in real danger of recession. Surely there must be a calming, knowledgeable and sturdy guide through this morass in which we have found ourselves. In an Irish market already worth over IR£200 million, is this an opportunity for Irish management consulting?

Ireland. An economic miracle – of that there is no doubt. Economic growth of six per cent is predicted for this year – last year's 11 per cent growth is impossible to maintain when the US recession and the foot and mouth crisis are taken into account. Ireland, the exemplary European state. A country equally at home in Boston, Berlin, Brazil or Brisbane. A country that has branded itself as the honest broker. A country that voted 'no' to Nice.

Notwithstanding this blip on our path to European integration there is no doubt of our country's respected global standing. In truth, as a nation we are firmly committed to European integration. A recent Deloitte & Touche poll shows that over 80 per cent of business people were disappointed by the referendum result. Our adoption and implementation of the best telecommunications technologies will determine whether this time is just a beautiful moment or the beginning of a golden age for our citizens.

Ireland has embraced the adoption of digital media and telecommunications technologies. The Department of Enterprise has been instrumental in the implementation of many of the country's most ambitious infrastructure projects. The Global Crossings project and the Digital Media District are examples of forward thinking, infrastructural investment. The Revenue Online Service has become a renowned international benchmark. Other examples of the Government's drive to adopt the new technologies are REACH and OASIS projects. David Hearn, Deloitte &

Touche's European e-Business Lead Partner said after a recent meeting with Mr. Brendan Touhy, Secretary General of the Department of Public Enterprise 'There is no doubt of the Irish government's commitment to establishing an exemplary digital infrastructure and service to its citizens. They are taking a long-term view and all aspects of society will be improved. Government is providing the lead in this area and the private sector must surely answer the call.'

Ireland has been through substantial socio-economic change in the past decade and in the process has become a nation with a focus on European and Global development. The Government is working to make Ireland the e-Hub of Europe. Ireland will be recognised as a global centre of digital excellence. Today Ireland offers the management consultant a wide range of opportunities. As Ireland has changed, so too has the face of management consulting.

The fires of the dotcom furnace are quickly cooling with three main results. Firstly, greater opportunity for established management consultants – now more than ever our clients need to know that they can trust us. Secondly, greater demand for our services due to the demise of those that concentrated on hype rather than the bottom-line. Finally, the realisation that there is only one economy and to succeed in it simple business principles like making a profit should be adhered to.

Nua and Oniva in Ireland, Razorfish, Organic, MarchFirst, Viant and Xpedior in the US have been affected by the recent market adjustment. A consequence of the dotcom bust has been less spending and fewer clients, resulting in less revenue for the small Internet consultancies.

The larger consulting firms have the fundamental attraction of stability and maturity that the remaining dotcoms need in order to develop – they provide a safe pair of hands. The Big Five consultancies, which were slow off the mark when the Net consultancies first entered the newly created market space, have now implemented marketing and business development strategies specifically targeting the Internet companies.

At the core of the dotcom bubble there existed a solid business e-strategy. Large enterprises were quietly implementing ERP and CRM systems, investing in huge sums in the process and these large enterprises sought the safety of large, proven consultancies for these important strategic projects.

The early call to arms during the dotcom era was 'first mover advantage' and this was a spur to companies to develop an Internet presence quickly. In the rush, companies primarily chose small consultancies for speed, agility and creative solutions. The Big Five consulting firms have invested significantly in the e-business market and can now offer all the necessary speed and innovation. Nowadays, companies have realised that first mover advantage was a myth and that, on the contrary, a lot can be learned from the mistakes of those at the 'bleeding-edge'. Companies are now aware of the power of the Internet as another channel for doing business. They now realise that an Internet promise is a business promise that must be kept.

The larger companies are now focusing on strategic initiatives, leaving reactive, ineffective and costly internet projects behind. These strategic initiatives are more complex and larger – and more mission-critical to the business. A consulting firm that can provide the depth and breadth of knowledge – from marketing and branding to ERP implementation, from tax advice to website design – provides a level of comfort to these companies.

Between the Big Five consulting firms and the dotcom consultancies there remains a vibrant group of mid-range consultancies (5–25 employees) like CHL Consulting Group and Farrell Grant Sparks. In Ireland, CHL have a complement of ten permanent staff in addition to nine associates and an extensive network of specialist consulting companies with whom we work on a regular basis. Overseas, CHL has a complement of twelve permanent staff in addition to some 35 associates in Belgium, Britain, France, Germany and the Netherlands. According to Mr. Michael Counahan, a CHL partner, the market has changed substantially in the last year or two. 'Our client base is mature and sophisticated.

They no longer expect a one-stop shop consultancy service – hence the increased number of team-bids we are involved in. We have led a bid this year, which involved Accenture's London and Paris offices and Peter Bacon. We see this trend becoming more and more prevalent'.

There is also the thriving Independent Management Consultant Group (ICG). This group comprises almost fifty practices with expertise across the complete range of management and business functions. To add to the substantial experience and specialist expertise, members of this group are exploring the new opportunities afforded by the digital technologies. Invest-Tech for example, run by Brian Flanagan has been developing and delivering its business planning software via its Planware website (www.planware.org) for over two years. These products are sold to a customer base in over 70 countries using Electronic Software Distribution (ESD).

Information Technology continues to drive the demand for management consulting, however not all management consulting is IT-centric. The implementation of a management information system requires many sophisticated skills in order to be successful. Business strategy, business process re-engineering, marketing strategy, manufacturing strategy, project management, human resources, logistics, economics and financial management are all vitally important considerations in projects of this scale in order to ensure a return on investment.

The management consulting market in Ireland has changed considerably in the period 2000–2001. The government is driving the adoption of the latest digital media infrastructure and this will have a knock on effect for management consulting. Clients have become more sophisticated and more willing to pick and choose the best that a management consulting practice has to offer. Within the industry itself, the changes within the Big Five are consolidating the market offering. The dotcom aftermath is still being felt but has presented an opportunity for the traditional practices. The glass does exist and it is fine Irish crystal. Now as to whether it is half full or not...

THE NETHERLANDS *Robert Florijn*

The Dutch National Institute of Management Consultants is one of the older national institutes. Founded before the Second World War, it has become the national Institute supporting professional consultants as well as academic studies and developments in the field of organisational change, change management, quality of working life, strategy and financial health. Since the beginning, the Institute has had an open mind regarding the definition of management consultancy. Professionals from different academic and professional backgrounds may become members provided they pass the rigorous and individual entrance procedure. Quality standards are high: of nearly 1500 total members almost 700 have CMC status.

After a period of stability, recent years have seen a modest but sure growth. Growth will get an extra boost by the planned takeover of the Dutch Organisation of Small Consulting Firms, hopefully at the end of 2001.

Currently, talks with the Dutch Council of Management Consulting Firms are warm and congenial, opening up the prospective of contacts with and entry for the employees of the Big Five and other leading firms.

UNITED KINGDOM *Ian Barratt*

The UK management consultancy sector is arguably the most sophisticated outside the United States, from where it came to the UK in the 1920s.

The US practices themselves only began to establish a presence in the UK in the 1950s and this coincided with the beginning of considerable growth in the UK market. It is difficult, however, to gauge the market as a whole (sole practitioners up to the global players) since no one collects the data in this way. UK Government statistics do not recognise management consultancy as a separate industry and, as the earlier chapter on self-regulation explains, the Inland Revenue in the UK regards management consultancy as a trade.

In addition, the structure of the representative bodies in the UK makes the task no easier. The Institute of Management Consultancy (IMC) is predominantly concerned with the qualification and standards of individual management consultants, while the Management Consultancies Association (MCA) is the trade body for the largest practices. Neither is concerned with the full range of practices, nor is membership compulsory. The picture is not helped by the lack of clarity in the UK about what constitutes a management consultant. Much of the statistical information about UK management consultancy is therefore built on the narrow membership base (in purely representative terms) of the MCA membership, although it is clearly the case that MCA members employ the majority of consultants in the UK. Bearing this in mind, the following figures demonstrate the overall growth in the UK market since the 1950s:

Table 5.2.1 Overall growth in the UK market since the 1950s

Year	Member firms	Consultants	Average number of consultants per firm
1956	4	684	171
1960	18	1,813	101
1976	23	2,009	87
1986	24	1,350	56
1996	32	7,267	227
1999	35	14,742	4,212

Source: MCA

What the table also demonstrates is the decline in demand for consultancy services during the 1970s and 1980s. This was reversed by a concerted move of the major accountancy firms into the field. These firms were also merging, enabling them to consolidate their position and absorb more established companies. The market was also given a significant boost by the growing importance of information technology. This has been accelerated by the development of e-commerce.

Expressed in financial terms, and again using MCA figures, the increases in fee income over the same period were even more dramatic:

Table 5.2.2 Increase in fee income since the 1950s

Year	UK revenues (£m)	Overseas revenues (£m)	Outsourcing (£m)	Total (£m)
1960	4	1	0	6
1970	43	17	0	61
1980	43	17	0	61
1990	706	103	0	810
1995	968	172	116	1,256
1999	1,627	578	871	3,076

Source: MCA (figures have been rounded to the nearest £)

Between 1996 and 1999, fee income in the UK grew by 68 per cent, compared with an 18 per cent increase in the UK's gross domestic product.

It is also true that, as a percentage share of GDP, the management consultancy market is the most vibrant in Europe. Services provided by firms in the UK have achieved a greater presence than in any other European country. The following figures (Table 5.2.3), quoted in a report from British Invisibles (due to be published at the time of writing) make the point.

Clearly, even the European market as a whole (USA $36.3 billion) falls behind that of the USA (USA $52 billion), which accounts for just over half the world total. Other developed countries, e.g. Canada, are significant but elsewhere the market is at an early stage of development.

As discussed earlier, there is a lack of clarity in the definition of a management consultant in the UK. The Institute of Management Consultancy's own definition is:

...an independent and qualified person who provides a professional service to business, the public and other undertakings by: (a) identifying and investigating

problems concerned with strategy, policy, markets, organisation, procedures and methods; (b) formulating recommendations for appropriate action by factual investigation and analysis, with due regard for broader management and business implications; (c) discussing and agreeing with the client the most appropriate course of action; (d) providing assistance where required by the client to implement these recommendations

but even this, in itself, may be broader than is desirable.

There are a variety of routes into the management consultancy profession. Many consultants started their careers as specialists in a technical field (eg accountancy or marketing), and are therefore members of another professional body (eg the Institute of Chartered Accountants or the Chartered Institute of Marketing) for their principal professional expertise. It is this 'base' qualification that is seen as giving the necessary credibility. As a result, the homogeneity produced by, say, a practising certificate in other professions does not exist. The Institute's position, as explained in the earlier chapter on self-regulation, is that consulting skills are both a separate discipline and capable of quite specific testing and accreditation mechanisms. Yet until this is universally accepted, the difficulties around definition and professional identity will remain.

Table 5.2.3 The management consultancy market

Country	Market ($bn)	per cent share of the market	per cent of GDP
UK	9.9	27.2	0.78
Germany	11.6	32.0	0.43
Sweden	1.0	2.6	0.36
Netherlands	1.2	3.2	0.28
Spain	1.5	4.0	0.22
France	3.2	8.9	0.19
Italy	1.8	4.9	0.15
Others	6.2	17.1	–
Total	**36.3**	–	–

Source: European Federation of Management Consulting Associations (FEACO), 1999

What is clear is that the industry is developing with the challenges posed by globalisation, e-commerce and changes in client demands. These have included a wish for a move away from advice alone, leaving implementation to the client themselves, towards the implementation of solutions. Clients are becoming more sophisticated and want long-term partnerships, while the large practices in particular see the taking of equity in their clients as a way of cementing the relationship. This creates challenges around independence and objectivity, but reflects a maturing of management consultancy from being seen as a 'jobbing' service into a fully-fledged industry with a major role to play in the development of the UK economy in a global context.

This growing maturity is also expressed in the sectors to which management consultants contribute. Taking MCA analysis, the picture is as follows in Table 5.2.4.

What must also be remembered, however, is the continuing role of the smaller practice and the sole practitioner in the marketplace. It is generally assumed that these smaller firms would show a different mix of specialisms, with IT playing a smaller role. A study carried out by the Institute of Management Consultancy on management consultants working for government tended to bear this out (Table 5.2.5).

So what is the future for the UK market? The rapid growth in demand is being driven by the constant change in the business world as a whole. This seems set to continue. The restructuring of whole industries, required by global competition and the opportunities presented by e-commerce, is unlikely to slow down. Management consultancy is now seen as an integrated service, matching the wide range of challenges currently faced. The key role of IT generally, in this context, is also pushing management consultancy firms towards alliances with IT-solutions providers, while consolidation amongst the practices themselves is also continuing.

Against this background, the debates continue on the regulation of the sector and as to whether or not it is a genuine profession. Codes of conduct, as a minimum, have been put in

Table 5.2.4 Management consultancy and its contribution to industry

Analysis by industry	UK (£m)	EU (£m)	Elsewhere (£m)	Total (£m)
Agriculture, forestry and fishing	9	0	0	9
Electricity/gas (excl. nationalised industries)	154	12	17	183
Water industry (excl. nationalised industries)	77	7	13	97
Extraction of minerals and ores including fuels: manufacture of metals and mineral products (excl. industrialised industries)	106	6	10	122
Chemical industry/man-made fibres	65	17	17	99
Mechanical engineering (i.e. mechanical industrial machinery and equipment)	36	2	2	40
Electrical and electronic machinery and equipment (incl. office machinery and data processing equipment)	45	13	4	62
Transport vehicles and equipment (e.g. motor vehicles, shipbuilding, aerospace)	63	6	7	76
Instrument engineering and other metal goods	35	2	1	39
Food, drink and tobacco	68	5	7	80
Textiles, footwear and clothing	15	2	4	21
Paper, printing and publishing	18	5	8	31
Other manufacturing	101	13	6	121
Construction	14	1	4	18
Wholesale, retail trades and repairs	61	6	15	82
Hotels and catering	36	4	3	43
Transport, storage and post	153	27	30	210
Telecommunications	281	31	27	338
Banking	323	22	33	378
Insurance	219	11	21	251
Other financial services	97	19	21	136
Business services	44	3	14	61
Private sector non-profit making bodies	8	1	1	9
TOTAL PRIVATE SECTOR	**2,027**	**216**	**265**	**2,509**
Central Government	437	19	37	493
Local Government	13	1	3	17
National Health Service	7	1	0	7
Other public bodies	7	0	0	7
Nationalized industries	4	0	0	4
International agencies	4	0	1	5
CEC	0	34	0	34
TOTAL PUBLIC SECTOR	**471**	**55**	**41**	**567**
TOTAL ALL SECTORS	**2,498**	**272**	**306**	**3,076**

Source: MCA

Table 5.2.5 Specialisms of management consultants according to company size

Specialisms	Sole	Small	Medium	Large	Total mentions
Strategy	2	2	4	1	**9**
HR	4	3	1	0	**8**
Programme/project management	1	3	2	0	**6**
Finance and audit	1	4	1	0	**6**
Change management	2	1	1	1	**5**
Business process re-engineering	2	1	0	1	**4**
Marketing	0	0	2	1	**3**
Organisational structure and strategy	0	2	0	1	**3**
Training	0	3	0	0	**3**
IT	0	1	0	1	**2**
Procurement	0	1	1	0	**2**
General operations and efficiency improvement	0	2	0	0	**2**
Quality systems	2	0	0	0	**2**
E-business	0	0	0	1	**1**
Entrepreneurship development	0	0	1	0	**1**
Facilitation	0	0	1	0	**1**
Governance	0	0	1	0	**1**
Report/document writing	0	0	1	0	**1**
Disaster recovery	1	0	0	0	**1**
Health and safety	0	1	0	0	**1**
Information management (not specifically IT)	1	0	0	0	**1**
Risk analysis	1	0	0	0	**1**
Social policy research	0	1	0	0	**1**
VFM	1	0	0	0	**1**

Source: IMC

place by the trade associations while the Institute of Management Consultancy in the UK and the International Council of Management Consulting Institutes (ICMCI) worldwide argue for and pursue professionalisation through qualification.

Commercially, then, the future looks bright for management consultancy in the UK. What will be critical to that future, as ever, will be the health of the global economy and the resilience and competitiveness of the UK economy within it.

SCANDINAVIA *Flemming Poulfelt*

The Scandinavian management consulting sector developed in the period following the Second World War. During its infancy, smaller domestic firms dominated the market. However, in the 1960s the market for management consulting services began to grow, focusing primarily on budgeting, time and motion, and marketing. The increase in demand allowed domestic firms to grow in size while also attracting new entrants onto the market. Although, several years were to pass before the domestic firms' market dominance would be challenged by large international firms, the duration of this period of dominance varied from country to country. Nevertheless, common to them all is the fact that over the past ten years, large and particularly American-based players have come to dominate the market. From this domination by international providers of consulting services has followed a certain standardisation in the methods applied, although many consultancies will argue for the customised approach. Furthermore, this internationalisation has also allowed the scope of the firms to widen. However, differences do exist in the way the markets have developed on a national level.

DENMARK

The Danish market for management consulting services began to grow during the 1960s as the demand for services such as budgeting, time-and-motion studies and marketing rose, thus allowing domestic firms to grow in both size and scope. In 1972 the American company McKinsey & Co entered the market by opening an office in Copenhagen, which was to serve as the company's foothold in Scandinavia, thereby making the Danish market the first in Scandinavia with the physical presence of an international player. Today, several of the big international players are represented in Copenhagen.

The industry has experienced high growth rates, primarily driven by growing internationalisation, the development of new technologies, outsourcing and rationalisation and privatisation in the public sector. In the period from 1988 to 1990 the rate of growth was around 14 per cent and then subsequently declined to 10 per cent between 1992 and 1994. However, during the past couple of years the rate has remained stable at around 20 per cent. This growth in the industry has attracted management consultants with diverse professional backgrounds, thus making the industry's boundaries increasingly difficult to define.

The size of the Danish market has traditionally been estimated by using a supply approach. In 1994, the Association of Management Consultants in Denmark estimated annual revenues to be in the region of US$260 million and identified 300 management consulting firms within the market. In order to be included in the industry, identified firms were required to earn the majority of their revenues through management consulting activities (FMK, 1994). A later survey from 1998, for which a broader definition of management consulting providers was applied, identified the number to be 460. Furthermore, the survey found the Danish market to have more than doubled in size since 1994 reaching annual revenues totalling US$630 million. This apparent growth experienced in the period from 1994 to 1998 reflects not only an actual growth in the market but also the fact that the scope of the providers had broadened.

Despite the presence of large international firms such as McKinsey & Co, Accenture, PricewaterhouseCoopers and PA Consulting Group, the market in 1998 was dominated by domestic firms. In terms of revenue the group of international players accounts for less than one-third of the market, while the large or medium-sized domestic firms account for close to 40 per cent. Another 20 per cent are accounted for by new players on the market stage such as firms with their origin in engineering or IT. However, during the last two years the international players have grown substantially in size through organic growth and acquisitions.

The profile of many consulting firms has become more and more heterogeneous. Even the firms that had previously been specialised have a broader profile today, and the tendency to narrow down the scope of a consultancy is less prevalent. Several of the large international firms have expanded the number of services they offer. This development has reinforced the lack of differentiation, at least at a generic level, between the different providers of management consulting services. A survey undertaken by Oxford Research A/S in 1998 revealed that the majority of firms, regardless of their size, primarily focus on strategy, organisational and management development. The only area in which the

Table 5.2.6 The leading consultancies on the Danish market in 1998 (not ranked)

	Revenues 1998 (million US$)	*Number of consultants*	*Country of origin*
PwC (PriceWaterhouseCoopers)	54.0	301	US/UK/Denmark
Andersen Consulting (Accenture)		265	US
PLS Consult A/S	17.0	180	Denmark
PA Consulting Group	31.4	160	UK/Denmark
Ernst & Young	22.4	130	US/Denmark
KPMG	13.5	101	US/The Netherlands
Deloitte Consulting	14.0	100	US/UK/Denmark
Mercuri Urval	21.0	89	Sweden
F.J. Gruppen A/S	16.0	80	Denmark
Teknologisk Institut	10.0	85	Denmark
TIC Denmark	8.6	80	Denmark
Lisberg Management A/S	8.6	60	Denmark
Fisher & Lorenz A/S	5.8	53	Denmark
PROMENTOR A/S	8.5	50	Denmark
McKinsey & Co		50	US
Kjaer &Kjerulf A/S		42	Denmark
Dansk Management Forum	7.1	38	Denmark
Andersen Management International A/S	7.2	35	Denmark
Mercuri International A/S	4.8	34	Sweden
A.T. Kearney		30	US/Denmark
Ankerhus	3.1	24	Denmark

Source: Information collected by the author based on a questionnaire to consultancies

focus of larger firms differs from that of the smaller ones is in the provision of IT related services. The focus on organisational and management development is a reflection of the type of consulting services most frequently sought by customers (Table 5.2.6).

The increase in scale and scope is likely to make the market for management consulting services more complex and less transparent as it grows. One of the driving forces behind this increase in complexity is the complexity in demand. It is becoming increasingly difficult to separate the majority of technical assignments from organisational assignments, which, in turn, cannot be separated from management development assignments, human resource assignments etc. Thus assignments are often interrelated and therefore require a multi-disciplinary problem solving approach.

NORWAY

The domination by national players of the Norwegian consulting market continued into the 1990s, although two larger international players, Mercuri Urval and PA Consulting Group, had entered the market back in 1977/8. This domestic domination is illustrated by the fact that in 1987, 15 out of the top 20 consulting companies on the Norwegian market were of Norwegian origin. Table 5.2.7 below illustrates how market leadership evolved in the following decade.

The internationalisation of the Norwegian consulting market only began during the latter part of the 1980s and continued into the 1990s. This is illustrated by the fact that even the international accountancy firms such as Arthur Andersen and PriceWaterhouse, which established offices in Oslo as early as 1956 and 1964 respectively, did not set up Norwegian branches of their consulting businesses until the latter part of the 1990s.

Despite the considerable growth experienced during the period from 1987 to 1998, the average size of the Norwegian consulting firms has remained relatively small. Thus, the international players have not been impeded by their late entry into the market and have been able to capture the rewards stemming from

Table 5.2.7 The top 20 consulting firms on the Norwegian market in 1987 and 1998

	1987	Ownership	Revenue (mill US$)	No. of consultants	1998	Ownership	Revenue (million US$)	No. of consultants
1	IKO-Gruppen	Norway	12.7	78	Andersen Consulting	US	117.2	
2	Habberstad	Norway	12.7	116	Arthur Andersen	US	42.4	
3	Harmark-Iras	Norway	9.2	73	PriceWaterhouse Coopers	US/UK	32.4	240
4	Mercuri-gruppen	Sweden	9.2	60	McKinsey & Co	US	30.1	
5	Resulting Kompetansesenter	Norway	5.8	32	PA Consulting Group	UK	23.4	130
6	VINN	Norway	4.6	33	Deloitte Consulting	US/UK	21.2	114
7	PA International Consulting	UK	2.3	16	Ernest & Young	US/UK	20.1	142
8	Semco	Norway	2.3	17	Gemini Consulting	France/US	20.1	38
9	Bedriftsrådgivning	Norway	2.3	13	Dovre	Norway International	16.7	120

10	Mercuri Urval	Sweden	2.3	18	KPMG	US/UK/Holland	16.7	
11	Asplan Analyse	Norway	2.3	23	A.T. Kearney	US	14.5	26
12	Barlindhaug	Norway	2.3	15	Stradec	Norway	6.7	25
13	UPK-Utviklingspartner	?	1.7	11	Guide	Sweden	-	43
14	AFF	Norway	1.7	15	Hartmark Consulting	Norway	5.6	30
15	Nissen-Lie	Norway	1.7	10	Arkwright Consulting	Norway	5.6	19
16	Indevo	Sweden	1.7	19	Mercuri International	Sweden	4.5	30
17	Pasco Ledelse	?	1.7	14	Mercuri Urval	Sweden	4.5	45
18	Enator	Norway	1.2	17	Prudentia	Norway	4.5	27
19	OSO Consult	?	1.2	20	Carta	Sweden	3.3	17
20	Bedriftsutvikling	Norway			Agenda	Norway	3.3	20

Sources: 1987 figures come from *Ledelse* No. 9, 1988 and the 1998 figures are from data collected by Fokus Publishing this rapid growth. To put the development into perspective, the size of the Norwegian market was estimated to be US$109 million in 1988, which was less than Andersen Consulting's annual revenue ten years on. This rapid growth in the Norwegian market continued in 1998 with revenues up 37 per cent on the previous year.

Looking at the business profile of the top 20 consulting firms as it stood in 1998, practically all the firms offered strategy and change management or change process type services. However, given the complexity of large change projects undertaken by the big international consulting firms, it is reasonable to assume that such assignments also entail strategy and IT related services as well as implementation.

SWEDEN

Sweden has a long tradition of international trade, which stems from the large number of international corporations the country has fostered through time.

The Swedish market for consulting services had already begun to develop during the 1950s as numerous Swedish companies adopted the time-and-motion method, causing a surge in the number of domestic consulting firms established during the period.

The provision of management consulting services was undertaken purely by domestic firms until the mid-1970s when competition from large American consulting firms began to grow. Although PA Consulting had been operating in the Swedish market since the 1960s through its acquisition of the Swedish firm Ekonomisk

Företagsledning, it continued to operate under that name until the 1980s, by which time several international consulting firms had made moves to establish a presence in Stockholm.

It was not until 1980 that the first international consulting firm, McKinsey & Co, opened an office in Stockholm. The 1980s were the decade in which the Swedish consulting firms' market dominance came to an end. The pivotal point for this structural change appears to have been 1990. However, the recession that hit the Swedish economy in the early 1990s made entry onto the market a hazardous venture and several international, as well as domestic, players were forced out. Because of the difficult economic conditions, the dominance of the national firms was broken. By 1998 large American players dominated the Swedish market. This development is illustrated in Table 5.2.8.

Furthermore, as Table 5.2.8 also indicates, the Swedish market for consulting services experienced a tremendous rate of growth during the 1990s. In 1996 the total turnover of the sixty largest consulting companies totalled US$450 million, of which the top 20 consulting companies accounted for US$250 million. Thus the top 20 companies initially accounted for 63 per cent of the total turnover in 1992. This share then subsequently dropped to 55 per cent in 1996 before rising to 80 per cent of the US$560 million turnover contributed by the top sixty firms in the industry in 1997. Therefore, not only did the market itself grow in size, but the majority of activities today remains concentrated within a few large American players.

A survey undertaken by *Konsulentguiden* in 1998 revealed that the main focus of the more classic US firms such as McKinsey & Co, BCG, Arthur D Little and Bain & Co is on strategy and business development services (63 per cent). Overall the emphasis on strategy and business/organisation development is very clear regardless of the type of firm. An exception, however, is the 'Big Five' (PriceWaterhouseCoopers, Andersen Consulting, Ernst & Young, Deloitte & Touche and KPMG) where strategy and business development services only account for 11 per cent of all services offered. This group of firms is the only one to display a wide diversity in the type of services offered. It is interesting to note that HR and competence development services are offered primarily by domestic consulting firms.

The Swedish consulting market has experienced an increased merger activity between medium and large-sized Swedish consulting firms in response to the increasing competition from

Table 5.2.8 The top 20 consulting firms on the Swedish market in 1988 and 1997

	1988	Origin	Revenue (Mill US$)	Number of consultants	1997	Origin	Revenue (US$m)	Number of consultants
1	Indevo	Sweden	56.1	254	McKinsey & Co	US	64.2	127
2	Invent	Sweden	8.5	54	Andersen Consulting	US	62.9	370
3	PA Consulting Group	UK	21.7	139	Boston Consulting Group	US	27.5	58
4	KcKinsey & Co	US	21.2	50	ALMI	Sweden	22.9	
5	Siar	Sweden	16.1	89	CARTA CA	Sweden	22.8	
6	Habberstad	Norway	16.0	94	Arthur D Little	US	22.3	39
7	Cicero	Sweden	13.2	77	Ernest & Young	US/UK	22.0	115
8	Maynard	US/Holland	7.7	53	KPMG Consultants	US	19.0	147
9	Sinova	Sweden	5.4	32	Coopers & Lybrand	US/UK	18.3	130
10	Bohlin & Strömberg	Sweden	5.1	28	Gemini	France/UK	17.7	50

11	Cepro	Sweden	4.7	25	Price Waterhouse	US	10.1	61
12	Sevenco	Sweden	4.6	21	Askus	Sweden	9.2	50
13	Nordic Management	Sweden	3.9	13	A.T. Kearney	US	6.8	20
14	Consultus	Sweden	3.9	18	SLG	US	8.3	70
15	Lagerquest & Partners	Sweden	3.9	10	IBM Consultants	US	7.3	
16	Semco	Sweden	2.9	18	Bain & Co	US	7.3	22
17	Ingemar Claesson	Sweden	2.0	14	Bohlin & Strömberg	Sweden	7.3	54
18	SMG	Sweden	1.6	7	Crepo	Sweden	7.3	27
19	Trim	Sweden	1.5	6	Deloitte & Touche	US	4.6	37
20	SRC	Sweden	1.3	4	Sinova	Sweden	3.7	23
Total			193.4	1000			349.4	1800

Source: Konsulentguiden 1989 and 1998

the large international players. Thus the Swedish market is becoming more concentrated and the level of competition is likely to become fiercer as large international consultancies, primarily American, enter the Swedish market through the acquisition of medium to large-sized Swedish counterparts.

Furthermore, the larger international consulting firms are increasingly using standardised methods enabling the firm to transmit the same image to a large number of customers. This development may pose a challenge for many of the Swedish consulting firms that traditionally have provided more process-based consultation.

Conclusion

During the last few years, the overall Scandinavian market has grown considerably. The growth has to a great extend been driven by the region's position as a European market leader in mobile telephony commerce, Internet technology and wireless applications along with the privatisation of public services. The emergence of the e-business market has greatly impacted the overall market. The current drivers behind e-business development in Scandinavia rest primarily within the new economy companies, which have had a significant impact on the market. This was reflected in the fact that the Scandinavian business-to-consumer (B2C) market was very strong around the turn of the century. However, a rapidly evolving business-to-business (B2B) market is now replacing the B2C one. This is a development which is most likely to benefit the more traditional consulting providers. Furthermore, as the region experiences an increased number of cross-border mergers, the clients will increasingly turn to the firms with the global capabilities and depth needed to assist them in their cross-border ventures. The Scandinavian consulting market is becoming more polarised, with the large consulting firms becoming even bigger and leaving the smaller players only the lower end of the market. This trend is set to continue, making it difficult for medium-sized consulting firms to survive unless they serve a niche market.

This trend will be further emphasised by globalisation, which is causing companies to look for international providers of consulting services. The reason being that as they grow and become more international they are seeking partners who have at least an equivalent presence globally. Furthermore, demand is becoming more complex. A general consensus prevails between leading management consultants and major buyers of consulting services that most technical assignments can no longer be separated from organisational assignments, which in turn cannot be separated from management development assignments, human resource assignments etc. Clients may define a certain assignment as being technical, managerial or human resource orientated. However, these assignments are often highly interrelated and therefore require a multi-disciplinary problem-solving approach. Hence the domination of the individual Scandinavian markets by the large, particularly American, consulting firms is likely to continue, further fuelling the trend of consolidation among the domestic consulting firms in their efforts to survive.

The trend towards consolidation is still predominant in Scandinavia as multiple companies attempt to position themselves as full-service providers. This lack of differentiation between the different providers on a generic level, coupled with the complexity in demand adds to the markets' complexity and lack of transparency. Efforts are currently being made to improve transparency within the individual Scandinavian consulting industries and to install a common code of conduct/industry ethics, and general professionalism through professional consulting organisations.

Despite the slowdown in the general economy, the outlook for the Scandinavian market is positive with the emergence of a cross-border and pan-Scandinavian market.

Other Western Europe

SWITZERLAND

*André Wohlgemuth,
Chairman, ASCO*

ASCO – The Swiss Association of Management Consultants since 1958

In the 1950s, the quality of management consulting was a hot topic. Swiss entrepreneurs and managers were more than sceptical about the value and purpose of the consulting profession. Some had suffered bad experiences with hard selling and unprofessional consultants. In response to this situation, eight leading management consultants founded ASCO in 1958 and established a clear code of conduct which is very similar to the International Council of Management Consulting Institutes' (ICMCI) code today. Our ethics committee is ready to become active on a client's request and, after hearing all parties involved, may recommend the exclusion of a member of ASCO. Our association also engages in all kinds of promotion and development activities for its members. The requirements for membership are stringent and each ASCO member must be able to communicate professionally with top management.

ASCO is also the association of the management consulting firms in Switzerland. Six of the ten largest Swiss firms are members, among them PricewaterhouseCooper, KPMG, Cap Gemini and Ernst & Young. The membership also includes the largest native Swiss consultancies such as ICME International AG, Helbling Management Consultants, Abegglen Management Partners AG and Visura.

In 1960 ASCO was one of the six founding members of FEACO, the European Federation of Management Consulting Associations. Today ASCO represents more than 1,200 management consultants, about 40 per cent of the total in Switzerland.

ASCO was very active during recent years in raising the value of membership. ASCO offers training programmes for consultants and was an initiator of the first German-Austrian-Swiss management consulting conference which took place in Munich in 1999 with 500 participants. In 1998 ASCO began to organise a recurring top event for managers and entrepreneurs. This new concept was so successful that it is now held on an annual basis. Additional professional public relations activities led to sharply increased name recognition in the business community.

A very competitive market

The Swiss market for management consulting services is not regulated but is highly competitive. Switzerland has the highest number of consultants per head of population, higher than in the developed markets like the Netherlands or the USA. All large global management consulting firms have offices in Zurich, the largest economic centre in the country. In 2000, Swiss consulting revenues were over SFr1 billion (US$588 million).

The export ratio of management consulting services is high and grows steadily: 25 per cent in 1995, more than 30 per cent in 2000. Swiss management consultants tend to speak several languages, have working experience with international clients and are used to dealing with different cultures.

Why is ASCO a member of the ICMCI?

ASCO wants to help members to improve their competitiveness in Switzerland and in other countries. In 1995 the annual general meeting of ASCO decided to support ICMCI and the Certified Management Consultant (CMC) procedure, the only international standard for professional management consultants. The task of implementation was delegated to a group of five experienced management consultants. Leading this group gave me the opportunity to contribute from my experience of receiving the CMC from the IMC USA in 1992/93. The group also benefited from experience and documentation received from Canada, New Zealand, the USA and others. ASCO was able to start operations in 1996 and became a full ICMCI member in 1997. Our certification documents are available in German and French. There were nine CMCs at the end of 1997, 13 in 1998 and 34 in 2000.

We didn't follow the approach of some other institutes which gave the CMC title to all their members. We only admit certified management consultants who actively promote the values of the CMC. Another important decision was to keep the CMC admission procedure open not only for ASCO members but for all consultants. As we see the CMC certification as a professional and fact-driven procedure we offer each individual the opportunity to prove his or her qualifications. The only difference consists in a higher certification fee for consultants who do not pay the annual ASCO membership dues.

Vision and expectations

ASCO will continue successfully to promote the CMC. Our goal is to double the number of certified management consultants within the next three to four years. We have established a professional infrastructure with an executive director. Our home page lists all CMCs and will be developed and linked to relevant addresses in the marketplace. We offer our experience to other institutes or associations. In 1997 we provided the BDU, the corresponding association in Germany, with all our documents. We are convinced that long-term success can be achieved not only from professionalism in our work but also from continuity in communication.

Our main expectation from the ICMCI is simple and clear: to concentrate the limited resources in promoting and pushing the CMC standards worldwide. We will support all activities with the aim to make the CMC a known brand of top management consultants everywhere.

CENTRAL AND EASTERN EUROPE

József Poór, Managing Director,
Hay Group Management Consultants,
Budapest, Hungary

General trends and recent developments

Generally speaking, before the political changes that took place at the end of the 1980s, in most East European countries consultancy services were supplied by research institutes controlled by the state, or by departments of various ministries. In numerous countries management training and consultancy centres were established by the International Labour Organisation (ILO) or by the UNIDO, an organisation of the United Nations (UN). Characteristics of modern management consultancy were pretty scarce in these countries in the framework of the previous system.

Since the change of regime, consultancy connected to privatisation has been developing significantly in all countries. Several billion ECUs flew to these countries in the framework of the European Union PHARE programmes, and consultants played a significant role in founding and executing various programmes. During this transition, Japanese Productivity Centres for Social and Economic Development were established in almost every Central and Eastern European (CEE) country in order to facilitate the influx of Japanese capital. Consultancy associations have been founded in almost every country with the initiation of FEACO – the European Federation of Management Consultancy Organisations. In addition, the books and publications of Milan Kubr have been translated into various local languages.

The transition from socialism to capitalism is a rare event in history. The difficult political and economic transition processes associated with this event were exacerbated by a dramatic decrease in the output performance of the region's economies. Today most of the national economies in the region have begun to grow. In a recent *Financial Times* report (Done, 1998), it was noted that for the first time since the beginning of this transition, the CEE region has at last returned to growth.

Table 5.2.9 Economic development and the consulting market in FEACO member countries

Countries	Bulgaria	Czech R.	Hungary	Poland	Romania	Russia	Slovenia
GDP per cent change	4.50 per cent	2.50 per cent	5.50 per cent	4.60 per cent	2.00 per cent	8.00 per cent	4.30 per cent
Consumer prices per cent change	11.00 per cent	4.00 per cent	9.50 per cent	9.50 per cent	40.00 per cent	21.00 per cent	9 per cent
Trade balance (in billion Euros)	−1.44	−3.6	−3.84	−18	−1.8	71.16	−1.44
FDI (in billion US$)	0.96	7.2	2.04	9	0.96	3.72	0.12
Number of consultants	2700	3000	3000	2300	2500	3900	490
Number of CMC designees	30	0	125	40	0	0	0
Average annual earnings per consultants 000'Euros	12,000	50,000	66,667	45,652	16,400	17,949	77,551

Sources: Central–Eastern European Economic Review and FEACO

A growing number of scholars and practitioners claim that privatisation does not automatically improve the effectiveness of governments, companies and social welfare systems. On the contrary, it may well increase opportunities for corruption and bribery. When a company is being privatised or governed by western-style business law, there is no guarantee that the values and mindsets of the people will change along with it. The adoption of all the financial, legal, technical and sales frameworks in a privatised local company or in firms with foreign participation represents only the first stage in the creation of a western-like enterprise.

Once all this is in place, one must start to consider how to get the people and the organisations to perform in a competitive way. The best financial infrastructure in the world will not change companies around from command economy to market economy if the people and the organisations do not deliver.

Today more and more signs show that in these countries, besides financial and privatisation consultancy, other areas of consultancy business will also emerge. Until the end of the 1990s the role of the consultant in the consultant-client relationship was in many ways similar to that of a supplier who provides different products and services. Over a period of time the consultant would draft a rather extensive report, which, together with an accompanying letter or in the framework of a presentation, he or she would 'deliver' to the client. During the last two to three years this relationship has gradually become a mutual partnership, aimed at improving the effectiveness of the client.

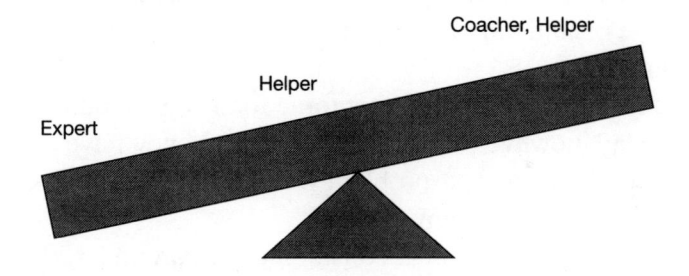

Figure 5.2.3 Development and change of the consultant role in emerging countries

Management consultancy in different CEE countries

I will now survey the fundamental concepts of consultancy and show the most important characteristics of the development of consultancy in the six FEACO member countries of Central and Eastern Europe. The following is not intended to be exhaustive, but will allow the reader to get acquainted with the practices of some of these countries.

Scientific and branch institutes, universities, the Institute for Industry Development and the Institute of Management formed the basis of management consulting in the previous system. These institutions followed the Soviet school in management, political economics and science management (NOT). Many projects and assignments were related to Management Information Systems (MIS). In a few cases state companies (Podem, Balkankar) used foreign consultants.

BULGARIA

The Bulgarian Association of Management Consultants (BAMC) was established in 1990 (Hristov, 2001).

Almost 250 consultancy firms operated at the end of the 1990s, most of which were small-sized local companies, employing only a few people. Besides these, there were also management consultancy units of large international auditing companies, and also the offices of some medium-sized companies.

Here, privatisation was a hot topic for a considerable length of time. Today, however, other areas of consultancy have also come to the fore. The greatest problem for the consultancy business is still the scarcity of foreign capital.

The average fee of local consultants was around 150 Euros in 2000. The market size of management consultants is about 48 million Euros per year. The average market growth was 15 per cent in the last year.

The Certified Management Consultant (CMC) certification was introduced with the active support of the British Management Consulting Association in 1999.

CZECH REPUBLIC

Management consultancy has very significant traditions in the Czech economy. Between the two World Wars factory management methods and procedures applied in the Czech industry were widely known. These traditions wasted away significantly within the framework of socialism. Since the change of regime, state and private frameworks for consultancy have been re-built.

HUNGARY

The development of the Hungarian consultancy business was fragmented. The beginnings here were connected to the spreading of the Taylor method. Following the German model, there was a strong rationalisation process between the two World Wars. Numerous organisations and consulting companies were established in Hungary, mainly in the area of office and administrative management. One of the most significant among them was Evolut Ltd, established in 1929. There were many domestic entrepreneurs in the consultancy area connected to administrative management and accountancy. The same can be said about the industrial sector, where mainly German and Swiss organisation experts worked for many Hungarian companies. The world-famous Bedaux Office has carried out consultancy work for Goldberger. Indorag Dutch engineering consultancy institute participated in several reorganisation projects between 1933 and 1943.

The development of the domestic consultancy business was very much hit by the fact that after the war, the Soviet Union's views – that the independent existence of a science of management and organisation was absolutely unnecessary – took over. At the beginning of the 1950s many institutions, which were created after the liberation for facilitating company management and organisation, ceased to exist. This situation improved slightly only at the end of the 1950s when the first sectoral organisation institutions were founded. This profession has changed since the end of the 1950s. One of the most important changes is that different sectoral organisation institutions have gradually transformed into companies. With the cessation of the sectoral ministries of industrial management, totally independent organisation and consultancy institutions were formed. The work of experts, working for various organisations, institutes or for their legal successors, was the target of much criticism, both just and unjust.

Professional management and business consultancy carried out by a third party (organisation) for different clients became fashionable again in Hungary in the middle of the 1980s. Numerous factors played their part in this change:

- foreign consultancy firms had a very important role in shaping the new type consultancy culture
- new and fast-moving privatisation has offered plenty of opportunities to consultants
- companies purchased by foreigners and big greenfield investments offered new consultancy tasks
- numerous publications were released in order to help university-level management consulting faculties (Budapest University of Economic Sciences, Faculty of Economics of Janus Pannonius University at Pécs, etc). The publications of Milan Kubr were translated into Hungarian (see above)
- in the meantime professional organisations, responsible for establishing basic professional and ethical conditions of management consultancy and other consultancy areas, have been formed

The first representatives of foreign consultancy firms appeared in Hungary at the beginning of the 1970s. These were needed more at the time of the launch of the World Bank's (WB) restructuring programmes. The first joint ventures in consultancy had already been established in the mid-1980s, mainly with the co-operation of German, Austrian and Swiss companies. Since the end of the 1980s, the expansion of consultancy firms with Anglo-Saxon origins has been continuously rising. However, a consultant working in an international business environment soon realises that what works in San Francisco may not be applicable to a Hungarian family venture.

As regards the number of consultancy firms and consultants, the Hungarian market has a ratio similar to more developed countries – 10 million inhabitants, and 2,000–3,000 consultants. There is a significant difference, however, between daily fees (one third to one quarter), and per capita annual sales incomes (about one half). On the domestic market, trends mentioned above are apparent: company mergers, rapid growth connected to information technology and growing market competition.

Hungary had been an associate member of the International Council of Management Consulting Institutes (ICMCI) since 1991 and full membership was awarded in 1996. The first certification took place in 1994 when six Hungarian consultants were certified by the UK Institute of Management Consultancy. Today there are 125 Certified Management Consultant designees in Hungary. The CMC committee works within the Hungarian Management Consultants Association.

POLAND

Management consultancy in Poland began at the end of the 1980s. The first local consulting companies emerged from institutions of university colleges. They were founded by lawyers and economists.

Consultancy has become a rapidly developing sector. According to the Association of Economic Consultants (SDG), at the beginning of the 1990s the most significant project financing institutions were typically PHARE, the Know-How Fund and US funds. Today these sources are slowly vanishing. Their roles are taken by the EU's projects that finance structural funds, and by the dynamically developing private sector. In the structure of the Polish consultancy market, the well-known big consultancy firms are represented (with 5–10 consultants); besides these are the management consultancy departments of the Big Five auditing and accounting companies (with 20–30 consultants). The number of local companies is estimated to be 200–300, and they each employ 1–10 consultant(s). Today there are almost 2,000 consultants working in this market.

There are no statistics of the consulting market available for Poland. The first attempt to research the market was undertaken by SDG this year. It is estimated that services worth about 105 million Euros can be sold on the market, and that about 2,300 consultants operate in management support.

The CMC certification was begun in 1997. Since then 40 designations have been awarded (Glowczki, 2001).

ROMANIA

In Romania, due to very strong over-centralisation of the economy, consultancy was virtually non-existent, even in the primitive form seen in the other ex-socialist countries. Since the change of regime however, potential conditions for modern consultancy have also been set up in Romania. In contrast with other Eastern European countries, further development is seriously hampered by the very sluggish pace of privatisation, resulting in a lack of state and private purchasing power needed to build up the consultancy business and market.

AMCOR, the Association of Romanian Management Consultants, was established in 1992 by the initiation of FEACO. The Romanian management consulting market consists of 1,200 companies. Within these companies there are 3,500–4,000 consultants, from which just 350–400 are certified at national and international level.

The majority of the Big Five consultancy firms are represented in Romania but involvement in the most important problems of the Romanian economy does not represent a relevant impact in the real market (Plesoianu, 2001). In addition, some smaller companies, mainly specialising in headhunting, and a selection of foreign companies have become established here. Besides these, there are dozens of small, local consultancy firms operating in the market. A local consultancy network has started to develop with government and foreign support. One of the most pressing problems of the consultancy market is the insolvency of clients and low contract fees. Not taking into consideration international projects, local daily allowances are no higher than 130–400 Euros.

RUSSIA

Russia is a vast country with a wealth of natural resources, a well-educated population and a diverse industrial base. In Russia, according to the estimates of ACEM, the Federation of Russian Management and Business Consultants, there are about 4,000 consultants working in a market with an estimated worth of 70 million Euros. The fee rate of a big and a medium-sized firm can range between 250–2,000 Euros per day. The small and medium-sized consultancies earn between 50–300 Euros per day.

On the one hand, the size of the country provides an excellent opportunity for large firms to establish offices in Moscow and in the country as well. On the other hand, the missing infrastructure and the undeveloped transport and logistics force the international firms to set up their offices in the capital only.

Russian companies spend between 30–70 million Euros per year on management consulting. Foreign Technical Assistance brings 1 billion Euros per year into the Russian economy. The average growth rate in terms of turnover of management consulting firms in Russia was 200 per cent in 2000 and 112 per cent in 2001 (Posadsky, 2001).

SLOVENIA

In 1960, nine Slovenian consulting companies established the Independent Business Consulting Association, which later became a member of the Yugoslav union – Yucor. There was a total of about 200 consultants at this time. With the disintegration of Yugoslavia in 1991, Yucor collapsed, as did the Independent Business Consulting Association (Arah, 2001).

Slovenia was among the first countries in transition to overcome the transition depression in the early 1990s. The local consulting companies in Slovenia began to offer services similar to those found in developed European nations, and the quality of the services they offered corresponded to that of foreign consultants. The introduction of modern working methods, the encouragement of new solutions and the high standard of consulting services is and remains the main principles of consultants.

The Association for Management Consulting of Slovenia (AMCOS) was created in 1992. AMCOS has been integrated into the framework of the Slovenian Chamber of Commerce. It has 35 members. AMCOS became a member of FEACO in 1993. The Association has 52 members employing a total of 284 consultants. In 2000, management consulting in Slovenia created a total income of 47 million Euros, or 0.24 per cent of GDP. Among the CEE countries, the average annual earning per consultant is highest in Slovenia.

The future

When looking to the future we must never forget that while some serious future research theories have come true, others have proved to be real blunders. However, trends so far have shown that revenues of consultancy business will increase further.

Let us start our analysis from this very positive future. Canbacks (1999) believes that this positive trend can only be sustained if consultants are willing to reconsider the contracts or practices that they have established during past years. It may be very important in this respect that consultants should use success fees in their work. Generally speaking, decentralisation of different organisations is a hindrance to the employment of consultants. Bureaucratic organisations employ more consultants than their less bureaucratic counterparts. The sale of consultancy services may greatly be facilitated by the reduction of uncertainty factors. It is very important that clients should not feel that the consultant is much better informed and is in a preferential situation to competent members of the client organisation. It may also strengthen the concepts of the positive scenario if consultants actively join the formation of operation networks within the company. We can assume that the relatively low revenue from CEE-based management consultancy will increase. The management consulting market of these countries has great market

```
        ┌─────────┐
        │         │
   ┌────┴────┬────┴────┐
```

| State bureaucracy | Local administration | SMEs |

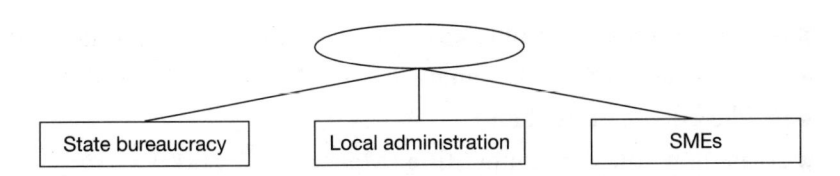

Figure 5.2.4 Future client groups of management consultants in CEE-countries

potential. The state bureaucracy, local public administration and the small and medium-sized enterprises (SME) will provide this business with great growth potential.

Now let us look at the possible outcomes of the negative scenario. It may be a serious problem if solutions advised by the consultant require a great deal of effort from the client organisation. Large companies frequently build up their own management services. If a problem emerges repeatedly, then the client organisation will devise its own solutions. It is not rare for the same client to be given an offer from the local office of a multi-national corporation (MNC) consultancy, the parent company of the consultancy firm and the internal advisory service of the client organisation.

| The local office | The parent company | The client's internal advisory service |

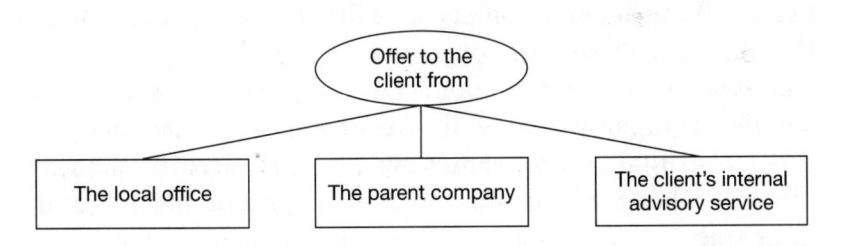

(Offer to the client from)

Figure 5.2.5 New client groups of management consultants in the future in CEE-countries

Experts who study the future of business life agree that those who will win in the 21st century will:

- lead change processes and be able continuously to redefine their branches of industry and within it their operation

- be able to create new markets
- not be afraid of new challenges
- handle clients individually
- create new rules of competition (Maister et al, 2000).

The developed world is on the threshold of an information and knowledge-based society (Gibson, 1997). Information technology and e-business will be determining factors in the lives of different organisations. Only those consulting companies which continually follow the development of information technology and adequately integrate it into their problem-solving methods will succeed. Markets will globalise. and the rigorous delimitation of internal, regional and world markets will cease to apply. Therefore, consulting companies will have to adjust their supplies and strategy development concepts to this global market. The knowledge of employees of client companies will grow continuously. More and more clients will learn how to use consultants. Consultancy companies will only be able to cope with this situation if they continually train their employees. 'Virtual' consulting will appear.

Kelley (1986) suggested in one of his earlier publications that 3–10 consultancy companies will rule an area, and it seems that this prediction will come true. In this publication he also mentioned that new technologies would leave enough space for smaller companies as well. According to some analyses, 3–10 consultancy companies will rule an area of management. We believe that this prediction is becoming more and more true.

Other predictions show that radical changes in information technology and telecommunications would considerably change our previously-held notions of companies and ventures. According to some opinions, those who will not be able to keep pace with the Internet revolution, even if they are the most successful ones today in their profession, would disappear or lag behind in competition. How effective and human this environment will be is largely up to the people who operate it.

Fiona Czerniawska (1999) writes about the future of consultancy and according to her, specialists will win the ongoing fight between generalists and specialists. As a result of this, however, demand for system or solution-integrator companies will appear. These general contractors will be the ones who will hold together the work of all consultants working on the given problem. In order to be successful, consultants will have to change their style.

The consultant of the future will be characterised by that odd, double linkage that he will be working for a certain company and organisation, but the most important link for him will be his profession and professional success. Besides full-time employees, freelancers will work in this profession in increasing numbers.

These changes, which today are largely assumptions, may in future be parts of our everyday life. However, we will have to work hard to attain this. Consultants can play an important role in this process, in the CEE countries as well as elsewhere.

The Middle East

JORDAN *Hatem Abdel Ghani*

Management consultancy has been a well-established industry in Jordan since the 1970s. It started with a few pioneering firms dealing mostly with governmental requests for various consulting services as important steps in implementing national infrastructure projects. This state of affairs encouraged many entrants to establish their own management consulting bureaux. Later, in the 1990s, it became apparent that there was a need to establish some sort of association that would be joined by eligible management consultants, as firms or individuals, and the Institute of Management Consultants (IMC) was established in September 1995. Its character was approved by a general assembly which also appointed a Board of Directors for a three year tenure. The second set of elections took place in September 1998 and the third is expected in September 2001.

The number of registered IMC members by the end of 2000 was 78 with 63 individual and 15 corporate members.

Types of consultancy

Jordanian management consultants deal with all types of consulting, such as:

- feasibility studies
- marketing and business development
- technical studies
- strategic planning
- quality systems
- development of organisational effectiveness
- HRD
- management systems
- organisational structuring
- strategic studies
- economic research
- tax consultancy
- financial and management consultancy
- evaluation studies and appraisal of companies
- formation of shareholding companies
- diagnostic studies
- trade marks and patents registration
- management and information systems
- re-engineering
- institutional analysis
- project management
- MIS/GIS software development
- environmental studies
- information technology
- marketing research
- restructuring and merging

- due diligence and valuation
- liquidation of companies
- telecommunications consulting
- financial consulting
- appraisal and inspection of technical and safety problems
- quality control and HACCP systems
- investment studies
- business strategy development

The industries that frequently commission consultancy are:

- government and other public agencies
- utilities
- manufacturing
- non-governmental organisations (NGO)
- bi/multilateral agencies
- banks
- insurance

Relevant education and qualification standards

To be accepted as a member of IMC-Jordan, a management consultant should have a university first degree or equivalent in addition to a minimum of seven years' work experience in his/her field of speciality, of which at least three should have been as a full-time management consultant.

Use of consultancy in government and state-aided projects

The government of Jordan and its public agencies are responsible for designing and implementing the major infrastructure projects in the country such as airports, seaports, electricity, water production and distribution, public health, energy and mining.

There are usually major activities requiring a considerable amount of consultancy. Government departments also use management consulting to upgrade their performance, enhance their efficiency and avoid red tape and similar bureaucratic problems.

Africa

NIGERIA
David Iornem

Population

With over 100 million inhabitants, Nigeria is the most populous country in Africa. Less than 30 per cent of Nigerians live in cities. The country covers an area of 923,768 km^2 with a population density of 103.9 per km^2. Life expectancy is 46.9 years for men and 50.2 years for women.

Nigeria has over 250 ethnic groups that speak different languages. The leading ones are Hausa, Yoruba, Igbo, Fulani, Kanuri, Tiv and Edo. The official language is English.

Major religions

Christianity and Islam are the major religions, arguably in equal strength. Recently, conflict between the two major religions has led to serious disturbances in the country.

Major diseases

Malaria, tuberculosis and AIDS.

Capital

Abuja is the new capital of Nigeria. Other large cities with thriving commercial and industrial activities include Lagos (the former capital), Port Harcourt, Kano, Warri, Kaduna, Ibadan, Enugu and Calabar.

Political structure

Nigeria is a Federal Republic. Due to years of military rule, the administrative structures have assumed unitary character with a great deal of central control. There are 36 states which are demanding more devolved powers, an issue that has become contentious with the return to democratic rule. Nigeria has an executive president modelled on the United States of America system, and executive governors for the states.

Recent history

The British territories of Northern and Southern Nigeria were merged in 1914 to form Nigeria. The country became independent in 1960. In 1966, the civilian government was toppled. The situation deteriorated rapidly leading to a civil war between the Federal Government and the Eastern Region, ending 30 months later. A return to civil rule in 1978 was terminated by the military in 1983. The military organised elections in 1993 which were free and fair, but reneged on the promise to hand over power, leading to a serious political crisis. Finally, a return to civil rule took place in 1999.

National economy

Agriculture used to be the mainstay of the economy, providing about two-thirds of the country's GDP in the early 1960s. The situation has changed since the late 1960s because of the huge growth in the volume and value of petroleum output. However, agriculture still employs about 66 per cent of the working population. There are very few large scale commercial farms and smallholdings are far more common. Minerals available in commercial quantity include tin, columbite, coal, iron ore, zinc, limestone, barrytes and uranium.

Types of consultancy

- *Human resource management:* Manpower development, industrial training, corporate head-hunt and Organisation Development (OD) engagements occupy the time of most consultants.
- *Project feasibility appraisal:* Being a developing country, both the Federal and State Governments have been the main initiators of large industrial projects. The future will change drastically as there is a trend towards privatisation.

- *Re-engineering:* Big companies in the organised private sector use management consultants in their re-engineering efforts. Foreign consultants have had an edge over local ones in this category of consulting – probably because the big companies involved have foreign origins.
- *Privatisation:* State-owned enterprises are undergoing privatisation under the surveillance of the World Bank. The process appears to be transparent, a situation that means a level playing field for consultants.
- *Marketing:* There are opportunities in marketing and advertising consultancy, especially with the big companies.
- *Quality management systems:* Many of the big companies are using consultants to introduce Total Quality Management (TQM) procedures and in attaining the ISO 9000 and ISO 14000 quality standards.

Consultancy sectors

- *Services sector:* This is a growing area covering financial institutions, information technology, tourism, political campaign management and transportation etc.
- *Government:* This is perhaps the juiciest of all the consulting sectors for those who are able to penetrate the system. The rewards are considerable and there are many opportunities. There is, however, a great deal of corruption associated with doing business with the government. An anti-corruption law has recently been introduced to sanitise the situation, but the effect of it is yet to be assessed.
- *Industries (or sectors) which commission the most consultancy:* In order of importance: the Federal Government and its agencies, the oil industry, information technology, financial institutions, the manufacturing sector and services.

Regulatory framework

No licence is needed to engage in management consultancy. However, there are regulatory professional bodies that relate to activities offered by various types of consultants. If you are offering financial services, you must be a member of one of the two chartered accounting bodies, ie the Association of National Accountants of Nigeria and the Institute of Chartered Accountants of Nigeria. The Securities Exchange Commission (SEC) also regulates aspects of financial services consultancy.

Consultants offering HRM services are required to be members of the Institute of Personnel Management of Nigeria while those offering advertising and marketing services are required by law to belong to the Advertising Practitioners Council of Nigeria (APCON). The National Council for Management Development, set up by the Federal Government, recently introduced an accreditation system for management consultants involved in manpower development and training. In addition to that, management consultants involved in industrial training need to get their programmes approved or endorsed by the Industrial Training Fund before marketing them to industrial organisations.

The main management consulting body is the Institute of Management Consultants (IMC), which is a voluntary regulatory body with a Code of Ethical Conduct that is rigorous and in line with standards approved by the International Council of Management Consulting Institutes (ICMCI).

Relevant qualifications

The Institute of Management Consultants admits members into the following grades:

- Associate (AMIMC)
- Member (MIMC)
- Fellow (FIMC)

Those who attain 35 credit hours of continuing education also gain the ICMCI qualification of Certified Management Consultants (CMC). There are, however, many management consultants practising legitimately who do not belong to the Institute. They are mainly professionals in their own primary fields of training such as accounting, information technology, banking etc.

Qualifications and standards of recruits

Members are recruited from those with basic qualifications in their respective fields, usually a Bachelors, Masters or equivalent professional qualification with relevant experience. An MBA with relevant practical experience is the ideal qualification for recruits. New entrants are examined.

Use of consultancy in government and state-aided projects

Consultants in management and other fields are highly patronised in government and state-aided projects. The defunct Petroleum Trust Fund (PTF) brought the value of the use of consultants to the fore. It is hoped that the newly created agencies like the Niger Delta Development Commission, Petroleum Equalisation Fund, Educational Trust Fund (ETF), the National Council on Privatisation, the Nigerian Industrial Promotion Council, etc will follow in these footsteps.

History of the Institute of Management Consultants – Nigeria

The Nigerian Institute of Management Consultants was incorporated in 1983 as an independent non-governmental organisation (NGO) to promote management consultancy, economic and social development and management education. It works as an international membership body and collaborates with other national institutes.

Membership

Membership is open to all nationalities as long as they have the requisite professional training and experience. Anyone involved in providing consultancy services – that is, 'services provided for diagnosis, guidance, training and education, and research concerning management', may join. Currently, there are almost 400 members.

Membership qualifications

Successful applicant consultants may be designated FIMC, MIMC, AMIMC or CMC according to their seniority, training and experience in consulting.

Membership services

There is continuing education for members. The newsletter, *The Consultant*, is circulated to members. Other services include a journal on planning board; regular seminars and participation in international management fora.

Code of Ethics

An effective code with a monitoring system to guarantee quality and high ethical standards.

Education programmes

There is a Postgraduate Diploma in Management Studies covering international management subjects and emerging issues such as quality management systems, environmental management issues, privatisation, globalisation and continuing professional development (CPD).

Joint degree programme with St Clements University

IMC teaches Master of Business Administration, Master of Science in Management and Doctor of Management degree programmes by distance learning. It also selects high profile candidates with quality publications for the St Clements University Doctor of Letters programme.

The IMC is helping to develop the curriculum for the Master of Science in Management Consultancy to be awarded by St

Clements University. The MSc will be based on the certification standards of the ICMCI, emphasising functional competence and the uniform body of knowledge developed by the ICMCI. Graduates of this MSc degree who also have appropriate experience will qualify for the CMC qualification of the ICMCI.

Publications

A recommended book entitled *The Marketing of Management Consultancy Services*, written by the current Director General, Professor Dr. David Iornem, FIMC, can be bought from the Nigerian IMC. It costs US$30 including packaging. Orders are welcome.

For further inquires, either fax us on +234 62 241048, write to Box 9194, Kaduna, Nigeria or e-mail: nimc@inet-global.com

SOUTH AFRICA *Angelo Kehayas*

A number of indigenous languages are spoken in South Africa, together with English, Portuguese, French, English, Afrikaans and German. The universal business language remains English.

South Africa is the economic powerhouse of the region and attracts the most investment.

Botswana and Namibia have small but healthy economies. There has recently been political turmoil in Zimbabwe and its currency has crashed. The economies of Zambia, Congo, Maputo, Angola and Malawi are all in crisis. Most of these economies are dependent on foreign aid, much of which generates consulting opportunities of sorts. Since many of these economies are command economies, relying on the exploitation of natural resources, much of the consulting work is to be found in the areas of:

- ecotourism
- community development
- infrastructure development
- power and communications utilities
- land banks
- manufacturing sector projects

South Africa still represents the lion's share of opportunities on its own, accounting for more than the combined GDP of all the other countries. South Africa's economy however, only accounts for approximately one per cent of the world's GDP, which makes it unattractive for some sectors.

Most of the global consulting firms have representation in South Africa, with some smaller satellites to the north.

Black empowerment has progressed significantly in 2001, especially in South Africa. There are many black consulting firms, but very few undersized firms. The market is dominated by the global practices.

It is difficult to assess consulting revenues due to the difficulty in defining consulting, plus the lack of focused market research in this area.

Consulting is still to be found in:

- government
- privatisation
- parastatals
- commercialisation
- financial Services Sector
- skills development
- utilities
- IT/e-commerce
- transportation
- urban and rural development
- education

South Africa tends, to a large extent, to follow trends in both the United States and United Kingdom. Thus, consulting firms based in these two countries tend to find favour. South Africa has experienced a loss in independent consultancies, with a shift to implementation and product focus in the larger firms.

IT still accounts for a large proportion of consulting revenues, with softer skills such as HR, IR and change management being abundant.

Importation of consultants remains expensive because of the exchange rates and it makes economic sense to use Rand-based consultants.

Communications infrastructure in South Africa, Botswana and Namibia is relatively sophisticated, with a booming internet business.

The Americas

BRAZIL
Eduardo de Macedo Rocha and Cristian Welsh Miguens

Management consultancy in Brazil has been growing consistently for the last 20 years. As in many other countries, the collection of data about this market is extremely difficult. The data in this chapter may not be entirely accurate, however IBCO has made an effort over the years to keep track of trends and the evolution of the industry. We periodically carry out polls (of members and non-members), exchange information with the largest consultancy firms and monitor the market through other private and government institutions. There are no official government statistics.

The downsizing process in big corporations in the 1990s pushed much of the laid-off middle management into management consultancy. Many of these act as sole practitioners.

However, many small firms are not listed as consultancies, because tax reduction benefits for small businesses are not applicable to consultancy firms. This makes the identification of players in the market extremely difficult.

With this in mind, Figure 5.2.6 shows our best estimates of growth in the consultancy market (estimated at US$ 500m):

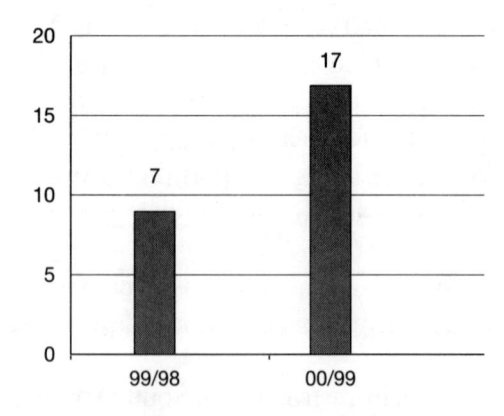

Figure 5.2.6 Estimated growth in the Brazilian consultancy market
Source: Consultancy Thermometer poll – IBCO

This growth rate is explained by two factors

- a growing trend in the private sector to outsource activities as a way of reducing labour costs (especially fringe benefits)
- small and medium sized companies facing growing competition in their markets need to achieve global performance levels

A 1998 poll revealed the following interest areas identified by consultancy clients (Figure 5.2.7):

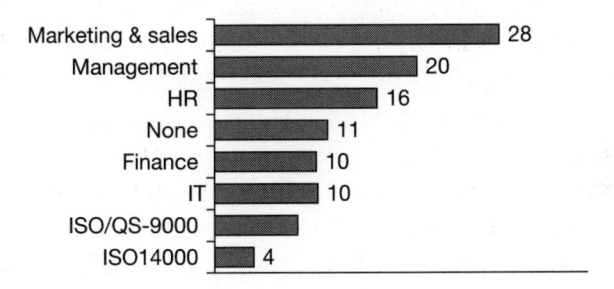

Area	Value
Marketing & sales	28
Management	20
HR	16
None	11
Finance	10
IT	10
ISO/QS-9000	
ISO14000	4

Figure 5.2.7
Source: Poll conducted by SENAC RS on behalf of IBCO in Nov/Dec 1998

Although this poll has not yet been repeated, our feeling is that little has changed in the interval.

Another poll conducted in 2000 among 5000 executives in the Training and Human Resources associated sector showed the following results (Figure 5.2.8):

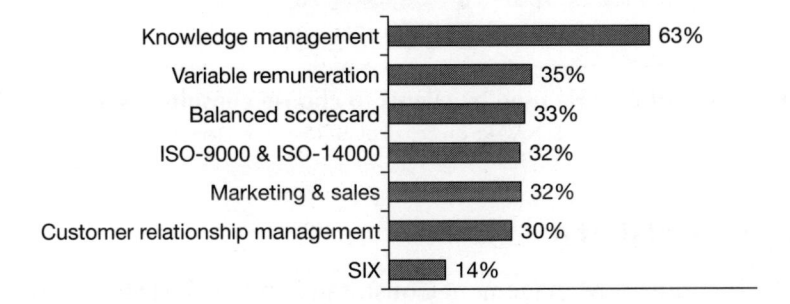

Area	Value
Knowledge management	63%
Variable remuneration	35%
Balanced scorecard	33%
ISO-9000 & ISO-14000	32%
Marketing & sales	32%
Customer relationship management	30%
SIX	14%

Figure 5.2.8 Interest areas among consultancy clients
Source: Poll conducted by Universo da Qualidade (SP) in Jan/Feb 2000

Two issues have always been major concerns of our institute regarding ethics and quality in consulting: client satisfaction and how clients choose consultancy. The following two charts illustrate the situation:

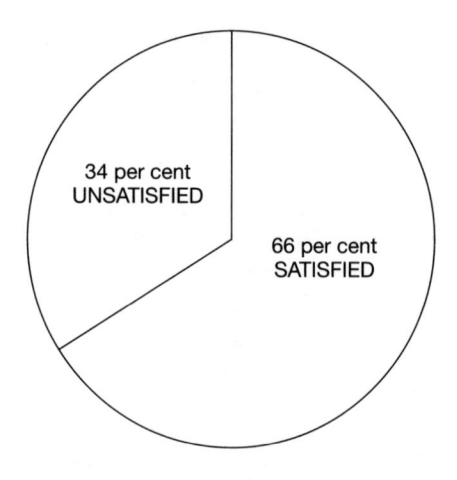

Figure 5.2.9 Client Satisfaction Poll
Source: Poll conducted by SENAC RS on behalf of IBCO in Nov/Dec 1998

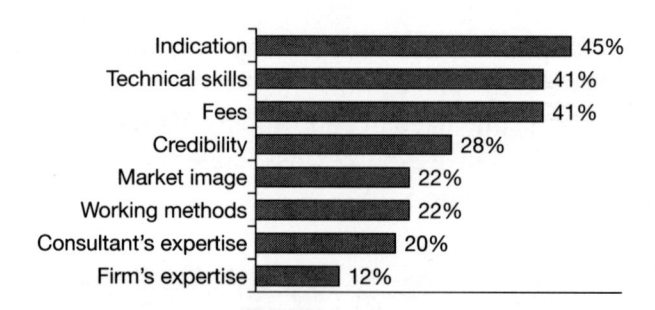

Figure 5.2.10 Criteria used by clients to choose consulting services
Source: Poll conducted by SENAC RS on behalf of IBCO in Nov/Dec 1998

The Institute

The Institute of Management Consultants in Brazil (IMC Brazil or IBCO (Instituto Brasileiro dos Consultores de Organisação)) was founded to promote quality and ethics in management consulting.

It began in São Paulo as INSCO in 1968, and merged with ABCO from Rio de Janeiro in 1981 when it acquired its current name. Its national headquarters are now in São Paulo. Local branches exist in the most important Brazilian states.

The board is chosen by a direct members' vote every two years. The current board was chosen in June 2000 and will manage the institute until 2002. Members contribute to the maintenance of the Institute with a quarterly fee.

The Board has a president and six directors in charge of finance, professional development, public relations, marketing and two executive vice-presidents.

The 170 members have been certified and they commit themselves to perform according to the Institute's mission and objectives as well as its Code of Ethics.

Branches promote regular seminars and debates between members, other management consultants, clients and institutes representing other professional areas, discussing matters of common interest and promoting development by sharing knowledge and experience.

The Institute offers many services to its members, all described on its website, www.ibco.org.br.

CANADA *Heather Osler*

Size of the consulting market

Management consulting is a dynamic and growing industry in Canada that not only generates significant revenues and profits, but also provides value to all types of organisations. Approximately 70 per cent of all business and government organisations in Canada have used the services of a management consultant at least once in the last five years.

There are many challenges in defining the size of the consulting market due to definitional issues around 'management consulting', and the fact that many firms in other industries also provide management consulting services. Management consulting comes under code 7771 of Statistics Canada's *Standard Industrial Classification* (SIC) system.Industry Canada also collects statistics based on the North American Industry Classification System (NAICS). The consulting codes are as follows:

54161	Management consulting services
541611	Administrative & general management consulting services
541612	Human resource & executive search consulting services
541619	Other management consulting services
5416A	Scientific & technical consulting services
54162	Environmental consulting services
54169	Other scientific & technical consulting services

Based on the NAICS categorisation, the Canadian market for management consulting services is estimated at $5.7 billion (all funds are in Canadian dollars unless otherwise stated).

Table 5.2.10 Revenue of all Canadian Management Consulting Firms, 1998

NAICS		Total Revenue $	
54161	Management Consulting	5,736,024	86 per cent
5416A	Scientific & Technical Consulting	940,033	14 per cent
5416	**Total**	**6,676,057**	

Source: 1998 Survey of Service Industries: Management, Scientific & Technical Consulting Industry, Industry Canada, March 2001

The consulting industry in Canada had grown significantly over the past two decades. The industry was growing at levels greater than 15 per cent per year up to the 1990–92 recession. In 1995, Industry Canada estimated the size of the Canadian market for Management consulting services (based on Canadian industry revenues) at between $2.3 billion and $3.0 billion. Although data is not available, annual growth rates for the late 1990s were estimated to be in the range of 20 per cent.

Consulting revenue in Canada is concentrated in the most populous regions, with more than half of all revenue from the province of Ontario. Many of the largest firms have offices in at least one or two of the larger cities (Vancouver, Calgary, Toronto, Montreal). In the last few years, the accounting based consulting firms have reduced the number of offices by exiting smaller communities. In addition, with the drive to have consultants billable, and working at the client site, larger firms are experimenting with 'hotelling' arrangements, which enable several consultants to share office workspace.

Table 5.2.11 Provincial Distribution of Consulting Revenue, 1998

	Total Revenue $000's	Total Canada per cent
Ontario	2,935,726	51.2 per cent
Quebec	1,160,266	20.2 per cent
British Columbia	710,579	12.4 per cent
Alberta	629,197	11.0 per cent
Manitoba	109,953	1.9 per cent
Saskatchewan	64,971	1.1 per cent
Nova Scotia	55,348	1.0 per cent
New Brunswick	39,472	0.7 per cent
Yukon & Northwest Territories	14,539	0.3 per cent
Newfoundland	9,543	0.2 per cent
Prince Edward Island	6,429	0.1 per cent
Canada	**5,736,024**	

Source: 1998 Survey of Service Industries: Management, Scientific & Technical Consulting Industry, Industry Canada, March 2001

Providers of consulting services

There are approximately 5,000 management consulting companies in Canada, and over 20,000 management consultants, depending on the definition used. According to the 1996 census, women account for 44 per cent of those employed in the Canadian consulting industry.

The number of consultants in Canada has increased over the last two decades. In the early nineties, much of the growth was attributed to the downsizing of senior executives. The Canadian situation mirrors that in the US where growth is also triggered by the blurring of boundaries with technology service providers. Increasingly traditional hardware, software and telecommunications companies are opening consulting divisions. In addition, other professional service firms such as law firms and advertising agencies are beginning to provide management consulting services to their clients.

According to Human Resource Development Canada, two thirds of consultants in Canada are employed by firms with more than 100 employees. Some 28 per cent of consultants work in firms with less than 20 employees, and many of these people would be sole practitioners.

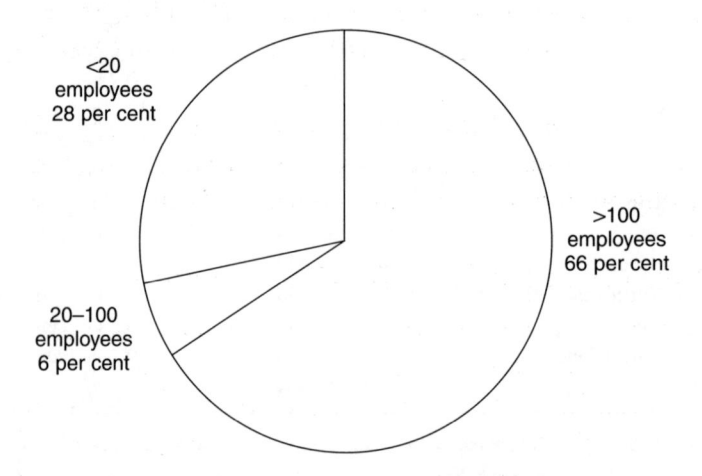

Figure 5.2.11 Where consultants work, by size of firm
Source: HRDC Industry Profile, Management Consulting Services

The largest consulting companies in Canada are the same large international players that one sees in developed nations around the world. Although some re-positioning has occurred, there has been little movement in the composition of the top firms over the past 10 years. The large consulting firms are becoming larger and the smaller firms more numerous, and this trend is likely to continue. Frequently firms which reach 20–50 employees are acquired by the larger companies. Currently, mid-sized Canadian firms include Western Management Consultants, Myers Norris Penny and Johnston Smith International.

The top 20 consulting firms in Canada represented more than one third of the total industry revenue in 1999. The largest consulting firm in Canada at the end of 1999 was PricewaterhouseCoopers with revenue of $44.1 million from a total staff of 1,749 (Table 5.2.12).

Of the firms listed, Andersen Consulting (now Accenture) had by far the highest leverage model, with a ratio of over 75 consultants for each partner. As a result, it also had the highest revenue per partner at over $16 million. The other major firms had an average of between four and twenty consultants per partner. Average revenue per consultant ranged from $110–780,000, with most of the top twenty companies billing between $200–300,000 per consultant.

Different consulting firms focus on providing different services. Over time, technology related services are becoming an increasing portion of most firm's offerings (Table 5.2.13).

Metrics on Consulting Service Providers

On average, management consulting firms in Canada earn 22 per cent profit before taxes, and scientific and technical consulting firms earn 20 per cent. Salaries and benefits are the largest component of expenses, accounting for 40 per cent of total expenses. Other main expenses include sub-contractor fees and occupancy costs.

Table 5.2.12 Major consulting companies by revenue and staff

Rank	Firm	Revenue ($Cmn)	Growth rate per cent	Effective date	Number of Consultants	Number of Partners	Total Staff	Revenue/ Consultant ($Cmn)	Revenue/ Partner ($Cmn)	Consultants/ Partner
1	PricewaterhouseCoopers	441.0	282	Jun-99	1511	81	1749	0.29	5.44	18.65
2	Deloitte Consulting/DTT	388.5	16	Aug-99	n/a	n/a	1825			
3	Andersen Consulting	226.4	28	Dec-98	1070	14	1350	0.21	16.17	76.43
4	William M. Mercer	208.0	22	Sep-99	697	n/a	1275	0.30		
5	Ernst & Young Consulting Services	187.0	15	Sep-99	463	67	620	0.40	2.79	6.91
6	KPMG Consulting	148.0	32	Sep-99	659	55	861	0.22	2.69	11.98
7	Aon Consulting	66.0	3	Dec-98	230	n/a	550	0.29		
8	Watson Wyatt Worldwide	62.6	2	Jun-99	289	0	375	0.22		
9	AT Kearney	60.0	20	Dec-98	77	4	119	0.78	15.00	19.25
10	Computer Sciences Corporation	60.0	16	Mar-99	400	n/a	600	0.15		

11	AMS Management Systems Canada	42.0	−3	Dec-98	50	9	230	0.84	4.67	5.56
12	Boston Consulting Group of Canada	36.0	63	Dec-98	63	n/a	n/a	0.57		
13	Arthur Andersen	31.5	24	Aug-99	n/a	n/a	182			
14	Bain & Company	29.8	19	n/a	60	6	80	0.50	4.97	10.00
15	DMR Consulting Group	28.0	33	Dec-98	260	0	n/a	0.11		
16	Hay Management Consultants	24.2	13	Sep-99	87	9	156	0.28	2.69	9.67
17	Eckler Partners	20.3	17	Dec-98	80	22	110	0.25	0.92	3.64
18	Ajilon Canada	9.2	70	Dec-99	60	5	n/a	0.15	1.84	12.00
19	RSM Canada	6.5	23	Dec-98	20	5	30	0.33	1.30	4.00
20	CPCS Transcom	4.0	33	Aug-99	12	2	15	0.33	2.00	6.00

Source: Management Consultant International: 12 January 2000, CAMC Analysis

Table 5.2.13 Leading Canadian Consultancies: Fee Split by Activity

	IT	Strategy & Organ- isation	Financial	Project Mgmt	HR & Search	Change Mgmt	Marketing	Operations Mgmt	Process Re-engineer	Facilities/ Out- sourcing	Others
Ajilon Canada	20	15		5	27	10	3		10	10	
Aon Consulting					14					86	
Computer Sciences Corporation	30	20	20			10		10	10		
Hay Management Consultants		15			80	5					
KPMG Consulting	30	8	0.5	7	29	2	0.5		21	1	1
Pricewaterhouse Coopers	60	10								30	

Source: Management Consultant International

Table 5.2.14 Revenue and expenses by province, Canada, 1998

NAICS 54161 Management Consulting	Total Revenue $000's	Salaries, Wages & Benefits[1] $000's	Total Expenses $000's	Profit before taxes per cent
Ontario	2,935,726	948,419	2,260,305	23
Quebec	1,160,266	397,342	938,837	19
British Columbia	710,579	258,233	568,786	20
Alberta	629,197	218,110	466,825	26
Manitoba	109,953	37,099	81,308	26
Saskatchewan	64,971	16,461	47,199	27
Nova Scotia	55,348	18,943	39,238	29
New Brunswick	39,472	8,724	26,928	32
Yukon & Northwest Territories	14,539	3,139	11,730	19
Newfoundland	9,543	2,647	5,819	39
Prince Edward Island	6,429	1,793	4,374	32
Canada	**5,736,024**	**1,910,910**	**4,451,349**	**22**
NAICS 5416A Scientific & Technical Consulting	940,033	311,808	752,850	20

Source: 1998 Survey of Service Industries: Management, Scientific & Technical Consulting Industry, Industry Canada, March 2001

See *Notes* after Table 5.2.15 overleaf

Table 5.2.15 Operating expenses by type as a percentage of total revenue, Canada 1998

NAICS		Salaries, Wages & Benefits[2]	Work sub-contracted to others	Repair & Main-tenance	Adver-tising	Depre-ciation	Occupancy & other rental[3]	Materials, Components & Supplies	Other[4]	Expenses
54161	Management Consulting	40	9	1	1	2	7	3	20	82
5416A	Scientific & Technical Consulting	39	9	1	1	2	6	2	23	83
5416	Total	40	9	1	1	2	7	2	21	82

Source: 1998 Survey of Service Industries: Management, Scientific & Technical Consulting Industry, Industry Canada, March 2001

Notes (applies to Tables 5.2.14 and 5.2.15):

1. Data for surveyed firms only, accounting for 89 per cent of incorporated firms' revenue, and 79 per cent of revenue overall
2. Fees paid to contract employees are not included
3. Includes rent or lease of land and buildings, rent/leasing of motor vehicles, computer equipment, machinery and other equipment, heat, light, power and water, insurance, taxes, permit and licenses. Mortgage payments are excluded.
4. Includes fees paid to contract employees, interest paid, office supplies, telephone, travel and entertainment, royalties, franchise fees paid, legal, accounting and consulting fees, and other operating expenses.

Consumers of management consulting services

Businesses are the largest consumers of management consulting services, representing 71 per cent of services based on revenue. It should be noted that the government portion (15 per cent) may be slightly overstated as it may include consulting services provided to private organisations, but funded by government or other public agencies. For example, organisations such as the Canadian Technology Network (CTN) and the Industrial Research Assistance Program (IRAP) contract consultants on behalf of small and medium sized businesses.

Table 5.2.16 Distribution of client base as a percentage of total operating revenue, 1998

		Households & Individuals	Business	Government	Foreign Consumers
54161	Management Consulting	3	71	15	11
5416A	Scientific & Technical Consulting	2	58	25	14
5416	Total	3	69	17	11

Source: 1998 Survey of Service Industries: Management, Scientific & Technical Consulting Industry, Industry Canada, March 2001

Canadian consulting companies provide services to a variety of industries, although some firms have much deeper penetration of different industry verticals. Based on the fee revenue of a selected group of the largest firms, the financial services and high tech firms are the largest private sector users of consulting services.

Trade in management consulting services

Canadian management consultants have been successful in work markets, and are a major source of export earnings. The exact dollar value of exports is difficult to track due to internal transfer payments between the different country offices of the large consulting firms.

Table 5.2.17 Leading Canadian consultancies: fee split by industry

	Financial Services	Mfg.	Telecom	Gov't	Energy/ Enviro.	Products	Utilities	Distri- bution	Trans- portation	Health- care	Tech- nology	Other
Ajilon Canada	5	5	25	30			5	5		5	20	
AMS Management Systems	60		9	30	1							
Andersen Consulting	21		9	22		25						23
Computer Sciences Corporation	10	10		40						5		35
DMR Consulting Group	23	13	29	13	8				4			10
Ernst & Young Consulting Services	22	20	4	3	20	14				4		13
Hay Management Consultants	29	15		16		5	4			11		20
KPMG	9	10	10	29	3	8	2	8	10	5	2	4
Pricewaterhouse Coopers	15		7		18						28	32

Source: Management Consultant International

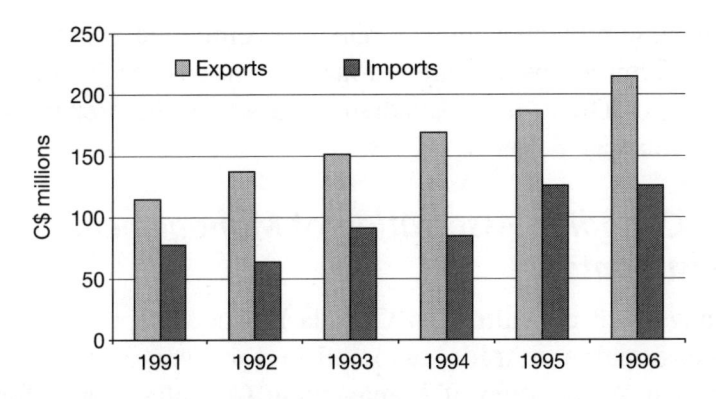

Figure 5.2.12 Trade in management consulting

Exports are more predominant in the larger firms. It is estimated that exports account for approximately 15 per cent of total billings, however they may reach over 20 per cent for the largest firms. The lower value of the Canadian dollar has made Canadian consultants economical in the US market, and this country is the source of most export revenue. The export of management consulting service to the US has also been facilitated by the North American Free Trade Agreement (NAFTA), and in a broader context by the General Agreement on Trade in Services (GATS).

Given the extent of cross border activity, many industry analysts see Canada not as a separate entity but as part of the larger North American market given the numerous affiliations between the major U.S. and Canadian firms and the significant, cross-border relationships held by the major consulting groups.

In addition to providing services in the United States, Canadian consultants do export their services around the world. Canadian consultants participate on large projects in the developing world, which are funded by the International Financial Institutions (IFIs), as well as the Canadian International Development Agency (CIDA). In the winter of 2001, CIDA replenished its Canadian Consultant Trust Funds (CCTFs) at the World Bank and the Inter-American Development Bank (IDB).

With these replenishments, CIDA has committed approximately C$ 26.5 million over the next four years to be used by the World Bank and IDB to hire Canadians to assist in the preparation of Bank-financed projects.

The Canadian Association of Management Consultants

Management consulting in Canada has been represented by a professional and trade association for over 30 years. The Canadian Association of Management Consultants was formed as a trade association in 1963 to promote professionalism in the industry.

CAMC has 10 regional chapters, which offer local networking and professional development benefits to members. While administration is centrally co-ordinated from the Toronto-based national office, each of the provincial institutes is still responsible for conferring the Certified Management Consultant (CMC) designation. This designation is given to practitioners who successfully complete a course of studies, academic requirements (university degree), and practical experience components. The CAMC Uniform Code of Conduct and the CMC designation serve to help differentiate those professional consultants from those who merely hang out a shingle while they are looking for other work.

The CAMC currently has over 4,500 members, of whom nearly half are in the province of Ontario. Of the members, over 2,200 are certified members. Membership includes representation from the large firms, the speciality boutique shops, and independent consultants.

As the 'Voice of Management Consulting in Canada', CAMC is active in government lobbying and promotes the interest of consulting in Canada.

This report was researched and prepared by Julie Lissaman May, CMC on behalf of the Canadian Association of Management Consultants in May 2001.

USA

The top US management consultancy firms were last surveyed by *Management Consultant International* journal in its September 2000 issue. The survey confirmed that industry growth rates in the US had slowed down in 1999 while at the same time a series of traumatic re-organisations and re-alignments was taking place among the major firms. Transformation among the top 10 firms is summarised in Chapter 1.3 and referred to elsewhere in Part One.

The survey also preceded the acknowledged downturn of the US economy, although the signs were probably there for those with 20: 20 hindsight, whose vision was obscured at the time by the continuing technology revoluton and the rapid growth of e-consulting. Plans for Independent Public Offerings (IPO's) were being made then by the larger consultancies, partly as a direct response to the hardened stance of the SEC towards consultant-auditor divestment.

Kennedy Information, the publishers of MCI, have declared global management consultancy revenues for 2000 of US$114 billion of which the USA accounted for some US$63 billion.

In the first half of 2001, as internet marketing businesses have continued to fail investors' expectations and the general malaise has spread further to all IT related businesses, notably to the telecommunications industry, e-consultancy in the US has nose-dived. With the continuing economic slow-down, it is expected that many individual firm's US growth rates revealed in the next MCI survey are likely to be significantly lower, particularly those with a high proportion of revenue derived from e-business.

Beyond the 69 US firms surveyed by *MCI* with revenues in excess of $US1 million, the management consultancy industry continues to consolidate and gather strength. The Association of Management Consultants (AMC) and the Institute of Management Consultants (IMC) which have been merged since 1986 now have a combined membership of 3,000 independent consultancies, of which approximately half have obtained their American CMC qualifications.

Asia and Australasia

ASIA REGIONAL OVERVIEW *Walter E. Vieira*

Management consultancy in Asia, except Japan and Australia, is in its infancy. This can be seen from the fact that 60 per cent of management consultancy revenues are from the USA; 25 per cent are from Europe; 7 per cent from Japan; 2 per cent from Asia; and 6 per cent from the rest of the world.

Yet it is also true that the highest rate of growth in management consultancy is in the Asian region. It is estimated that there will be an increase of over 30 per cent in comparison to a 20 per cent increase in the West.

Countries pass through different stages. The initial period is when the role of agriculture is pre-eminent. The next period is when the role of industry is most important. Finally, the most sophisticated period is when the role of services is the highest.

A country like India has graduated into the third phase. In 1950–1951, the economy broke down into agriculture at 55 per cent, industry at 32 per cent and services at 13 per cent. In 1999–2000, this had changed to 26 per cent agriculture, 22 per cent industry and as much as 52 per cent services.

The trend towards services also applies to China, Sri Lanka, Bangladesh, Thailand, Indonesia, South Korea and Taiwan. However, Sri Lanka is still at the agricultural stage while China, Thailand, Indonesia and South Korea are at an advanced industry stage.

The stage of development of a country reflects on the development of the management consultancy profession. An indicator is the table opposite.

Table 5.2.18 A country's stage of development reflects upon the management consultancy profession

Country	IMC Members	Estimated Consultants in Practice		IMC Formed
India	700	8,000	All Big 5 present	1989 (from association in 1962)
China	20	Unknown	Unknown	1998
Taiwan		Unknown		
Bangladesh	31	200	All Big 5 present	1996
Thailand		Unknown		Being formed
Sri Lanka		Unknown		Being formed
Indonesia	60	300	Some Big 5 present	Irregular (dissolved)
S. Korea				
Malaysia	60	200	All Big 5 present	1992
Japan	700	8,000	All Big 5 present	1999
Australia		25,000	All Big 5 present	1969
New Zealand				
Philippines			Big 5 + local firms	Have only MC association
Jordan	77	100		1995
Hong Kong	45	3,000	All Big 5 present	October 2000

AUSTRALIA

Management consultancy in Australia has achieved a high level of development. The IMC-Australia is well regarded and recognised by government. They have a proper system of certification, re-certification and on-going training and development; and the rate of the Institute of Management Consultants' (IMC) membership growth is high. There is also a committed and effective leadership. Australia, with its achievements, casts a shadow over New Zealand and its IMC.

JAPAN

Japan has all shades of consultancy – management and technical – covered under the umbrella organization Zen-Noh-Ren. This has about 8,000 members, of which about 700 are management consultants. The management consultancy branch of Zen-Noh-Ren is now affiliated to the International Council of Management Consulting Institutes (ICMCI). Zen-Noh-Ren conducts its own entrance examinations, but will soon follow the ICMCI model for their management consultants.

PHILIPPINES

The IMC-Philippines went into oblivion in 1997. It had survived for four years. The Philippines now only have an association of MC firms, which is a trade body and does not involve itself in the certification of individuals or impose a code of conduct.

INDONESIA

The IMC-Indonesia has gone under after eight years as a result of the financial crisis and political instability. It is now a defunct organisation and will have to bide its time and re-start when the situation stabilises. However, the Big Five continue to operate, reasonably successfully, in Indonesia.

MALAYSIA

IMC-Malaysia seems to coast along neither making progress nor regressing. It has yet to become a dynamic organization.

CHINA

IMC-China seems to have many problems with regard to starting and expanding an organisation. Such organisations are looked upon with suspicion by the authorities as perhaps the beginnings of trouble.

SINGAPORE AND INDIA

Singapore and India have dynamic IMC organisations which have a process of certification in place, a focus on training and development and the imposition of a code of conduct. Both Singapore and India have a programme for the Diploma in Management Consultancy.

HONG KONG

Hong Kong formed an IMC in October 2000 and has already got off to a good start with a Diploma in Management Consultancy and plans for training.

The other countries in the region have yet to start effective operations.

Certification

Because of the amorphous nature of management consultancy, which includes a wide range of disciplines, there is always resistance to a certification process. There seems to be little understanding that the examination covers consulting skills and ethical practices and not the specialisation of the consultant.

A large number of management consultants in Asian countries are those who have retired and have gone into consultancy as an extension of their working life. This section of consultants, many of whom are senior managers, resist the IMC's efforts to introduce certification.

Also, in developing countries, a major market share is held by the Big Five and many successful individual consultants or small firms work on an assignment basis for some of the Big Five. The Big Five assert that they have their own induction and training programmes and do not need assistance from the local IMC. With the development of the Certified Practice model, this may now change.

A large proportion of the potential consultancy market in Asian countries is government, public sector or non-profit organisations. Yet often none of these really understands their own needs – and what is worse, most consultants do not realize the potential and the opportunity. So they restrict themselves to the private sector and impose boundaries on the possibilities.

The lead for forming institutes generally comes from successful individual consultants or small local firms. If these are too few in number, then there is great difficulty in getting an institute started. This is the difficulty in South Korea, Sri Lanka, Thailand and Vietnam. In these countries even forming a core group of 20 consultants who meet the criteria set down by the ICMCI seems to be an insurmountable problem.

Some of the countries do not encourage the setting up of associations as a national policy. China, Kuwait and other countries in the Middle East are examples. These have been described and registered as limited companies, and operations are conducted under this umbrella.

Conclusion

Management consultants will be increasingly needed in Asian countries – as the growth rate indicates. As clients and consultants themselves become more savvy, there will be a compulsion to separate the wheat from the chaff and certification of individuals and firms will gradually become the norm. With the explosion of knowledge and the globalisation of businesses, management consultants will find it necessary to keep updating themselves – ongoing training will become a necessity rather than remain a choice. They will have to learn, in order to provide a service.

With management consultancy evolving into a profession, the ethical dimensions will become increasingly important, as they are in any other 'profession'. Ongoing learning, outsourcing and networking will all become the currency of operating as a management consultant in the Asian environment.

AUSTRALIA AND NEW ZEALAND

Richard Elliott

Background to Australian consultancy

Old land, new ways

Forty thousand years ago, the Australian aborigines employed management techniques to invigorate the land. In those days, they regularly used fire to generate new growth and life in an otherwise harsh and unforgiving environment. Little changed until the second settlement about 200 years ago when Sydney and Hobart were established as colonial outposts of the British Empire. In the subsequent period, the vast mineral and renewal resources were developed almost exclusively for export to the United Kingdom, Europe and the United States.

While we can identify the use of management techniques by aborigines in the past, it is difficult to identify the start of any formal management consulting in Australia other than its first reference in the 1930s when WD Scott and Co was established by the cost accountant Sir Walter Scott.

When Britain entered the Common Market in 1964, it closed the door on its supply chain from Australia and New Zealand and looked to internal sources in Europe. This caused many years of adjustment and difficulty for Australia as it came to grips with establishing new trade relationships in a highly competitive market.

Until recently, Australia was primarily viewed as an asset-rich country and the raw material supply source for major manufacturing countries such as Japan. But such a simple assessment does not take into account the extraordinary changes that have occurred in the last 30 years.

During this time, strategic planners and advisers underwent considerable soul searching, many false starts and complex modelling to determine a suitable way forward. The result is that Australia is now a stronger, more independent society which is relaxed and confident in its overall ability, both within Australia and the global market. Today, the management tool used to invigorate the land is creative thought and planning.

2000 saw the longest period of economic growth for over 50 years, which resulted in the following:

- unemployment at its lowest level for 25 years
- federal and state government budget surpluses
- standard of living a third higher than in 1990
- the lowest interest rates for 25 years
- four per cent GDP annual growth

What makes this trend more impressive is that it has happened despite the collapse of nearly two-thirds of Australia's major export markets in the late 1990s due to the Asian financial meltdown. The resilience of the economy is due to deep structured changes to the economic and social management of this young nation carried out by the Hawke Government in the early part of the 1980s.

The central strategy of this revolution – and subsequent developments which will have important implications for both domestic and regional economies for the next 20 to 50 years – was largely the work of political advisers and economic strategy consultants. Their work, while well-couched and researched, was high-risk as it challenged the fundamental principles of how Australians worked and were rewarded. It required a change of focus from a resource-based economy to a service-based one, open to highly competitive world trade and investment with a current account deficit and high foreign debt.

The key elements of this strategy were:

- deregulation of financial markets and the banking system
- floating of the Australian dollar
- changes in work practices and union philosophy
- a consultative accord between the Australian government and the Australian Council of Trade Unions
- deregulation of many government controls including reduction of tariffs and import duties

- disappearance of high-subsidised protection of labour intensive industries such as the clothing and footwear industry
- enterprise bargaining for award wages rather than industry-wide agreement

While political parties will debate the success and benefits of these and other elements in the re-organisation of the economy, the final result has clearly been increased wealth, more choice and new hope.

Value of the regional market

Government statistics do not provide sufficient breakdown of data to allow a precise valuation of the consulting industry in Australia. However, economic activity has seen management consultancy and business services grow at a rate of between 20 and 30 per cent per annum over the last 10 years. Little attention has been paid to consultancy as an industry sector until recently, so an accurate indication of market size is difficult. However, a recent survey suggested that the market has annual billings of A$6 billion and employs over 22,000 people. New Zealand annual billings are approximately NZ$55–65 million and the sector employs between 2,000 and 3,000 people.

Value of types of consultancy (or proportions)

The proportion of government business is around A$2.5–3 billion in Australia and probably about NZ$30 million in New Zealand.

There may be a further A$10–20 million per annum in revenue from Papua New Guinea, largely derived from advertising agencies.

Management consultancy is still an evolving profession with a rapid trend away from the technostructural approach of delivery to a more humanised style of strategy, scenario modelling and performance improvement. With these changes comes a greater range of services and a move towards providing 'expert' services rather than general advice and problem solving services. There has been a move towards more specialised 'niche' services, which can achieve sustainable competitive advantage.

These trends are not only true for private sector firms, but also for internal consultants in government or not-for-profit organisations.

Under the recently introduced national competition policy in Australia, many internal consultants are now having to engage in competitive tendering with the private sector for their own work. The outcomes, while disastrous for some, have been encouraging in terms of better solutions, tighter time frames and improved value for money. The other noticeable result has been that the improved relationship between consultants and their clients has become central to most long-term arrangements.

Another major trend is the growing provision of non-consulting activities to capture greater project fees. Typically, these products include software development, systems integration, outsourcing and training.

According to a recent survey undertaken by the IMC of its members in Australia, the most popular services provided by management consultants are business strategy, change management, performance improvement, IT and telecommunications, human resources and business re-engineering.

Main industries employing management consultants

The federal, state and local governments are the major buyers of consulting services in Australia and New Zealand, followed by transnational companies and the service sector.

In terms of delivery of consulting services, Australian management consultancy firms are divided into the following categories:

- large multi-functional consulting firms – capable of providing a range of complex services delivered to a wide range of industry sectors
- major accounting firms with management consultancy departments – providing national and transnational services with regional specialisation such as human resource management, organisational development and IT

- small to medium sized firms – focusing on a regional coverage of general management and business development services with growing interest in specialisation
- sole practitioners – generalists with broad management experience
- consulting academics – involved in part time work on a regular basis
- non-traditional suppliers – such as investment bankers, brokers, IT specialists, project managers

The three tiers of government are largely serviced by the relative sized tiers of management consultants, although in more recent times the concept of project teams or smaller firms has become increasingly popular.

The Australian consulting profession is dominated by small firms. However, there is now a noticeable trend towards networking for larger projects which has resulted in some remarkable work.

As the market grows, the industry is becoming more formalised and clients are looking for competency standards to aid selection of both individuals and consulting firms.

Activities outside the region by consultancies located within it

The export of consultancy services falls into two areas. IT services are provided to governments in New Zealand and the Asia Pacific Region by Accenture, PwC and several small specialist firms. This market is thought to be worth approximately A$30–35 million per year. Agriculture, economic and social consulting services are provided under NGO aid programmes to various countries in Africa, Asia and the Asia Pacific Region. The value of this business, of which a large percentage is linked with AusAid programmes, is in excess of A$20 million per year

Human resource aspects

Main sources of recruitment

Based on government figures, it is estimated that approximately 13,000 people are employed by smaller firms of less than 20 employees. This accounts for 95 per cent of the industry, while the balance (mostly large multi-national firms) employ the remaining 9,000.

While the small firms sustain employment, the large firms usually hire new graduates and train them.

Hiring is usually directly through universities, normally up to six months before graduation. The attrition rate of this process is high, with 70–80 per cent leaving these firms within three years.

Educational standards

A university degree is a basic criterion for most applications, with firms such as Accenture preferring MBAs and double degrees.

Local management consultant training

IMC Australia was established in 1967 and provides a range of internal and outsourced professional development. The CMC designation was introduced in 1992. This competency mark and post-nominals are conferred after appropriate training and an eight hour case study examination.

The Australian and New Zealand institutes are both members of the ICMCI and have adopted the international competency model approved in Amsterdam in 1999.

The Australian institute is in the process of trialling the new global, individual and practice CMC model to be introduced in late 2001.

Outlook

In a survey of Australian CEOs undertaken in 2000, IMC Australia asked them what they thought were the most important issues and challenges facing them over the next five years.

Twenty-nine percent responded that they felt people were their greatest concern, especially in relation to

- building strong leadership
- retaining key staff

- building enthusiasm
- effective succession planning
- recruiting staff and attracting enough new/young entrants

The next most important issue related to competitiveness and how they should deal with
- competitive pressures
- maintaining competitive cost structures
- squeezes on margins
- identifying and maintaining competitive advantage

The third area of major concern was e-business growth and how to
- meet competition in export markets
- build growth and revenue
- identify growth opportunities
- extract value from products
- develop new markets

All of this suggests that the demand for consulting services in Australasia will continue to be strong with good, competent consultants in high demand.

The trend towards downsizing and outsourcing is likely to continue and with it will come a sustainable market for the management consulting sector.

PR CHINA *Li Yong*

Management consultancy as a concept was introduced into China in the 1980s but had been confined to the ivory tower for a considerable length of time and only became a business practice in the last few years. In the 1980s, 'idea kings' and 'masters of planning' seemed to create miracles and people were led to believe that one good idea could save a business from the brink of collapse.

Indeed, some businesses did survive as a result of these ideas, however they were nothing more than simple product/service concepts that temporarily solved the problems of the businesses' inability to improve their product/service offerings. Because of the lack of systematic management propositions in those ideas, the fundamental problems that existed in the operating systems of the Chinese businesses were not eliminated. The symptoms were alleviated but the ailment was still there. Therefore, it is not difficult to imagine that those businesses will eventually fall into another round of difficulties, which cannot be solved by any ideas.

With the collapse of many well-known companies, who had created miracles as a result of past ideas, people started to realise that improvement of their core competence and management capabilities was essential. At the same time, however, most businesses did not have the required management resources within themselves, a legacy of flawed competition from the planned economy. With the entry of more and more foreign businesses, introducing modern management and marketing concepts, competition has intensified. Local Chinese businesses are beginning to feel the pressure of their eroding market shares, and China's imminent entry into the World Trade Organisation (WTO) has made them re-examine their competitive positions in the market as well as the effectiveness of their current operating systems. While efforts have been made to tempt management talent with high salaries, many businesses are beginning to look at other options, such as the use of technical consultants, economic advisors, marketing experts and management consultancies from outside, called 'external brains'.

Some of these external brains – consisting of scholars, industry experts, economists, professors and journalists – are invited to perform the function of an advisor on issues of product development, market strategies, management control, training of senior staff, etc. Other external brains – which are basically management consulting firms – are employed to establish systems of production management, research and development, organisational set-up, human resources management, corporate strategy, marketing strategy, financial control, management information, corporate culture, etc. The general lack of management resources in China has created a potential demand for management consultancy; and the effort to transform the operating mechanism of Chinese companies at both government and business levels has spelled out the need for management consultancy. However, the unique features of the ongoing economic reforms pose challenges not only to foreign consulting companies, but also to local ones, in terms of their ability to make the correct diagnosis and prescription.

The potential demand for management consultancy has prompted both international and local firms to enter the market. No official statistics are available on the total number of management consulting companies in China but one estimate indicates that there are about 3,000 companies registered under the name of management consultancy. It is believed that there are many more companies that may not call themselves management consultants, but perform a similar role. It is also generally believed that management consulting companies are largely concentrated in key commercial centres such as Beijing, Guangzhou, Shanghai and Shenzhen. The local companies vary greatly in staff size, from 5–6 staff to up to 200. In terms of revenue, there are only a few who have total revenues exceeding RMB 10 million (about US$ 1.2 million), with many more struggling to make ends meet.

In the battlefield of the management consulting market, we can see the familiar names such as McKinsey, Arthur Andersen, Roland Berger, A T Kearney, Boston and Bain. All of these are actively exploring the market and have now established a strong foothold. These foreign consulting firms brought new management theories, methodologies and tools to China, while at the same time putting competitive pressure on local management consulting firms. Due to their established reputations in the world and their superiority of knowledge, foreign management consulting firms enjoy favourable competitive positions over their local counterparts. While no one is really clear about the size of the management consultancy market in China, a multinational management consulting firm believes that the current market size is about US$100 million. The same company forecasts that the market will increase to US$10 billion in about 10 years time – an even more attractive picture.

The prospects for management consultancy in China in the years to come are bright. But to capture this growth is quite another matter, and will require a great deal of effort. The current market size is the combined result of years of education by both foreign and local consulting firms and of increased exposure of Chinese businesses to the outside world. Chinese companies have only just begun to recognise the value of management consultancy and the level of acceptance of it is still being built up. Such recognition and acceptance are reflected in a number of consulting assignments to foreign management consulting firms, which include

- a contract of RMB 5 million (about US$0.62 million) between Wangfujing Department Store Group of Beijing and McKinsey
- the consulting services of Anderson to Heguang Group of Shenyang involving a total price of RMB 10 million (about US$1.2 million)
- the purchase of McKinsey advisory services by China Pingan Insurance Company for a price of nearly RMB 100 million (about US$12 million)
- an agreement between A T Kearney and Shenzhen Overseas Chinese Town Enterprise Group

These cases are positive signs of growth in the demand for management consultancy in China. Therefore, the focus of international management consulting firms has now shifted from its previous emphasis on servicing the needs of foreign companies in China to include Chinese companies. As local management consulting firms are still in their infancy in terms of growth and development, they have not yet built up the strength needed to fight for a significant market share. Foreign management consulting firms are believed to have taken over 90 per cent of the current market.

There has been no direct conflict between foreign and local consulting firms in this market segment. This is partly because few companies in China can afford to pay high professional fees for management consultancy. The picture may become clearer in about 3–5 years time.

However, the prohibitively high prices charged by international management consulting firms are considered to be a major weakness by industry people and experts, who maintain that such high professional fees may suffocate the demand for foreign management consultancy. There are also concerns about whether such expensive investments would bring the expected returns.

These concerns are a result of cases where foreign management consulting firms have failed to help their clients achieve their strategic goals. Industry analysts have pointed out that some of the consultancy services provided by foreign consulting firms had seemed to be a kind of highbrow game with concepts and spreadsheets but which gave little consideration to the unique economic and societal conditions in China. Many simply 'copied' the Western management models and 'pasted' them on to the Chinese companies. Some Chinese companies who had purchased foreign consultancy services were bewildered at being told to implement unfeasible strategies. Some of them felt they had spent money to be told facts that already knew, without realistic and practical solutions. Of course, there are also arguments in favour of the efficacy of foreign management consultancy services. The consensus is, however, that as well as their high fees, foreign consulting firms need to overcome other weaknesses, such as:

- lack of insight into and understanding of the external political and social environment in which a business operates
- inability to interpret the implications of macro-economic and industrial policies and their likely impact on a business
- failure to adapt western management models to local conditions
- insufficient understanding of cultural differences and a tendency to provide western experience-based solutions

Both foreign and local management consulting firms need to make efforts to overcome their respective weaknesses in order to become qualified 'doctors' for business 'patients'. In China, there are four categories of 'patients' that may need the treatment of management consultancy. One category is foreign invested businesses, who will need therapies for developing a management structure and marketing strategy suitable to the local conditions while at the same time meeting their global objectives. Another is the state-owned businesses (including collective-owned), who have complex symptoms that need to be treated with appropriate therapies to improve not only corporate governance, but also operating systems. A third category is the joint-stock companies, which are dynamic and fast-growing and will need more comprehensive therapies for sustained development. The fourth category is those private businesses, which will eventually face a transition from paternalistic management to rule-based corporate governance.

At present, the competition for top-class, deep-pocketed Chinese companies is between foreign management consulting firms. As the competition intensifies, these foreign firms may move down the pyramid to offer their services to smaller companies where they will meet competition from local firms, who will make every possible effort to sharpen their competitive edge. The meeting of foreign management consulting firms with the local ones in competition is unavoidable as the former localise their management resources and the latter internationalise their business norms. It is hard to say who will win the race at this early stage. But for those who are eyeing the opportunities in China, it is important to know where the opportunities lie.

HONG KONG AND THE PEARL RIVER DELTA

Gregg Li

The management consultancy industry is one of the fastest growing industries in China, and one of the fastest growing locations for this industry is the Pearl River Delta (PRD) region which includes Hong Kong, Macau, Shenzhen, the landmass alongside the Pearl River estuary and Guangzhou. Over the years, the demand for these services has moved from primarily one-off strategic studies such as the installation of an ERP system, overview of a privatisation strategy, or a new airport strategy to include process improvement such as the installation of ISO 14000 quality systems, supply chain improvements and market extension research. In other words, implementation and turnkey projects are now more in demand, as they are in other countries.

As the local manufacturer base migrated north over the border, which historically has never used much consultancy (except perhaps production and quality systems consultancy), the demand for training and applications of such consultancy blossomed north of Hong Kong. Hong Kong is now a service economy struggling to stay afloat of the changes imposed upon it from China, the US, the UK, Japan and surrounding countries. It is like a cork floating in an ocean, always on top of the turbulence beneath it. It had done well under the British administration prior to July 1997 and has continued to prosper under the One Country-Two System of Beijing.

Hong Kong is home to a vast number of international and local management consultancies, firstly due to the high number of multinationals headquartered in Hong Kong which often demand international levels of consultancy, and secondly due to the almost exponential speed of change in the Territory. Past research estimates that there are now over 120 management consultancies in Hong Kong, with a total of about 1,500 consultants working out of Hong Kong. After adding to a range of consultants over the border, ranging from those working in 'management hospitals' to professors moonlighting and to accountants providing management advice as an add-on, we can safely assume there are several thousand management consultants practising within the Pearl River Delta area at this stage.

However, there has been little research and data gathering about the industry in Hong Kong or the catchment area that it affects. Information on the consultancy industry in the PRD (outside Hong Kong) is even more difficult to come by as statistics are not collected and/or are difficult to verify. Therefore, this report is based on anecdotal evidence, past research and personal experience.

The demand for consultancy throughout China is generally more sophisticated in the Pearl River Delta region due to the presence of Hong Kong, which is an international financial city with an eye to becoming the London and New York of China. The presence of a high number of multinational offices (7,300 according to the Hong Kong Government Industry Department) has given Hong Kong a special status and much of the consultancy work has tended to revolve around the financial industry, government, transport and infrastructure, and the retail and consumer goods industries which are still vibrant in Hong Kong. Increasingly, however, the local multinationals (which started in Hong Kong and are extending their reach into mainland China and Asia) like Hutchinson Whampoa and even the local non-governmental organisations (NGO) have become sophisticated users of consultancy themselves, and this trend has been favourable for the industry. Hong Kong has become a sophisticated user of consultancy in mobile telecommunications, privatisation strategy, network governance, supply chain management, property development, infrastructural development, hyper-growth strategy, and in due course environmental venture strategy.

But this supremacy is rapidly changing as Shanghai flexes its muscles and opens its doors to multinationals, which frequently bring in their most favoured international consultants. The consultancy firms in Hong Kong are handling this challenge by using Hong Kong as a base of knowledge, ie by keeping their headquarters in Hong Kong, using Shenzhen or Guangzhou as the base for hiring and training, and marketing these skills into other parts of Greater China. Nevertheless, the larger firms are more aggressive and have established solid bases of operations in Shanghai, Beijing or Guangzhou to service mainland China. The smaller firms, increasingly finding Hong Kong too expensive to operate in, are downsizing their Hong Kong offices in favour of establishing larger offices in Shenzhen or even Macau. The latter is more popular and many are moving out of Hong Kong and into China.

The nature and type of consultancy is also changing with the clientele. As business moves north from Hong Kong, there is an increasing need from local clients who do not speak English, for example, and who want to communicate with competent Putonghua speaking consultants, who are difficult to find. English used to be the dominant language of choice, but this is no longer the case. Increasingly, clients want to see reports in both English and Chinese, or simply in Chinese. This impacts directly on the skills of those consultants who operate best in English, but allows more opportunity to the local recruits, from whom many international consultancies would have shied away from five years ago.

Historically, the charge-out rates prevailing in the market are some of the highest in the world, partly because of the high costs of living in Hong Kong and also because of the dearth of competent international-level consultants, together with a sophisticated client base that typically has a long list of demands. These factors combined have encouraged high fees. Nevertheless, fee rates are beginning to go down as consultants must now sell to a large client base that is not familiar with service charges, intangible results and the price/value relationship that quality consultants have enjoyed. On the other hand, consultants who must work increasingly over the border into the mainland pay higher transactional costs and worry constantly about their payment. In Hong Kong, where the rule of law has remained effective, contracts are generally honoured and consultants do not need to worry too much about delinquent payments. Hence, for many local consultancies Hong Kong has remained, and must remain, a cash cow while the PRD (outside Hong Kong) is less reliable.

Over the next few years, members of the Institute of Management Consultants (IMC) have expressed the view that, as a reflection of its industrial and expansion policies in China (and to a lesser extent in Hong Kong), the following types of consultancy services will probably be in high demand *inter alia*:

- speed and supply chain
- quality control and assurance, more ISO 9000 than total quality management (TQM)

- competitive benchmarking and market intelligence (particularly when China's trade is liberalised after it joins the WTO
- innovation, knowledge management and retention
- human resources administration and management, including training
- functional areas like finance, marketing and sales (turnkey projects)
- change management and diversity (cultural differences)
- core competencies
- strategy and regional co-operation studies
- privatisation or commercialisation
- corporate governance and infrastructural development
- market entry studies
- environmental impact and self-funding environmental ventures
- e-commerce and m-commerce

HONG KONG

In late 1997, the Hong Kong Coalition of Service Industries commissioned the Poon Kam Kai Institute of Management at the University of Hong Kong to undertake research in understanding the size and needs of the management consultancy sector in Hong Kong (Enright and Thompson, 1998). A total of 1,660 questionnaires were sent out, with a final response rate of 16 per cent. The survey results were supplemented with findings through focus groups, structured interviews and secondary sources – all of which included users and non-users of consultancy. One of the aims of the survey was to identify obstacles to expanding the management consultancy industry.

The survey began in early 1998 and the final report was available to the public in July 1998. Although the survey was conducted a few years ago, immediately after the Asian Financial Crisis, much of the domestic economics in Hong Kong remained relatively stable during this period and we can assume that little has changed in terms of the demand or the supply for such services. (One notable exception would be the slow migration of services upwards into China, with consultants servicing the Pearl River Delta region as explained earlier).

Industry growth

According to the survey, in early 1998 the consultancy industry was expected to grow in double-figure terms over the following five years. Information technology was thought to have the highest overall growth prospects (26 per cent per annum), followed by strategy (22 per cent), then sales and marketing (21 per cent). For consultancy work in China, the highest expected growth was thought to be in the operations and process management fields (30 per cent).

Despite the difficulty of identifying and certifying the number of management consultancies, the survey estimated that there were approximately 95 self-identified management consulting firms, with a total employee base of about 705 staff. Together, the estimated market size was HK$1,520 million in revenue (US$194 million). These figures, however, were little more than best guesses.

When interviewees were asked about their own firms in the study, they were optimistic. Despite the prevailing 'Asian Crisis' during the period of research, very few firms were expecting any major or long term loss of business. 'Most interviewees foresaw a difficult two years ahead, but those firms answering survey questions relating to growth during the next two to five years were more sanguine…'

Even when the five most optimistic and pessimistic views of the projected future were deleted, the average overall growth rate expected by firms that responded was as high as 36 per cent. Average annual growth of 23 per cent was expected in Hong Kong, 27 per cent in China and 16 per cent in the rest of the Asia-Pacific area. The vast majority of this growth was expected to be in the private sector in all three geographical areas. While such forecasts (or guesses) must be taken with at least a pinch of salt, they indicate that Hong Kong management consultancies tend to be optimistic about their own futures.

Table 5.2.19: Expectations of average annual percentage growth in turnover over the next 2–5 years (from 1998)

Type of management consultancy service area	Overall growth	Hong Kong	Mainland China	Asia-Pacific
All areas	59 (36)	52 (23)	47 (27)	27 (16)
Corporate and business strategy	33 (22)	20 (12)	43 (27)	31 (12)
Information technology management	60 (26)	39 (16)	33 (22)	16 (8)
Financial management	43 (19)	33 (14)	23 (15)	12 (5)
Human resource management	16 (14)	16 (11)	23 (19)	13 (12)
Operations/process management	36 (16)	31 (15)	33 (30)	20 (10)
Marketing/distribution/sales management	24 (21)	13 (10)	34 (18)	13 (7)
Other	27 (19)	21 (14)	36 (24)	20 (17)
Private sector	75 (45)	41 (26)	46 (43)	38 (25)
Public sector	23 (10)	15 (7)	10 (5)	5 (3)

In surveys of users and non-users, and also of consultants, the researchers attempted to gauge how important management consultancy in a more general sense is to Hong Kong. It was thought that the sector was necessary to the profile of Hong Kong as an international business centre, likely to attract and retain multinationals by both users and non-users of management consultancy services, as well as by the consultants themselves.

One notable suggestion that came out of the survey was that it was felt that a first-class management consulting sector is important to the success of both the manufacturing and service sectors in Hong Kong. Somewhat surprisingly, users and non-users indicated that the presence of first class consultancy services was more important to Hong Kong overall than to their firms or sectors. In addition to the direct benefits to Hong Kong of the business generated by Hong Kong management consultants, 'there are many additional benefits'. Although they were difficult to quantify, these 'public goods' aspects of management consulting were real, worthy of note and wider understanding.

Table 5.2.20
1= strongly disagree, 2 = disagree, 3 = neutral, 4 = agree, 5 = strongly agree

Importance (on a scale of 1–5) of the availability of first-class management consultancy services to the future competitiveness of:	Consultants	Non-users	Users
Your firm	–	2.98	3.32
Your firm's sector generally	–	2.91	3.31
Manufacturing industry generally	3.91	3.32	3.54
Service industry generally	4.10	3.41	3.69
Hong Kong in attracting foreign multinationals	3.85	3.49	3.74
Hong Kong as a modern, international business city	4.18	3.68	3.89

Obstacles to growth

Interviews with Hong Kong based management consultants revealed a number of factors generally thought to retard the growth of the management consultancy industry in Hong Kong. Some related to the nature of potential buyers, some to the structure and capabilities of the management consultancy industry itself, and others to supply factors, essentially availability of suitable personnel and/or development programmes for local consultants.

In many senses, however, the management consultancy industry in Hong Kong was seen to be in a very good position. Consultant interviewees generally gave the impression that the industry was in robust health. Few complained of excessive competition or lack of market demand. On the contrary, several suggested that demand outstrips supply due to a shortage of good quality consulting staff. Nonetheless, nearly every interviewee thought that the local market still held plenty of potential, in the form of local businesses that currently do not fully appreciate, or are reluctant to use, management consultancy services.

Table 5.2.21

Your firm would have more clients if: (on a scale of 1–5)	All consultants	HK HQ firms	Non-HK HQ firms
Local business understood management consultancy more	4.17	4.19	4.11
It individually promoted its services more	3.70	3.68	3.78
Qualified local Hong Kong personnel were more available	3.64	3.57	3.89
Management consultants had more professional reputations	3.61	3.70	3.26
More foreign (non-consultant) multinationals located here	3.49	3.42	3.68
Qualified international personnel were more available	3.44	3.36	3.74
Management consultancies collectively promoted services	3.41	3.53	2.95
Foreign businesses understood management consultancy more	3.35	3.47	3.00
Fewer foreign management consultancies were here	2.97	2.99	2.95
Fewer local management consultancies existed	2.90	2.96	2.74

Professionalism

One factor generally thought by consultant interviewees to put potential clients off using management consultants was the belief that the industry lacked a reputation for professionalism. Unprofessional practice was generally stated to be perpetrated by 'rogues' and 'cowboys' masquerading as management consultants, but some respondents were none too complimentary about the industry in general. The survey results on the degree of professionalism and its impact on the market were mixed, as reflected in the survey findings which reportedly contain apparently contradictory data.

The Hong Kong Government does not require management consultants to be registered or licensed. Given that it has been difficult to define what a management consultant is in other parts of the world, Hong Kong is not alone in having its share of charlatans. 'Anyone with a business card can call themselves management consultants', Professor Enright commented, 'but anyone who can still give out a business card with that title after a year in service in Hong Kong's competitive environment should be given a fair chance.'

Overall, the survey report concluded that consultants agree their firms would have more clients if management consultants had more professional reputations. Noticeably, members of Hong Kong headquartered consultancies were inclined to this view more strongly than members of firms headquartered elsewhere. However, the consultants do not agree that some firms are reluctant to use management consultants because they have a poor reputation, despite remarks by both interviewees and focus group participants contradicting this. These data are possibly not inconsistent with each other as any industry can improve on an already high reputation for professionalism and thereby gain more clients.

The survey report further concluded that when the respondents were asked directly comparative questions on professionalism, management consultants as a whole rated their professionalism as relatively high – as might be expected – second only to accounting firms, slightly above law firms and well above public relations firms. 'Reassuringly for the industry, users/non-users also associated reasonably high levels of professionalism with management consultancy firms. Non-users rated consultants' professionalism less favourably than users, and law and accountancy firms were still rated more highly, but public relations firms significantly lower.'

Hong Kong headquartered users/non-users have a higher regard for the professionalism of management consultancy than do firms headquartered elsewhere. Manufacturing firms rated management consultancy on a par with law firms in terms of professionalism. Service firms ranked the consultancy industry less highly than either manufacturers or import/export wholesaler firms, and these latter rank consultants as relatively far behind law and accountancy firms, as the next table from the report reveals.

Table 5.2.22

High levels of professionalism are associated with the services offered by: (on a scale of 1–5)	All consultants	HK HQ firms	Non- HK HQ firms	All users/ non-users	Non- users	Users
Accountancy firms	3.92	3.96	3.79	3.90	3.82	3.95
Law firms	3.73	3.69	3.89	3.87	3.84	3.88
Management consultancy firms	3.81	3.78	3.89	3.60	3.44	3.71
Public relations firms	3.22	3.17	3.37	3.26	3.17	3.31

Table 5.2.23

High levels of professionalism are associated with the services offered by: (on a scale of 1–5)	All users/ non-users	HK HQ U/n-u	Non-HK HQ U/n-u	Import Export	Service firms	Manu-facturer
Accountancy firms	3.90	3.95	3.83	4.02	3.87	3.91
Law firms	3.87	3.89	3.84	4.04	3.87	3.73
Management consultancy firms	3.60	3.71	3.47	3.65	3.51	3.70
Public relations firms	3.26	3.39	3.10	3.27	3.16	3.43

Conclusion

In summary, the surveys confirmed the development of management consultancy as a growing industry. Industry growth did not appear to be hampered by an over-supplied marketplace. On the contrary, the prime constraint on growth would seem to be an inability to supply market demand due to a dearth of qualified and professional personnel.

The survey has had an impact on the overall strength of the industry. Six months after the survey, the University of Hong Kong launched Hong Kong's first 6-month Diploma in Management Consultancy and Change through its Institute of Management. It was novel for that time and was well-received. According to Walter Viera, the ICMCI's former chairman, it was the only structural education programme available for management consultants in Asia outside India. As of 2001, this diploma was in its fourth intake and already 90 students have graduated, about half of whom have joined a management consultancy firm.

A year later, the Institute of Management Consultants in Hong Kong was formed, with a clear mandate to raise the level of professionalism in the industry. As of May 2001, there was a total of 60 members and rising (see www.imchk.com.hk).

All in all, the management consultancy sector in the Pearl River Delta region has a far wider range of services than anywhere else in south-east Asia and, perhaps most importantly, the widest availability of services throughout Greater China. Despite a relatively stable period of slow growth since 1998, principally as a result of the financial crisis, the level of sophistication in services has grown, pushed by a dotcom and e-commerce mania, to a level that is probably one of the highest in terms of delivery anywhere in Asia and Australia. Globalisation has made Hong Kong and the PRD one of the important centres in the world of management consultancy.

JAPAN

Matsui Shigeki

Since its establishment in 1949, Zen-Noh-Ren (All-Japan Federation of Management Organisations) has been operating as a focus body of management-related professional institutions engaged in the dissemination and guidance of management consultancy (MC) for the purpose of promoting management as a science in Japan.

In recent years, Japan has begun to show serious signs of a prolonged recession due to the 'burst bubble' economy. To cope with the situation, local companies have been proceeding with restructuring and re-engineering at a quickened pace. Despite this, Japanese businesses are in a difficult position in terms of adjusting employment and restoring the economy as a whole. To survive in the competitive markets, they are facing many managerial problems, particularly in developing their overall business strategies. We are certain, therefore, that the demand for management consultancy will grow.

The history of management consultancy in Japan dates back to the days of production efficiency improvement such as in the field of mechanical engineering, and now the management consulting industry is contributing to the efficiency improvement in various other industries. The need for management consulting services is expected to increase with the growing diversification, complexity and computerisation of management tasks along with recent economical globalisation, while the effectiveness and credibility of management consulting services is being closely examined.

In 1994 and 2000, Zen-Noh-Ren, in co-operation with the Japanese government, conducted an extensive survey into management consulting firms, sole management consulting practitioners and user companies of management consulting services in Japan for the purpose of defining the position and the future direction of business enterprises and management consultancy in the context of a changing environment. This chapter contains a summary of these survey results as well as the current status of the management consulting industry in Japan.

The theme of the 1994 survey was 'The Current Status and Overview of Management Consulting'. The survey was carried out into 2,500 management consulting firms, 5,400 sole practitioners and 1,200 client companies. Those who actually responded included 280 firms, 1,750 sole practitioners and 90 client companies. The first three sections of this chapter are based on an analysis of the survey results of those respondents. These results may be slightly dated, but they do help to identify the trends and direction of the management consulting business in Japan.

The 2000 survey was conducted under the theme of management problems companies face in the changing business environment and what user companies expect from the management consulting industry. The survey was carried out on 2,600 companies, 250 intellectuals/experts/professionals and 300 management consulting firms. This time 200 companies, 30 individuals and 70 management consulting firms responded. The survey results were analysed and the summary of the analysis is given below.

Japanese management consulting firms

Overall characteristics

An accurate calculation of the number of management consulting firms in Japan has not been established.

Length of operation

Since management consultancy was born in Japan after the Second World War, half of the firms are about 20 years old and approximately 30 are over 30 years old. The size of firms has grown and the number of employees has also increased.

Type of incorporation

Most of the firms are corporations while some are limited companies. Several large public corporations are included. Zen-Noh-Ren has 62 members, which comprise 28 private corporations, 27 public corporations and seven others.

Number of employees

Seventy companies or more have more than five employees, and the number is growing every year. Another characteristic is that the firms employ a large number of temporary workers in addition to regular employees, and that the larger the firm, the bigger the ratio of sales staff to other employees.

Annual sales

The sales of 20 of the firms are less than 50 million yen; and 50 of the firms reported sales of over 100 million yen. More than 40 firms record annual sales of over 1 billion yen. Compared by type of incorporation, sale proceeds of most of the limited companies and the sole practitioners are less than 50 million yen, while about 70 of the corporations have annual sales of 100 million yen. There is therefore a distinct gap between the two groups.

Types of MC services requested

The range of management consulting services varies depending on firm size. As a whole, diagnosis/guidance is the most sought after, followed by survey/research, education/training and management consultancy/advice, which account for over 50 of the total services. Others include information-providing, data service, public seminars etc.

Small firms

Small firms mainly seek services such as diagnosis/guidance, survey/research and management consultancy. Most of the small firms are self-employed individuals, such as tax accountants and social insurance specialists, many of whom offer management consulting services alongside their other services. Long-term management consultant/adviser contracts are on the rise.

Medium or large firms

Medium or large firms request more information seminars and less management consultancy. The ratio of diagnosis/guidance increases for medium/large firms, making them more like professional management consulting businesses. Some large firms focus on think-tank services with an emphasis on surveys.

Client business types

In order of size, clients include wholesale/retail, construction, service industry, governmental/public bodies, manufacturing and information.

Types of contracts

The various types of contracts are – in order of size – adviser contract, project contract and quantity-based contract. Under the adviser contract, the management consultant in charge visits the client for a long period of time on a regular basis. Many smaller firms choose this kind of contract.

Contract value

The value of each contract ranges from 1 to 5 million yen per order. Fifty per cent of small management consulting firms with fewer than five employees make contracts under 1 million yen per order, while 60 per cent of firms with 100–500 employees earn 5 million yen or more per order, and firms with over 1,000 employees earn a much larger amount. There are clear differences between firms of different scales.

We presume that the differences depend on contract contents and size of client companies. In other words, large MC firms tend to get big project orders from big corporations.

Recruitment, training and management

Recruitment

The majority of new employees are experienced. Small firms do not usually hire new college graduates. The job of a professional management consultant requires experience and technical knowledge and if an inexperienced person is sent to a client's office, it could damage the firm's reputation.

For this reason, small firms that are not equipped to provide new employees with proper education and training refrain from recruiting new college graduates.

Screening criteria

The screening criteria cover three areas: common sense, technical knowledge and aptitude. The most weight goes to aptitude – creativity, persuasiveness, analytical ability and sincerity. It is critical how the three abilities are evaluated in actual screening tests.

Sixty per cent responded that their test items include business ethics and conduct guidelines.

Duration of education and training

Many firms train new college graduates for one to three months or one to two years, and experienced hires for three months. Moreover, three-month on-the-job training is provided by experienced employees at many firms.

Internal organisation of firms

Many firms are organised on a by-job basis (diagnosis, education, research, etc) and some are organised on a by-industry basis (manufacturing, commerce, finance, public, etc). Management philosophies and other managerial characteristics of each firm seem to be reflected in its organisational structure.

Performance, evaluation, quality control and problems

Overall performance of a firm

The overall performance of a firm is measured by its sales/profit rate, repeat order rate, operation rate etc. Quality reports, repeat contract rates, operation rates, delivery times, new technology developments and so on are used as yardsticks to evaluate the performance of an individual professional. Since there are no standard or industry averages of these yardsticks, performance evaluation is made based on past records or individual comparison.

Quality control

Quality control is not a simple task. Consultation is divided into the following three stages:

- Planning
- Execution
- Follow-up

Quality control at small firms is not easy to check because some have no records of quality control, and others pay little attention to it. Bigger firms, however, tend to give a high priority to quality control and take a systematic approach in its operation phase.

Causes of problems

The four main causes of problems are the following:

- changes in the management strategy of clients due to unexpected change of business environment or client's overestimation of consultants
- insufficient preparation by clients, partly due to lack of explanation from consultants
- clients and consultants do not get on. Both are responsible for poor relations
- lack of understanding clients' needs due to insufficient communication at preliminary stages of negotiation or due to differences in ways of thinking and expectations on both sides

The above remarks seem to hold the client responsible, but later we will see that the survey of client companies shows that responsibility rests with consultants.

Measures taken to improve consulting skills

Concrete methods

'Internal Study Meeting' is the most common concrete method used to improve management consulting skills. The second most common is 'Readiness to Develop New Techniques'.

Here again, we can see a clear difference depending on the size of firms. Study meetings and new technique development are used at 30 per cent of firms with five members of staff or less. About 50 per cent of firms with more than 5 staff use these approaches in order to help improve consulting skills. This shows that the bigger the firm size, the more they employ these measures to improve consultants' skills. Among larger firms of more than 50 persons, over 30 per cent attend 'Academic Meetings' to acquire technical knowledge.

Practical methods for technical development

'Encouragement of Individual Research and Study', 'Formation of Project Teams', 'Tie-Up with Outside Institutions/Universities' and 'Setting Up Internal Research Functions' were mentioned. 'Individual Research Study' is the favourite in small firms of less than five people. Larger firms put more emphasis on whole-company systematic approaches.

Internationalisation

Smaller firms (less than five people) are becoming more international but without significant economic results. Included are such activities as research study, diagnosis, education, consultancy and lecture-giving.

Many requests for market research are also received. The contents are guidance to foreign business, overseas market surveys, guidance to developing nations and tie-ups with foreign businesses.

The foreign countries involved are Korea, Taiwan, South-East Asia, China and North America in that order. Most of the firms wish to become international. The larger the organisation, the more willing it is to spread overseas. Some of these have already begun operations in other countries and are planning to expand their overseas business further.

Individual management consultants

The number of management consultants

Some management consultants are self-employed working as individuals, while others are employed by firms. The self-employed MCs are sometimes concurrently tax accountants, social insurance specialists or engineers. In terms of income, some earn the majority of their income as a management consultant, while others earn as much money engaging in some other profession. Furthermore, management consultancy has not yet been established as a profession in Japan and so is frequently referred to by different names. This being the case, it is difficult to obtain an accurate idea of the number of MCs in operation.

Firms use temporary consultants in addition to their regular consultants. This trend causes the number of concurrent consultants to increase. The 1988 survey estimated approximately 60,000 consultants by adding employees supplemental to 37,000 self-employed and firm employed management consultants. We cannot say, however, that this figure is accurate. The same can be said about the number of firms. Very small firms, for example, cannot be defined as sole practitioners or firms.

There is another thing to note. Recently some large firms have tended to diversify into general education, open seminars, research, publishing, etc, in addition to their original business, namely management consulting in the narrow sense of the word. Also, it is to be noted that other businesses are advancing into the management consulting business, which makes it hard to define the industry classification.

It was under such circumstances that the 1994 survey was conducted on management consultants and management consulting firms.

Professional areas

Along with the economic development and structural change in recent years in Japan, the business strategy and priorities of corporations have changed. As a result, consulting needs have also changed, and consultants' areas of competence are changing too. The management consultant's main areas of competence are as follows:

- management planning – mid-range and long-range plans
- management strategies
- new business development
- marketing

- production control
- human resources/labour relations
- education/training
- system development/employment
- management development

Age and experience

Due to the nature of the occupational characteristics of the management consultant, the average age of management consultants is rising compared with other professions. Those who have over 15 years' experience make up 50 per cent of the consultant population, and those with experience of less than five years comprise only 10 per cent. This profession requires many years of experience. In general, young consultants often lack the poise which generates persuasiveness on the job. This is the reason why so many experienced people are hired and also why retirement age consultants are entering the market. They are mostly self-employed.

As to their academic background, approximately 70 per cent are university graduates, and the percentage of junior college graduates is increasing slightly.

These have acquired consulting knowledge and experience by:

- working on the staff at general business corporations.
- acquiring the professional MC certificate while working for a company.
- working as accountants and adding consulting services to their own job.

Only a few new graduates are employed by consulting firms. Many of the self-employed consultants also work as tax accountants, accountants or social insurance specialists. Most of these consultants have taken up management consultancy after practicing as self-employed management consultants for some time.

Earnings and work days

Most of the self-employed consultants earn 5 million to 20 million yen a year. The largest age group – in their forties and fifties – earn 10 to 20 million yen per year. Of these earnings, the proportion of income from concurrent jobs is unknown.

Many self-employed consultants work under the advisor contract. Others are paid by the project or work according to the framework of the budget.

It seems that management consultants work harder than generally expected. The higher the income they get, the more days they work.

Areas of business/types of industries

The self-employed consultants operate in the following industries:

- Secondary industries – construction, manufacturing, machinery, foods, electricity.
- Tertiary industries – commerce, wholesale, retail, other service businesses, government related education, information.

Commerce covers the largest proportion, which suggests that many of these clients are small/medium businesses.

Overseas operation

About 20 per cent of self-employed consultants have overseas experience. Generally, however, they do business in Japan. Sixty-five per cent of those with overseas experience have worked in Korea, Taiwan and South-East Asian countries. In addition, assignments in China are on the rise.

In order to increase overseas operations, it is essential to acquire foreign language skills. In this respect, they are at a disadvantage as compared with larger organisations.

The overseas contracts include education/training, management strategy, production control, system development/employment, mid-/long-range planning etc.

Problems with clients

The causes of problems with clients are as follows:

- poor preparation of clients and their lack of co-operation
- change in client's business conditions
- change of client's business strategy
- change in social environment/external conditions
- poor relations with client's top management/executives

While some or all of the above observations may be true, it should be noted that they are one-sided opinions of the consultants.

Aptitudes of consultants

Some of the important aptitudes of the competent management consultant are as follows:

- sincerity
- persuasiveness
- analytic power
- creativity
- health
- professional ethical conduct
- business ethics

There are slight differences of opinion as to the above order of importance. It is noteworthy that 'health' is included in the list, agreed upon by firms as well as clients. As mentioned earlier, consultants work longer than ordinary company employees, leaving little time to spend with their families. It is their personal conviction that the consultants cannot do a good job without good health.

User companies

Market/users of consulting services

Based on user's company size

Bigger MC users are bigger companies. The bigger the companies, the more problems they have. These companies have a sufficiently large budget to outsource the task of solving their management problems.

By type of business/industry

Secondary industry is the biggest client, covering 60 per cent, followed by chemicals, transport machinery and manufacturing of other products. The third industry covers 45 per cent, of which the wholesale/retail industry is the biggest customer. Two-thirds of wholesale/retail companies use management consulting services. The construction industry and the service industries are bigger clients to the smaller firms. These results are almost the same as that of the previous survey.

Reasons that some companies do not use MC services

Some companies do not use MC services because:

- they have no work to outsource
- they can handle their company staff
- they are unsure as to whether management consultants are really effective

Each of the above was given approximately equal importance.

Selection criteria for hiring management consulting firms/consultants

The selection criteria are as follows:

- higher priority given to those consultants who have worked for the client before
- reputation through books/theses produced by the consultant
- recommendation by others/acquaintances

The above three points carry roughly equal weight in consultant selection. It appears that past performance records and the credibility of the consultant are the key elements.

The most commonly used type of contract is the advisor contract or the project blanket contract. The average fee of the latter is 5 million yen or less per order.

Contents of MC service

Clients use consultants for the following reasons:

- personnel/labour relations
- education/training
- management planning
- system development/empowerment
- management strategy
- marketing
- CI

The above shows that the client companies' biggest concerns are personnel matters, training and system-related problems. On the other hand, manufacturing, sales and administrative work, which were the mainstream of management consulting in the past, have not increased greatly. The needs for computer applications such as OA, FA, CAD, CAM etc, and financial accounting have decreased. We presume that clients are now handling these areas by employing professional contractors in these fields.

Scope of service implementation stage

We will now look at how the management consultants get involved in the client business to help it solve its problems. There are four stages, which consist of:

- research analysis, problem identification
- problem identification to presentation of solutions
- implementation of solutions/guidance
- education/training only

The current trend is that clients usually request the consultant's services ranging from the first stage (research and analysis, problem identification) to the third (implementation of solutions/guidance). In other words, clients want to get practical results through MC services.

The 1988 survey showed that the second stage (presentation of solutions) was favoured. Judging from the results of the 1994 survey, we believe that user companies have begun to value the consulting services. In the case of self-employed individuals, the third stage (implementation of solutions/guidance) is the most common. In the case of foreign-affiliated companies, banking and think-tank institutions, they use the second stage (problem identification to presentation of solutions). This is because these organisations put more emphasis on research work and also because there are not many consultants experienced in consulting practices to solve problems.

Clients' evaluation of management consultants' performance

The survey shows that about 50 per cent of the clients are 'satisfied' or 'somewhat satisfied', but 20 per cent are 'not satisfied'. The 'not satisfied' customers have given the following reasons:

- client companies are responsible – not sufficiently prepared or lack co-operation
- consultants are responsible, not sufficiently capable of solving problems

As stated earlier, the consultants looked at this differently and cited the following reasons for their dissatisfaction:

- sudden change in the management conditions of client companies
- change in the management strategies of client companies
- clients do not get along well with consultants

The dissatisfaction on the part of the client may have been caused by differences of opinion or viewpoint between the two. Even if it is evident that the clients are at least partly to blame, the consultant party should reconsider the matter to improve mutual relations and restore their reputation.

Capabilities and nature required as management consultants

The following table shows responses made by client companies, consulting firms and sole practitioners to the question 'What are the five essential capabilities and/or natures required for an individual management consultant?'

Table 5.2.24 The five essential capabilities/natures required for individual management consultants

Response	No.1	No.2	No.3	No.4	No.5
client companies	analysing power	sincerity	ethical conduct	persuasiveness	creativity
management consulting firms	sincerity	creativity	analysing power	persuasiveness	ethical conduct
sole practitioners	sincerity	persuasiveness	analysing power	creativity	health

Management consulting firms and sole practitioners ranked 'sincerity' as most important just as they did in the 1988 survey, which shows that clients' credibility in an individual professional management consultant is the key factor of success in this business. What is a very interesting fact is that 'ethical conduct', which client companies regarded as more important, is less valued by the other parties while health is ranked number five by sole practitioners. Different viewpoints generate different responses.

Use of in-house management consultants

In-house management consultants are increasingly being utilised not only for their companies but also for their affiliated and co-operative companies, subcontract factories and client enterprises.

The main services that they provide include management planning, management strategy, information systems, marketing, production management, education/training and organisation development.

It is presumed from their responses that in some cases in-house consultants may have been confused with administrative staff.

In order to cope with such remarkably improved in-house consultants, independent MC practitioners are strongly required to elevate their professional competencies through professionalisation and through widening their scope.

Future utilisation

The survey regarding the use of consulting services in the future discovered that about half of clients intend to continue using management consultants at the present level or are planning to increase the use of consulting services; but there are not many clients who are thinking of limiting usage to specific issues, nor to a specific range of services.

The following indicates four reasons to use professional management consulting services, in order of importance:

- clients want to undergo business diagnosis of their companies from the third party
- use of external professional consultants is more effective
- use of external professional consultants gives a stimulus to in-house staff
- no qualified and capable staff in the company

Meanwhile, the most common reason given by user companies for not using the services of consultants is that there are adequate staff capable of handling MC services in the company. Another reason clarified by a number of companies is that they are unsure of the effectiveness of using MC firms. It is, therefore, an absolute necessity for MC firms and sole practitioners to concentrate more of their energy more on exploiting the market.

Prospects for the future of management consultancy

In 2000, at the request of the Ministry of Economy, Trade and Industry, Zen-Noh-Ren conducted a research survey that would contribute to formulating a 21st century vision of management consultancy. One of the research studies regarded how to create the base of Japanese industries' international competitiveness while coping with a changing internal and external economic environment.

Three points were identified as a result of surveying industries, well informed people and consulting firms, and seeking their opinions on extensive themes:

- Japanese industries' need for management consulting services is increasing as they are losing their competitive advantages over other countries in a growing globalised market.
- Management consultancies are becoming so markedly diversified now that it is difficult for client companies to grasp a clear picture of their status.
- It is highly desirable to exchange students/consultants among enterprises/universities etc, in order to help develop their consulting capabilities and to recruit well trained capable consultants. Social recognition of management consultancies is not necessarily enough to ensure the clients' reliance on them.

Management issues of customer companies

- Globalisation of management activities is creating various influences in many aspects of businesses:
  - borderless market competition
  - global standardisation of business rules and technology
  - deregulation, exchange risk
- In order to tackle squarely management challenges posed by growing globalisation, businesses have been focusing their energies on the following issues:
  - reform of the management system
  - modification of accounting standards
  - avoidance of exchange risk
- Measures necessary in the future will include:
  - Recruitment and education/training of capable/qualified staff
  - Strengthening of corporate governance
  - Reform of the management system

The key factor that influences industries most in the context of globalisation is borderless market competition, which is urging them to establish new business rules.

Utilisation by companies of management consulting firms

Companies have a strong desire to take advantage of management consulting services in future for the following purposes:

- management strategy/planning of business strategy
- personnel system restructuring
- ISO relation
- establishment of management system
- building management information system

The result of the survey is that under the strong influence of the changing business management environment, the clients' greatest needs for management consultants are concentrated on 'planning of management strategy and business strategy'. Amid the changing competition rules and the weakening superiority of Japan in product and cost competition globally, Japanese industries are now urged to establish new strategies to cope rapidly with the changing economic and industrial environment. We believe, however, that some Japanese businesses lack the planning capability needed to create effective strategy.

This reflects the recognition described above that recruitment and education/training of capable/qualified professional consultants is the first priority.

Hopes for the consulting industry

All industries and well-informed people hope that management consultants will play a key role in providing information. All clients also hope that they can rely fully on management consulting businesses for management consulting services; and well-informed people want them to upgrade their consulting competencies and to establish an integrated MC certification system. Professional management consultants want to maintain free competition and to establish institutions that can train and develop capable professional consultants.

Issues in IT activities

Both client companies and MC practitioners emphasised the following three points as challenges to be solved:

- insufficiency of IT utilisation planning
- lack of basic understanding about IT
- insufficient leadership in taking advantage of IT.

In addition, the proposal of a new strategy successfully to meet IT change and the achievement of such a plan are widely regarded as the main challenges confronting the management consulting industry.

References

Arah, J (2001) Association of Management Consulting of Slovenia – AMCOS Profile for the FEACO/VTMSZ Seminar, Budapest 1st June 2001

Canbacks, S (1999), The Logic of Management Consulting, *Journal of Management Consulting*, November, May, pp 3–12, (Part Two), pp 7–8

Czerniewska, F (1999), *Management Consultancy in the 21st Century*, Macmillan Business, pp 83–89

Done, K (2001), Investing in Central and Eastern Europe, *Financial Times*, 8 May 2001, 1998, p 10.

Enright, Michael and Thompson, Edmund (1998) 'Promotion of Management Consultancy Sector in Hong Kong', Hong Kong Coalition of Service Industries

Erhvervsfremmestyrelsen (1999), *Managementkonsulenter – kortl'gning af en branche v'kst*, EFS, Copenhagen

Gibson, R (1997), *Rethinking the Future*, Nicholas Brealey Publishing, p 10

Glowczki, A (2001), The consulting service market in Poland, FEACO/VTMSZ Seminar, Budapest, 1st June

Hristov, D (2001), Management Consulting in Bulgaria, FEACO/VTMSZ Seminar, Budapest, 1st June

Industry Canada (1997), Sector Competitiveness Survey – Management Consulting

Kelley, R (1986), *The Gold Collar Worker: Harnessing the Brainpower of the New Workforce*, Addison-Wesley, Reading Mass, p 5

Kipping, M and Armbrüster, T (1999), The consultancy field in Western Europe

Management Consultant International Survey (134) (2000), 'Scandinavia – Doom and gloom for local internet consulting firms, but strong growth overall', November 2000, pp 12–15

Maister, D C H, Green, R M, Galford (2000), *The Trusted Advisor*, The Free Press, 2000, p 10

Management Consulting Services, Industry Sector Analysis (1998), US & Foreign Commercial Services and US Department of State

Poulfelt, Flemming (2001), *The (R)Evolution of the European Management Consulting Industry*, International Conference of the Management Consulting Division, Academy of Management, Lyon

Posadsky, A (2001), Consulting Business in Russia, FEACO/VTMSZ Seminar, Budapest 1st June 2001

Plesoianu, G (2001), Management Consultancy in Romania, FEACO/VTMSZ Seminar, Budapest 1st June 2001

Statistics Canada (March 2001), 1998 Survey of Service Industries: Management, Scientific & Technical Consulting Industry

Acknowledgement

Tables 5.2.14 and 5.2.15 reprinted with permission from Management Consultant International January 2000 issue © Kennedy Information, Fitzwilliam NH 03447 USA, tel: +1 800 531 0007, website: www.consulting-central.com

Appendices

Appendix I: ICMCI National Members

Argentina

Consejo Asesor de Empresas Consultoras
Leando N. Alem 465 4 'g'
1003 Buenos Aires
Argentina
Tel: +54 11 4311 6299
Fax: +54 11 4311 2722
Email: mz@lvd.com.ar
Chairman: Mario Humberto Zelarayan
Executive Director: Alfredo E. Blousson

Australia

Institute of Management Consultants – Australia
Level 2 The Mansions
40 George St.
Brisbane QLD 4000
Australia
Tel: +61 7 3229 7636
Fax: +61 7 3229 1838
Email: imc@imc.org.au
Website: www.management-consultants.com.au
President: Bruce Crowe
Secretariat: Carlie Polinski

Bangladesh

Institute of Management Consultants Bangladesh (IMCB)
c/o Survey Research Group of Bangladesh [SRGB]
396 New Eskaton Road, P O Box 7092
Dhaka 1000
Bangladesh
Tel: +880 2 9351102, +880 2 9351321 or +880 2 832450
Fax: +880 2 9351103 or +880 2 9560310
Email: mshaq@bangla.net
Chairman: Hafiz G A Siddiqi
President: M Saidul Haq

Brazil

Instituto Brazileiro dos Consultores de Organizacao
Av. Paulista, 326-Conj. 77-Bela Vista
01310–902 Sao Paulo -SP
Brazil
President – Eduardo Rocha
Executive Director – Rosi Mazanati
Tel: +55 11–289–4152
Fax: +55 11–289–4152
Email: ibco@uol.com.br
Website: www.ibco.org.br

Bulgaria

Bulgarian Association of Management Consulting Organizations (BAMCO)
1 Macedonia Square
1040 Sofia
Bulgaria
Tel: +359 2 917 0506
Fax: +359 2 986 1279
Email: bamco@delin.org
Website: www.delin.org/bamco
Chairman: Gergana Mantarkova
Executive Director: Ekaterina Ignatova

Canada

Canadian Association of Management Consultants
BCE Place, 181 Bay Street
Box 835
Toronto, Ontario M5J 2T3
Canada
Tel: +1 416 860 1515 or +1 800 268 1148
Fax: +1 416 860 1535 or +1 800 662 2972
Email: camc@camc-consult.org
Website: www.camc-consult.org
Chairman: Jan Grude
President & CEO: Heather Osler

Cyprus

Institute of Management Consultancy-Cyprus
Cyprus Technology Foundation
Ionion Nison No. 1
1st Floor, Akropoli
p.O. Box 20783
1663 Nicosia
Cyprus
Tel: +357 2 317288
Fax: +357 2 318087
Email: idrymatech@industry.cy.net
Website: www.industry.cy.net
Chairman: Nicos Rolandes
Executive Director: Dr. Costas Y. Konis

Denmark

Danish Institute of Certified Management Consultants
Chr Richardts Vej 3
P.O. Box 782
DK-5230 Odense M
Denmark
Tel: +45 70 262 002
Fax: +45 70 262 003
Email: info@dicmc.dk
Website: www.dicmc.dk
Chairman: Peter Sorensen
Executive Director: Peder Friis

Finland

The Finnish Management Consultants LJK
Etelaranta 10
00130 Helskinki
Finland
Telephone: +358 9 622 4442
Facsimile: +358 9 6220 1009
Email: ljk@ljk.fi
Website: www.ljk.fi
Chairman: Pentti Harmanen
Executive Director: Jani Kekkonen

Germany

Bundesverband Deutscher Unternehmensberater – BDU e.V
Zitelmannstrasse 22
53113 Bonn
Germany
Tel: +49 228 9161 0
Fax: +49 228 9161 26
Email: wey@bdu.de
Website: www.bdu.de
Chairman: Remi Redley
Executive Director: Christoph Weyrather

Greece

Hellenic Association of Management Consulting Firms
13 Elikonos str.
GR 152 34 Chalandri
Greece
Tel: +301 68 58 653
Fax: +301 68 40 784
Email: sesma@hol.gr
Chairman: Lambis Dolkas
General Secretary: Napoleon Karantinos
Administrative Director: Kitty Louropoulou

Hong Kong

Institute of Management Consultants – Hong Kong
c/o The Poon Kam Kai Institute of Management
University of Hong Kong Town Centre
3/F Admiralty Centre, 18 Harcourt Road
Hong Kong
Tel: +852 2865 2108
Fax: +852 2866 7052
Email: info@imchk.com.hk
Website: www.imchk.com.hk
President: Gregg Li
Administrative Secretary: Betty Wong

Hungary

Association of Management Consultants in Hungary – Vezetési Tanácsadók Magyarországi Szövetsége
Szent István krt. 11.
Budapest H-1055
Hungary
Telephone: +36 1 302 7681 or +36 30 685 826
Facsimile: +36 1 302 7681
Email: vtmsz@mail.datanet.hu
Website: www.datanet.hu/~vtmsz
Chairman: Dr. Gabor Kornai
Executive Director: Sándor Hetyey

India

The Institute of Management Consultants of India
Centre 1, 11th Floor, Unit 2
World Trade Centre, Cuffe Parade
Bombay 400 005
India
Tel: +91 22 218 5319
Fax: +91 22 218 5319
Email: imci@vsnl.com
Chairman: Dr Dilip Sarwate
Executive Secretary: Vishakha Desai

Ireland

Institute of Management Consultants – Ireland
Confederation House
84/86 Lower Baggot Street
Dublin 2
Ireland
Tel: +353 605 1600
Fax: +353 638 1600
Email: robert.grier@ibec.ie
President: Gerry McLarnon
Executive Director: Robert Grier

Italy

APCO (Associazione Dei Consulenti Di Direzione E Organizzaione)
Corso Venezia, 49
20121 Milano
Italy
Tel: +39 2 77 50 449
Fax: +39 2 77 50 480
Email: segreteria@apcoitalia.it
Website: www.apcoitalia.it
Chairman & Executive Director:
Claudio Antonelli, CMC

Japan

Zen-Noh-Ren
Kindai Building 6F 12–5
Kohimachi 3Chome
Chiyoda-Ku
Tokyo 102–0083
Japan
Tel: +81 3 3221 5051
Fax: +81 3 3221 5054
Email: imcj@zen-noh-ren.or.jp
Website: www.zen-noh-ren.or.jp
Chairman: Akira Hattori
Executive Director: Kasio Uehara

Jordan

Institute of Management Consultants of Jordan
9 Mogadishu Street – Um Uthaina
P.O. Box 926550
Amman 11110
Jordan
Tel: +962 6 553 0856 7
Fax: +962 6 553 0858
Email: imc@go.com.jo
Website: www.imc.com.jo
Chairman: Tayseer Abdel Jaber
Executive Director: Hatem Abdel Ghani

Malaysia

Institute of Management Consultants – Malaysia
Level 1, Menara Sungei Way
Jalan Lagun Timur, Bandar Sunway
Petaling Jaya
Malaysia 46150
Tel: +60 3 735 2811
Fax: +60 3 736 4048
Email: musghaz@m.net.my
Chairman: Dr Datuk Paduka; Saleha bt Mohd Ali
Executive Director: Mustapha Ghazali

Netherlands

Ooa, Orde van organisatiekundigen en-adviseurs
Postbus 302
1170 AH Badhoevedorp
Netherlands
Tel: +31 20 658 02 55
Fax: +31 20 658 01 00
Email: ooa@wispa.nl
Chairman: Robert Florijn
Executive Director: Joke van Iperen

New Zealand

Institute of Management Consultants New Zealand Incorporated
P.O. Box 6493
Wellesley Street
Auckland
New Zealand
Tel: +64 9 427 4443
Fax: +64 9 427 4400
Email: ron.evans@hawkeye.co.nz
Chairman: Philip Verstraaten
Executive Director: Ron Evans
National Secretary: Colin Kropach

Nigeria

IMC, Nigeria
P O Box 9194
Kaduna
Nigeria
Tel: +234 62 214073
Fax: +234 62 241048
Email: nimc@inet-global.com
Chairman: Dr. Philemon Agashua
Executive Director: David Iornem

Norway

Norges Bedriftsr†dgiverforening-NBF
Interforum Partners AS
Askerveien 61
N-1370 Asker
Norway
Tel: +47 6698 9990
Fax: +47 6678 9993
Email: nbf@interforum.no
Chairman & Executive Director: Cato Musaeus

Poland

Association of Economic Consultants
Stowarzyszenie Doradcow
Gospodarczych
Warszawska Street 39/41
61–028 Poznan
Poland
Tel: +48 61 650 32 32
Fax: +48 61 650 32 16
Email: dgasa@dga.com.pl
Website: www.dga.com.pl
Chairman: Andrew Glowacki
Executive Director: Krzysztof Broniatowski

Singapore

Institute of Management Consultants – Singapore
20 Maxwell Road
#08–09, Maxwell House
Singapore 069113
Tel: +65 372 1728
Fax: +65 372–1727
Email: imcsec@mbox3.singnet.com.sg
Website: www.imcsin.org.sg
Chairman: Garry Ng
Executive Secretary: Emily Tay

South Africa

IMCSA
P O Box 798
Hurlingham Manor 2070
South Africa
Tel: +27 83 2632579 or +27 11 7893241
Fax: +27 11 7893232
Email: imcsa@global.co.za
Website: www.imcsa.org.za
President: Laurie Hall
Executive Director: Angelo Kehayas

Spain

Instituto de Consultores de Organizacion y Direccion
Orfila, 5 – Escalera 1 – 4 D,
28010 Madrid, SPAIN
Tel: +91 308 01 61
Fax: +91 308 23 27
Chairman: Luis Herrera Carrero
General Secretary: Edwardo Mendiciutti

Sweden

Swedish Association of Management Consultants
Box 7469
S-103 92 Stockholm
Sweden
Tel: +46 8 20 83 30
Fax: +46 8 21 25 40
Email: anders.grufman@grufman-reje.se
Chairman & Executive Director: Anders Grufman

Switzerland

ASCO, Association Suisse des Conseils en Organisation et Gestion
Forchstrasse 428
Postfach 923
8029 Zurich
Switzerland
Tel: +41 1 395 24 04
Fax: +41 1 395 24 05
Email: office@asco.ch
Website: www.asco.ch
Chairman: André Wohlgemuth
Executive Director: Marianne Senti

United Kingdom

Institute of Management Consultancy
17–18 Hayward's Place
London EC1R 0EQ
United Kingdom
Tel: +44 20 566 5220
Fax: +44 20 566 5230
Email: consult@imc.co.uk
Website: www.imc.co.uk
President: Penny Bickersaffe
Deputy President: Brian Ing
Chief Executive: Ian Barratt

United States

Institute of Management Consultants – USA
Suite 800
2025 M Street
Washington DC 20036–3309
USA
Tel: +1 202 367 1134 or +1 800 221 2557
Fax: +1 202 367 2134
Email: office@imcusa.org
Website: www.imcusa.org
Chairman: E. Michael Shays
Executive Director: David Rohn

Appendix II: FEACO membership

Fachverband Unternehmensberatung und Datenverarbeitung (FUD)
Wiedner Hauptstrasse 63
A – 1045 Vienna
Austria
Tel: +43 1 50 105 35 39
Fax: +43 1 50105 285
Email: office-ubdv@wko.at
Website: www.ubdv.or.at
Contacts: Herbert Bachmaier; Hans-Jurgen Pollirer

Association Belge des Conseils en Gestion et Organisation (ASCOBEL)
Place des Chasseurs Ardennais 20
B – 1030 Brussels
Belgium
Tel: +32 2 743 41 50
Fax: +32 2 742 17 85
Email: ascobel@skynet.be
Website: www.ascobel.be
Contact: Roland Van den Berghe

Bulgarian Association of Management Consultants (BAMCO)
1 Macedonia Square, 17th floor
Sofia 1040
Bulgaria
Tel: +359 2 9170 506
Fax: +359 2 986 1279
Email: bamco@delin.org
Website: www.delin.org/bamco
Contacts: Gergana Mantarkova; Ekaterina Ignatova

Cyprus Association of Business Consultants
30, Grivas Dhigenis Ave.
P.O. Box 1657
1511 NICOSIA
Cyprus
Tel: +357 2 665102
Fax: +357 2 669459
Email: oeb@dial.cylink.com.cy
Contacts: George Phedonos; Chris Michaelides

Association for Consulting to Business (APP)
Veletrzni 21
CZ – 170 01 Praha 7
Czech Republic
Tel: +42 02 87 90 43
Fax: +42 02 87 90 43
Email: asocpor@asocpor.cz
Website: www.asocpor.cz
Contacts: Ivo Ulrych; Miroslav Kobza

Dansk Management Råd (DMR)
14 A, 2. sal, Amaliegade
DK – 1256 Copenhagen K
Denmark
Tel: +45 33 18 16 20
Fax: +45 33 18 16 25
Email: kh@danskmanagementraad.dk
Fax: www.danskmanagementraad.dk
Contacts: Mr Jannick Pedersen; Mr Karsten Hillerstøm

Management Consultancies Association (MCA)
49 Whitehall
London SW1A 2BX
England
Tel: +44 20 7321 3990
Fax: +44 20 7321 3991
Email: mca@mca.org.uk
Website: www.mca.org.uk
Contacts: Bruce Petter; Pippa Wylde

Liikkeenjohdon Konsultit LJK
Eteläranta 10
FI – 00130 Helsinki
Finland
Tel: +358 9 622 4442
Fax: +358 9 6220 1009
Email: ljk@ljk.fi
Website: www.ljk.fi
Contacts: Liisa Nakari; Pentti Harmanen

Syntec Conseil en Management (Chambre Syndicale des Sociétés de Conseil)
3 Rue Léon Bonnat
F – 75016 Paris
France
Tel: +33 1 44 30 49 20
Fax: +33 1 40 50 73 57
Website: www.syntec-management.com
Contacts: Brigitte David-Gardon Mr Alain Donzeaud

Bundesverband Deutscher Unternehmensberater e.V. (BDU)
Zitelmanntrasse 22
D – 53113 Bonn
Germany
Tel: +49 228 91 61 0
Fax: +49 228 91 61 26
Email: info@bdu.de
Website: www.bdu.de
Contacts: Christoph Weyrather; Rémi Redley

Hellenic Association of Management Consulting Firms (SESMA)
115 Vas.Sophias Avenue
Mavili Square
GR-115 21
Greece
Tel: +30 1 64 70 660
Fax: +30 1 64 70 661
Email: sesma@hol.gr
Website: www.sesma.gr
Contacts: Athanassios Mavros; Alexandra Rapakoulia

Association of Management Consultants in Hungary (VTMSZ)
11 Szt. István Krt
H – 1055 Budapest
Hungary
Tel: +36 1 302 76 81
Fax: +36 1 302 7681
Email: vtmsz.iroda@mail.datanet.hu
Contacts: Sándor Hetyey; Kornai Gábor

Associazione delle Società di Consulenza Direzionale e Organizzat. (ASSOCONSULT)
Plazza Velasca 6
I – 20122 Milan
Italy
Tel: +39 02 866 686
Fax: +39 02 890 12750
Email: assoconsult@fastwebnet.it
Website: www.assoconsult.com
Contacts: Patrizia Marino; Federico Butera

Raad van Organisatie Adviesbureau (ROA)
P.O. Box 85515
NL-2508 CE The Hague
Netherlands
Tel: +31 70 313 1311
Fax: +31 70 364 3748
Email: harriet.baars@cmg.nl
Website: www.roa-advies.nl
Contacts: Harriet Baars; Pim Zoeteweij

NBF – Norges Bedriftsrådgiverforening
c/o Interforum Partners AS
Askerveien 61
N-1384 Asker
Norway
Tel: +47 6698 9990
Fax: +47 66789993
Email: catom@online.no
Contact: Cato Musaeus

Stowarzyszenie Doradcow Gospodarczych w Polsce (SDG)
ul. Chalubinskiego 8 p. 38/68
PL 00–613 Warsaw
Poland
Tel: +48 22 8301 422
Fax: +48 22 8301 423
Email: sdg@sdg.com.pl
Website: www.sdg.com.pl
Contacts: Mikolai Illukowicz; Andrzej Glowacki

Associaçao Portuguesa de Projectistas e Consultores (APPC)
Avenida Antonio Augusto Aguiar 126
7th Floor
P – 1050 Lisbon
Portugal
Tel: +351 21 358 0785/6
Fax: +351 21 315 0413
Email: info@appconsultores.pt
Website: www.appconsultores.pt
Contacts: Fernando Rolin; Manuela Lourenço

Asociatia Consultantilor in Management din Romania (AMCOR)
7–9 Piata Amzei, Sc. C, ap. 6
70174 Bucharest
Romania
Tel: +40 1 3126891
Fax: +40 1 3127094
Email: svasta@mail.kappa.ro
Website: www.amcor.ccir.ro
Contacts: Mihai Svasta; Mihail Dumitrescu

Association of Consultants for Economics and Management (ACEM)
12 Petrovka
103 756 Moscow
Russia
Tel: +7 095 928 26 16
Fax: +7 095 200 44 52
Email: acemsr.ru
Contacts: Alexander Posadsky; Sergey Vasiliev

Association of Management Consultants of Slovenia (AMCOS)
Dimiceva 13
1504 Ljubljana
Slovenia
Tel: +386 61 1898253
Fax: +386 61 1898200
Email: cernjac@hq.gzs.si
Website: www.gzs.si
Contacts: Albin Cernjac; Janko Arah

Asoc. Espanola de Empressa de Consultoria (AEC)
Orfila 5 – Esc. 1 – 4§ C
E – 28010 Madrid
Spain
Tel: +349 1 308 0161
Fax: 349 1 308 2327
Email: aec@wanadoo.es
Website: www.consultoras.com
Contacts: Eduardo Mendicutti; Gil Gidron

SAMC, Sveriges Managementkonsulenter
Kungsgatan 48
S-11135
Sweden
Tel: +46 820 8330
Fax: +46 821 2540
Email: info@samc.se
Website: www.samc.se
Contact: Anders Grufman

Association of Management Consultants (ASCO)
Forchstrasse 428
Postfach 923
CH – 8029 Zürich
Switzerland
Tel: +41 1 395 2404
Fax: 41 1 395 2405
Email: office@asco.ch
Website: www.asco.ch
Contacts: Marianne Senti; Leonhard Fopp

Appendix III: Zen-Noh-Ren (All-Japan Federation of Management Organisations)

Zen-Noh-Ren was founded in 1949. Like FEACO in Europe and AMCF in the United States of America (previously known as ACME), Zen-Noh-Ren is playing a key role as the only federation of management consultancy organisations in Japan.

Our main objective is to disseminate management efficiency for the improvement of Japanese industry as a whole. Specifically, Zen-Noh-Ren's goal is to contribute to the development of Japan's industry and economy, not only through the enhancement of communication and the exchange of information among its members, but also the provision of helpful and substantial management consulting services.

A few of our past activities include hosting Parts I and II of the National Efficiency Conference, dispatching a Japanese delegation to the FEACO Conference and creating a registration system for certified management consultants (CMC). For this last, we dissolved the previous system – which had dealt exclusively with consultants belonging to a member organisation – in 1999, and worked to set up a new system so that non-member consultants could also be certified. As of April 1 2001, 780 management consultants have been certified and received international management consulting licences at the same time.

Now, the world pays close attention to Japanese management (which has successfully overcome innumerable difficulties since the end of the Second World War) to see how it will change in the future. Corporations in Japan can no longer survive world competition without making efforts to revamp their corporate management style.

Thus, in this time of economic hardship, not only the industrial sector but other sectors of the economy as well are looking to management consulting organisations with great expectation of economic solutions. As Zen-Noh-Ren entered the new century, we planned to chart our course to broaden and improve our activities with the underlying goal of promoting 'cutting edge management style'.

We would appreciate continued support from all related organisations, the industry as a whole and the population in general.

Major tasks of Zen-Noh-Ren

National Efficiency Conference

Part I: main conference

The National Efficiency Conference has been held every year since 1949. Business owners, managers, management consultants and many others who are interested in business management get together from all over the country and attend lectures by top-notch speakers who suggest solutions to the important problems facing business. The conference also serves as a place where corporations present their cases. At the 52nd National Efficiency Conference in 2000, we made a new start with the theme of 'Pursuit of state-of-the art management' with the aim of contributing to the enhancement of Japanese industrial competitive power.

Part II: thesis presentation session

This session is for presentation and discussion of the research theses submitted from all over Japan for the purpose of exchange and study of management techniques and theories. The session is divided into five subdivisions: management strategy, research development/manufacturing, distribution/marketing, personnel/organisation and IT.

Opportunities are given not only to management consultants but also to those who aspire to be management consultants and those people who are in charge of practice, guidance and management improvement in the area of business management.

'The Economy, Trade & Industry Minister Award', the only award of its kind in the area of management, is given to the best thesis. The 'Director-General Award of Economic & Industrial Policy Bureau, the Ministry of Economy, Trade & Industry' awards are given to the rest of the selected theses. Furthermore, all the selected theses receive cash awards/prizes from the Ueno/Godoh/Yamashita Foundation. These three names are great pioneers in the area of productivity improvement in Japan.

Management consultant certification programme

The Management Consultant Registration System has been in effect since 1986. It registers management consultants who belong to member organisations – in accordance with given criteria – with Zen-Noh-Ren. Initially this programme was limited to members, but this was recently changed and since April 1 1999, the Management Consultant Certification System has been the only system in Japan to evaluate and certify active management consultants regardless of nationality.

Since Zen-Noh-Ren joined the ICMCI in 1998, those management consultants certified by Zen-Noh-Ren have been automatically qualified for the CMC certified by ICMCI.

There are approximately 780 management consultants certified by Zen-Noh-Ren as of April 1 2001.

Registration/publication of professional qualifications by voluntary regulation of management consultant qualifications

In order to differentiate management consultant qualifications given out by Zen-Noh-Ren member bodies from unqualified low grade certifications, and at the same time enhance the quality of the Zen-Noh-Ren certifications, Zen-Noh-Ren established Voluntary Regulations Concerning Management Consultant Certifications in 1977 under the guidance of the Ministry of Economy, Trade and Industry and has been registering approved qualifications after rigorous evaluation. At the end of 1999, the above rules were changed in such a way that those certifications created by Zen-Noh-Ren members can play more important socialroles in line with changing times.

As of January 2001, a total of 51 certifications and 23 certifying bodies were registered with the Federation.

A group of Japanese representatives sent to the World Convention

FEACO is the ruling body of management consultancies in Europe. In 1984, Zen-Noh-Ren sent the Japanese inspection group, as a non-regular FEACO member, to the FEACO Convention – the world convention of management consultants held every year in Europe. Since then, the Japanese delegation has attended the Convention every year.

Management consultants in America, Europe and other parts of the world are keenly interested in Japanese management, and significant discussions and exchange of opinions on the subject are ongoing.

The first World Management Consultants Convention was held in France in May 1987, the second convention in the US in 1990, the third in Italy in 1993 and the fourth took place in Yokohama, Japan, when Zen-Noh-Ren acted as host under the co-sponsorship of FEACO and ACME. In October 2000, the sixth world convention was held in Berlin and Zen-Noh-Ren sent a group of 20-plus members to exchange ideas with management consultants from various countries.

Foundation of Zen-Noh-Ren Research Institute

In 2000, the Zen-Noh-Ren Research Institute was newly founded to undertake research into 'cutting-edge management'. The research work of the first year was focused on a business model, and the research results were compiled into a report entitled 'Pioneering 21st century – creating values in anticipation of future change'.

Management consulting survey and other research work

In 2000 Zen-Noh-Ren conducted research into Japanese/foreign consulting bodies, management consultants, intellectuals and client companies. The surveys were themed 'Setting the Management Consulting Vision for the 21st Century', and aimed at developing international competitive power to cope with change in the business environment in Japan as well as overseas. The survey work was assigned by the Ministry of Economy, Trade and Industry (METI).

Code of Professional Conduct

Code of Professional Conduct (Excerpts)

Zen-Noh-Ren is a combined body of professional institutes aimed at the dissemination and enhancement of management concepts and practices. As the only industrial body of its kind, Zen-Noh-Ren has contributed to the development of industry.

We recognise that the activities of our member organisations should be carried out in accordance with high-level ethical standards, and so established these guidelines for the purpose of gaining the trust of industrial society as a whole through social responsibility.

Basic platform

- **Be trustworthy** – observe the high-level code of conduct and work for the benefit of the public.
- *Enhance the reliability process* – develop higher and more effective technology/processes and enhance efficiency to ensure that good results are obtained.

History of Zen-Noh-Ren

Purpose of the Federation

The primary purpose of Zen-Noh-Ren is to make a major contribution to the sound development of the Japanese economy through giving maximum support to management consultancy. It is engaged in study, dissemination, guidance and practice of 'the most advanced concept, technologies and methods concerning management to the Japanese industries facing accelerating economic globalisation'.

Establishment

Zen-Noh-Ren was established in 1949, succeeding the former All-Japan Management. The inaugural meeting and the First All-Japan Management Annual Conference were held in Tokyo in November 1949. Historical sketches are shown in the following table.

Table III.1 Chronological record of major events

1923–	The Japanese Management Research Association was established to develop and disseminate scientific management methods in Japan. Subsequently, management research groups with the same purpose were organised in several Japanese cities, including Tokyo, Osaka and Aichi, and also in Manchuria.
1927–28	The Japanese Federation of Management was created by consolidating management research groups in various locations. The First All-Japan Management Conference was held in October 1928.
1931	The Japanese Industries Association – a combination of the Factory Association and the Factory Councils – was established.
1942–43	The Japanese Federation of Management and the Japanese Institute Association merged into the Japanese Management Association. In 1943 the First All-Japan Management Conference was held in Osaka.
1949	Zen-Noh-Ren (All-Japan Federation of Management Organisations) was established after the end of the Second World War on May 16 1949 by consolidating all management organisations across the country.
1950	The establishment of the Japanese Management Association (Zen-Noh-Ren, an abbreviation of the Japanese name) was officially approved by the Minister of the former MITI, presently METI.
1977	Voluntary regulation on management-related qualifications and designations was formulated, and a registration service of qualifications and designations began.
1984	The Federation sent the first Japanese delegation to the FEACO Conference.
1986	A voluntary registration system for management consultants was created and the first round of registration carried out.
1987	First Management Consultant World Conference held in Paris under the co-sponsorship of FEACO, ACME and Zen-Noh-Ren.
1990	Second Management Consultant World Conference held in New York
1993	Third Management Consultant World Conference held in Rome
1996	Fourth Management Consultant World Conference held in Yokohama, Japan.
1998	The Management Consultant Registration System was dissolved, and the Management Consultant Certification System set up.
1999	50th anniversary of Zen-Noh-Ren. The first round of certification under the Management Consultant Certification System was carried out. Zen-Noh-Ren revised the voluntary regulation of management consultant qualifications and designations to give more authority to this regulation and also to make it more widely used.
2000	The middle range project plan started. The delegation was sent to the Sixth Management Consultant World Conference. The Zen-Noh-Ren Research Institute was founded.

Index

Page references in italics indicate tables or figures

Accenture   35, 37–38, 39, 435
accountancies   26–27, 35
added value   335–36
Africa
   Nigeria   420–26, 501
   South Africa   426–27, 501
AI *see* appreciative inquiry
All-Japan Federation of Management Organisations (Zen-Noh-Ren)   473, 474, 500, 507–13
alliances, consultant and 'others'   67–69
AMCOR (Association of Romanian Management Consultants)   412, 505
AMCOS (Association for Management Consulting of Slovenia)   414, 505
Amsterdam standard   74
Andersen Consulting   34–35, 36, 435
anticipatory principle   205
appointment process   161
appreciative inquiry (AI)   202–03
   4D cycle   206–09, *206*
   benefits   212
   conditions for   210–11
   consultants role   211
   five core principles   204–06
   outcomes   209–10
   power of dialogue   203–04
   power of image   204
Argentina   497
Arthur Andersen   30, 34–35, 36, 393
ASCO (Association of Management Consultants), Switzerland   402–03, 403–04, 502
Asia   446–49, *447*, 450
   certification   449–50
   IMCI members   498, 499, 500, 501
   see also Australia; China
assignments *see* projects, consulting
Association of Management Consultants (ASCO), Switzerland   402–03, 403–04, 502
Association for Management Consulting of Slovenia (AMCOS)   414, 505

Association of Romanian Management Consultants (AMCOR)   412, 505
audit services   27, 35, 65–66
Australia   447, *447*, 451–57, 497
Austria   367–70, 503

BAMC (Bulgarian Association of Management Consultants)   408, 498
Bangladesh   498
BCG (Boston Consulting Group)   25–26
BDU, Germany   370–3
Bedaux consultancy   22, 23
Belgium   503
'Big Five' consultancies   30, 34, 35, 381, 397, 449
board of directors   139–40, 142, 146
   appointing directors   146
   challenges and responsibilites   140–41
   and change and continuity   257–58
   and evaluation process   197–99, 200–201
   executive directors   143, 145–46
   key purpose   140
   non-executive directors   142–45, 146
   tasks   141–42
Booz Allen   24
Boston Consulting Group (BCG)   25–26
Brazil   428–31, *428*, *429*, *430*, 498
Breakthrough ThinkingÅ   221–22, 222–23
Bulgaria *406*, 408, 498, 503
business schools   30
   see also HE

CAMC (Canadian Association of Management Consultants)   444, 498
Canada   431–44, *432*, *433*, *434*, *436–40*, *441*, *442*, *443*, 498
Cap Gemini   28, 35, 350
capital, consultancies and   36–38
Central and Eastern Europe (CEE)   405–08, *406*, 414–17, *415*
   Bulgaria   408, 498, 503

Czech Republic   408–09, 504
Hungary   409–11, 499
Poland   411–12, 501, 505
Romania   412, 505
Russia   413, 505
Slovenia   413–14, 505
Certified Management Consultant (CMC)   72–3, 74, 87, 101, 120
  competency tests   75–80
  Switzerland and   403–4
Certified Practices   81, 86, 120, 120–1
change management   214–15, 226, 255
  anticipating impact of change   255–56
  change and continuity balance   257–60
  and coaching   292
  focus on customer   218–19
  goals   217–18
  involve stakeholders   219–20
  leadership   274–75, 276–84
  match expectations   215
  minority interests and   260–61
  post-merger integration   263–73
  prepare people   224–25
  process improvement   215–16
  purposes   216–17
  and risk   225–26
  sponsorship   220–1
  think forward, innovate backward   222–4
  using to organise consultancy profession   136
  see also appreciative inquiry
China   *447*, 448, 457–62
  Hong Kong   *447*, 449, 466–73
  Pearl River Delta   462–66, 473
CHL Consulting Group   381–82
Cisco Systems   71, 350
civil society groups   48–49
client-consultant relationship   152, 154, 353
  closing off the project   227–34
  consulting styles and   153–54
  evaluating advice and recommendations   195–201
  getting the most from consultants   152–53, 154–55, 180–81
  getting value from consultants   170–74
  levels   179
  managing the project   175–85
  phases of   186–88, *187*
    engagement   188–91, *189, 191*
    management   181–82, 191–93
    transformation   193–94, 228, 229–30
clients   179–80
  Japanese   484–92
  legal basis for work   88
  reasons for using consultants   152
  sanctions, arbitration and redress   88–89
  selecting consultants   82–3, 154–5, 156–69
CMC *see* Certified Management Consultant
coach-mentor consulting style   154, 231
coaching   192–93, 285–86, 293–94
  assessing the coach   292–93
  definition   287–89

forms and use of   290–92
codes of conduct
  IMC   91–98
  MCA   66–67
  Zen-Noh-Ren   511–12
Commodity consulting scenario   58–59
communication
  during mergers   265–66
  see also Internet; m-commerce
communication consulting
  advice and services available   304–6
  assessing consultants   306–07
  growth and development   303–04
  sample case   310–11
  standards   307–08
  typical assignments   308–09
  value of   310
competency, consultant   74, 86–7
competition
  competitor analysis   253
  in consulting   13
    and regulation   119, 120
  sustainable competitive advantage   240–44
conflicts of interest   35, 85
constructionist principle   204–05
consultancies   9, 33–34, 40–41
  alliances   67–69
  Certified Practices   81, 86, 120
  e-commerce and IT   39–40, 42–47
  emergent   13, *14*
  and ethical issues   85–86
  evolution of   28–31, *29*
    first generation   22–24
    second generation   24–26
    third generation   26–28
  the future   40–41, 56–60
  Internet   350
  IPOs and capital   36–38, 350–51
  Japan   475–80
  middle market   73, 381–82
  ownership and identity   34–36
  sanctions, arbitration and redress   88–89
  staff and skills   39
consultancy   7–8, 19
  definitions   11–13, 16, 66, 127–28
  fields of   16
  future scenarios   56–60
  global industry   8–10, *9*
  growth as an industry   10–11, *11, 12*, 21–31, *29*, 122–24
  growth and ethical issues   83–87
  growth and IT   42–47, 344–45, 353–54
  independent advice   66–67, 68
  as a profession   125–27, 128–29, 134, 134–36
    internationally   15–17
  and sustainability   54–55
  in transition economies   14–15
consultants   9–10, 16, 16–17
  assessing coaches   292–93
  competency   74, 86–87
  definition   183, 385–86

freelance 72
getting the most from 152–53, 154–55, 180–81
getting value from 170–74
internal 72
Japan 480–84, *488*
perceptions of 18–19
as professionals 123–24, 125–27, 128–29, 134, 134–36
reasons for using 152
regulation 115–21
roles 17–18, 183
   in AI 211
   in managing change 214–26
selecting 154–55, 156–69
   communication 306–7
training, development and qualifications 73–4, *75–80*, 81, 101–12
see also client-consultant relationship
consulting projects *see* projects, consulting
contracting 164–65, 165, 167–68
   costs 168–69
Cooperrider, Dr David 202–03
corporate governance 138–39
   board of directors 140–46
   national models 139–40
corporate transformation *see* transformation programmes
costs 168–69, 172, 179
counsellor-therapist consulting style 154, 192–93
creativity 238, 239
CRM (customer relationship management) 339–40
currency exchange 363
customer relations 312–13, 321–22
   business partnering 313–16
   customer-focused processes 317–21
   and m-commerce 336–37, 339–40
customer segmentation analysis 252
customers 218–19
   and mergers 269–70
Cyprus 498, 503
Czech Republic *406*, 408–09, 504

Deloitte Consulting 36, 39, 350
Denmark 390–93, *392*, 498, 504
developing world 357–9, 365–6
   follow-on 365
   identifying work 359–60
   initial procedures and pitfalls 363–4
   partners 359, 361–2
   payment 362, 365–6
   piggy-backing 360–1
   project delivery 364
   project planning 364
   taxation and currency 363
development
   and coaching 287, 290–1
   see also training and education
dialogue, power of 203–04
differentiation 331
directive coaching 288
directors *see* board of directors

discussion, power of 204
doctor-patient consulting style 153, 231
Doomsday scenario 57–58
dotcom era 36, 37, 380–81
   see also e-business

e-business 39–40, 335, 348–50, 381
   adapting to market demand 45–46
   first decade 43–45
   the future 46–47, 353–54
   marketing aspects 250
EAI (Enterprise Application Integration) 346, 347, 351
EAPs (Employee Assistance Programmes) 297–98, 302
Eastern Europe *see* Central and Eastern Europe
economies, transition 14–15
EDS (Electronic Data Systems) 27, 351
education *see* training and education
EEDE (Hellenic Society of Management Consultants) 378
efficiency experts 22
efficiency, operational 240
Emerson, Harrington 22
emotional competence 282–84
Employee Assistance Programmes (EAPs) 297–98, 302
employees
   communication support 304–05
   of consultancies 39
   international support services 295–7, 302
      counselling 297–98
      emergency resources 298–99
      employee benefits 300–301
      for expatriates 299–300
      specialised 301–02
   managing during projects 178
   and mergers 265–66
engineer consulting style 154, 231
Enterprise Application Integration (EAI) 346, 347, 351
enterprise resource planning *see* ERP
environmental accounting 53
Ernst & Young 35
ERP (enterprise resource planning) 43, 344
   development 345
   recent trends and 346–47, 348–49, *348*, *349*, 351
ethical issues 85–86
   client-consultant relationship 231–2
   codes of conduct 66–7, 91–8, 511–12
   IMC guidelines 89–91
   IMC helpline 84–5
   social responsibilities 48–50, *49*, *50*
   see also sustainability
Europe, ICMCI members 498, 499, 500, 501, 502
European Federation of Management Consultancy Organisations (FEACO) 405
   membership 503–06
European Union (EU)
   Austria 367–70, 503

Germany   140, 370–5, *373*, *374*, 499
Greece   375–8, 499
Ireland   379–83, 500
Netherlands   383, 500, 505
United Kingdom   383–90, *384*, *385*, *386*, *388*, *389*, 502
evaluation process   195–96, 201
   board's role   197–99
   final report   199–201
   setting criteria   196–7
Evolut Ltd   409
Executive Coaching   285–86
   see also coaching
executive directors   143
   remuneration   145–46
executive education programmes   103–04
expatriate support   299–300
expectations   191
   managing   181
   matching   215
   understanding   182–83

FEACO (European Federation of Management Consultancy Organisations)   405
   membership   503–06
Federal Association of German Management Consultants (BDU)   370–3
fees   119, 168–9, 170, 172, 179
final reports   199–201, 229
Finland   499
flotation   37–38, 350–51 4D cycle, appreciative inquiry 206–09, *206*
France   140, 504

Germany   140, 370–75, *373*, *374*, 499
Global Reporting Initiative (GRI)   53
goals   217–18
   and coaching   290, 292, 293
Greece   375–78, 499

HE (higher education)   100, 101–02, 102–03, 111–12
   executive programmes   103–04
   future provision   108–11
   masters and postgraduate programmes   107–08
   masters programmes for specialists   105–06
   MBA electives   104–05
   quality of   108
Hellenic Association of Management Consulting Firms (SESMA)   377, 378, 499, 504
Hellenic Society of Management Consultants (EEDE)   378
High Tech, High Touch scenario   57
higher education *see* HE
Hong Kong *447*, 449, 466–73, *468*, *469*, *470*, *472*, 499
   and Pearl River Delta   462–66, 473
human capital   295
human relations consultants   22–3
Hungary *406*, 409–11, 499
Hybrid consultancy scenario   58

IBCO (Instutito Brasileiro dos Consultores de Organisaçao)   430–31, 498
IBM Global Services   34
ICG (Independent Management Consultant Group)   382
ICMCI (International Council of Management Consulting Industries)   15–16, 17, 72–3, 87–8
   national members   497–502
IFIs (International Financing Institutions)   359, 360, 365
IIP (Investors In People)   322
image, power of   204
IMC, Australia   447, 456, 497
IMC, Austria   367–68
IMC, Brazil   430–31, 498
IMC, Hong Kong   473, 499
IMC, Jordan   417–18, 500
IMC, the Netherlands   383
IMC, Nigeria   423, 424–26, 501
IMC, UK   84, 89, 384, 502
   Codes of Conduct   91–98
   and education and qualifications   73–74, 81, 86–87, 101
   ethical guidelines   89–91
   and regulation   120–21
implementation   193–94, 223–24, 228–30
   marketing project and plans   251
Incite, Austria   369–70
incubators   350
Independent Management Consultant Group (ICG)   382
Independent Public Offerings (IPOs) and consultancies   37–38, 350–51
India   446, *447*, 448–49, 499
Indonesia *447*,   448
industrial engineers   22
information management *see* knowledge management
information technology *see* IT
Institutes of Management Consultancy   15
   ICMCI members   497–502
   see also IMC
integration *see* mergers
intellectual capital   295
   enhancement   332
   management of   327–31
International Council of Management Consulting Industries *see* ICMCI
International Financing Institutions (IFIs)   359, 360, 365
Internet   44, 261, 350, 381
   advertising projects   360
   see also e-business; m-commerce
Invest-Tech   382
Investors In People (IIP)   322
IPOs (Independent Public Offerings) and consultancies   37–38, 350–51
Ireland   379–82, 500
IT   14, 40, 416
   and alliances   67–68

development 345, 345–46, *347*
and evolution of consultancy 27–28, 29, 30, 344–45
the future 353–54
future investment in 351, *352–53*
and mergers 272
recent trends 346–51
see also e-business; Internet; m-commerce
Italy 500, 505

Japan 447–48, *447*, 473–74, 500
consulting firms 475–80
individual consultants 480–84, *488*
user companies 484–92
Zen-Noh-Ren 473, 474, 507–13
Jordan 417–20, 500

K-Frame 329
knowledge management 323–24
corporate learning strategy 324–26
and differentiation 331
intellectual capital enhancement 332
management 327–31
software 347
KPMG 35, 70

leadership
changing challenges 279–82
defining 275–76
emotional competence 282–84
transformational 274, 276–79
learning
and coaching 287
corporate strategy 324–6
see also knowledge management; training and education
letter of agreement 171

M-commerce 342–43
market forces 334–37, *336*
impact of 337–40
strategies 340–42, *341*
M-form company structure 24
McKinsey & Co. 24, 25, 390
McKinsey, James O. 24–5
Malaysia *447*, 448, 500
Management Consultancies Association *see* MCA
management consultancy *see* consultancy
market migration analysis 253
market segments 241–2, 252
marketing 246–47
aspects of e-business 250
and m-commerce 337–9
marketing audit 247–9
outsourcing 250
plans 251
project evaluation 250
project and plan implementation 251
specific investigations 249
and sustainable competitive advantage 240–44

tools and techniques 251–53
masters degrees 105–07
Maynard, Harold B. 23
MBA electives 104–05, 108
MCA (Management Consultancies Association) 23, 66–67, 84, 85, 89, 384, 504
mergers 263–64, 272–73
appropriate pace 264–65
integration partners 271–72
organisation stability 265–6
realistic targets 266–7
successful integration features 267–71
Methods-Time Measurement (MTM) system 23–24
Middle East *see* Jordan
minority interests 260–61
mobile communication 334–35
see also m-commerce
multi-divisional company structure 24
MVNOs (Mobile Virtual Network Operators) 336–37

Netherlands 383, 500, 505
New Zealand *447*, 453, 454, 455, 456, 501
NGOs (non-government organisations) 49
niche suppliers 259
Nigeria 420–26, 501
non-directive coaching 288–89
non-executive directors 142, 146
context 142–43
functions 143–44
key responsibilities 144–5
Norway 393–6, *394–5*, 501

off-shore development companies (ODCs) 43
one-to-one development coaching 290–91
one-to-one performance coaching 290
operational thinking 239, 239–40
organisational change *see* change management
outsourcing 12, 250, 345
partnering strategy 351, *352*, 353
partners
consultancy 37, 37–8
developing world 359, 361–2

Pearl River Delta (PRD) 462–6, 473
see also Hong Kong
Performance Coaching 285–86
see also coaching
personal introductions 157
Philippines *447*, 448
piggy-backing 360–61
pitches, competitive 157–58
poetic principle 205
Poland *406*, 411–12, 501, 505
Portugal 505
positive principle 205–06
postgraduate certificates 107–08
PR China *see* China
PRD *see* Pearl River Delta
presentations 157, 163, 166

PriceWaterhouseCoopers (PwC)   35, 36, 71, 393, 435
privatisation   406
problem solving   239
process improvement   215–16
product portfolio analysis   252–3
products, consultancy   10–11, *11*, 12–13, *12, 13, 14*
professional associations   116
professionals
   consultants as   123–24, 125–27, 128–29, 134–36
   Hong Kong   470–72, *472*
   ideal types of profession   131–34
   regulation   115–21
   theories about professions   129–31
   see also consultants
project leaders   189
project teams   198, 200
projects, consulting
   closing off   227–33
   commissioning   157
   in developing world   364–65
   evaluation   195–201
   generic stages   152
   managing   175–85
   see also client-consultant relationship
purpose hierarchy   217
PwC (PriceWaterhouseCoopers)   35, 36, 71, 393, 435
qualifications   72–73, 73–74, 81, 87
   see also HE

quality assurance   100–102, 107–08

recommendations, consultant's
   evaluation   195–201
   implementation   193–94, 228–30
regulation of consultants   114–21
Request for a Proposal (RFP)   159–60
risk monitoring and control   225–26
Romania *406*,   412, 505
Russia *406*,   413, 505

Scandinavia   390, 400–401
   Denmark   390–93, *392*, 498, 504
   Norway   393–96, *394–95*, 501
   Sweden   396–400, *398–99*, 502
scientific management   22–24, 83–84
selection of consultants   154–55, 156
   appointment process   161
   competitive pitches   157–58
   contracting   164–65
   costs and contracting   167–69
   decision   163–64
   educating the consultants   162
   overall choice   165–66
   personal introductions   157
   presentations   163
   short-listing   158–61
   written proposals   162–63
self-change   283
self-regulation of consultants   115–21
SESMA (Hellenic Association of Management Consulting Firms)   377, 378, 499, 504

Shell   48–49
simultaneity principle   205
Singapore   448–49, 501
Slovenia *406*,   413–14
Small is Beautiful scenario   59
social accounting   53
social constructionism   203
social responsibilities   48–50, *49, 50*
   see also sustainability
social trends   52
software, business   30
   see also ERP
South Africa   426–27, 501
South America
   Brazil   428–31, *428, 429, 430*, 498
   ICMI members   497, 498
Spain   502
sponsorship   220–1
staff *see* employees
stakeholders   52
   and change   219–20
steering groups   162, 178
strategic marketing   338–39
strategy consulting   237–39, 244–45
   operational versus strategic thinking   239–40
   sustainable competitive advantage   240–44
sustainability   51–52
   a business issue   48–50
   consultancy and   54–55
   managing   52–54
Sweden   396–400, *398–99*, 502
Switzerland   402–04, 502
synergy   192

taxation in developing world   363
Taylor, Frederick W.   22
teacher-pupil consulting style   153, 231
team coaching   291
technology   14, 42–43, 243
   see also e-business; Internet; IT; m-commerce
trade associations   116
training and education   73–81, 101–12
   corporate learning strategy   324–26
transformation phase (client-consultant relationship)
   193–4, 228, 229–30
transformation programmes   274–5
   emotional competence   282–4
   leader's role   276–82
transition economies   14–15

United Kingdom   140, 383–9, *384, 385, 386, 388, 389*
   see also IMC, UK; MCA
universities *see* HE
USA   445, 502

validation   220
value webs   335–36, *336*, 338
venture capital   36–37, 350

written proposals   162–63

Zen-Noh-Ren   473, 474, 507–13